ANTI-DRUG POLICIES IN COLOMBIA

A Vanderbilt University Center for Latin American Studies volume.
Edward G. Fischer, director

Anti-Drug Policies in Colombia: Successes, Failures, and Wrong Turns,
edited by Alejandro Gaviria and Daniel Mejía (2016)

VANDERBILT UNIVERSITY
Center for Latin American Studies

ANTI-DRUG POLICIES IN COLOMBIA

Successes, Failures, and Wrong Turns

Edited by Alejandro Gaviria and Daniel Mejía
Translated by Jimmy Weiskopf

Vanderbilt University Press
Nashville

Originally published as *Políticas antidroga en Colombia: Éxitos, fracasos y extravíos* by Ediciones Uniandes, Bogotá, Colombia, in April 2011.

This book is printed on acid-free paper.
Manufactured in the United States of America
Translation coordinator: Nicolas Vaughan

Library of Congress Cataloging-in-Publication Data on file
LC control number 2014045942
LC classification number HV5840.C7A5813 2015
Dewey class number 362.29'1609861—dc23

ISBN 978-0-8265-2071-5 (hardcover)
ISBN 978-0-8265-2073-9 (ebook)

CONTENTS

Part IV. Legal and Institutional Aspects of the War on Drugs

Part V. Institutions and Narcotics Trafficking

ACKNOWLEDGMENTS

First of all, we would like to thank the former rector of Universidad de los Andes, Dr. Carlos Angulo Galvis, who came up with the idea of creating this book. During the process of its realization, Dr. Angulo gave us his constant support and guided us toward the objective which he himself had formulated: to undertake an academic publication that would allow Universidad de los Andes to contribute to an objective, constructive, and informed debate on a subject that is crucial for the future of Colombia. We would also like to express our thanks and acknowledgments to former president of Colombia, César Gaviria Trujillo, who supported this project in many ways and stimulated our interest in and curiosity about an in-depth treatment of the subjects dealt with in this book. We would further like to thank the general manager of the Central Bank of Colombia (Banco de la República), Dr. José Darío Uribe Escobar, and the Open Society Institute for the partial funding of this book.

During the first semester of 2010 at the University de los Andes two events were held in which the preliminary versions of the chapters were presented and discussed. We would like to especially thank the former director of the National Police (Policía Nacional de Colombia), General Óscar Naranjo, for his participation in both events, as well as that of other persons who have been actively involved in the formulation of anti-drug policies in Colombia, among them Ómar Figueroa, Sergio Jaramillo, Alberto Lozano, Inés Elvira Mejía, Augusto Pérez, and Ricardo Vargas. Academics of international renown also participated in these events. Among them, it is worth mentioning Jonathan Caulkins of Carnegie Mellon University, Beau Kilmer of RAND, Elvira María Restrepo of the University of Miami, Peter Reuter of the University of Maryland, and Juan Tokatlian of the Torcuato Di Tella University.

This book would not have been possible without the active and enthusiastic participation of the twenty-four authors of the fifteen chapters that compose it. To all of them we would like to express our sincerest thanks for their effort to bring this project to completion and their infinite patience in complying with all the requirements needed for its publication. We would also like to thank Felipe Castañeda, general editor of Ediciones Uniandes, and his work team, made up of Eduardo Franco, Felipe Rubio, Carolina Mazo, and Alejandra Muñoz. Their support and cooperation was indispensable in turning the publication of this book into a reality. Finally we would like to thank Guillermo Díez, who revised the final version of the Spanish manuscript with a critical eye, along with María José Uribe.

PREFACE

The publication of this book represents a landmark in the manner of confronting the problem of illegal drugs in Colombia. In the course of three decades, Colombia has acted in line with the prohibitionist policies promoted by the United States, generally based on the war against drugs inaugurated by President Richard Nixon forty years ago. No country in the world has paid as high a cost as Colombia in terms of the lives of its political leaders, judges, police officers, soldiers, journalists, and tens of thousands of innocent civilians, nor suffered a graver damage to its democratic institutions.

Is it fair that this happens in the name of a failed and worn-out policy? The same thing is happening in Mexico, where the deaths run into tens of thousands. Our country has paid an immeasurable economic cost in this still unfinished fight against narco-terrorism. Even during the period when we have received significant aid from the United States, under what is known as Plan Colombia, nine out of ten dollars have come from the Colombian government, according to the United States Congressional Budget Office.

The moment has come to evaluate the results of this strategy, which has so few results to show beyond statistics about interdiction efforts, drugs seizures, the persecution of drugs cartels, deaths, and prisoners in jails. Nothing has been achieved in reducing consumption in the United States, by far the biggest market for drugs. It is just the opposite: the use of methamphetamines has shot up and more people are addicted to this drug now than to cocaine. There the US government has just officially dropped the term "war on drugs" because it does not allow for the designing of effective policies. The US government has said that the strategy of controlling the problem through the reduction of supply does not work and that the only viable solution is to reduce consumption by 15 percent during the Obama administration. More than 70 percent of the population in the United States thinks that the war on drugs has failed. President Obama said it himself in his campaign for the Senate. And the growing tolerance toward the use of marijuana is evident, to the point where many people, even unconditional adherents of prohibitionism, believe that its legalization is just a matter of time.

The United States has made an extraordinary effort in the battle against all illegal drugs. The problem is that the $40 billion in question is spent more on judicial, police, and prison system than on policies for treatment and prevention. More people are imprisoned for narcotics trafficking in the United States (more than 500,000) than those jailed for all crimes in the Europe as a whole. When the war began there were 50,000 such prisoners; now the figure has multiplied by ten, without any visible effects on consumption. It is frankly incredible that $450,000 is spent each year on the jailing of a youngster who, at worst, once tried marijuana. Despite that, 60 percent of US prisoners use marijuana, according to the latest study by the Inter-American Dialogue.

From my own experience on the Latin American Commission on Drugs and Democracy, I learned that, except for Sweden, European countries do not jail consumers because they regard consumption as a health problem and not as a crime. That policy is much less harmful and onerous for that continent and has a much lower social, economic, and institutional cost. These countries do not maintain that these policies are very good or ideal, but that they are the ones that do the least harm to humanity. The differences in these policies basically lie in the support for addicts and youngsters, which are meant to reduce the clandestine drug business and free such people from the clutch of criminal networks. Holland, Switzerland, and, recently, Portugal, have had excellent results with this approach; consumption has not risen while violence has declined. This is not to the detriment of the fight against organized crime, which no one proposes to abandon.

The term *legalization* is unfortunate. It is a simplistic, libertarian expression that implies that drugs do not cause any harm or do not require controls, or that people have the right to damage their health. This approach does not have any political future, as it leads to many kinds of phantoms and fears. It is a policy as mistaken, radical, simplistic, and attractive as prohibitionism. Both are based on ideological principles and fundamentalism and not on scientific research and well-documented experiences.

What Colombia, Latin America, and the United States need to do is not legalize drugs, but start from the premise that consumption is a health problem, not a crime. We have to investigate the harm done by each drug, the manner in which it alters human conduct, how addictive it is, and what the campaigns of prevention and treatment should be like. These are questions where there has been a great deal of progress in other regions.

We have reached this point because of our passivity and because of the inability of the US government, Congress, and media to even enter into the debate and discuss ways of finding alternatives to a policy that, after four decades, has shown so few results.

Several major newspapers in the United States have asked for a review of the current prohibitionist regime, but they are not listened to. The lack of courage of the political leaders in the United States is startling. They are blindly bound to a mistaken and costly policy, the same fundamentalism that led the country to ban alcohol in the past and confront the criminal organizations that came into being as a result. They say that even debating the subject is dangerous, as they take crime to be equivalent to narcotics trafficking, and they don't want to be soft on crime because of the electoral risks. They also say there is no alternative, even though the European one is at hand. Moisés Naím has said that in the United States it is prohibited to even think about the issue.

Colombia, for its part, should revise its policy in the following ways. First, President Santos, together with President Calderón of Mexico, should address the public in the United States and call for a serious public debate on its policy and the adoption of corrective measures. Second, Colombia should abandon the traditional criteria for the success of US policy, such as how much money is spent, how many people are put in jail, and how many deaths result from its prohibitionist policies, or how much the street price of drugs has risen in New York or Los Angeles, a figure that, like many statistics on the subject, is of doubtful veracity.

None of that is of any use to Colombia or Mexico. The rhetoric of the US government so far is useless. The United States should tell us why they are not willing to debate the matter, and if they are willing, what results were obtained: how much of that $40 billion went into treatment and prevention policies. They should tell us how much the consumption of drugs was reduced, with figures confirmed by an independent institution. Colombia and Mexico have an undeniable moral authority to ask these questions, and I am certain they will be heard. President Santos cannot keep waiting for the California resolution on legalization to be passed before changing our policy; he has changed policies in many other fields with singular good judgment and success.

César Gaviria Trujillo
Former President of the Republic of Colombia

INTRODUCTION

Forty years ago, in June 1971, the President of the United States, Richard M. Nixon, declared the "war on drugs." In a now famous speech, Nixon repeated his commitment to the prohibition of the consumption of psychoactive drugs and announced a package of military aid to the countries that produced and exported illegal drugs. "The consumption of drugs has assumed the dimensions of a national emergency . . . the danger will not disappear with the ending of the war in Vietnam. It existed before Vietnam and will exist after it," Nixon said in an emphatic way.

At that time no one foresaw the devastating consequences of a political decision motivated by Nixon's dislike for the youngsters who were opposed to his anticommunist crusade, many of whom were habitual users of marijuana and other drugs, and the rise in drug use by veterans of the Vietnam War.

President Nixon's reasons are now a distant historical subject, buried in the presidential archives. The consequences of the war on drugs, on the other hand, are still clearly with us, as evidenced in the daily news reports all over the world. The declaration of the war on drugs probably had to do with a transitory political situation, but it has had permanent, long-term effects. The war on drugs unleashed a series of events that within a few years led to the consolidation of Colombia as the main exporter of cocaine to the United States. The contemporary history of Colombia began to unfold in 1971. Or, better put, that is when drugs began to skew the fate of our country in a slow but definitive manner.

Paradoxically, the war on drugs produced a considerable increase in the consumption of cocaine in the United States. "Nixon focused his legendary political rage on marijuana" (Gootenberg 2008, 308). The first repressive measures increased the fines and prison terms for the use of marijuana, LSD, and heroin (Robbins 1969, 51), but not for the use of cocaine. In 1975, an official White House document stated that cocaine had a low priority: "it does not have serious consequences such as crime, hospitalization or death" (Gootenberg 2008, 310).

The consumption of cocaine was openly tolerated by Nixon's administration and by US society. In the early 1970s, cocaine was regarded as a relatively harmless drug used by glamorous people: businessmen, Hollywood actors, and rock stars, those who belonged to what is now known (the anachronism is justifiable) as the *creative class.* The demand grew in line with its toleration by the government and society as a whole. Consumers had little to fear: cocaine was neither punished nor stigmatized. In fact it was just the opposite. Cocaine was regarded as the champagne of drugs. Fashionable parties in Manhattan began with martinis and ended with "a hit of coke" (Demarest 1981).

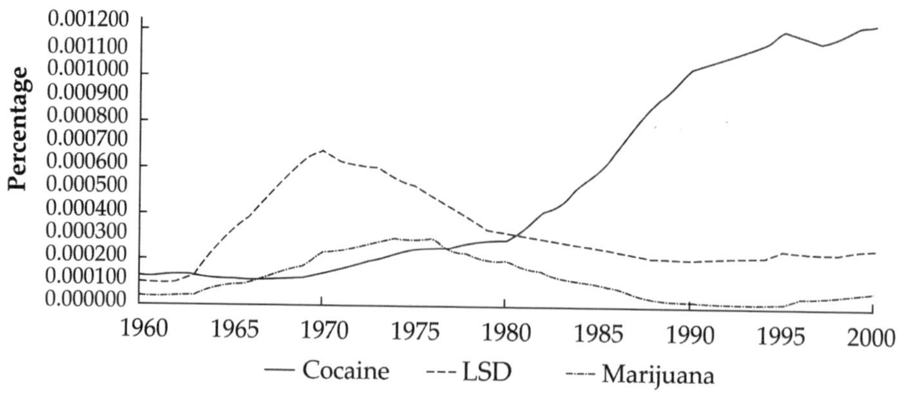

FIGURE 1. Frequency of the appearance of the words "cocaine," "LSD," and "marijuana" in English-language publications. Source: *ngrams.googlelabs.com*

As the demand for cocaine grew, the supply of marijuana, heroin, and other psychoactive drugs fell considerably, mainly as a result of the repressive measures undertaken by the government of the United States. Thousands of hectares of marijuana in Mexico were fumigated in the 1970s. A number of international networks for the distribution of heroin, among them the famous "French Connection," were dismantled in the same period (Gootenberg 2008, 308). Marijuana began to grow scarce on the streets of the United States, as did heroin and LSD. The fall in supply opened the way for the emergence of cocaine.

The rise of cocaine (and the corresponding fall in other psychoactive drugs) may be measured in quantitative terms. Figure 1 shows the frequency of the use of the words "cocaine," "LSD," and "marijuana" in hundreds of English-language publications. Up to the beginning of the 1970s, the word "cocaine" barely appeared in the literature or the print journalism of the English-speaking world. By the beginning of the 1980s, it was being used more frequently than the words "LSD" or "marijuana." From the point of the view of literature and the media, cocaine quickly displaced other psychoactive drugs. The boom in this attention to cocaine paradoxically began with the declaration of the war on drugs.

At the beginning, the growing demand for cocaine was handled by traffickers without much experience who took advantage of the absence of controls in the airports of the countries where it originated and where it was sold. They bought the raw material from growers of coca leaf, processed it locally, and exported it by means of casual couriers, recruited from among middle-class travelers. The Chileans initially dominated the cocaine trafficking business. But their lead came to an abrupt end as a result of the coup d'état against the Chilean government in September 1973 (Gaviria 2000, 1–25). In a matter of months, nineteen Chilean narcotics traffickers were extradited by the new military regime. It had only needed a hint from the US authorities that the traffickers might be financing the activities of left-wing groups that had gone into hiding. The war against drugs and the fight against communism were closely linked at this point.

At first, Colombian traffickers did not dominate the cocaine export market. Cubans living in the United States, Argentines, and Italians, among others, were the first to actively participate in the business after the Chileans were displaced. In May 1974, in one of its first articles on cocaine trafficking, the Colombian daily newspaper *El Tiempo* reported that several Americans, Argentines, Chileans, Italians, and Venezuelans had been arrested at Bogotá's El Dorado airport when they tried to bring cocaine on board flights to the United States (*El Tiempo* 1974). They usually spent a few days in Colombia, bought the drug in Leticia or another border city, and carried the cocaine when they flew back to the United States or Europe. The Colombian traffickers were one group among many others. "On the world map of drugs trafficking Colombia is one of the three or four most important countries," *El Tiempo* wrote in the same period (1973).

Within a few years, for reasons that are still not fully understood, Colombian traffickers had turned into the main exporters of cocaine to the US market. Some academics cite geographical reasons; others mention sociological reasons (Colombians' supposed liking for illegal activities). But such determinism, whether geographical or cultural, is not wholly convincing. The dominance of Colombia might have been due to fortuitous events, historical accidents that were then exploited and maintained for economic reasons, and the experience and specialization that resulted might have created a competitive advantage.

The role of chance in the rise of Colombia as the main cocaine-producing country makes what happened after that—the many adverse effects of narcotics trafficking on the country's political, social, and economic life—even more tragic. Narcotics trafficking unleashed an unprecedented wave of violence. The homicide rate rose from less than 30 per 100,000 inhabitants in 1978 to more than 70 by 1990 (Gaviria 2000, 1–25). Other types of criminality—extortion, arms trafficking, car theft—also flourished as a result of the consolidation of organized crime and the resulting weakening of the judicial system. In short, narcotics trafficking led to a rapid growth of violent crime, first limited to a number of areas and then spreading throughout the country.

But narcotics trafficking also affected the country's institutions. Initially, it infiltrated the traditional political parties, then it waged an open war against the state and the media. It later financed the expansion of guerrilla groups and paid for the growth of paramilitary ones, and most recently sponsored the emergence of what are known as the *bandas criminales* (crime gangs), as former president César Gaviria correctly notes in the preface to this book. During the past thirty years, the greatest challenges to Colombian institutions have come from groups directly involved in drug trafficking activities.

From the early stages, narcotics trafficking corrupted the judicial system, politics, and many public and private activities. In March 1978, in the middle of the presidential campaign of that year, a reporter from the *New York Times* wrote a lengthy article on the subject, in which he noted, among other things, that

> the drug traffickers have arisen not only as a new economic class, but also as a powerful political force, with corrupt links on all levels of government. . . . Illegal money affected the congressional elections in which many votes were bought for a price of ten dollars each, especially on the Atlantic coast. (Vidal 1978, E2)

Now, more than thirty years later, the corrupting power of narcotics trafficking is just as evident as it was then. Little has changed in that respect.

But the consequences did not end there. The foreign relations of the country were "narcotized" and came to be completely dominated by the subject of drugs. Colombia began to be regarded simply as a country that produced and exported cocaine. Every export, every movement of capital, every journey to a foreign country by a Colombian, was considered to be suspicious. The export of cocaine not only transformed our internal reality, it also distorted the world's perceptions of the country.

To sum up, narcotics trafficking profoundly transformed Colombian society. In the words of the historian Mary Roldán, the cocaine business "broke up tradition, transformed social customs [and] restructured morality, thought and expectations" (Roldán 2002). The consequences are still visible; they form part of the economic, social, and institutional reality of Colombia. The causes are harder to determine. It is a complex and not fully resolved story, a history that began in 1971 with the declaration of the war on drugs.

Colombia has suffered the consequences of the war on drugs more than any other country. It has felt it on its own flesh. Forty years' experience of being the epicenter of a futile war grants Colombia (and Colombians) the moral and intellectual authority to promote an open, worldwide debate about anti-drug policies and to identify their successes, failures, and lost opportunities. This book is inspired by that conviction.

This publication gathers together research undertaken by a diverse group of professors, diverse insofar as they employ a broad range of methodological, conceptual, and even ideological approaches. But there is also an obvious guiding thread, a constant feature in all chapters: a respect for the facts, a tendency to analyze the data and judge the policies not by their intentions or adherence to a given doctrine, but by their results, their effects on the country's economic, social, and institutional reality.

STRUCTURE AND CONTENT

This book is divided into five parts. The first, titled "The Dimensions of the Drug Problem in Colombia: Production, Trafficking, and Consumption," is made up of two chapters. Chapter 1 describes the chain of production and trafficking of cocaine in Colombia, quantifies the aggregate value produced by each link in the business, and analyzes the macroeconomic importance of the production and the trafficking of cocaine in the Colombian economy. Chapter 2 studies the evolution of drug consumption in Colombia during the past fifteen years, characterizes the consumers of illegal drugs, and presents a preliminary analysis of the effects on internal consumption of a mid-1990s ruling by the Constitutional Court that decriminalized what is known in Colombia as the *personal dose*.

The second part, titled "Policies for the Reduction of Supply and Demand," deals with anti-drug policies in Colombia. It presents an exhaustive analysis of three policies: the recent one for controlling the production and trafficking of cocaine under Plan Colombia, alternative development policies, and those policies aimed at reducing demand by implementing treatment and prevention programs.

More precisely, Chapter 3 analyzes the costs, effectiveness, and efficiency of drug policies implemented under Plan Colombia to reduce the supply of drugs, and it also evaluates the different possibilities for intervening in the activities of producing and exporting illegal drugs in the country. Chapter 4 is devoted to programs for alternative development, particularly the most recent efforts to control the cultivation of illegal drugs through the promotion of legal agricultural activities. Finally, Chapter 5 describes the generally meager and disjointed programs that have been implemented in Colombia for reducing the demand and treating addicts. The chapter presents some specific recommendations, based on scientific evidence and sound practices discussed in academic studies on this subject.

The third part of the book, "International Relations and Anti-Drug Policies in Colombia," deals with the interrelation between Colombia's foreign policy and the drug problem. This part is made up of three chapters, which, taken as a whole, show how the efforts to "narcotize" the foreign policy agenda, undertaken by several administrations with the main objective of obtaining aid and funding for the anti-drug fight, have led to wrong decisions, disagreements with countries that have a different approach to the drug problem, and the neglect of other foreign policy objectives.

Chapter 6, for example, shows how, with the aim of counteracting the lack of interest in the subject of illegal drugs shown by some multilateral organizations, different Colombian administrations have followed a deliberate (rhetorical, it might be said) strategy of emphasizing the link between the production and trafficking of illegal drugs and other subjects that are priorities for these organizations, such as terrorism, the environment, and human rights.

Chapter 7 speaks of the recent "disagreements" between the European Union and Colombia on drug policy. Whereas Colombia has repeatedly insisted on a more repressive approach, the European Union has tended to emphasize more balanced policies, focused, for example, on what is now known as harm reduction. This lack of understanding has led Europe to reduce its cooperation, limiting it to specific areas like alternative development, environmental cooperation, and the economic development of remote rural zones. Finally, Chapter 8 shows the manner in which the emphasis on security (*securitización*) in anti-drug policies has kept Colombia and the United States from engaging in a broader and more constructive discussion about the drug problem. The chapter argues that, among other things, Colombia should take advantage of the current political situation in the United States to promote an open and frank debate about the prohibitionist stance and an objective evaluation of the cost-benefit of the anti-drug policies implemented under Plan Colombia.

The fourth part covers the legal and institutional aspects of the war on drugs in Colombia. Chapter 9 presents a detailed study of the Constitutional Court ruling that ordered the decriminalization of the possession and consumption of small doses of narcotics. Basing itself on a description of the day-to-day enforcement of the abovementioned ruling on the streets of Bogotá, the chapter shows the discrepancy between the written norm and the way it is put into practice in the streets, especially in cases involving homeless people and youngsters from poor families. These people are singled out from the start by the police as possible perpetrators of violent crimes and the source of social problems.

Chapter 10 discusses the state's different juridical responses to the challenge of narcotics trafficking and the crimes associated with it. The chapter shows that new penal laws and harsher punishments have not led to a significant reduction of the crimes associated with narcotics trafficking. Finally, Chapter 11 deals with the subject of money laundering. The chapter attempts to quantify the laundering of such assets in Colombia and to identify the means used to channel the earnings from narcotics trafficking into the Colombian economy.

The final part of the book, "Institutions and Narcotics Trafficking," consists of four chapters. Chapter 12 shows the manner in which narcotics trafficking penetrated different ambits of the political, social, and economic life of Colombia, thus altering the course of its history. The second part of the chapter analyzes a more recent problem: the conjunction of narcotics trafficking, the activities of the paramilitaries, and the policy that gave rise to the "*parapolítica*" scandal about links between political leaders and paramilitary forces.

Chapter 13 discusses the effect of narcotics trafficking on the opinions and political behavior of Colombians. The chapter shows how the inhabitants of areas where illegal crops are grown tend to participate less in political processes and have less trust in state institutions; the aerial fumigation campaigns, for example, led to a significant decline in their trust in institutions like the National Police. Chapter 14 analyzes the interrelation between narcotics trafficking and organized crime. In particular, it shows that the criminal violence initially caused by the outbreak of drug trafficking proliferated in an endogenous manner due to the weak and dilatory response of the police and judicial authorities to the initial shock. Finally, Chapter 15 deals with the links between organized criminal organizations and the drug trafficking industry during the past thirty years. It presents two case studies that clearly show the role of criminal organizations and illegal armed groups in the chain of the production and trafficking of cocaine at the present time.

SOME GENERAL RECOMMENDATIONS

While each chapter deals with aspects of the drug problem and makes specific recommendations for the formulation of more effective anti-drug policies, there are a series of general recommendations that derive from the book as a whole. A summary of them is as follows:

1. The formulation of anti-drug policies should be based on the available information about what works, what does not work, and at what cost. Policies based on evidence are not only more effective, they also encourage a more open debate on the best way of confronting a complex and, to a certain extent, unsolvable problem.
2. Existing anti-drug policies in Colombia suffer from a lack of coordination. This is not a recent phenomenon; it has been an eternal, continuous problem in the design of anti-drug policies in Colombia. There is thus a need for a different institutional arrangement, one that allows for a coordinated formulation of anti-drug policies. In particular, the government should consider the possibility of creating an independent institution that would replace the National Narcotics Administration (Dirección Nacional de Estupefacientes) and that would have the technical and operational capacity to design and coordinate the application of anti-drug policies based on available scientific evidence.
3. The war against the production and trafficking of cocaine should be reoriented. The available evidence shows that aerial spraying and the manual eradication of

illegal crops have been extremely costly and not very efficient in reducing the production of cocaine. By contrast, interdiction seems much more effective, because it mostly hurts the profitability of the business and thus has a greater dissuasive power on this illegal industry.

4. Drug consumption in Colombia has grown rapidly. Although the current rates of consumption are lower than those of other Latin American countries, they have been rising and will doubtless continue to rise. Given this context, the absence of policies aimed at preventing the consumption of drugs and treating addicts is worrying. It is not only the responsibility of the government; nongovernmental organizations (NGOs) and the civil society play a leading role in this in many of the countries that are leaders in the design of treatment and prevention policies. One of the functions of government should be to support the work of the NGOs and civil society and partly fund their activities.
5. In the international sphere, the Colombian government has the knowledge and authority to promote an open debate on the effectiveness of the current prohibitionist regime. The present situation in countries like Mexico and Brazil, where drug-related violence has substantially increased, should help to promote a global dialogue about anti-drug policies and seek new strategic allies in this enterprise.
6. The links between narcotics trafficking and organized crime in Colombia justify the Colombian government's recent call for a rationalization of the war against drugs. As former president César Gaviria rightly points out in the preface to this book, the successes of Colombia's anti-drug policies cannot be measured by the rises in the price of drugs in consumer countries. Anti-drug policies should aim at reducing the profits associated with the producing and selling illegal drugs and should generally reduce the harm done to society. The question is, how? The answer would be through the implementation of effective treatment and prevention policies that reduce the demand for drugs; the design of supply-reduction policies that attack those links in the chain that produce the highest aggregate values and thereby reduce the profit margins of narcotics trafficking; mechanisms that make money laundering more and more difficult; and providing judicial bodies with adequate tools and the resources needed to engage in a large-scale fight against the crimes associated with narcotics trafficking.

Forty years after the formal declaration of the "war on drugs," the debate about the effectiveness and high costs of the current prohibitionist regime is more alive than ever. Several former presidents from Latin America and well-known intellectuals from all over the world have called attention to the ineffectiveness and adverse effects of the current prohibitionist stance. This book is a contribution to an unavoidable debate that, now more than ever, needs informed analyses that transcend the prejudices and inertia of political decisions.

Alejandro Gaviria
Daniel Mejía

REFERENCES

Demarest, M. 1981. "Cocaine: Middle Class High." *Time*, July 6. Retrieved from *content.time.com/time/magazine/article/0,9171,922619,00.html*, accessed May 12, 2015.

El Tiempo. 1973. "Lo único cierto es que sube." May 13.

———. 1974. "Cae cocaína avaluada en 27 millones." May 10.

Gaviria, A. 2000. "Increasing Returns and the Evolution of Violent Crime: The Case of Colombia." *Journal of Development Economics*, vol. 61: 1–25.

Gootenberg, P. 2008. *Andean Cocaine: The Making of a Global Drug*. Chapel Hill: University of North Carolina Press.

Robbins, W. J. 1969. "Congress Gets Nixon's Bill to Curb Drug Abuses." *New York Times*, July 16, 51.

Roldán, M. 2002. *Blood and Fire: La Violencia in Antioquia, Colombia, 1946–1953*. Durham, NC: Duke University Press.

Vidal, D. 1978. "Colombia Is Still the Gem of the Cocaine Traffic: The U.S. Is Both Chief Consumer and Principal Worrier." *New York Times*, March 19, E2.

PART I: DIMENSION OF THE DRUG PROBLEM IN COLOMBIA

Production, Trafficking, and Consumption

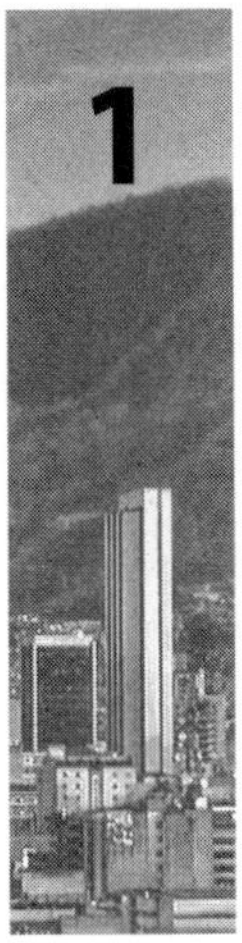

1 The Microeconomics of Cocaine Production and Trafficking in Colombia

Estimates Updated through 2012

Daniel Mejía and Daniel M. Rico

This chapter presents a detailed X-ray of the microeconomics of cocaine production and trafficking in Colombia and presents the estimates updated through 2012. The chapter first presents a brief description of the evolution over time of the aggregate figures on cocaine production and then focuses on a detailed description of each link in the cocaine production and trafficking chain. In particular, it describes the main costs and revenues in each link of the production chain and, on the basis of the available information, provides an estimate of the flows through the Colombian economy of the money that results from these illegal activities. The phases of the production of cocaine chlorhydrate include transformations of the raw material (coca leaf), undertaken in the peasant-farmer (*campesino*) economy and aimed at the small- and medium-scale production of coca base; the involvement of illegal armed groups in the links that produce the greatest aggregate value; and complex networks for the distribution of chemical precursors and the control of the routes for narcotics trafficking.

Our estimates indicate that, on the basis of data for 2012, the size of the illegal drug business in Colombia is between \$4.5 and \$5.5 billion per year, which corresponds to about 1.2 percent of Colombian GDP. While a small part of this aggregate figure is produced in the initial stages of production (coca cultivation and coca paste and base production), the bulk of it (approximately 70 percent) is produced in the trafficking stage (e.g., when cocaine is transported from the processing labs in remote areas of the country to the Pacific coast or the border with Venezuela to be shipped to the main consumer markets in North America and Europe).

DANIEL MEJÍA: Associate professor and director of the Research Center on Drugs and Security, Economics Department, Universidad de los Andes.

DANIEL M. RICO: PhD student at the School of Public Policy at the University of Maryland.

INTRODUCTION

As cocaine is an illegal substance, one should be cautious when analyzing the figures on its production and trafficking. The existing academic literature on this subject has focused on describing the evolution over time of aggregate ("macro") figures for the production of coca leaves and cocaine, and the prices at the intermediate and final stages of the production chain (Mejía and Posada 2010). The two main sources for these aggregate indicators are the United Nations Office on Drugs and Crime (UNODC) and the US Office of National Drug Control Policy (ONDCP). Given the large amount of information and analysis available on the aggregate indicators of the cocaine market in Colombia (Mejía and Posada 2010; US Government Accountability Office [GAO] 2008; and several annual reports of the UNODC), this chapter presents a brief description of them only to give the reader a perspective on the evolution over time of the size of this illegal business in Colombia. Next, the chapter concentrates on making as detailed an X-ray as possible of the microeconomics of cocaine production and trafficking in Colombia, which had not been sufficiently done so far by academic studies on this subject. In particular, this chapter gives a detailed description of each step in the cocaine production chain, the agents involved in it, the inputs and production costs in each of the stages, the types of contracts that the different agents enter into, and the value of the production at each stage.

Behind the nearly 48,000 hectares where coca is grown and the 410 metric tons of cocaine that is produced according to the most recent estimate from UNODC[1] for 2012 (the ONDCP figures for the same year are nearly 175 metric tons of pure cocaine produced on 78,000 hectares[2]), there are almost 60,000 families who have decided to earn money from growing coca leaves and are linked with complex networks of buyers of coca base (mostly illegal armed groups), distributors of inputs and chemical precursors, and local chains of corruption and transnational mafias dedicated to trafficking cocaine.[3]

To help the reader understand the flows through the economy associated with the cocaine production chain in Colombia, from planting the seeds to the first stage of wholesaling, this chapter divides production into four stages: (1) the phase of growing and harvesting coca leaves; (2) the primary transformation of coca leaves into coca paste and coca base; (3) the phase where coca base is transformed into cocaine chlorhydrate; and (4) a final stage where wholesalers move the final product (cocaine) to the country's coasts and borders.[4]

The first two stages are characterized by the haphazard nature of a peasant-farmer economy, where approximately one-third of the smallholders who grow coca do not directly sell the leaves but transform them into coca paste by means of a relatively simple artisanal process and then sell the paste as an input to the large-scale producers of cocaine (UNODC 2005–2012). This figure has dramatically changed during the past six years; whereas in 2008 two-thirds of coca farmers transformed the leaves into coca paste and base and then sold these products, in 2012 this figure was close to one-third.

It is in the third phase of production where the large flow of money characteristic of the cocaine business begins. Here the profitability of the process increases in terms of both the per-kilogram profit margin and the volume of what is being processed. This stage is characterized by high fixed costs of production, such as the mounting of a workshop for processing cocaine (*cristalizadero*), which often requires an investment of more than a million dollars. It is in this phase where illegal armed groups, which have the capacity to assume these fixed costs, become directly linked to the cocaine production chain, in some cases by providing security to cocaine-processing facilities and in others as the direct owners and operators of the *cristalizaderos.*

The final stage consists of the transportation of cocaine to the borders and coasts, where Colombian producers sell the product to intermediary traffickers or join with them to sell it in final markets in the consumer countries.

The sources of information used for the analyses of each of the four stages are mainly the studies published since 2000 by the UNODC and the Integrated Crops Monitoring System (SIMCI) for illegal crops. To develop some of these estimates, the information from the UNODC was complemented with the records of the Colombian Presidency's Program for the Manual Eradication of Illicit Crops (PCI). Another important source of information are the records, kept by the US government since the 1980s, on production, yields, and the area sown with coca leaves, which are useful for providing reference points for establishing ranges of estimates for revenues from the narcotics trafficking value chain in Colombia.

Finally, the analyses and estimates of domestic cocaine trafficking were based on official records of confiscations of cocaine and chemical precursors kept by the Colombian authorities, which are compiled and validated by the Drugs Observatory in Colombia (Observatorio de Drogas de Colombia) of the Colombian Ministry of Justice.

This chapter is made up of four sections, beginning with this introduction. The following sections describe the aggregate data on the production and prices of cocaine in Colombia, as well as their evolution during the past decade. Section 3 focuses on the quantification of production costs, revenues, and value added in each link of the production chain. Finally, Section 4 summarizes the main results and presents the main conclusions.

AGGREGATE INDICATORS FOR THE PRODUCTION AND PRICES OF COCAINE IN COLOMBIA

According to the UNODC,[5] the area devoted to coca growing in Colombia fell from approximately 163,000 hectares in 2000 to nearly 48,000 in 2012. Likewise, the ONDCP estimates that the number of cultivated hectares declined from approximately 140,000 to 78,000 during the same period (Figure 1.1). The figures of the US government (ONDCP) show a cultivated area 50 percent larger on average than the one found in the estimates of the UNODC. The main cause of the difference between the two sources lies in the use of different methodologies for measuring coca plantations (Correa 2007). More precisely, the two methodologies differ in the coverage of the satellite images, the corrections made when interpreting the satellite images, and in the methodologies used for extrapolating the estimates in regions where the satellite images are not very accurate.

The growing of coca leaves is highly concentrated in Colombia (see Figure 1.2). Half of all coca cultivation in Colombia takes place in only three of the thirty-two departments, and 80 percent of all coca cultivation is concentrated in just eight of the departments (UNODC 2013). There were 163 municipalities that had positive levels of coca cultivation in 2011. Half of the cultivation of coca is concentrated in only fourteen municipalities (1.2 percent of total municipalities and 8.6 percent of the municipalities where coca is grown).

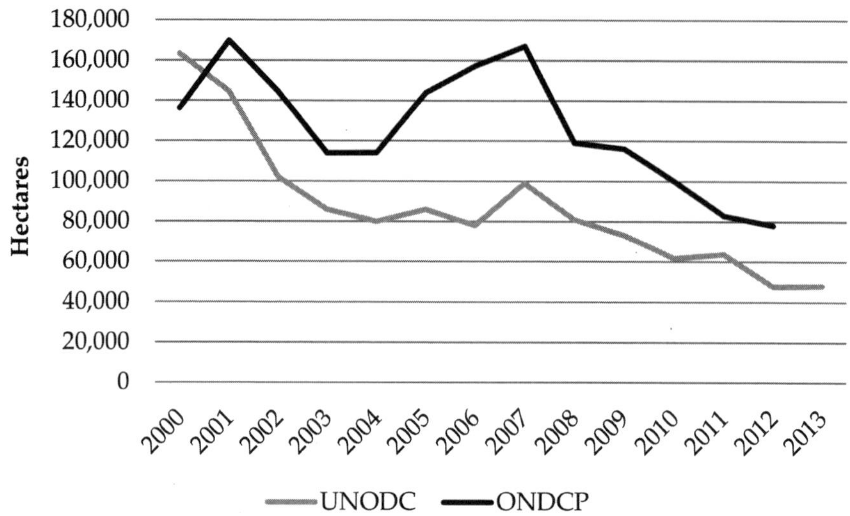

FIGURE 1.1. Coca cultivation in Colombia (hectares). Source: SIMCI-UNODC and ONDCP

One way of measuring the evolution of the concentration of coca crops in Colombia is by means of the Gini coefficient.[6] The high concentration of the cultivations of coca in Colombia can be seen in Figure 1.2A, which shows the Lorenz curve associated with the distribution of coca plantations in Colombia in 2011,[7] and Figure 1.2B, which shows the evolution of the Gini coefficient for the distribution of coca crops between 2000 and 2011. The Lorenz curve for the distribution of coca plantations shows that there is no coca in 85 percent of the municipalities, whereas they are highly concentrated in the remaining 15 percent of the municipalities. As can be seen in Figure 1.2B, the concentration of coca plantations is high but had been steadily declining until 2009, when it started increasing again. This reduced concentration may be due to the strategy that coca growers have adopted to deal with the intensification of aerial and manual eradication campaigns, since the more separated the plantations are, the more difficult and costly it becomes for the government authorities to detect and destroy the plantations.

The two sources of information about the data on cocaine production in Colombia estimate the potential production of cocaine on the basis of statistics on productivity per hectare per year (e.g., the number of kilograms of cocaine that can be produced in a year on each hectare where coca is grown).[8] Using these figures, the UNODC estimates that the potential production of cocaine in Colombia in 2012 was approximately 310 metric tons. The ONDCP, for its part, estimates that the potential production of pure cocaine in the same year was approximately 175 metric tons, which, with an average purity of 85 percent in Colombia, amounts to about 205 metric tons. Figure 1.3 shows the evolution over time of the estimates for the potential cocaine production in Colombia between 2000 and 2012 according to the two sources of information. As can be seen, the production of cocaine in Colombia has fallen by approximately 55 percent since 2000 according to UNODC and by 75 percent since 2001 according to ONDCP estimates.

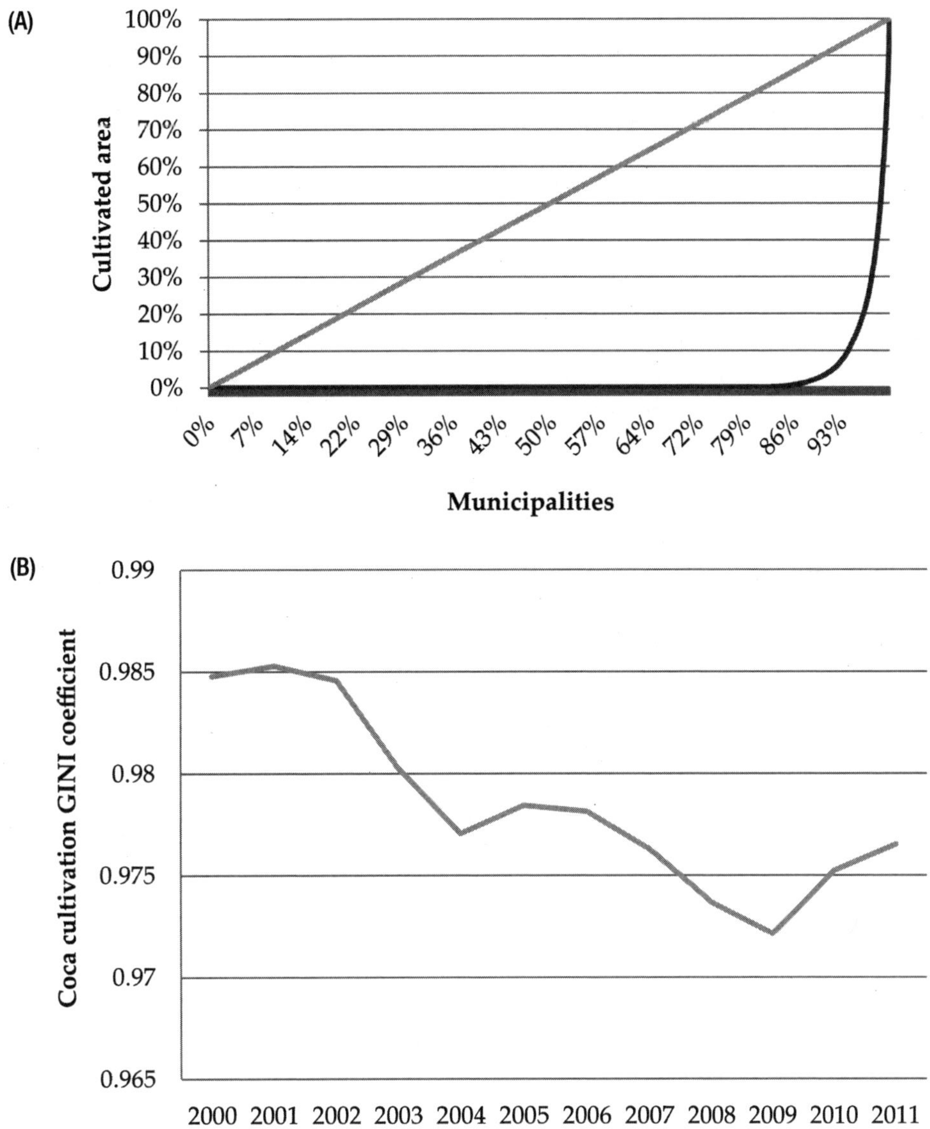

FIGURE 1.2. Concentration of coca crops in Colombia (2000–2011). (A) Lorenz curve—coca crops (2011); (B) Gini coefficient of coca crops (2000–2011). Source: Our own estimates based on data from SIMCI-UNODC

Finally, the prices of coca leaves, coca base, and cocaine in Colombia, in line with the estimates of the UNODC, have been increasing steadily since 2000 (Figures 1.4A and 1.4B). This pattern is consistent with the decline observed in both coca cultivation figures and cocaine production estimates (shown in Figures 1.1 and 1.3 respectively).

The following section provides a detailed description of the microeconomics behind the chain of cocaine production and trafficking in Colombia, focusing on a description of the costs in each link, the required inputs and manpower, revenues, and the total value added in each stage of the process of producing and trafficking cocaine.

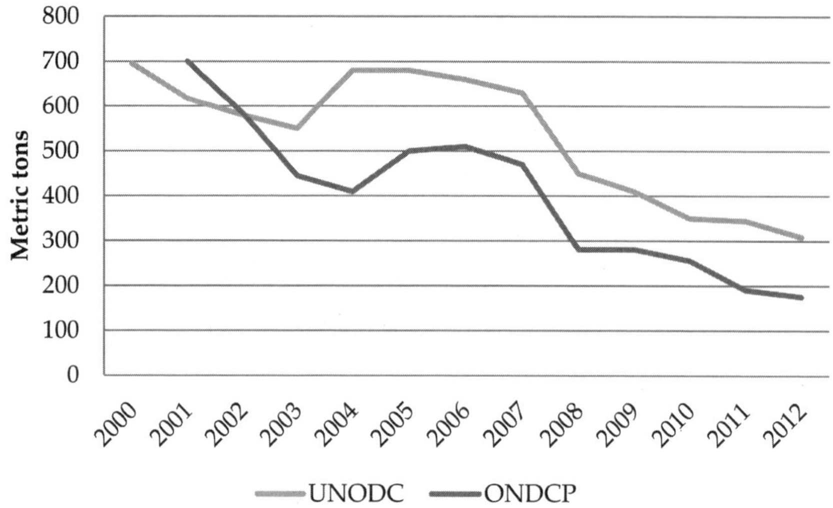

FIGURE 1.3. Potential cocaine production in Colombia. Source: UNODC and ONDCP

THE MICROECONOMICS OF COCAINE PRODUCTION AND TRAFFICKING IN COLOMBIA

The Cultivation of Coca Leaves: Peasants' Specialization

Coca is a bush that grows at altitudes of between 0 and 1,700 meters above sea level. The time required before it can be harvested varies between two and six months, depending on the variety of the coca plant, its age, and the geographical and climatic conditions of the terrain, among other environmental conditions. According to UNOCD studies carried out in Colombia, the average size of a coca plot fell from approximately 2.2 hectares per family in 2002 to less than a half of one hectare per family one decade later.

In turn, the production costs require paying for approximately 5.8 million working days for the cultivation of the nearly 60,000 hectares sown with coca in Colombia (97 working days per hectare per year),[9] with a total mean cost of US$0.7 billion (US$1,300 per hectare). Preparing the terrain requires approximately 459,000 working days per year (7.6 per hectare), with a per hectare cost of about US$65 per year. In the country as a whole, sowing coca requires 494,000 working days per year (8.2 per hectare), with a per hectare cost of about US$75 per year. Maintaining the plots requires 2.1 million working days per year (35 per hectare), with a per hectare cost of about US$390. Finally, harvesting the leaves requires approximately 2.7 million working days per year (46 per hectare), with an approximate per hectare cost of US$725 (UNODC 2005–2013).

Growing coca remains an uncertain source of income with significant risks, largely due to the far from negligible possibility of a total or partial loss resulting from aerial or manual eradication or the hazards of agriculture itself.

We found during the field interviews that the main incentive to stay in the production of coca for the rural farmers is not the expected gain extracted from coca leaf production, which is low or negative in aggregate terms as a result of low profitability and high risks. Instead, peasants maintain coca fields as the result of two conditions:

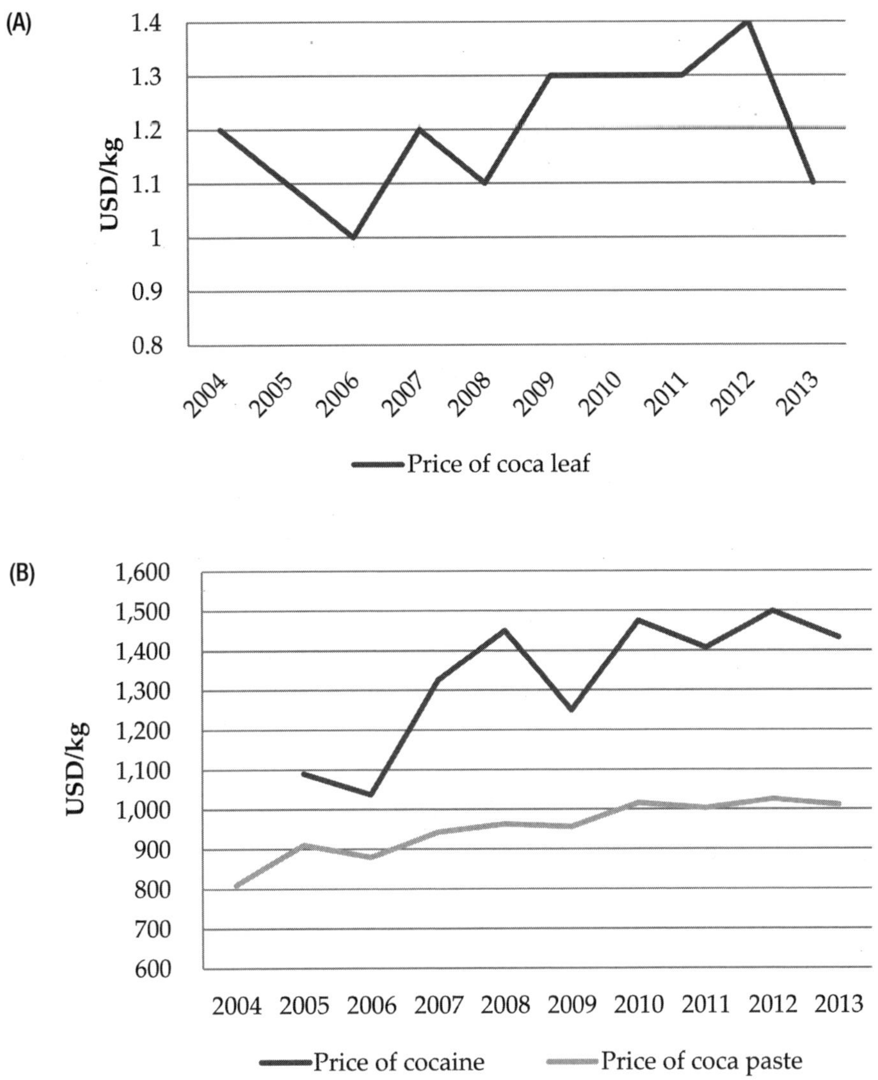

FIGURE 1.4. (A) Price of coca leaf. (B) Price of cocaine and base. Source: SIMCI-UNODC

First, the pressure of illegal armed groups, and second, the use of coca to access the local economic systems, where coca leaf or coca paste became the only commodity that has constant exchange value. For the peasants, possessing coca is the opportunity to enter the economic circuit and make exchanges; otherwise they are excluded from a deeply isolated rural economy, where there are no currency or stable markets for other products. As a result, coca assumes the institutional role of money, for which the grower had to assume the costs and risks of entry into this market.

The decline in revenues for coca growers sharpened during the second administration of Uribe and current president Santos (Uribe's minister of defense between 2006 and 2009), when spraying campaigns, the control of chemical precursors, and manual eradication expanded to critical areas of coca leaf production. Expanding the areas of coca cultivation to more remote areas increased the costs of production and the environmental damage and deforestation of national parks and indigenous reserves.

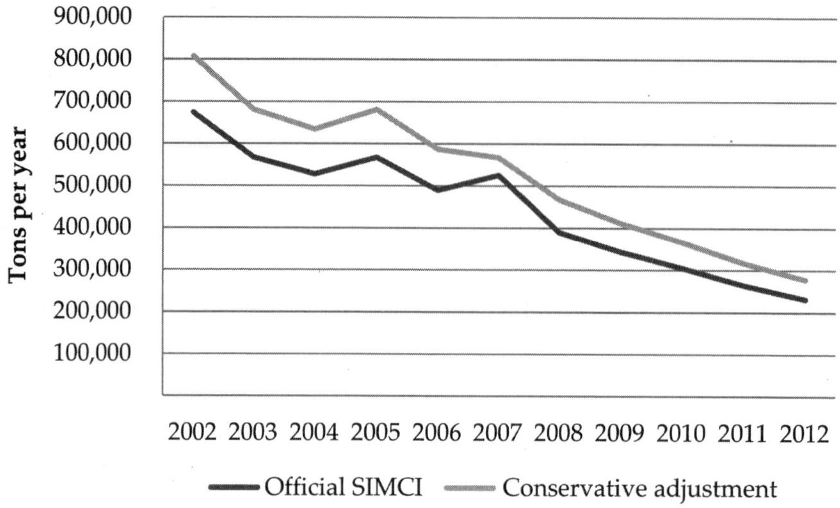

FIGURE 1.5. Production of coca leaf (MT) in Colombia: 2002 to 2012. Source: Our own estimations based on SIMCI-UNODC (multiple reports), CNC, and manual eradication reports

For the estimations presented in this chapter we include the estimated losses that coca growers confront as a result of aerial spraying campaigns and manual eradication. Having Mejia, Restrepo, and Rozo's (2014) work as reference, we assume that, on average, it is required to spray nearly 32 hectares to successfully destroy 100 percent of the production of coca leaf of one hectare. For the case of manual eradication there are no estimates available and we assume that this figure is 3:1. That is, for every three hectares of coca bush manually eradicated, one is permanently destroyed. We observe that the costs of eradication campaigns and aerial spraying per hectare are several times greater than the economic loss suffered by the farmer.

In order to quantify the monetary value of the production of coca cultivation in Colombia, we use the data on per hectare productivity, sown area, and prices of coca leaf. Although these figures vary from one region to another, due to limitations of space we will concentrate in this chapter on describing the aggregate (average) national figures and assess their reliability in the face of the differences between the available sources by constructing the appropriate confidence intervals for our baseline estimations. In 2012, a hectare sown with coca produced approximately 4.2 tons of coca leaf per year, with a minimum of 3.7 tons and a maximum of 4.7 tons per hectare. On the basis of these figures on the per hectare yields and the sown area given in the previous section, we calculate that the total production of coca leaf in Colombia in 2012 was approximately 297,728 tons, with a minimum of 278,000 and a maximum of 317,000, an amount less than half of what we estimated was produced in 2008. Figure 1.5 presents the estimates for the production of coca leaves in Colombia during the past decade.

Based on any of the two estimates presented in Figure 1.5, it can be seen that the reduction in the production of coca leaf in Colombia has been large and steady: 63 percent during the past decade. Our estimates are based on the SIMCI reports, but we made some methodological changes to correct some assumptions used by SIMCI that generate a bias in the estimations and reduce the real cultivated area. These biases are the result of taking the satellite images only one time at the end of each year and discounting from them the hectares that are reported as having been eradicated.

Starting in 2008 we identified a worrying trend of concentration of the spraying campaigns and eradication efforts in the last quarter of the year, precisely at the time when the satellite images are taken, which has the temporary effect of reducing the estimated area of coca cultivation. Also, the coca that is eradicated a few weeks before the end of the year is considered as having had no production throughout the year, which clearly generates a bias in the estimates. Lastly, another bias arises because SIMCI's analysts have also detected inconsistencies in the reports procedures for manual eradication conducted by the Colombian army and police, indicating an overestimation of the number of hectares eradicated. For these reasons, we include a conservative adjustment in Figure 1.5 that corrects these inconsistencies.

Five years ago about one-third of coca growers directly sold coca leaf; the other two-thirds of the farmers processed the leaf into coca paste (*pasta)* or coca base and then sold it to the large-scale producers of cocaine. In the past few years the structure of production has changed and peasants have specialized only on coca leaf production. In the most recent coca cultivation census, 65 percent of coca producers sell the leaf without any processing. This transformation of the peasants' role in the initial stages of cocaine production occurred quickly and has been a result of the increase in the prices of the raw materials needed for processing coca leaf into paste and base (mainly gasoline and cement) and of the emergence of a new generation of local criminal entrepreneurs—"intermediaries"—that now make money by transforming the leaf into coca base in large-scale operations, increasing efficiency and purity levels achieved and reducing the risks of being detected.

The terms of trade in the initial production stages vary a great deal from region to region, according to the conditions imposed by the buyer. The available evidence indicates that this market acts as a monopsony (Cano 2002), where, depending on the region, the only buyers are the Revolutionary Armed Forces of Colombia (hereafter FARC for its Spanish acronym) guerrillas, the paramilitaries, or another illegal armed group that dominates the territory in question. Gallego and Rico (2014) show that the prices of coca leaf, coca paste, and coca base are not affected by aerial spraying or manual eradication, indicating that farmers are able to successfully include the costs of these losses on their expected earnings, also indicating the monopsony role of the FARC and criminal bands in the purchasing of coca leaf.

On the basis of the available data on the prices of coca leaf, we calculate that the total value of coca leaf produced and sold by the peasants in Colombia in 2012[10] was approximately US$189 million. Based on this estimate, the value of the coca leaf sold by the peasants in Colombia as a percentage of GDP is about 0.05 percent. Now, the value of the coca actually transacted by coca growers has increased and more peasants are now directly selling the leaf (two-thirds of the total) at now higher prices (see previous section), but the net income for coca farmers has steadily declined over time.

Figure 1.6 shows the estimates for the three sources of income for the peasants that cultivate coca leaf during the past decade. As can be seen, the income made by the peasants has been falling as a result of a lower participation in the trade of coca paste and coca base, a role that is now assumed by other actors—local criminal entrepreneurs—that are capturing the rents that used to be appropriated by the farmers.

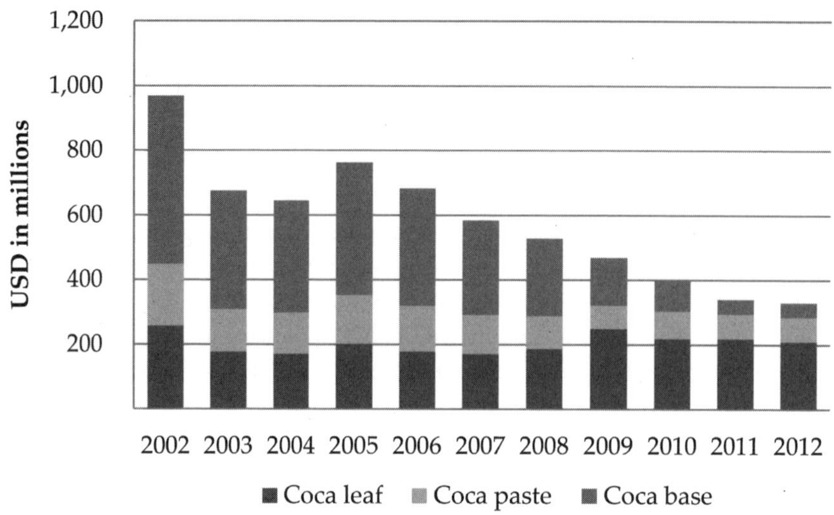

FIGURE 1.6. Total income for coca growers by type of product sold: 2002 to 2012. Source: Our own estimations based on SIMCI reports

The Processing of Coca Leaves into Coca Paste and Base

The processing of coca leaves into coca paste goes through two stages. First, once the leaves are harvested, they are chopped up and mixed with cement, urea, or lime (caustic soda) in order to "basify"[11] the coca leaves before turning them into a mixture of gasoline and an acid solution, which reduces the lead content. This mixture is allowed to steep for a few hours. The process extracts the alkaloid (cocaine sulphate) from the coca leaves. After that, the mixture is drained and organic residues are removed through the use of one or more oxidizing agents in artisanal processes of acidification-basification. The result of this process is coca paste, a gelatinous coffee-colored substance.

Next, the coca paste is mixed with a considerable amount of gasoline and sulfuric acid (the two are reusable), and a smaller amount of sodium carbonate, potassium permanganate (or ammonia),[12] and other inputs to whiten the coca base and eliminate impurities.

It is important to emphasize that the division between paste and base is now much more complicated; the traditional division (made with the use of potassium permanganate) is more diffuse now because of the emergence of new substances that have been substituted for potassium permanganate and the methods used to transform coca paste into coca base. In the past, this process was mainly conducted by the peasants, but less than one-third of them are now dealing with the processing of the coca leaves into coca paste and base. In the past few years other actors associated with criminal bands and guerrilla groups have taken control of this process and are extracting large rents out of controlling this intermediate stage of cocaine production. Implementing large-scale processes for transforming coca leaves into coca paste and base has led them to significantly improve the efficiency of the process. The most conservative estimates indicate that they have been able to improve efficiency by at least 10 percent over the past few years.[13]

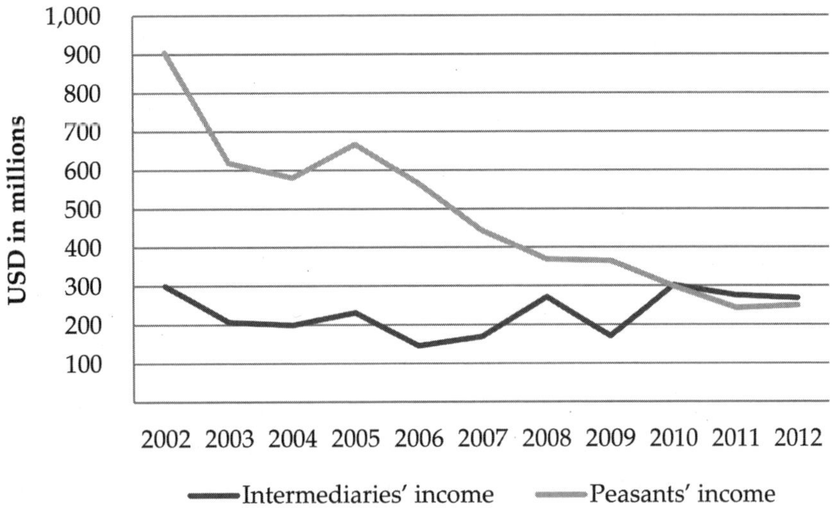

FIGURE 1.7. Total income of the peasants and intermediaries in the cocaine chain. Source: Our own estimations based on SIMCI reports

The main actors at this stage are no longer the peasants, but a small group of intermediaries that operate as a franchise for the FARC or the so-called criminal bands (*bacrim*[14]), where the intermediaries pay for the monopoly of producing and selling large amounts of coca base to the armed group or drug trafficker that controls the region where they operate. These middle-level players in the cocaine chain have not been the target of antinarcotics operations (eradication affects mainly the peasants and interdiction the traffickers) and, as a result, they have been able to expand their economic role in the local and rural economies. Figure 1.7 compares the evolution of the income received by the farmers (who only cultivate coca) with that of the intermediaries that specialize in coca paste and coca base production and that are not under the radar of antinarcotics operations.

As can be observed in Figure 1.7, in the past few years, the income obtained by the intermediaries (who total less than a thousand) is higher than the income of all the peasants (about sixty thousand rural households). This clearly indicates a rebalancing of power inside the intermediate stages of the cocaine production chain that has occurred during the past decade, the concentration of the coca profits into more and more urban actors and the impoverishment of coca growers that in some regions are no longer part of the transformation economy.

The increased economic power of this emerging group of intermediaries relies on the fact that they can produce coca paste and base at higher efficiency levels (over 85 percent purity for coca base) and can purchase large amounts of low-quality coca paste and base made by one-third of the peasants and improve the product in a process that they call "reoxidation," which extracts the impurities and "standardizes" the quality of the base that will later be transformed into cocaine. This process of reoxidation is an expanding business, as the intermediaries have found a profitable business out of standardizing the coca base that is used to produce cocaine. By having a standard base, cocaine producers are able to save time and lower the risks of losing the product by using low-purity coca base.

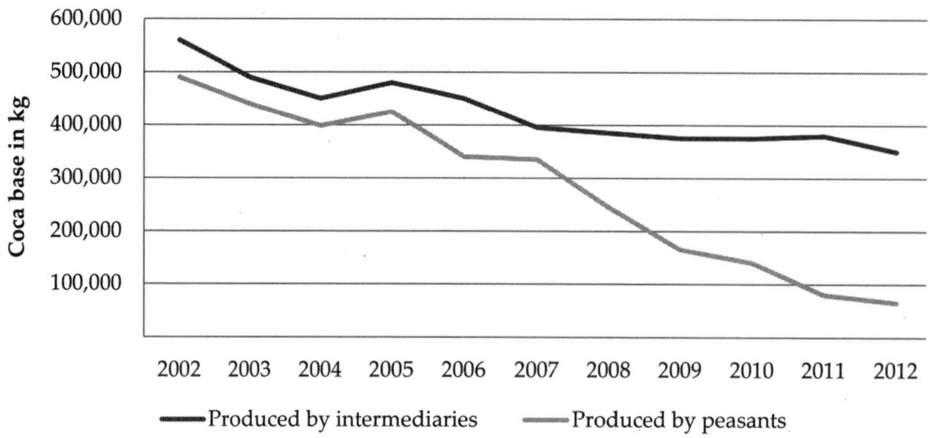

FIGURE 1.8. Production of coca base by intermediaries and peasants. Source: Our own estimations based on SIMCI reports

In 2012, one ton of coca leaves produced, on average, approximately 1.65 kilograms of coca base, an increase of nearly 400 grams per ton compared with the estimations for 2008, indicating a more efficient system of transformation and not a more efficient cultivation process.

The recent changes in the conditions governing access to inputs and chemical precursors in the regions where coca is grown have led to an important increase in the price that farmers face for the inputs required to process cocaine. This is yet another factor that has increased the power of the so-called intermediaries.

The price of coca base has steadily increased in the past years (see Figure 1.4B). The structure of this market and the conditions of payment are influenced by multiple factors, such as the charging of a tax per unit of weight (*gramaje*) by the armed groups, the presence of brokers (*chichipatos* and *maseros*), and payments in cash or kind.

For the past two years the areas of expansion where coca base is paid at the highest prices or in advance for the production (35 percent above the national average) are the borders of the country (in the departments of Nariño, Putumayo, and Norte de Santander), where the FARC has its most important zones of influence.

As observed in Figure 1.8, today less than 15 percent of the entire coca base produced in Colombia is produced by the peasants: six of every seven kilograms of base are produced now by middle-ranked intermediaries.

The Production of Cocaine

The available data on the microeconomics of cocaine production are much more meager than those for the production of coca leaves, paste, and base. This is partly explained by the risk implicit in any kind of fieldwork, since it is at this stage that the illegal armed groups are most directly involved in the production process. The only references in this respect are those we find in sporadic studies by Colombia's National Narcotics Administration (hereafter DNE for its Spanish acronym)[15] and the rigorous estimates, made under laboratory conditions, by the US government. Nevertheless, this evidence, joined to the reports on confiscations and other activities included in the processing and trafficking of cocaine, allow us to make some inferences and estimates about the process of transforming coca base into cocaine chlorhydrate.

The process of transforming coca base into cocaine is simple and takes about six hours if the required infrastructure and chemical precursors and the appropriate security conditions are present.[16] In the first part of this process, the base is dissolved in a solvent that is later shaken and filtered with calcium chloride, and the mixture is then combined with activated carbon and potassium permanganate. In the next step, the mixture is filtered through activated carbon and then is gently heated in a bain-marie. Once the boiling point is reached, a mixture of concentrated hydrochloric acid and another solvent is added to obtain cocaine chlorhydrate. The final step is filtering, drying, and packing. At the end of the process, in addition to cocaine, there are a number of chemical residues that must be separated and recycled (through a repeated boiling process) so that they can be reused. In the whole of this process, the main difficulties for the producer are obtaining the highest grades of purity and ensuring that the production centers are secure. The workshops (*cristalizaderos*) where cocaine sulphate (base) is transformed into cocaine chlorhydrate require an important investment in physical infrastructure, lodging and food for the operatives, distribution networks and storerooms for chemical equipment, early warning systems to avoid attacks by the authorities or even other criminal gangs, and a supply of electricity and safe (and dry) places to store the final product.

The size of these *cristalizaderos* varies in accordance with the production needs and their scale. In most cases, the cost of mounting such a laboratory can reach a million dollars, and its operations are cyclical (depending on the harvests that determine the availability of coca base). Each processing facility has a chief chemist and about a dozen workers whose wages depend on the amount produced. The available information indicates that the labor costs in a *cristalizadero* are about US$200 per kilogram of processed cocaine.

In terms of production capacity and number of laboratories, the *cristalizaderos* in the jungle and isolated rural areas continue to be the norm in this part of the production chain. When we look at the records of the destruction of *cristalizaderos*, however, we see an increase in laboratories located in urban areas, close to the country's main roads, which indicates a tendency to place these production centers in those places where there is an easier access to inputs and chemical precursors, even at the risk of detection.[17]

The information available from the interception of communications from illegal armed groups in Colombia serves as a reference point for estimating the sales price of a kilogram of cocaine in the production centers in Colombia. According to this information, the illegal armed groups (the FARC and the *bacrim* in the great majority of cases) sell the cocaine at a price that varies from US$2,300 to US$3,000 per kilogram. It is worth noting that this is the price in the lab and does not include the profits derived from cocaine trafficking. Based on the available figures on cocaine prices and potential cocaine production (see Figure 1.9), we can calculate the economic size of cocaine production in Colombia. On this basis, we estimate that the market value of the cocaine produced in Colombia is approximately US$820 million (nearly 0.2 percent of GDP), with a maximum value of US$930 million (0.23 percent of GDP) and a minimum of US$710 million (0.16 percent of GDP).

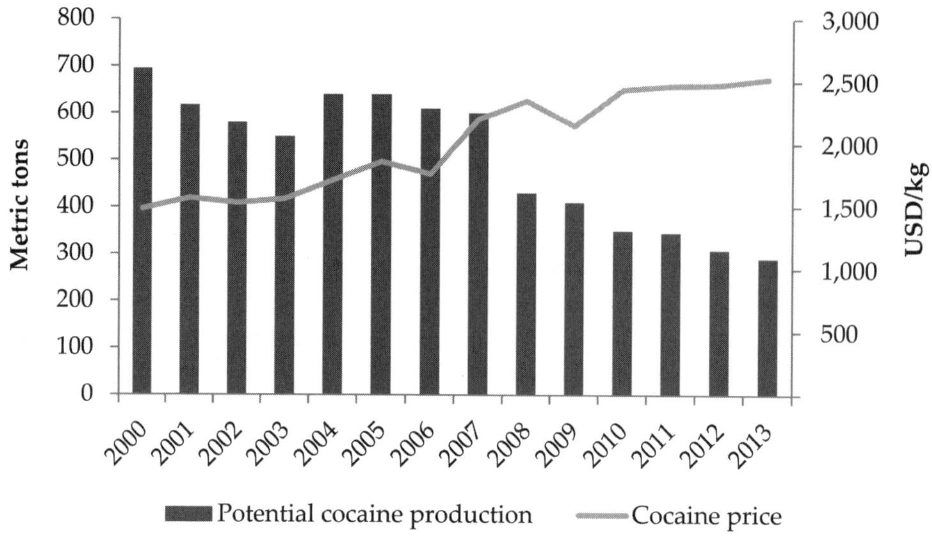

FIGURE 1.9. Potential cocaine production and cocaine prices. Source: SIMCI-UNODC

The improvements achieved in the efficiency rates in the cocaine-production process (10 percent according to SIMCI) do not compensate for the decrease in the amount of cocaine production (about a 60 percent reduction), so the size of the economy of cocaine transformation has decreased significantly over the past six or seven years in Colombia.

It is also worth noting that in the past few years, drug trafficking organizations have started to export coca base from Colombia to Central America (Rico 2013) in order to carry out the last stage of transformation in countries that have less controls on chemical precursors, thus reducing the costs and associated risks.

The Trafficking of Cocaine

The level of involvement of Colombian groups in the trafficking of cocaine has changed over time. There are several schemes that the *bacrim*, the FARC, and other illegal groups use to sell the cocaine they produce. Under the first scheme, these groups sell the cocaine at the gate of the laboratory to drug traffickers, who are responsible for collecting the product in planes or riverboats in the jungles of Colombia and then transporting it out of the country. Under this scheme, widely used by the FARC in the late 1990s, the risk is low, but achieving significant profits requires economies of scale. The sales price under this scheme varies from US$2,300 to US$3,000 per kilogram. In an alternative system, more frequently used by the illegal groups recently, a strategic alliance is formed with Colombian cartels to transport the cocaine to other countries. Under this scheme, drug producers put up the product and the drug traffickers take charge of exporting the cocaine. In this scheme of shared risk, the producers benefit from an average rate of return higher than that of the profit derived from selling the product at the laboratory gate. The available evidence indicates that the sales price for those who transport the cocaine to the consumer countries under this scheme varies from US$9,000 to US$12,000 per kilogram when the cocaine is shipped to markets in North America via

Mexico or Central America. The per kilogram transport cost to Honduras (the main port of entry for cocaine in the region) is, on average, US$3,500. When, on the other hand, the cocaine goes to European markets, the level of involvement of Colombian groups is less, but the prices vary from US$25,000 to US$30,000 per kilogram (this route involves many more brokers, the need to pay more tolls—*derechos de piso*—in different places, and a much longer time to transport the cocaine). On this route the average transport cost per kilogram of cocaine is much higher, nearly US$15,000. Additionally, while a shipment along the route to North America may take a few weeks to reach its final destination (eight weeks approximately), it takes much more time on the route to Europe (six months, on average). Therefore, while the sales price is much higher in Europe, the costs are also much higher and the transport takes more time.

When the illegal groups control the whole production chain, from the growing of coca leaves to the production of cocaine, the approximate cost of producing a kilogram of cocaine is US$1,250. In these cases, all the links in the production process are vertically integrated and the producers of cocaine obtain the greatest possible profits. The per kilogram profit, if the drug is not confiscated, may reach US$5,500 if the cocaine goes to North America and US$11,500 if the cocaine is sent to European drug markets.[18]

Cocaine markets have shifted south, with the biggest port of export of cocaine in the world now being Brazil (UNODC 2012). Also, the increase in cocaine consumption in other countries (mainly Spain, Italy, Argentina, and Brazil) has expanded the trafficking routes to new countries.

Based on available reports of UNODC and interviews with Colombian authorities, we assume that 3 percent of the cocaine produced in Colombia stays in Colombia to satisfy local consumption, nearly 10 percent is smuggled to the United States by Colombians using their own routes (without paying the Mexican cartels), 34 percent of the cocaine goes to Central America and from there to the United States and Europe without the control of the Colombian traffickers, and the remaining 53 percent goes to rest of the regions (South America, Europe, Asia, etc.).[19]

The microtrafficking of cocaine and coca paste (*bazuco*) is increasing in Colombia. Our estimates indicate that this market has more than doubled in the past decade, but its size is still marginal in comparison to other destinations. The biggest decrease is observed in the profits made by Colombian drug trafficking organizations (DTOs) that, avoiding the Central American and Mexican cartels, attempt to smuggle cocaine into the United States.

Considering the official reports, the estimated value of the DTOs' loss as a result of interdiction is US$479 million in 2012, more than double the value of the cocaine seized in 2002 (during the early stages of Plan Colombia), when the traffickers lost fifty-two tons of cocaine (adjusted for purity) and its value was US$217 million. The peak of interdiction and losses for the DTOs was 2009, when we estimate that traffickers lost about US$665 million.

There are several reasons for not deducting confiscations when we make our estimates of the amount of money entering the Colombian economy from cocaine production and trafficking. First, the figures for cocaine seizures are not comparable with the estimates for production, since the two may have very different levels of purity.[20] Second, it is not possible to determine with certainty who owns the cocaine when it is confiscated, so it is impossible to know if the revenues from the trafficking of the confiscated cocaine would or would not have returned to Colombia. In other words, it is not possible to know if the loss of income from the confiscations is assumed by Colombian or by foreign cartels. Third, the growing number of processing laboratories in countries where coca leaves are not grown (especially in Central America and Ecuador) leads us to think that many of the recorded seizures of cocaine are in fact of high-purity coca base, the value of which is different from cocaine chlorhydrate.

Our best estimates using potential cocaine production and average cocaine exporting prices indicate that the amount of money entering the Colombian economy from drug production and trafficking business lies between US$4.5 and US$5.5 billion. These estimates take into account that on the one hand, cocaine production has fallen, but on the other hand, cocaine prices have increased. Our estimate of the size of the cocaine production and trafficking business back in 2008 was US$7.8 billion. This implies that the illegal business has decreased by about 35 percent between 2008 and 2012.

SUMMARY AND CONCLUSIONS

This chapter has presented a detailed description of the microeconomics behind the process of producing and trafficking cocaine in Colombia. This process has many stages, not always integrated, which range from the relatively simple ones found in the peasant-farmer economies responsible for growing the leaves to the large-scale production, with high fixed costs, of cocaine chlorhydrate. Our estimates suggest that the size of the business of producing and trafficking cocaine in Colombia is approximately US$5 billion (approximately 1.3 percent of Colombian GDP).

It is worth noting that the previous estimates (done for other periods) suggested that the business of producing and trafficking cocaine had a much bigger role in the Colombian economy. In particular, Steiner (1997) estimated that the share of narcotics trafficking in the GDP for the period from 1982 to 1995 was approximately 5 percent. Rocha (2000), for his part, estimated that the total revenues from narcotics trafficking were 4 percent of GDP on average during the period from 1982 to 1992, when the author calculated that nearly 70 percent of that amount returned to Colombia, that is, 2.9 percent of GDP (Rocha 2001). Our own estimates for 2008 indicated that the size of this business was US$7.8 billion, implying a reduction of about 35 percent between 2008 and 2012.

Colombia, with the help of other countries (mainly the United States) has invested large amounts of money in the war against the production and trafficking of cocaine. Up to now, however, the academic literature had revealed little about the microeconomics of this illegal business (the agents involved in each link, the costs, profit margins, etc.). The main contribution of this chapter has been to provide a detailed description of this sector and quantify the size of this illegal business, as precisely as possible with the information available.

NOTES

We would like to thank María José Uribe for her valuable help in the preparation of this chapter and the comments of Miguel García and Peter Reuter. The authors would also like to thank the Banco de la República and Narcotics Section of the US Embassy for funding the writing of this chapter.

1. Monitoring of illegal crops, 2013, UN Illicit Crop Monitoring Program (SIMCI). The metric tons unit (t) of cocaine refers to cocaine with a purity of 100 percent, which is used as a reference for measurement although it is not technically possible to produce it at that level of purity. As a reference point, the purity of the cocaine produced in Colombia is nearly 85 percent.
2. Source: *www.whitehouse.gov/ondcp/targeting-cocaine-at-the-source*, accessed July 15, 2014.
3. These transactional narcotics trafficking networks are analyzed in detail in Tickner, García, and Arreaza (2014).
4. The other phases of the supply of cocaine, like its international trafficking, retail distribution in the consumer countries, and laundering of assets, are not included in this chapter. Chapter 11, by Carlos Caballero and Alfonso Amaya, deals with the subject of asset laundering in Colombia.
5. See various annual reports of the UNODC.
6. The Gini coefficient is a measure of inequality defined between 0 and 1. The closer to 1 the coefficient is, the more unequal is the distribution of coca plots among Colombian municipalities (i.e., the more concentrated are the coca plots).
7. The Lorenz curve is way of graphically representing the distribution of a variable (in this case, coca plots) in a given domain (in this case, the total number of municipalities in the country).
8. These estimates of productivity are based on field visits to study the efficiency of the process of transforming coca leaves into cocaine chlorhydrate.
9. For the purposes of the following estimates, we will assume that there were approximately 60,000 hectares devoted to growing coca in Colombia in 2012. This is the simple average of the estimates of the two available sources (UNODC and ONDCP).
10. This value refers to the hypothetical case where all the growers would sell their coca leaves without any kind of subsequent processing. It is essentially a regional distinction. For example, while 91 percent of the growers in the Sierra Nevada de Santa Marta and 86 percent in the Catatumbo sell coca leaves, in el Meta and Guaviare only 22 percent of the growers sell coca leaves.
11. The popular term for this stage of the process is "salting" the coca (*salar la coca*).
12. According to the United Nations definition, it is the utilization of potassium permanganate, ammonia, or another substance to eliminate organic substances that marks the difference between coca paste and cocaine base. The efficiency of the process is 93 percent. In other words, a thousand grams of coca paste afterwards become the equivalent of 930 grams of cocaine base.
13. Based on interviews and workshops made by the Colombian Police and UNODC, with professional workers of real cocaine labs from different regions of Colombia.
14. The term "*bacrim*" is a syllabic abbreviation of the expression "bandas criminales," criminal bands. It broadly denotes the various delinquent groups that grew out of the dismemberment of several paramilitary groups in 2006.
15. One of the main difficulties in the analysis of how many cocaine production centers were destroyed is that the term "laboratory" covered every kind of production facility, without distinguishing between those that produced paste, base, or cocaine. The DNE has worked to refine its records so that the figures for the past four years will be much more reliable.
16. When this chapter was written, the SIMCI was undertaking a detailed study in the field of precursors, needed chemical inputs, associated costs, and productivity estimates related to the process of transforming coca base into cocaine.

17. The number of captures per laboratory (*cristalizadero*) is less than one in the case of those located in remote rural zones.
18. The quantitative information that underlies the estimates of the prices at which the traffickers sell cocaine on the different routes comes from several press articles that cite information found in the computers belonging to Raúl Reyes and other *capos* of the narcotics trade.
19. This assumption is consistent with the global estimates of the respective share of the United States and Europe in the consumption of cocaine, reported in the World Drug Report.
20. Although there are no detailed records of the levels of purity of the cocaine seized in Colombia, the little evidence that is available indicates ranges of purity that run from 60 percent to 95 percent.

REFERENCES

Cano, C. G. 2002. *Reinventando el desarrollo alternativo*. Colección Puntos de Vista. Bogotá: Corporación Colombia Internacional.

Correa, H. L. 2007. "Contribuciones para entender las diferencias entre cifras de cultivos de coca en Colombia." Technical working document. Bogotá: United Nations.

Gallego, J., and D. Rico, D. 2014. "Eradication and the Price of Coca in Colombia." Working Paper. Bogotá: Universidad del Rosario.

Mejía, D., and C. E. Posada. 2010. "Cocaine Production and Trafficking: What Do We Know?" In *Innocent Bystander: Developing Countries and the War on Drugs*, edited by P. Keefer and N. Loayza, 253–300. Washington, DC: Palgrave Macmillan/World Bank. Retrieved from *www-wds.worldbank.org/external/default/WDSContentServer/IW3P/IB/2010/03/25/000333037_20100325005015/Rendered/PDF/536410PUB0Inn01010fficia10Use00nly1.pdf*, accessed May 12, 2015.

Mejía, D., P. Restrepo, and S. Rozo. 2014. "On the Effects of Enforcement on Illegal Markets: Evidence from a Quasi-Experiment in Colombia." Mimeo, Universidad de los Andes, October.

ONDCP (White House Office of National Drug Control Policy). 2007. *National Drug Control Strategy*. 2007 Annual Report, Washington, DC: ONDCP.

Rico, D. 2013. "Las dimensiones internacionales del crimen organizado en Colombia: Las Bacrim, sus rutas y refugios." In *La diáspora criminal: La difusión transnacional del Crimen Organizado y cómo contener su expansión*, edited by J. C. Garzón and E. L. Olson. Washington, DC: Wilson Center. Retrieved from *www.wilsoncenter.org/sites/default/files/LA_DIASPORA_CRIMINAL_0.pdf*, accessed May 12, 2015.

Rocha, R. 2000. *La economía colombiana tras 25 años de narcotráfico*. Bogotá: Siglo del Hombre-UNODC.

———. 2001. "Antecedentes y perspectivas del narcotráfico en Colombia: Una mirada a las políticas." *Problemas del Desarrollo* 32, no. 126: 59–109.

Steiner, R. 1997. "Los dólares del narcotráfico. Cuadernos de Fedesarrollo," no. 2. Bogotá: Tercer Mundo Editores.

UNODC (UN Office on Drugs and Crime). 2004–2009. *World Drug Report*, vol. 1, Analysis; vol. 2, Statistics. Vienna: United Nations. Retrieved from *www.unodc.org/unodc/en/data-and-analysis/WDR.html*, accessed May 12, 2015.

———. 2005–2009. *Coca Cultivation Surveys for Bolivia, Peru and Colombia.* Vienna: United Nations Office. Retrieved from *www.unodc.org/unodc/en/crop-monitoring/index.html*, accessed May 12, 2015.

———. 2012. *World Drug Report 2012.* New York: United Nations Office. Retrieved from *www.unodc.org/documents/data-and-analysis/WDR2012/WDR_2012_web_small.pdf*, accessed May 12, 2015.

———. 2013. *Análisis multitemporal de cultivos de coca. Período 2011–2012.* Bogotá: SIMCI. Retrieved from *www.biesimci.org/Documentos/Documentos_files/informes_analisis_multitemporal_1112_internet.pdf*, accessed May 12, 2015.

US Government Accountability Office (GAO). 2008. "Plan Colombia Drug Reduction Goals Were Not Fully Met, But Security Has Improved; U.S. Agencies Need More Detailed Plans for Reducing Assistance." GAO 00-71, Washington, DC: GAO.

2 Drug Consumption in Colombia

Adriana Camacho, Alejandro Gaviria, and Catherine Rodríguez

INTRODUCTION

Historically, the study of the drug problem in Colombia has focused on the dynamics of production and trafficking and their effects on the country's institutions and society in general (Grossman and Mejía 2008; Mejía and Restrepo 2010). There are also some studies of the relationship between the production and commercialization of drugs and violence in particular and the armed conflict in general (González and Smith 2009; Echeverry and Partow 2005; Medina and Martínez 2003; Gaviria 2000). The evolution of the consumption of drugs has been less studied. For example, there are no systematic studies in the country of the socioeconomic characteristics of drug consumers, nor about the risks associated with their consumption, and even less about perceptions of the individual and social consequences of consumption. These gaps in the analysis of the problem have made it difficult to design and put in place public policies aimed at the prevention of drug consumption and the treatment of addiction, as is documented in Chapter 5.

Among the few studies of the consumption of drugs, the following should be singled out: (a) the nationwide studies of the consumption of psychoactive substances in the years 1992, 1996, 2008, and 2013 undertaken by the National Narcotics Administration (DNE) in collaboration with the Colombian School of Medicine (Escuela Colombiana de Medicina), the Center for Studies and Information on Health of the Fundación Santa Fe (CEIS), the Ministry of Social Protection, and the Ministry of Justice;[1] (b) the surveys of the Programa Rumbos (Directions Program), and (c) some qualitative investigations recently carried out (UNODC 2006; Pérez 2009). Although all of them contribute to our knowledge of the situation of the consumption of psychoactive substances in Colombia, the analyses have for the most part been descriptive and have not examined the causes or determining factors of the observed phenomena.

The present chapter analyzes the evolution of the consumption of drugs on the basis of the information from national surveys by the DNE in the years 1992, 1996, 2008, and 2013. The chapter has four main objectives. To begin with, it describes the evolution of the consumption of psychoactive substances in Colombia. It then analyzes the demographic and socioeconomic characteristics of the typical drug user. Then it studies the perception of the risks and problems suffered by consumers of marijuana, cocaine, and *bazuco*, the Colombian slang for crack cocaine. Finally, it uses the above

Adriana Camacho: Associate professor, Faculty of Economics, Universidad de los Andes.

Alejandro Gaviria: Minister of health and social protection, 2012–present. Earlier he was dean and associate professor, Faculty of Economics, Universidad de los Andes.

Catherine Rodríguez: Associate professor, Faculty of Economics, Universidad de los Andes.

results to throw light on the validity of the reasons given by the Colombian government and Congress, toward the end of the administration of President Uribe,[2] to harden the prohibition of the personal use of drugs into a constitutional norm. Specifically, it presents some indirect and suggestive evidence that contradicts the main justification for the above legal reform, the supposed effect of the Constitutional Court's 1994 decision (Sentence C-221, May 1994) to decriminalize the consumption of the personal dose of drugs in Colombia.

The main findings of this chapter show that the consumption of psychoactive substances has significantly increased in Colombia in recent years. This increase is found in both genders and in all age groups, social classes, and occupational groups. Men from a prosperous background who steadily consume alcohol and cigarettes and are between the ages of eighteen and twenty-four are the ones most prone to consume drugs. The consumers of psychoactive substances are more likely to suffer from conflicts with their families and friends than from other kinds of problems. Finally, the dynamics of drug consumption in the course of the past thirty years, and comparisons between Latin American countries and between Colombian cities, suggest that the decriminalization of drug consumption was not a major factor in the increased use.

THE COLOMBIAN CONTEXT AND CHANGES IN THE LEGISLATION RELATED TO DRUG USE

During the past few years there has been a heated debate on the consumption of psychoactive substances and the role of the state in this problem. The administration then headed by Álvaro Uribe repeatedly argued, first, that the consumption of drugs had substantially increased, and second, that the increase had been a direct result of a Constitutional Court ruling of 1994 that decriminalized what is known as the personal dose. The Uribe government also asserted that the increased consumption of drugs was responsible for heightening the country's violence as criminal organizations fought for the control of what is known as the microtrafficking of drugs.

The following declaration of the Uribe administration typified its position:

> [T]he subject of consumption is not only a concern of the industrialized countries. Consumption is growing a great deal in our own society. We have a lot of problems here and this is linked to criminality. . . . [Likewise] . . . all of the studies show that the consumption of illegal drugs significantly increased in the country from the time the Constitutional Court authorized and decriminalized consumption.

In December 2009, the Colombian Congress passed a constitutional reform that explicitly prohibited the consumption of drugs in Colombia,[3] but the measure still lacks a regulatory framework. At the present time, the Congress is considering a bill that, among other measures, would stiffen prison sentences for drugs sellers and order the obligatory treatment of consumers. In principle, the initiative aims to reduce not only the consumption of illegal drugs but the violence associated with their trafficking. In line with the constitutional reform, the bill assumes that the decriminalization of the personal dose, and the tolerance underlying the court's ruling in general, had a substantial influence on the increase in consumption.

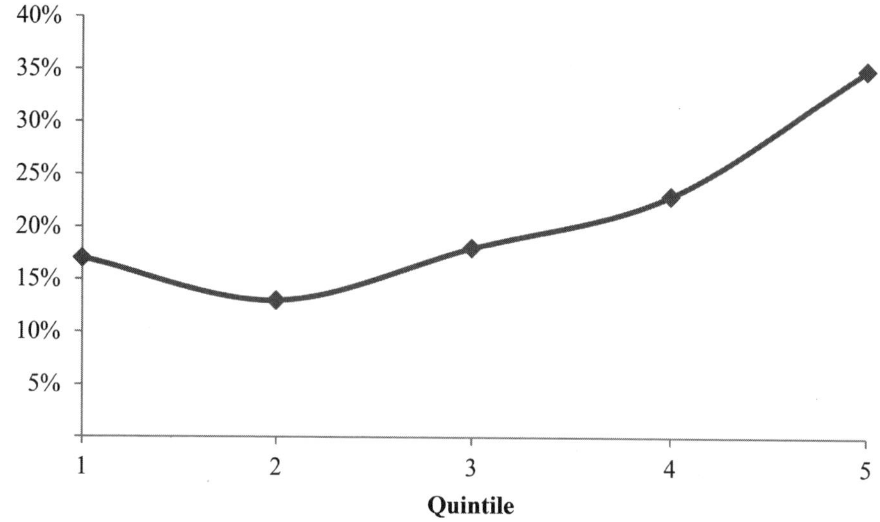

FIGURE 2.1. Support for the legalization of drugs, in quintiles. Source: Encuesta Social y Política (2006) and our own estimates

For the most part, the debate about the increase in the consumption of drugs has been characterized by the absence of empirical arguments. The proponents of prohibition have assumed, without proof, that there is a direct link between decriminalization and the growth of consumption. Its critics, for their part, have cited general principles of a typically libertarian kind that oppose the paternalism of the state or its arbitrary attempts to regulate the private life of citizens. No one has sought, for example, to study the alleged impact of the Constitutional Court's decision on the consumption of drugs in the country. There has not even been an attempt to make a contextual analysis of the increase in drug use in Colombia by comparing it, for example, with what is happening in other countries in Latin America.

The purpose of this chapter is to fill this empirical gap. It examines the available data and offers some conclusions that are relevant to this crucial debate on drug consumption in the country. In general, it is prompted by the conviction that public policy on the consumption, production, and trafficking of drugs must take the available evidence into account and not be based simply on supposed causal links or unquestioned philosophical principles.

It is also worth going beyond the data and statistical evidences to take a brief look at the climate of opinion about decriminalization or in more general (and ambiguous) terms, the legalization of drugs. The Social and Political Survey (ESP) from Universidad de los Andes, an opinion poll undertaken for the first time in 2006, originally included a question about the legalization of drugs: 2,600 people from the country's four major cities were asked whether they were or were not in favor of legalization. Figure 2.1 shows the results for each quintile of socioeconomic strata (the quintiles were based on housing conditions and the ownership of durable goods). Those in favor of legalization barely passed the level of 20 percent. In addition, the differences between the rich and the poor are substantial. From those in the lowest quintile, 16 percent were in favor of legalization, compared to 35 percent in the highest one. These differences are not surprising since, according to the same survey, there is a general difference between the attitudes of the rich and the poor in other areas like the market economy, interest in politics, and support for harsher judicial measures. Nevertheless, of all the variables included in the survey, the legalization of drugs shows the greatest difference between the opinions of the rich and the poor.

DATA

As was mentioned in the introduction, to analyze the evolution of the consumption of drugs in Colombia in recent years, we used the information found in the national surveys undertaken by the National Narcotics Administration (Dirección Nacional de Estupefacientes, or DNE) in 1992, 1996, 2008, and 2013. In this respect we need to clarify that these surveys are not wholly comparable since they used different methodologies for sampling and compiling data. The population in the first two surveys was made up of people between the ages of twelve and sixty. The 1992 sample is representative of the six main regions in Colombia. The 1996 survey includes people who live in 150 municipalities with a population of seven thousand or more inhabitants. In the 2008 and 2013 survey, the group was made up of people between the ages of twelve and sixty-five who live in departmental capitals and large municipalities with thirty thousand or more inhabitants.

The four surveys contain information about the consumption of both legal and illegal psychoactive substances. Among them we find tobacco, alcohol, nervous system stimulants, marijuana, cocaine, *bazuco* (crack), heroin, ecstasy, and LSD.

The informants were asked whether they had once tried any of the substances. If the answer was yes, they were also asked how frequently they had consumed the substance or substances in the year and month before the survey. The surveys also included a series of questions about the risks and problems caused by drugs consumption (problems with family, friends, work, and the law). In this chapter we focus on the five drugs most frequently used in Colombia: marijuana, cocaine, *bazuco*, heroin, and ecstasy (on the latter there is only information for 2008 and 2013). The surveys of the DNE show that, generally speaking, there has been a substantial increase in drug consumption in Colombia during the past twenty years. Whereas 3.4 percent of the population had consumed drugs at least once in their lives in 1992, this percentage had already risen to 5 percent by 1996, to 8.7 percent by 2008, and to 12 percent in 2013. The consumption of alcohol (five or more drinks per week) was 3.2 percent in 1996 and rose to approximately 6 percent in 2008 and 2013. The consumption of cigarettes, on the other hand, showed a slight decline during the past seventeen years.

All surveys contain questions about the socioeconomic characteristics of the individuals: gender, age, educational level, marital status, among others. Table 2.1 shows that in all surveys men accounted for less than half of those polled, their average age gradually increased in each survey, and hence the percentage of those who said they were employed also increased. For all surveys more than half stated they belonged to the poorer classes while, on average, less than 5 percent belonged to a rich household. A comparison of the surveys shows important differences in the educational attainment of the people polled.

TABLE 2.1. Descriptive statistics of the variables used in the regression analysis

Variable	1992 Proportion/ average %	1996 Proportion/ average %	2008 Proportion/ average %	2013 Proportion/ average %
Consumption of a traditional drug in his or her lifetime	3.4	5	8.7	12.0
They smoked six or more cigarettes a day in the previous month	5.0	6.9	6.3	5.0
They drank five or more glasses of liquor in the previous week*	8.4	3.2	5.9	5.7
Men	44.7	48.4	46.8	48.5
Between the ages of 12–17	30.6	21.4	16	14.3
Between the ages of 18–24	26.5	18.6	17.7	17.1
Between the ages of 25–34	16.7	22.6	21.8	21.5
Between the ages of 35–44	12.7	17.7	20.2	18.7
45 years or older	13.5	19.4	24.1	28.7
Uneducated	23.3	25.3	8.3	1.2
Complete primary education	15.7	17.8	9.8	16.1
Incomplete secondary education	36.0	30.6	28.3	17.0
Complete secondary education	15.7	15.6	25.1	36.3
Incomplete university education	4.5	4.4	17.7	13.6
Complete university education	4.6	6.1	10.4	15.6
Workers	37.7	45.9	45	53.0
Students	30.9	22	21.1	18.9
Housewives	24.1	27.8	20.7	14.5
Unemployed	6.0	4.1	13	13.6
Married women or common-law marriage	34.9	45.1	47.9	47.1
Widows or separated	5.6	6.8	7.7	8.0
Bachelor	58.3	47.9	44.2	44.4
Live in a rented room	3.1	2.6	NA	NA
Live in a shack or similar	7.7	7.5	NA	NA
Has a toilet	72.0	75.7	NA	NA
Access to public aqueduct	87.3	80.2	NA	NA
Low stratum	60.1	63.2	54.6	63.9
Middle stratum	37.7	34.3	39.7	31.3
High Stratum	2.2	2.3	5.7	4.7
Bogotá	6.1	10.6	18.4	24.1
Medellín	1.1	3.5	6.4	9.2
Cali	1.4	3.3	5.6	7.3
Barranquilla	2.2	3.1	4.4	3.9
Number of members of home	3.6	3.9	3.6	3.4
Number of observations	18,769	18,571	29,164	32,605

* The 1992 survey asks the question regarding how many times the individual drank five or more glasses of liquor in the past two weeks, and therefore we take those who reported drinking this amount twice or more times in that period of time.

Source: DNE (1992, 1996, 2008), OCD (2013), and our own estimates.

TABLE 2.2. Average consumption of drugs in Colombia (1992–2013)

	1992			1996		
Type of drug	Once in his or her life (%)	Previous year (%)	Previous month (%)	Once in his or her life (%)	Previous year (%)	Previous month (%)
Marijuana	4.00	0.39	0.34	4.68	1.24	0.59
Cocaine	1.86	0.1	0.1	1.13	0.29	0.13
Crack (*bazuco*)	1.68	0.11	0.03	0.83	0.20	0.16
Heroin*	1.19	ND	ND	0.11	0.01	0.01
Ecstasy	ND	ND	ND	ND	ND	ND
Some kind of drug	3.42	0.52	0.42	5.06	1.41	0.74

	2008			2013		
Type of drug	Once in his or her life (%)	Previous year (%)	Previous month (%)	Once in his or her life (%)	Previous year (%)	Previous month (%)
Marijuana	7.99	2.27	1.60	11.48	3.27	2.18
Cocaine	2.48	0.72	0.43	3.23	0.70	0.40
Crack (*bazuco*)	1.09	0.17	0.10	1.18	0.21	0.17
Heroin*	0.19	0.02	0.02	0.14	0.03	0.02
Ecstasy	0.91	0.28	0.11	0.71	0.19	0.02
Some kind of drug	8.70	2.68	1.82	12.04	3.52	2.32

*The 1992 survey asked about the joint consumption of heroin, opium, and its derivatives (such as morphine).
Source: DNE (1992, 1996, and 2008), OCD (2013), and our own estimates.

Whereas 75 percent had not finished high school in the first survey and 9 percent had some university education, these percentages changed to 34 percent and 29 percent, respectively, in the last one. This difference is not only due to the progress of the country's educational system between the first and last survey, but also due to the difference in their geographical coverage. For example, the percentage of informants who lived in the major cities of the country was 10 percent in 1992, 21 percent in 1996, 35 percent in 2008, and 45 percent in 2013.

CHARACTERISTICS OF DRUG CONSUMERS IN COLOMBIA (1992–2013)

Table 2.2 presents some figures on the consumption of drugs in Colombia obtained from the four surveys described in the previous section. From each survey, we take the percentage of people who answered that they had consumed the different types of drugs mentioned above. In 1992, the percentage of those who consumed marijuana at least once in their lifetime was 4.0; the percentage of those who consumed cocaine, 1.86; for *bazuco*, 1.68; and for heroin, 1.19.[4] The percentages of those who answered that they had consumed drugs in the previous year are obviously smaller: 0.39 for marijuana and 0.1 for cocaine and *bazuco.* The percentages for people who answered that they had consumed some kind of drug in the month before the survey were 0.34 for marijuana, 0.1 for cocaine, and close to zero for *bazuco*.

Table 2.2 also shows these same percentages just described for 1992, but corresponding to the years 2006, 2008, and 2013. The figures show a substantial increase in the consumption of most of the psychoactive substances during the period 1992–2013. The reported consumption of marijuana at least once reached 4.68 percent in 1996, 7.99 percent in 2008, and 11.48 percent in 2013. That of cocaine reached 1.13 percent in 1996, 2.48 percent in 2008, and 3.23 percent in 2013. That of *bazuco* decreased to 0.83 percent in 1996 but then increased gradually to 1.09 percent in 2008 and 1.18 percent in 2013. Finally, the consumption of heroin and ecstasy decreased since 2008 from 0.19 percent and 0.91 percent to 0.14 percent and 0.71 percent in 2013, respectively. These percentages imply a growth between 1992 and 2013 in the "at least once in their lifetime" consumption of marijuana and cocaine by 187 percent and 74 percent, respectively. Heroin consumption increased between 1996 and 2013 by 27 percent, while crack consumption decreased by 30 percent between 1992 and 2013 and ecstasy consumption decreased by 22 percent between 2008 and 2013.[5] The figures show a similar increase for consumption in the previous year, except again in ecstasy, where there was an important decline. For consumption in the previous month for the period between 1992 and 2013, that of marijuana grew by 541 percent; of cocaine, 300 percent; of *bazuco* by 467 percent; and that of heroin by 100.0 percent between 1996 and 2013. Finally, between 2008 and 2013 the consumption of ecstasy declined by 82 percent.

These figures show that the consumption of most psychoactive substances in Colombia substantially grew in the period between the years 1992 and 2013. As we mentioned before, the administration headed by President Álvaro Uribe repeatedly argued that this increase was mostly due to the decriminalization of the personal dose (Sentence C-221, May 1994). This hypothesis will be analyzed indirectly later in this chapter. The available figures suggest that the hypothesis is doubtful in the best of cases, and false in the worst.

Regardless of the debate about the causes or determinants of the increased use of drugs, the trend is worrying and indicates the need to strengthen policies for preventing consumption and treating addiction. An epidemiological characterization of drug consumers is a fundamental factor in the design of these policies. In particular, it is important to understand the risk factors associated with consumption and the manner in which they have changed over time.

Figure 2.2 shows the average age when people began to consume drugs. The informants were grouped into eleven cohorts, each spanning approximately seven years. This grouping allows one to analyze the changes in the age of first use in different generations. As is seen, there are significant differences both in the prevalence of consumption and the age at which people began to use drugs. Over time, a bigger percentage of individuals in the younger generations report having consumed drugs once in their lives. In addition, the starting age is increasingly younger. For example, on the basis of the 2013 survey, one finds that 7.77 percent of those born between 1943 and 1949 answered that they had consumed drugs at least once. In this group the average age of first use was 24.45. But for those born between 1992 and 1996, the percentage of those who consumed drugs at least once is 17.25 percent and the average age of initiation was 14.7 years.[6]

The information in Figure 2.2 suggests that prevention policies should focus on people of increasingly younger ages. But it is still incomplete or insufficient. It does not take into account other characteristics of these people, apart from age, that may also have an influence on the consumption of drugs. Up to now the studies done in

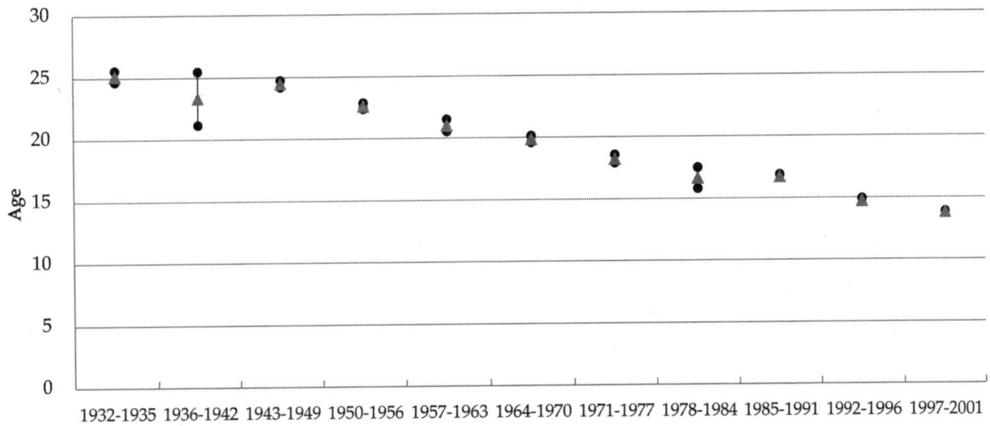

Proportion of consumers	1932–1935	1936–1942	1943–1949	1950–1956	1957–1963	1964–1970	1971–1977	1978–1984	1985–1991	1992–1996	1997-2001
1992	2.23%	2.19%	3.70%	4.22%	4.64%	5.17%	3.39%	0.67%	NA	NA	NA
1996	NA	2.88%	4.74%	5.49%	6.16%	6.14%	5.77%	2.30%	NA	NA	NA
2008	NA	NA	5.65%	7.08%	7.92%	7.30%	7.54%	11.16%	12.21%	3.48%	NA
2013	NA	NA	7.77%	8.53%	11.14%	9.27%	9.85%	13.00%	18.64%	17.25%	4.78%

FIGURE 2.2. Average age when people began to consume drugs. Source: DNE (1992, 1996, and 2008), OCD (2013), and our own estimates

Colombia provide some evidence in this respect, but because they are based on simple correlations, they do not achieve an adequate identification of the main risk factors. With this aim in mind, we made some estimates on the basis of some binary response models that study the relationship between the demographic and socioeconomic characteristics of people and the likelihood that they will consume drugs. In general terms, our main interest is to estimate how the different individual characteristics affect the probability of consuming drugs. In the specific case of this chapter, our variable of interest is a binary variable that takes a value of one if the individual reports having consumed drugs at some point in his or her life and takes a value of zero otherwise.[7] Due to this definition of the variable of interest, the exercise in question does not characterize a typical addict but only those who report having consumed illegal psychoactive substances at least once in their lives. In order to undertake an analysis of the characteristics of an addict, a more detailed survey would be necessary, one that would oversample drug consumers and thus allow one to identify habitual consumers in a more exact way (World Health Organization 2005).[8]

Among the variables included in the estimations are some demographic and socioeconomic characteristics of the people, such as age, gender, educational level, main source of income, and the economic stratum to which the person belongs, among others. Additionally, all the estimated models include dummy variables that identify the residents of the country's four major cities (Bogotá, Medellín, Cali, Barranquilla). These latter variables enable one to control for nonobserved characteristics of the cities, which do not change over time and which may affect the average level of consumption of the people who

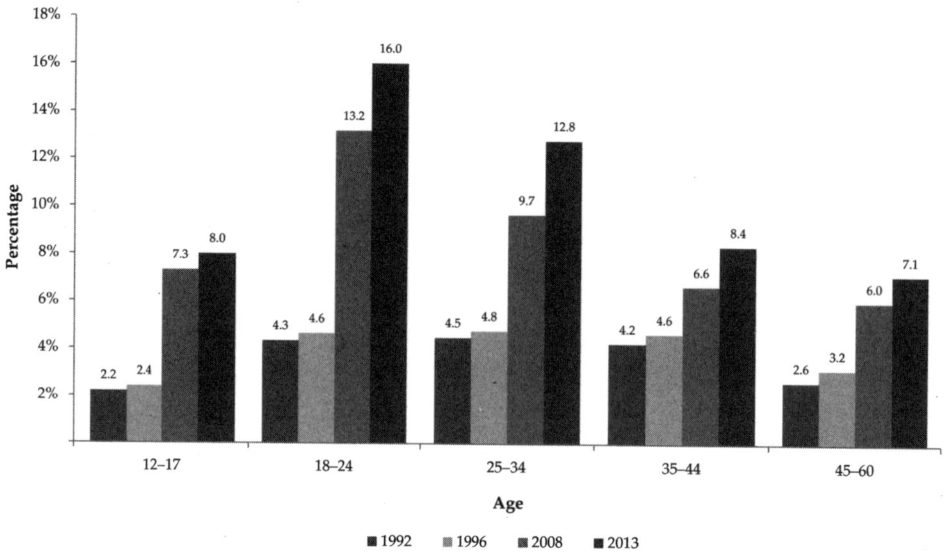

FIGURE 2.3. Likelihood of consumption of drugs according to age. Source: DNE (1992, 1996, and 2008), OCD (2013), and our own estimates

live there. The models presented in this chapter are based on Probit models (Wooldridge 2008). The models were separately estimated for each survey, which allows for an analysis of the way the profile of the typical drug consumer has changed in this period. The main results are shown in the table in the chapter's appendix.[9] The estimates show that while the characteristics associated with the probability of consuming drugs have remained relatively constant over time, the magnitude of their influence changed during the period in question. The figures and numbers shown below describe these changes.

The first thing that stands out, evident in Table 2.2, is that the percentage of people who report having consumed drugs once in their lives increased between 1992 and 2013. In percentage terms, although not shown, the increase in consumption was similar for men and women. For men, the percentage rose from 5.7 percent to 17.3 percent, an increase of 203 percent in the past twenty years. For women, the consumption changed from 1.6 to 4.6 percent, an increase of 195 percent for the same period. These numbers also show that, on average, men in Colombia are more prone to consume drugs than are women.

Figure 2.3 shows the change in the consumption of drugs according to the age of the people after the direct effect of the other variables in the model has been taken into account. In general, in all the cohorts the consumption of psychoactive substances rose between 1992 and 2013. As was to be expected, the younger cohorts have a higher probability of reporting that they consumed drugs throughout their lives than the people older than forty-four. But the differences between cohorts were accentuated over time. In particular, the consumption of drugs was much higher among youngsters between the ages of eighteen and twenty-four than in any other of the groups under consideration. In this group, reported consumption nearly quadrupled. Age, which has always been a risk factor, seems to have become even more important in recent years.

The person's educational level does not seem to have an important influence on the probability of consuming drugs at some point in his or her life. Although a larger

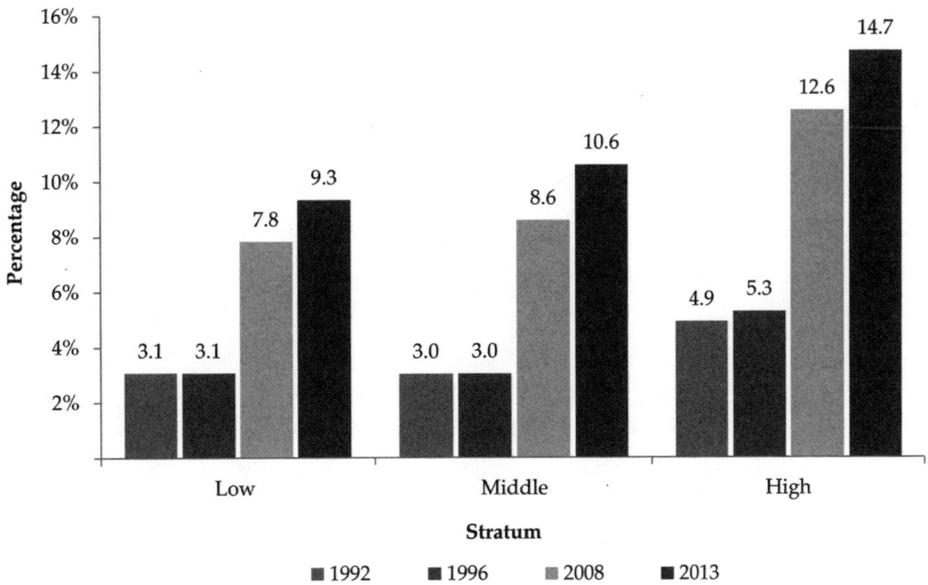

FIGURE 2.4. Likelihood of consumption of drugs according to stratum. Source: DNE (1992, 1996, and 2008), OCD (2013), and our own estimates

proportion of uneducated people reported having consumed drugs in comparison with those who have high school or university diplomas, this difference, less than one percentage point, is not statistically significant. The results of the estimation show, in particular, that the effect of education occurs in terms of the socioeconomic level, possibly because of its effect on people's acquisitive powers. Once the socioeconomic level is controlled for (social strata in this case), the effect of education disappears or even becomes negative. Figure 2.4 shows that the consumption of drugs increased in a proportional manner in all strata.[10] In general, however, consumption is greater in the higher strata than in the others. Specifically, in the higher strata, consumption increased by nearly 226 percent over the past twenty years. Thus, belonging to the higher strata is an important risk factor nowadays.

It is interesting to note that the unemployed are more likely to consume drugs than students, employees, and housewives in all surveys analyzed. As shown in the appendix, the differences are statistically significant and by 2013 they amount to around two and three percentage points on average when compared with housewives or students respectively.

Finally, Figure 2.5 shows that the consumption of psychoactive substances is strongly linked with the habits of drinking and smoking cigarettes. For example, for the year 2013, a person who has more than five drinks a week is 8.4 percentage points more likely to have consumed drugs than one who does not (this effect takes into account the effects of the other variables in the estimation). Something similar happens with the consumption of cigarettes. For the year 2013, a person who smokes more than six cigarettes a week is 15.5 percentage points more likely to have consumed drugs than one who does not.

The results discussed above enable us to identify some of the risk factors associated with drug consumption. The most important factors are the following: being a man, being between the ages of eighteen and twenty-four, belonging to high social strata,

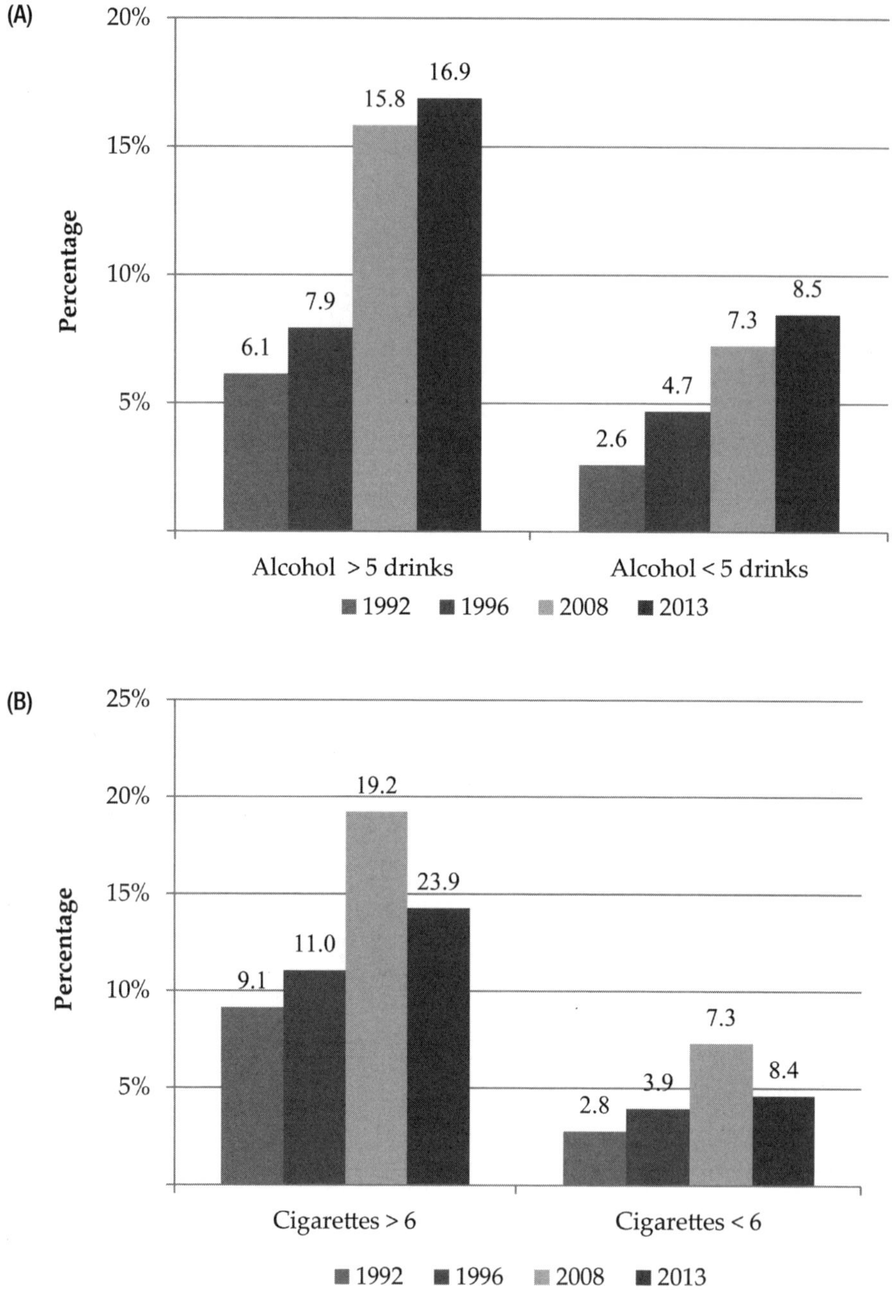

FIGURE 2.5. Likelihood of consumption of drugs according to consumption of alcohol and cigarettes. Source: DNE (1992, 1996, and 2008), OCD (2013), and our own estimates

having more than five drinks a week, and smoking more than six cigarettes daily. These factors appear significant in all four surveys, but the importance of age seems to have grown over time. In general, policies for the prevention of drug use should take these factors into account, and specifically they should be aimed at young men from the middle and higher social strata.

PROBLEMS AND RISKS ASSOCIATED WITH THE CONSUMPTION OF DRUGS

One of the arguments most frequently mentioned by those who uphold the penalization of drug consumption are the problems and risks consumption may bring both to the consumer and third parties. The DNE surveys for 2008 and 2013 have some questions that allow one to evaluate the dimensions and the frequency of the problems and risks associated with drug consumption. Both surveys asked those who consumed some psychoactive substance during the previous year if they had any problem at home, at work, in the place where they studied, or with the authorities, or if the drugs affected their physical health.

Figure 2.6 shows descriptive statistics on the percentage of consumers of marijuana, cocaine, or *bazuco* who reported being involved in some kind of problem in 2008 or 2013. There are no significant differences in the number of problems drug consumers report in both surveys, but for both years the kind of problem varies with the type of drug consumed. Problems at home, at work, with the family, with the authorities, or with their own physical health are more common among consumers of *bazuco* (or at least more commonly reported). The problems mentioned by the consumers of marijuana and cocaine are similar, but with two statistically significant differences. For 2008, the consumers of cocaine report significantly more problems with their physical health. For 2013, the consumers of cocaine report significantly more assaults to other individuals while under the influence of the drug.

The questions used in Figure 2.6 were only asked of drug consumers, which hinders the possibility of making a comparative analysis of the extent to which drugs use caused the reported problems. We do not know, for example, if nonconsumers are less prone to get involved in these kinds of situations. Future surveys should ask all the individuals about these problems in order to make case comparisons.

The 2008 and 2013 surveys included a question about the level of risk toward the individual associated with the consumption of different amounts of marijuana, cocaine, or alcohol. Those surveyed (both consumers and nonconsumers) were asked to grade the risk they would bear associated with consumption on a scale from 1 to 4, that is, from lowest to highest.

Figure 2.7 shows the average value of the answers for consumers and nonconsumers related with the risks of consuming different types of drugs. The first fact that should be noticed is that nonconsumers believe that the consumption of alcohol and drugs have significantly higher risk levels than what consumers believe. Differences between these two groups are particularly stark for the risks of trying some type of drug and the consumption of marijuana, reaching 12 percent and 21 percent respectively. For nonconsumers, the highest risk levels are those associated with the use of *bazuco* and cocaine, while the lowest is for the use of alcohol. For the consumers of some drug, the highest risk level is likewise attributed to the consumption of *bazuco.* The consumers nevertheless believe that the risk associated with trying some drug or the consumption of marijuana is low, even less than the risk associated with the frequent use of alcohol. Interesting results emerge when the answers from 2008 and from 2013 are compared. While the perception on the levels of risks associated with drug consumption did not change for nonconsumers in the past five years, for consumers these same beliefs changed considerably in the case of marijuana, decreasing by 6 percent in the past five years.

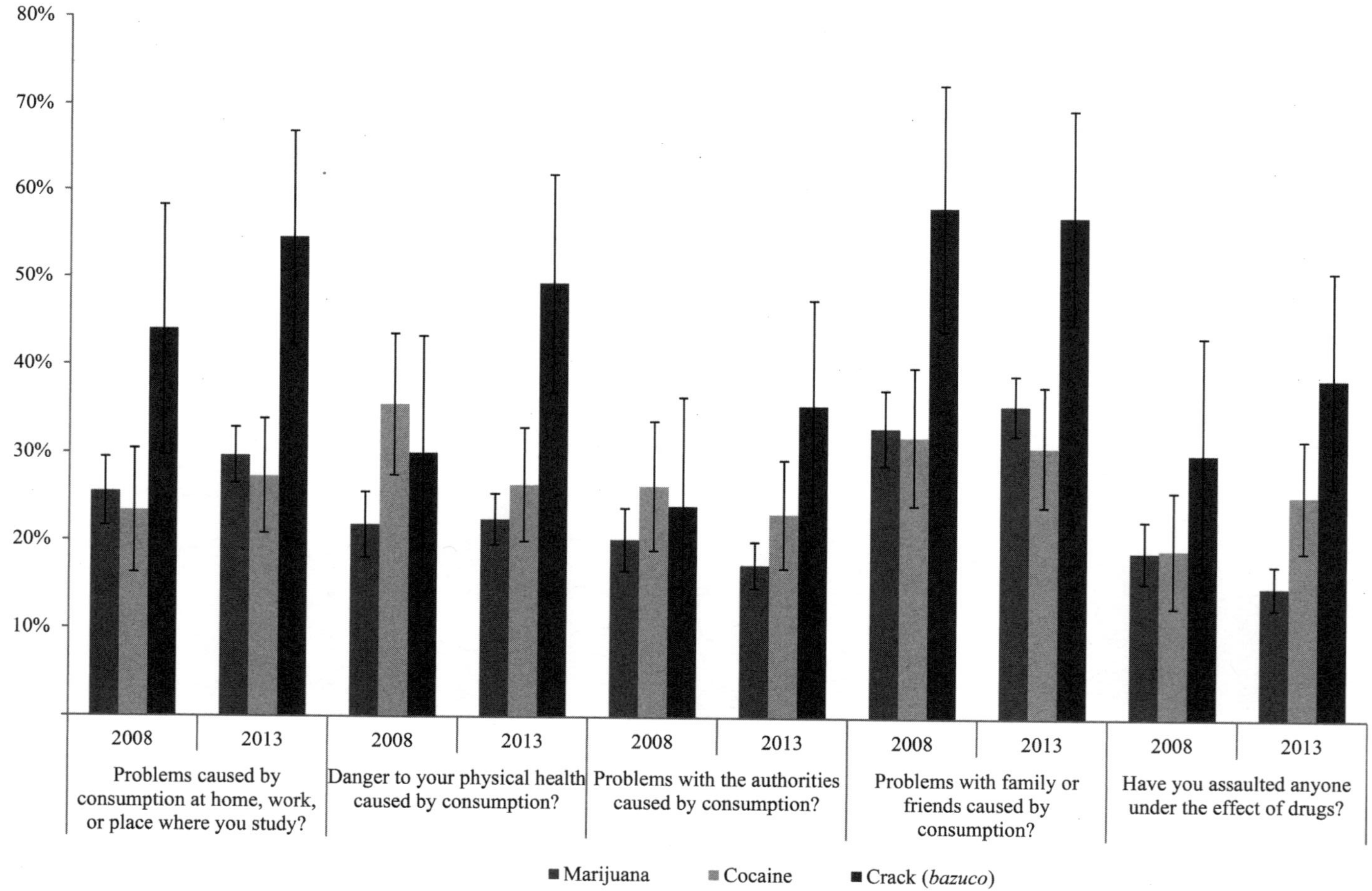

FIGURE 2.6. Problems related to the consumption of traditional drugs. Source: DNE (2008), OCD (2013), and our own estimates

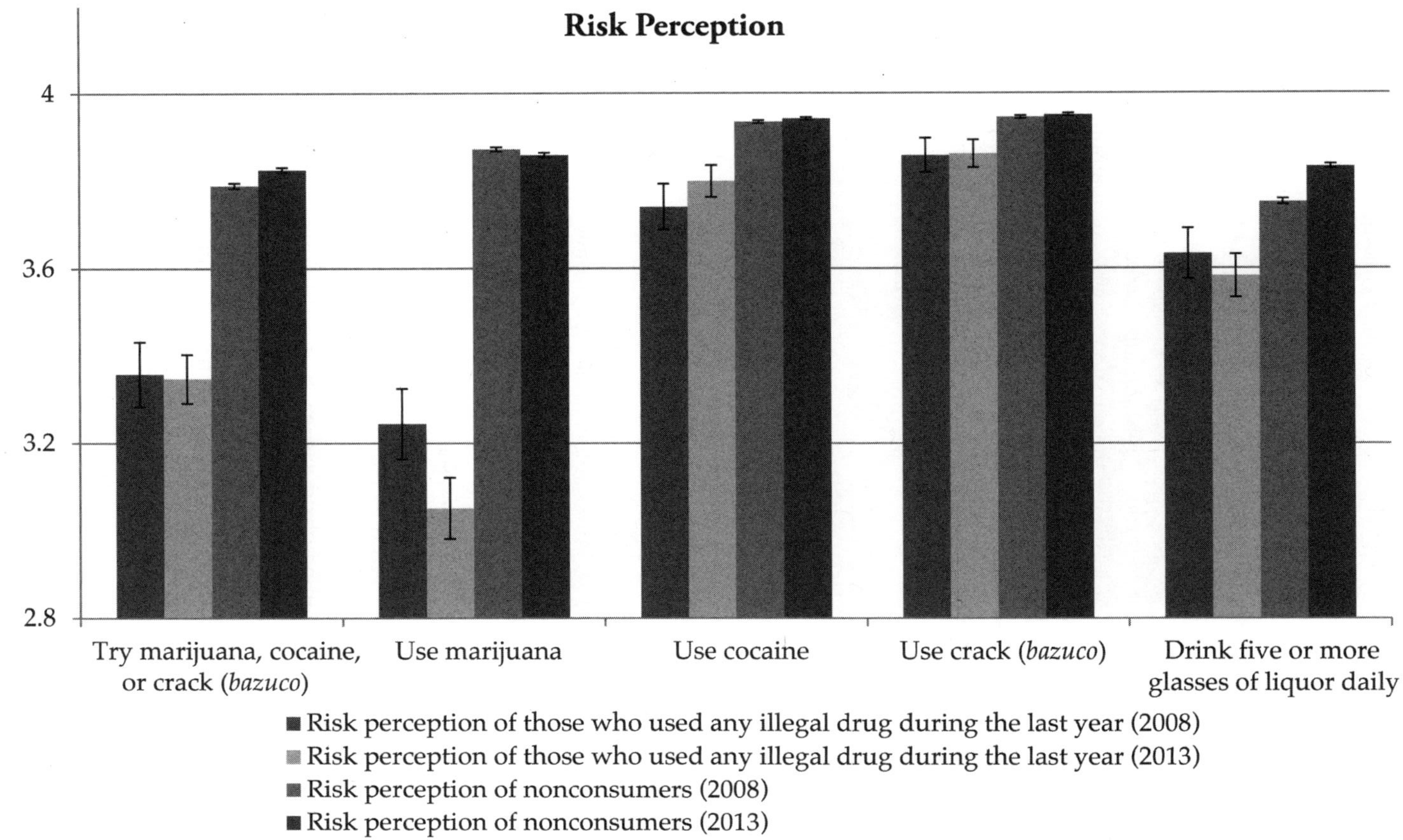

FIGURE 2.7. Problems related to the consumption of traditional drugs. Source: DNE (2008), OCD (2013), and our own estimates

THE IMPACT OF DECRIMINALIZATION ON DRUG CONSUMPTION IN COLOMBIA

This section evaluates, in an indirect manner, the possible consequences of the ruling (Sentence C-221, May 1994) that decriminalized the personal dose. The analysis includes three independent but complementary arguments. First, on the basis of the 2008 survey, we reconstruct the evolution of the new consumers since the early 1980s and, through a simple time series methodology, we examine whether the rapid growth in the number of new consumers in this period did in fact coincide with decriminalization. Second, we ask whether the growth in drug consumption in Colombia is in line with what has occurred in other countries. If it is, the supposed effect of Sentence C-221 would be doubtful or would at least raise the question of why consumption rose in a similar manner in other countries where there were no legal changes. And third, we analyze whether the growth of consumption has been different in the center of the country, or much greater in some cities than others, for example. If that were so, it would likewise raise doubts about the argument that a uniform legal change, which in theory affected the whole country equally, was a major factor in the rapid growth of consumption.

The Evolution of Consumption

On the basis of the information in the surveys undertaken by the DNE in 2008, we built a variable that shows, for each year, the percentage of people between the ages of eighteen and twenty-five who consumed drugs for the first time. To do that we used two sources of information: the age of the individual at the time of the survey and the reported age when the person first consumed drugs. On the basis of these two figures, it is possible to calculate the time elapsed since the first use, and, in addition, the year when consumption first occurred. For example, if the figures show that a person began consuming ten years before, that person will be classified in the group of new consumers corresponding to the year 1998, taking into account that the survey was carried out in 2008. The total number of new consumers for each year obtained in this way is divided by the number of people surveyed. As was already indicated, the analysis was limited to people between the ages of eighteen and twenty-four, taking into account that the results discussed in the previous section show a higher frequency of drugs use in that age range.

Figure 2.8 shows the evolution of the variable in question (percentage of new consumers between the age of eighteen and twenty-four) and a change of trend in 1994, the year when the consumption of drugs was decriminalized in Colombia. The figure shows that consumption, measured by the appearance of new consumers, doubled between the mid-1990s and 2008 and tripled between the end of the 1980s and the end of the previous decade. These figures are consistent with those presented in a previous section, which were based on a comparison between the 1996 and 2008 surveys.

One way to empirically determine whether the increase in consumption was actually due to the 1994 decriminalization decree is to verify if there was a structural change in the trend of the series of new consumers. With that aim in mind, twelve models with different changes of trend were constructed. The first assumed that the change in trend

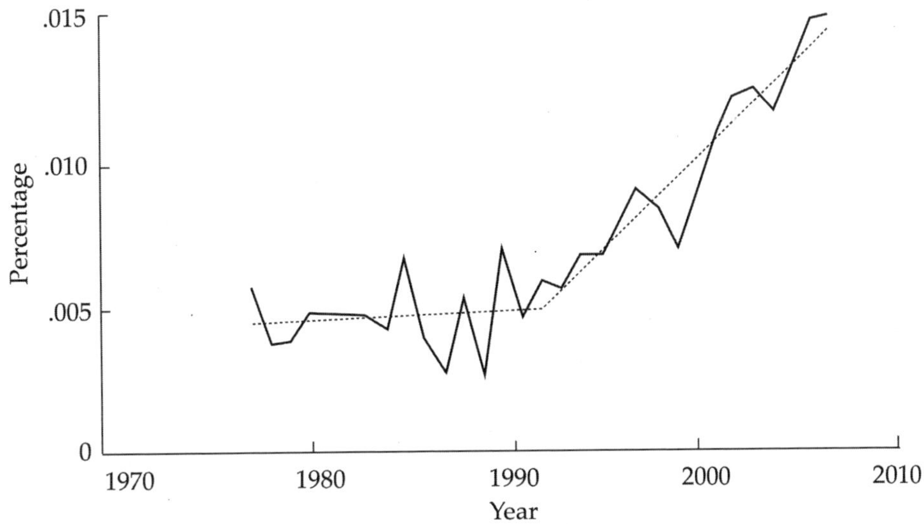

FIGURE 2.8. Evolution percentage of new consumers between the age of eighteen and twenty-four. Source: DNE (2008) and our own estimates

occurred in 1992, the second in 1993, the third in 1994, and so forth until the year 2003 is reached.

For each estimated model, the explanatory power was tested by means of the R2.[11] Figure 2.9 shows this statistic for each of the estimated models. The best adjustment is obtained at the beginning of the 1990s. The results are not definitive enough to identify a structural change in the trend of drug consumption. It seems equally probable that the break might have occurred before 1994 or a little later. In the end, the available evidence does not allow for a definite confirmation that the consumption of drugs suddenly and drastically rose from the time that the personal dose was decriminalized. The data are perfectly consistent with an alternative hypothesis, with a break in the trend toward the growth of consumption before, not after, Sentence C-221 of 1994.

An International Comparison

As was already noted, the comparison between the growth of drug consumption in Colombia and other countries may throw some light on the effect of decriminalization on internal consumption. Once again, if the growth and level of consumption observed in Colombia does not differ from that seen in other countries, it would be more difficult to argue that decriminalization had a substantial effect. In other words, an international comparison partly addresses the contrafactual question asked in this section, that is: what would the growth of drug consumption in the country have looked like if the personal dose had not been decriminalized in 1994?

There are comparable international figures for all the surveys in four additional countries in the region. Figure 2.10 compares the consumption of cocaine in Argentina,

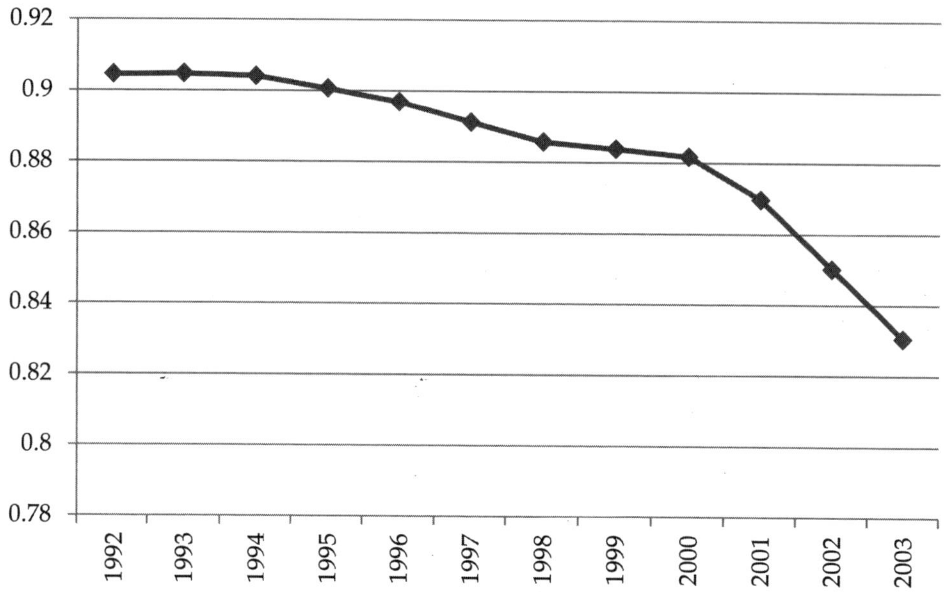

FIGURE 2.9. Year with the best adjustment in the change of the trend of drug consumption. Source: DNE (2008) and our own estimates

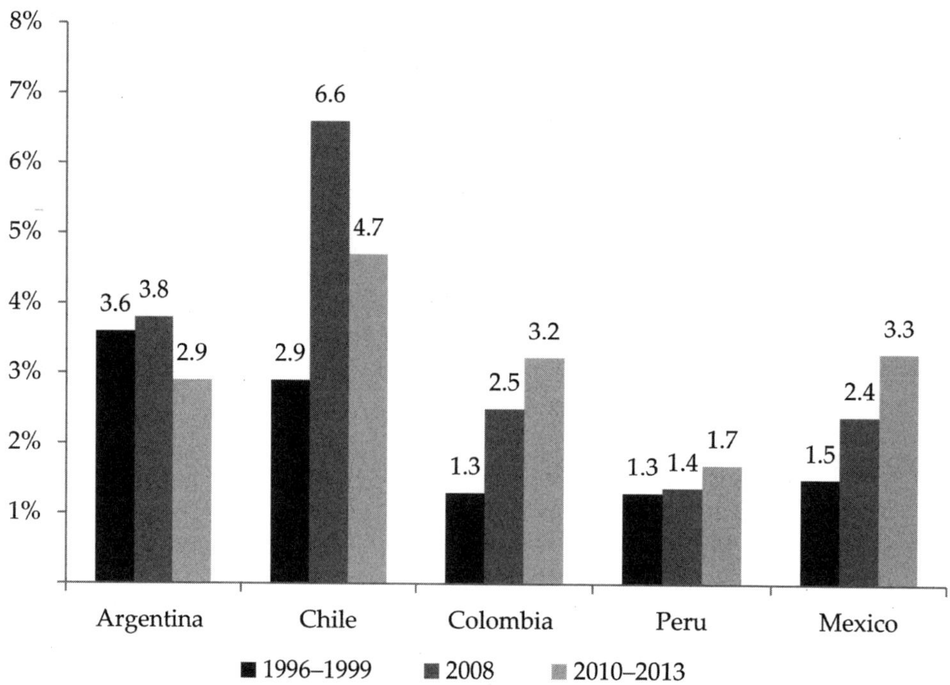

FIGURE 2.10. Consumption of cocaine at least once in one's life, international level (1996–2013). Source: For Argentina see Míguez (1999) and Ahumada (2011). For Chile see SENDA (2013). For Colombia see DNE (1992, 1996, and 2008), OCD (2013), and our own estimates. For Peru see Contradrogas (1999), CICAD (2008), and Comisión Nacional para el Desarrollo y Vida sin Drogas (2011). For Mexico see Brower (2006) and Villatoro-Velazquez et al. (2012)

Chile, Colombia, Peru, and Mexico for the years 1996–1999, 2008, and 2010–2013.[12] The figure shows the percentage of people who reported that they had consumed cocaine at least once in their lifetime. In the late 1990s consumption of cocaine was higher in Argentina and Chile, while Colombia, Peru, and Mexico had comparable figures. For the growth of consumption between the mid-1990s and 2008, Argentina and Peru had a growth rate of 5 percent, while Chile, Colombia, and Mexico had much higher growth rates of 127 percent, 92 percent, and 60 percent respectively. Comparing this same group of countries between 2008 and 2013, there is an evident reduction in the growth rates of cocaine consumption for Argentina and Chile of 23 percent and 28 percent respectively. For their part, Colombia, Peru, and Mexico had an increase in their growth rates of 29 percent, 24 percent, and 37 percent respectively.

The comparison reveals, on average, a greater level of consumption in Argentina and Chile by the mid-1990s compared to the other three countries. By 2013 however, consumption in Mexico and Colombia increased to levels similar to Argentina but still lower than Chile. Peru shows a much lower level of consumption compared to other countries in the region, while Argentina is the only country in which consumption decreased between 1996 and 2013. Finally, it is worth noting that the trends and levels of consumption for Mexico and Colombia are very similar.

As previously mentioned, in 1994 the Constitutional Court decriminalized the consumption of the personal dose of drugs in Colombia, but in 2009 the Colombian Congress passed a constitutional reform explicitly prohibiting the consumption of drugs in Colombia. As has been said, if the effect of decriminalization (or later criminalization) had been significant, the growth of consumption in Colombia would have been, in relative terms, much greater (or lower) than that in other countries. The data is not consistent with that story, which throws much doubt on the supposed importance of such laws. Between 1996 and 2008 the growth rate of drug consumption in Colombia was similar to the growth rate of Mexico, a country that during that period had not decriminalized consumption. Similarly, between 2008 and 2013, when drug consumption was criminalized again, Colombia did not have the lowest consumption growth rate in the region. In fact, after Mexico it had the highest consumption growth rate, while consumption in Argentina actually decreased in this period even though consumption in this country was decriminalized in 2009.[13]

A Comparison Between Different Colombian Cities

The surveys done in 1992, 1996, 2008, and 2013 allow us to compare the growth of consumption in different Colombian cities. Figure 2.11 illustrates the change in the percentage of people who reported consuming drugs in the cities of Bogotá, Medellín, Cali, and Barranquilla, and in the rest of the country. The differences in the frequency of consumption are notable. In Medellín, for example, the consumption registered in 2013 was three times that observed in Barranquilla in the same year.

But we would like to emphasize another fact. The growth of consumption was quicker in the cities where consumption was lower in 1996. For example, consumption grew by 382 percent in Barranquilla (where it was initially very low) and 82 percent in Medellín (where it was initially very high). Figure 2.11 suggests, in particular, a certain convergence of the regional rates of consumption. In other words, Figure 2.11 suggests a reduction of the formerly significant differences between regions. This fact suggests

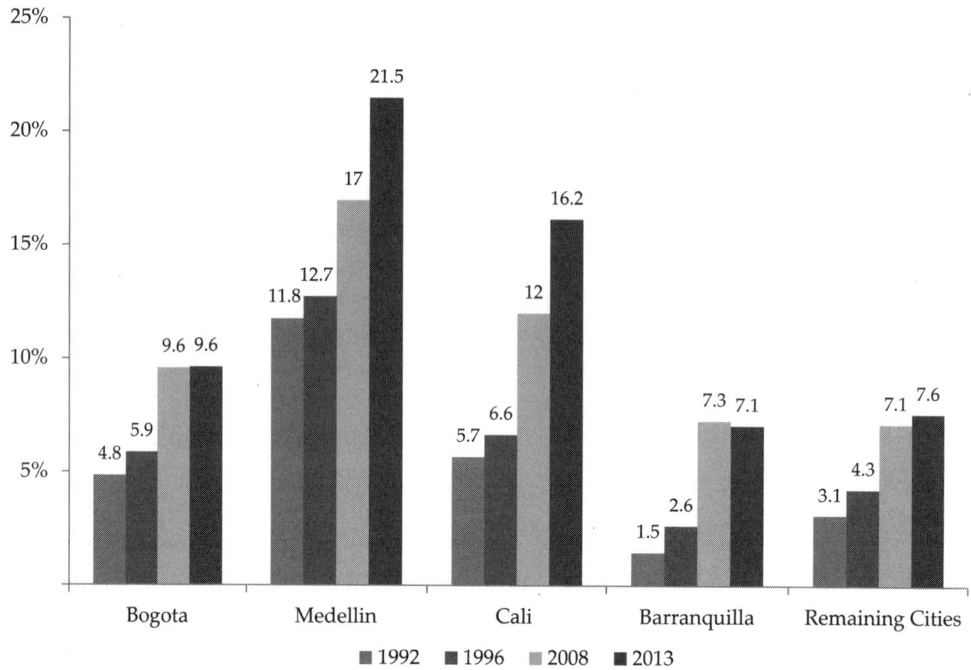

FIGURE 2.11. Consumption of drugs, by cities (1996–2013). Source: DNE (1992, 1996, and 2008), OCD (2013), and our own estimates.

that the growth of consumption may be associated either with regional factors or with endogenous processes of change. Whatever the case, the regional pattern of growth does not seem consistent with the hypothesis that consumption mainly grew as a result of a legal change that by definition uniformly applied to all the country's regions.

CONCLUSIONS

On the basis of the best available figures, this chapter documents the growth of drug consumption in Colombia. Between 1992 and 2013 consumption almost quadrupled. Young men who were habitual consumers of liquor or tobacco and were members of the middle and upper classes were the most frequent consumers of psychoactive substances, but the growth of consumption occurred in all demographic groups and in all regions.

The available evidence—which is indirect and suggestive and not definitive—casts much doubt on the idea that the increased use of illegal drugs in Colombia was due to the decriminalization in 1994 of the personal dose. The causes of this increased consumption are not fully known. The literature on other countries obliges us to be modest about our conclusions. As occurs with many social phenomena, the consumption of drugs has diverse causes that mutually reinforce one another. Often, small changes are enlarged through mechanisms of contagion and are thus undetectable in retrospect.

This chapter is barely a starting point, an initial contribution to the understanding of a complex and pressing subject. We hope this chapter will help bring about an informed discussion, based on the facts and evidence, of the consumption of drugs in particular and anti-drug policies in Colombia in general.

NOTES

The authors would like to thank Daniel Mateo Angel, Mauricio Romero, and Andrés Felipe Salcedo for their excellent work as research assistants, as well as the Ministry of Social Protection, and especially Jenny Constanza Fagua and Luis Alvarado of the DNE for providing us with the databases and allowing us to use them in our investigation.

1. DNE, Fundación Santa Fe de Bogotá, Fundación Escuela Colombiana de Medicina, and Ministerio de Justicia 1992; DNE and CEIS 1996; DNE and Ministerio Protección Social 2009; Ministerio de Justicia and Ministerio de Salud y de la Protección Social 2014.
2. See Chapter 9.
3. The norm, however, has not been completely applied and in many cases depends on the discretional nature and degree of understanding of its possible application. See reference in Chapter 9.
4. According to the study published by the DNE, these percentages are a little different from the ones calculated by the authors of this chapter. Specifically, the percentages for national consumption are marijuana (5.4 percent), followed by cocaine (1.6 percent) and *bazuco* (1.5 percent). These differences may be due to small variations in the observations that were finally employed in both studies. It is worth clarifying that the present study used all the available information.
5. For heroin and ecstasy these percentage are not estimated for the whole period between 1992 and 2013 due to differences in the questions in each survey as detailed in the footnote of Table 2.2.
6. The differences seen for the last cohort, those born between 1997 and 2001, may be because they are still at a young age and it is thus necessary to wait a few more years to have more accurate information about drug consumption. Furthermore, due to restrictions on the information, this final cohort is constructed on the basis of a lesser number of years. It should also be taken into account that the starting age reported by older cohorts may face more problems of memory.
7. The same regressions were estimated for each kind of drug in a separate manner. This chapter, however, only shows the combined version, since the predictive power of these models is low, due to the low number of observations of consumers per specific drug.
8. As may be seen in Table 2.2, all surveys allowed for the obtention of information about those people who consumed some kind of drug in the past year and the past month. Nevertheless, the available information does not allow us to exactly determine whether they are or are not addicts under the World Health Organization's definition of addiction.
9. The table shows the marginal effects estimated on the basis of the survey made in the years 1992, 1996, 2008, and 2013, respectively.
10. Strata 1 and 2 correspond to lower; 3 and 4 to middle; 5 and 6 to upper.
11. The R2 corresponds to the goodness of fit of the econometric model employed. The R2 is a value between 0 and 1, which will be higher when the explicative variables contain more information about the explained variable.
12. Data were obtained from different sources and hence we do not have it for the same years in all countries. For Argentina we have data for 1999, 2008, and 2010; for Chile we have data on 1996, 2008, and 2012; for Peru we have data on 1996, 2008, and 2011, and for Mexico we have data on 1996, 2008, and 2011. The sources are listed in the references.
13. See for example *www.eltiempo.com/archivo/documento/CMS-5995507*.

REFERENCES

Ahumada, Graciela. 2011. "Tendencia en el consumo de sustancias psicoactivas en Argentina 2004-2010." Observatorio Argentino de Drogas y Presidencia Argentina.

Brower, Kimberly C. 2006. "Trends in Production, Trafficking and Consumption of Methamphetamine and Cocaine in Mexico." *Subst Use Misuse* 41, no. 5: 707–27.

CICAD/OAS. 2008. *Primer estudio comparativo sobre consumo de drogas y factores asociados en población 15 a 64 años.* Lima: Tetis Graf E.I.R.L.

Comisión Nacional para el Desarrollo y Vida sin Drogas. 2011. *Informe Ejecutivo. Encuesta Nacional de Consumo de drogas.* Población General Perú 2010.

Comunidad Andina de Naciones. 2009. *Estudio epidemiológico andino sobre consumo de drogas sintéticas en la población universitaria de Bolivia, Colombia, Ecuador y Perú, 2009.* Lima: Tetis Graf E.I.R.L.

Conace. 1996. *Estudio nacional de drogas en la población general de Chile.* Gobierno de Chile.

Contradrogas. 1999. *Informe final de la encuesta nacional sobre prevención y uso de drogas.* Lima: Fondo Editorial Contradrogas.

DNE and CEIS. 1996. *Consumo de sustancias psicoactivas en Colombia 1996: Informe final.* Bogotá.

DNE, Fundación Santa Fe de Bogotá, Fundación Escuela Colombiana de Medicina, and Ministerio de Justicia. 1992. *Estudio nacional sobre consumo de sustancias psicoactivas, 1992.* Bogotá: Editorial Carrera 7ª Ltda.

DNE and Ministerio de la Protección Social. 2009. *Estudio nacional de consumo de sustancias psicoactivas en Colombia 2008: Informe final.* Bogotá: Editora Guadalupe S.A.

Echeverry, J. C., and Z. Partow. 2005. *Why Justice Is Unresponsive to Crime: The Case of Cocaine in Colombia.* Bogotá: Banco de la República, Borradores de Economía, n. 003778.

Gaviria, A. 2000. "Increasing Returns and the Evolution of Violent Crime: The Case of Colombia." *Journal of Development Economics* 61, no. 1: 1–25.

González, T., and R. Smith. 2009. *Drugs and Violence in Colombia: A VECM Analysis.* London: Birkbeck Working Papers in Economics and Finance No. 0906.

Grossman, H., and D. Mejía. 2008. "The War against Drug Producers." *Economics of Governance* 9, no. 1: 5–23.

Laufer, J. 1996. *Segunda encuesta nacional sobre consumo de drogas en el Ecuador.* Quito: Consep.

Medina, C., and H. Martínez. 2003. *Violence and Drug Prohibition in Colombia.* Munich: MPRA Paper No. 6935.

Mejía, D., and P. Restrepo. 2010. "The War on Illegal Drug Production and Trafficking: An Economic Evaluation of Plan Colombia." Bogotá: Documentos CEDE 005123, Universidad de los Andes-CEDE.

Míguez, H. 1999. *Encuesta epidemiológica sobre prevalencia de consumo de sustancias psicoactivas en Argentina 1999.* Observatorio Argentino de Drogas.

Ministerio de Justicia y del Derecho and Ministerio de Salud y de la Protección Social. 2014. *Estudio nacional de consumo de sustancias psicoactivas en Colombia 2013: Informe final.* Bogotá: Ministerio de Justicia. Retrieved from *www.unodc.org/documents/colombia/2014/Julio/Estudio_de_Consumo_UNODC.pdf*, accessed May 12, 2015.

ONUDD. 2006. *Jóvenes y drogas en países suramericanos: Un desafío para las políticas públicas. Primer estudio comparativo sobre el uso de drogas en población secundaria de Argentina, Bolivia, Brasil, Colombia, Chile, Ecuador, Paraguay, Perú y Uruguay.* Lima: Tetis Graf E.I.R.L.

Pérez, A. 2009. "Transiciones en el consumo de drogas en Colombia." *Adicciones* 21, no. 1: 81–88.

SENDA. 2013. Decimo estudio Nacional de Drogras en Poblacion General. Principales Resultados. Observatorio Chileno de Drogas, Servicio Nacional para la Prevención y Rehabilitación del Consumo de Drogas y Alcohol (SENDA).

Substance Abuse and Mental Health Services Administration. 1997. Results from the 1996 National Survey on Drug Use and Health: National Findings, OAS Series #H-13, DHHS Publication No. (SMA) 97-3149, Rockville, MD.

UNODC (UN Office on Drugs and Crime). 2006. *2006 World Drug Report. Volume 2: Statistics.* Vienna: United Nations. Retrieved from *www.unodc.org/pdf/WDR_2006/wdr2006_volume2.pdf*, accessed May 12, 2015.

Villatoro-Velazquez, J. A., et al. 2012. "El consumo de droga en México: Resumen de la Encuesta Nacional de Adicciones 2011." *Salud Mental* 35, no. 6.

Wooldridge, J. 2008. *Introducción a la econometría: Un enfoque moderno*, 2nd ed. México, D.F.: Paraninfo.

World Health Organization. 2005. *Neurociencia del consumo y dependencia de sustancias psicoactivas.* Washington, DC: World Health Organization.

APPENDIX

PROBIT

Marginal effects resulting from Probit regression model

Variables	Consumption of traditional drugs during the person's lifetime 1992 (1)	1996 (2)	2008 (3)	2013 (4)
Man	0.02374***	0.02811***	0.06123***	0.09664***
Age 12–17	–0.00432	–0.00761*	0.01292	0.00862
Age 18–24	0.01696***	0.01474***	0.07168***	0.08904***
Age 25–34	0.01836***	0.01595***	0.03649***	0.05654***
Age 35–44	0.01597***	0.01472***	0.00637	0.01226**
Middle stratum	–0.00047	–0.00023	0.00765***	0.01263***
High stratum	0.01836*	0.02209**	0.04745***	0.05391***
Has job	–0.00877***	–0.01093***	–0.00812**	–0.00797**
Studying	–0.01217***	–0.01372***	–0.03217***	–0.03452***
Housewife	–0.01270***	–0.01499***	–0.02224***	–0.02379***
Six or more cigarettes daily in the previous month	0.06379***	0.07102***	0.11918***	0.15550***
Has drunk five or more glasses of liquor in the previous week	0.03534***	0.03244***	0.08572***	0.08422***
Complete primary education	–0.00499*	–0.00539*	–0.00556	–0.00688
Complete secondary education	0.00009	0.00031	–0.00812*	–0.00101
Complete university education	–0.00008	0.00095	–0.01191**	–0.00837
Married or common-law marriage	–0.00451*	–0.00492**	–0.00010	–0.01606***
Widower or separated	0.00242	0.00335	0.00698	–0.00991**
Lives in a rented room	–0.00172	–0.00043	NA	NA
Lives in a shack or similar	–0.00826**	–0.00807**	NA	NA
Home has indoor toilet	0.00887***	0.00816***	NA	NA
Access to public aqueduct	0.01143***	0.01154***	NA	NA
Number of people between the ages of 16 and 65 who live in the home	0.00073	0.00025	–0.00372***	–0.00261**
Bogotá	0.01745***	0.01600***	0.02460***	0.02047***
Medellín	0.08656***	0.08465***	0.09839***	0.13902***
Cali	0.02568**	0.02385**	0.04877***	0.08563***
Barranquilla	–0.01637***	–0.01624***	0.00137	–0.00534
Observations	18,769	17,991	29,164	32,605
Pseudo R-squared	0.146	0.153	0.149	0.162

Significance levels with respect to p-value. ***p<0.01, **p<0.05, *p<0.1

Source: DNE (1992, 1996, and 2008), OCD (2013), and our own estimates.

3 Anti-Drug Policies under Plan Colombia

Costs, Effectiveness, and Efficiency

Daniel Mejía

This chapter presents the main results of the anti-drug policies implemented in Colombia between 2000 and 2008 under Plan Colombia. The chapter summarizes the results of several studies done in the past few years and is aimed at understanding the effectiveness and costs of anti-drug policies in Colombia. In particular, after presenting the main facts about these policies, the chapter focuses on a description of the main factors that explain the effectiveness of eradication and interdiction campaigns and alternative development policies. Finally, it makes some specific recommendations about the focus that should be given to strategies aimed at reducing the supply of illegal drugs, in order to strengthen their effectiveness and lower their costs, both direct and indirect.

INTRODUCTION

The Stylized Facts of Anti-Drug Policies in Colombia (2000–2008)

In 1999, the Colombian government announced a strategy for the fight against illegal drugs and organized crime, known as Plan Colombia (PC).[1] The main objectives of this strategy were first to reduce the production of illegal drugs (mainly cocaine) by 50 percent in a period of six years, and second to improve security conditions in Colombia by regaining the control of large areas of the country that were in the hands of illegal armed groups (DNP 2006; GAO 2008).

According to the available data from the National Planning Department (Departamento Nacional de Planeación or DNP), US aid for the military component of PC, aimed at reducing the production and trafficking of drugs from Colombia, was US$472 million per year on average between 2000 and 2008. The Colombian government, for its part, has invested approximately US$812 million per year in the fight against drugs and the organized crime associated with this illegal business. Taken

Daniel Mejía: Associate professor, Faculty of Economy, Universidad de los Andes.

together, these expenditures represent approximately 1.1 percent of average annual GDP between 2000 and 2008.

Figure 3.1A shows the evolution of US and Colombian expenditures on the military component of PC, and Figure 3.1B shows the joint spending of the United States and Colombia on each on the three components of this plan. The allocations to the military component were stable between 2003 and 2007, but in the final year (2008), the allocation of resources to the social and institutional components rose and the allocation to the military component significantly fell. In particular, while the military component represented nearly 80 percent of total US aid under the plan, in 2008 that component fell to 61 percent of the total.

Despite the large amount of resources invested, the results of the anti-drug policies implemented under PC are mixed. In particular, the number of hectares devoted to the growing of coca fell between 2000 and 2005 from approximately 160,000 to 80,000. Since 2005 the number of hectares where coca is grown has remained relatively stable, at an average level of between 80,000 and 85,000 hectares. With regard to the available estimates of potential cocaine production, the results have been different. According to estimates of the United Nations Office on Drugs and Crime (UNODC), the potential production of cocaine remained relatively stable between 2000 and 2006, and it was only in 2007 and 2008 that significant reductions began to be seen in the production of cocaine in Colombia (UNODC 2009).

The main tool for reducing the amount of cocaine produced between 2000 and 2008 was the aerial fumigation of coca plantations with herbicides. For about the past three years, as a result of the pressure from groups that oppose the aerial fumigation campaigns because of their potentially negative collateral effects, manual eradication campaigns of illegal crops have also been implemented, where squads of workers move to different zones where coca is grown and manually uproot and destroy the crops. In this way, the Colombian government has sought to guarantee that the targeted plots of land do in fact have coca and avoid possible damages to the environment and human health that may result from aerial spraying with herbicides. Figure 3.2 shows the number of hectares where coca is grown, the number of hectares sprayed in the aerial eradication campaigns, and the number of hectares subjected to manual eradication between 2000 and 2008. This figure shows that despite the strong efforts to reduce the number of hectares where coca is grown through intensive campaigns for the eradication of illegal crops, especially between 2005 and 2008, the number of hectares where coca is grown has not significantly fallen. Many observers have argued that the main result of the campaigns to eradicate illegal crops is to displace the crops, not to permanently eliminate them. This result, which is known as the "balloon effect," has not been measured in a precise way on a local level, however, and the proofs of its existence have been based on aggregate or "macro" observations of the evolution of coca crops in the three producer countries: Bolivia, Colombia, and Peru.

Other strategies used between 2000 and 2008 to reduce the supply of cocaine in Colombia have been focused on the control of the chemical precursors needed to process coca leaves into coca base and cocaine chlorhydrate, and to detect and destroy the laboratories used to produce cocaine. On the trafficking front, the authorities have tried to block the routes used to transport cocaine to consumer countries and to detect and impede the shipments of cocaine to the consumer countries. Figure 3.3 shows the evolution over time of the confiscations of gasoline and cement meant for the production of

(A)

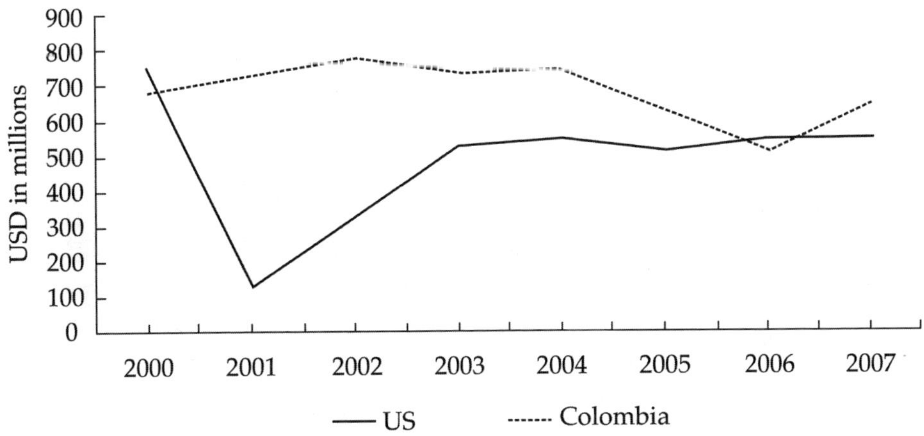

Note: Since 2007 the DNP has referred to the "fight against organized crime and illegal drugs" component as "the fight against terrorism and narcotics trafficking" component in the case of Colombia. In the case of the United States the DNP describes this component as security aid, which includes the resources of the State Department and the Department of Defense.

(B)

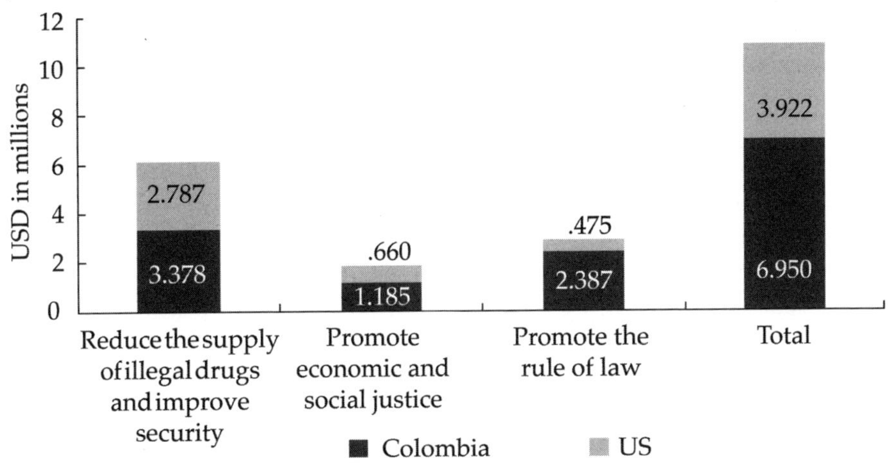

FIGURE 3.1. Resources assigned to Plan Colombia by the United States and Colombia. Source: Mejía (2009), DNP (2006). (A) Resources of the United States and Colombia for the military component of Plan Colombia (2000–2007). Source: Author's estimates based on information from the DNP. (B) Resources of the United States and Colombia by components of Plan Colombia (2000–2006). Note: The names of the components of Plan Colombia are in line with those used by the GAO

cocaine in Colombia. Large amounts of these two products are essential in the first stages of cocaine production (see Chapter 1) and their control by the authorities has proved important in stopping and preventing it. Figure 3.3B shows the evolution over time of the confiscations of cocaine in Colombia. Based on the figures for potential production

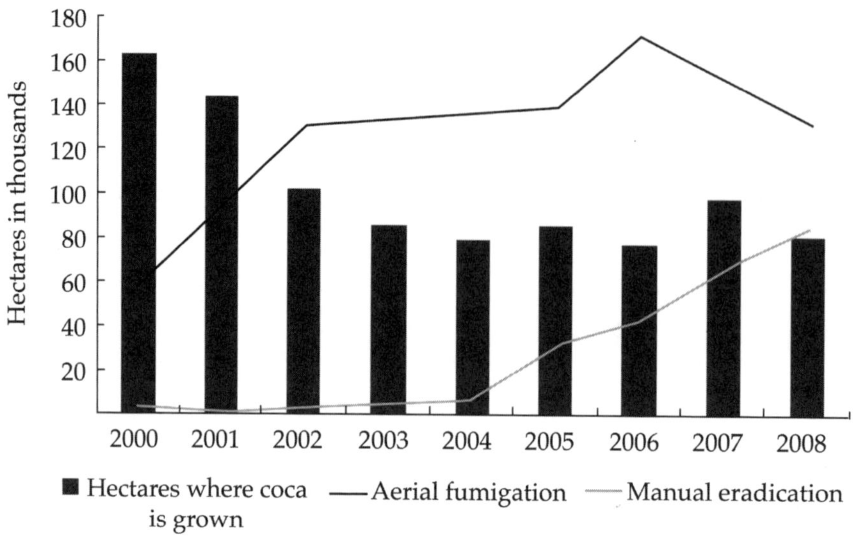

FIGURE 3.2. Coca crops and campaigns of aerial fumigation and manual eradication (2000–2008). Source: UNODC (2009)

estimated by the UNODC, the ratio between the seizures and production of cocaine has grown over time. In particular, according to the UNODC, while 13 percent of the potential cocaine production in Colombia was confiscated in 2000, this figure rose to approximately 46 percent in 2008.

Finally, it is worth noting that the evolution over time of the prices of coca leaves and base and cocaine in Colombia is consistent with the patterns just described. In particular, both the intermediate and final prices have remained relatively stable during the past years, with the price of cocaine in Colombia slightly rising in the past two years, as shown by Figure 3.4.

Using the above evidence and other, more specific indicators on the production and trafficking of cocaine in Colombia, it is possible to come up with concrete and specific measurements of the costs of reducing the amount of cocaine that is produced and exported from Colombia. Although this chapter does not aim to give a detailed description of the methods for estimating these costs and the different measures of the effectiveness of the anti-drug policies implemented in Colombia under PC (Mejía and Restrepo 2010; Mejía and Restrepo 2011; Mejía, Restrepo, and Uribe 2010), the following section summarizes the studies that have focused on measuring the effectiveness and costs of the different fronts of the war on drugs in Colombia.

The 'Sticks' of Anti-Drug Policies Under PC: Eradication Versus Interdiction

To simplify the analysis of the effectiveness and costs of the anti-drug policies as much as possible, those policies may be divided into two major categories: those aimed at the production of drugs and those aimed at fighting drug trafficking. Whereas the former seek to hinder the production of drugs by controlling the inputs needed to produce

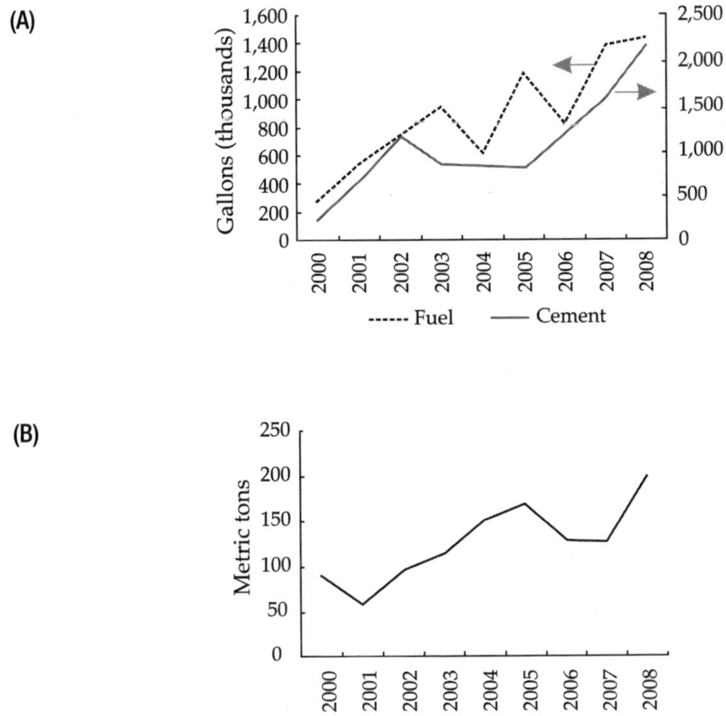

FIGURE 3.3. Seizures of inputs and cocaine in Colombia (2000–2008). (A) Seizures of fuel and cement (2000–2008). Source: Colombian police. (B) Seizures of cocaine in Colombia (2000–2008). Source: UNODC (2009)

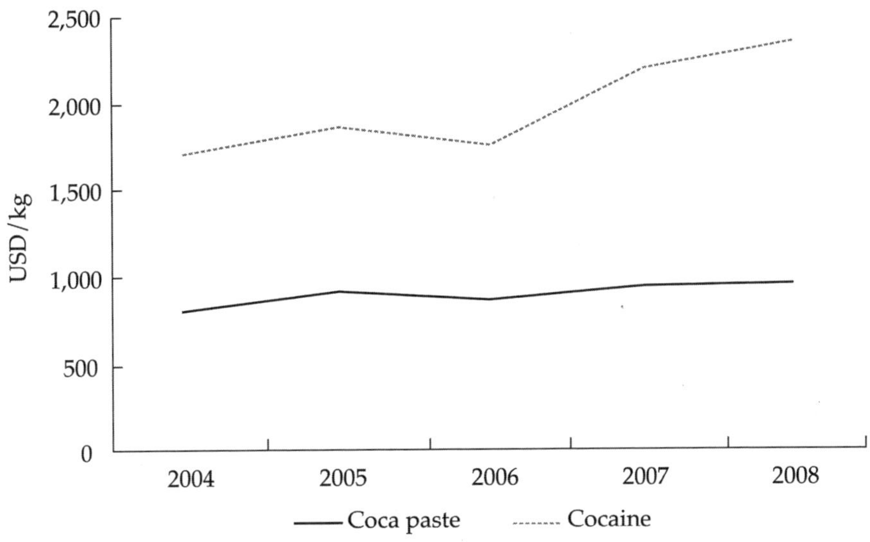

FIGURE 3.4. Price of coca paste and cocaine in Colombia. Source: UNODC (2009)

them, the latter seek to block the routes used to transport the drugs to consumer countries and prevent drugs shipments from reaching their final destination.

This breakdown of the two main fronts of the war on drugs facilitates an evaluation of the effectiveness and costs of the main anti-drug policies implemented under PC. With that aim in mind, Mejía and Restrepo (2010) built an economic model, using the tools of games theory, of the war on drugs under PC. This model captures several important aspects of this war, such as the partial funding of PC by the United States; the fight between cocaine producers and the Colombian government for the control of territories where coca can be grown; and the fight between the traffickers and the Colombian government for the control of the routes used to transport drugs to consumer countries. Finally, by explicitly modeling illegal drug markets, the model also captures important feedback effects between anti-drug policies and the strategic responses of the different agents involved in the production and trafficking of cocaine. In order to build a model of the war on drugs one must explicitly define the objectives of each of the agents involved in it. That of the producers and traffickers is relatively easy to define: to maximize profits. The objective of the governments involved in the war on drugs, on the other hand, is not so obvious. In particular, we assumed in our study (Mejía and Restrepo 2010) that while the objective of the government of the United States is to minimize the amount of drugs transacted in international wholesale markets, the objective of the Colombian government is to minimize the costs associated with the struggle against the production and trafficking of drugs and the costs of fighting on the two fronts of this war. For that reason, we set up a relatively simple structure in which the Colombian government faces a net cost, c1, for each dollar that the drugs producers receive, and a net cost, c2, for each dollar received by the traffickers. Readers who are interested in the specific details of this model may consult the original article or one by Mejía (2010), which gives a detailed but nontechnical summary of the original article. Table 3.1 in Mejía (2009a), summarizes the information used for estimating the model.

In particular, the information needed to estimate the model relates to data such as production before and after the implementation of PC,[2] the prices of the intermediate inputs and the final product (cocaine) before and after the plan's implementation, and the expenditures on the plan by the governments of Colombia and the United States.

The results of the estimates of the model indicate that between 2000 and 2008 the United States funded about 42 percent of the war against the drug producers (largely corresponding to US funding of the aerial spraying campaigns of illicit crops) and around 67 percent of the war against the drug traffickers for the control of the routes (through financial and technical support of the intelligence aimed at detecting cocaine shipments, including the satellite and radar technology used against planes and other means of exporting drugs from Colombia). We also estimate that the Colombian government faces a net cost, c1, of 55 cents for each dollar the producers receive (mainly, the FARC guerrilla and different paramilitary groups) and 2 cents for each dollar the traffickers receive, c2. We further estimate that the relative importance of land in the production of cocaine is about 22 percent (the remaining 78 percent corresponds to the importance of the chemical precursors, laboratories, and manpower), while the relative importance of the routes in the trafficking of cocaine is around 92 percent (the remaining 8 percent corresponds to the relative importance of cocaine itself).

Other results can be derived from the estimations of the model. The first significant result is that those policies aimed at reducing the production of cocaine by fighting for control of the territories used by the drugs producers are considerably more costly than those meant to reduce trafficking through the blocking of the routes along which the traffickers transport drugs. Or, to put it precisely, we estimate that the marginal cost to the United States of reducing by one kilo the amount of cocaine transacted in international wholesale markets by attacking production (e.g., by funding the Colombian government in its eradication campaigns), is approximately US$163,000, whereas the same cost, applied to the attack on trafficking, is approximately US$3,600. Another way of looking at this result is in terms of the elasticity of the amount of cocaine transacted in international drug markets to increases in the funding for each of the fronts in the war on drugs. To be more precise, we estimate that a 1 percent increase in US military aid for the fight against the production of drugs (that is, the battle over territorial control with the producers) reduces the amount of cocaine transacted in international drug markets by approximately 0.007 percent, whereas the same 1 percent increase in military aid spent on the battle over the control of routes with the traffickers reduces the amount of traded cocaine by nearly 0.3 percent. In short, to reduce the amount of drugs successfully produced and exported, it would be much less costly (that is, more efficient) for the United States to subsidize Colombia's fight with the traffickers over the control of routes than its fight with the producers over territorial control.

There are several reasons to explain this first result: (a) We estimate that the Colombian armed forces are more effective at fighting for the control of routes against producers than for territorial control against drug traffickers. In particular, in accordance with our estimations, while drug producers are approximately three times as efficient as the Colombian armed forces in the fight for territorial control, the Colombian armed forces are approximately four times as efficient as the traffickers in the fight for the control of narcotics trafficking routes; (b) the factor in dispute when production is attacked (land) is relatively less important than the factor in dispute when the attack is aimed at trafficking (the routes). As was mentioned above, our estimates indicate that the relative importance of land in the production of cocaine is approximately 22 percent, while the relative importance of the routes in the drug trafficking technology is nearly 92 percent. In light of this result, the war against the production of drugs has focused on a factor that is relatively unimportant (land) in the production of cocaine, while the war against trafficking has focused on the factor that is critical in the cocaine trafficking business (the drug routes); and (c) the capacity of the producers to counteract and mitigate the effect of anti-drug policies is much stronger than that of the traffickers. On the one hand, we estimate that when faced by a 1 percent reduction in the land they control, the producers are able to increase the productivity of the land they are left with by approximately 0.8 percent by improving the yields of crops and using more efficient chemical precursors and production methods. On the other hand, we estimate that when faced by a 1 percent reduction of the routes they control, the traffickers can only increase the productivity of the remaining ones by 0.1 percent. To sum up, the traffickers' ability to adapt themselves to the anti-drug policies, at least in the period between 2000 and 2006, was much less than that of the drug producers.

The second important result has to do with the price elasticity of the demand for drugs, an additional determinant of the effectiveness of the anti-drug policies under

PC. Price elasticity measures the fall in the demand for drugs when there is a 1 percent increase in their price.[3] While the economic literature had already identified this factor as one of the fundamental determinants of the effectiveness of anti-drug policies aimed at reducing supply (Becker, Murphy, and Grossman 2006), it reappears in our model as one of the crucial factors in determining how effective anti-drug policies are at reducing the amount of drugs traded in international drug markets. The intuitive reason for this result is easy to explain. The more inelastic the demand for drugs is, the less the amount of drugs traded in equilibrium will respond to reductions in supply caused by the war on drugs in the consumer countries. With regard to this parameter, our results indicate that the price elasticity of the demand for cocaine traded in wholesale markets at the frontier of the United States is approximately -0.6, which means that if there is a 1 percent increase in the price of cocaine, the demand for this product in international wholesale markets only falls by 0.6 percent. This result corroborates the available estimates on the price elasticity of the demand for cocaine in the retail markets in consumer countries and shows that this same inelasticity is also observed in the wholesale markets for this illegal product.

The third result of this study has to do with the benefits for Colombia of fighting on each of the fronts of the war on drugs. As was already explained, for the United States it is more efficient and less costly to reduce the amount of drugs transacted in international drug markets by subsidizing Colombia's fight for control of the narcotics traffickers' routes, rather than its fight with the producers for territorial control. Nevertheless, and although (a) Colombia is more efficient at the fight against the traffickers than the fight against the producers, (b) the factor under dispute in the fight with the traffickers is relatively more important than the factor under dispute in the fight against the producers, and (c) the producers are better able to counteract the anti-drug measures than are the traffickers, our results overwhelmingly suggest that Colombia would still prefer to use all the subsidies deriving from US military aid under PC for the war against the producers of cocaine (in the fight for territorial control). This apparently controversial and paradoxical result occurs because, according to our estimates, Colombia faces a much higher cost from the production of cocaine than from the activities associated with illegal drug trafficking. In particular, and as was already mentioned, we estimate that for every dollar the drugs producers (mainly the FARC and self-defense groups) receive in Colombia, Colombia faces a net cost of approximately US$0.55, while for each dollar the traffickers receive, Colombia faces a net cost of around US$0.02. This difference in the perceived costs of the activities of producing cocaine (vis-à-vis the activities of trafficking it) compensates for the three factors mentioned above, which in principle should lead Colombia to prefer an attack against the activities of trafficking and not so much those of production. When we look at this result from a historical perspective, we note that the groups responsible for violence in Colombia have changed over time. Whereas the major perpetrators of violence in Colombia in the 1980s and 1990s (those responsible for the highest costs of violence) were groups of narcotics traffickers, like the cartels of Medellín and Cali, who were then more involved in trafficking than in production activities, at the present time the groups that produce the highest costs of violence in the country have been the FARC and the paramilitaries, who, by virtue of their rural character, are more involved in the activities of production than those of trafficking. To a certain extent, this result explains the Colombian government's recent insistence that the way to reduce the production of cocaine is to concentrate on campaigns to eradicate the coca plantations. As we shall see in the final section on policy recommendations, however, this does not mean that there may not be less costly and more effective ways to reduce the production of cocaine that should be implemented with a greater intensity.

Finally, the other main result that derives from the estimates in Mejía and Restrepo (2010) has to do with the costs of achieving significant advances in the war on drugs. That is, we can ask the model, by means of simulation exercises, what are the costs (for Colombia and the United States) of reducing the amount of cocaine that reaches the consumer countries? To answer this question, we use the results of the model and, with exercises of counterfactual simulations, ask what would happen to the different variables of the model (amounts produced and exported, prices, the intensity of the war on drugs in Colombia, etc.) if US military aid were to increase to US$1.5 billion annually.[4] The results of these simulations[5] indicate that the amount of cocaine transacted in international drug markets would fall by around 19.5 percent (around 60,000 kilograms), whereas the wholesale prices of cocaine would rise by approximately 30 percent. These results suggest that if US military aid under PC were tripled (from about US$500 million per year to US$1.5 billion), the amount of cocaine traded in international drug markets would fall by approximately 20 percent.[6] In view of this result, the average per-kilogram cost of reducing the amount of cocaine reaching the United States would be nearly US$17,300.[7] Furthermore, the intensity of the war on drugs in Colombia, measured as the sum total of the resources invested by all the agents involved in it, would rise from around US$6 billion annually to US$10 billion, an increase of nearly 65 percent.

To summarize, it is possible to make an exhaustive analysis of the effectiveness and costs of the anti-drug policies implemented under PC, which also allows us to understand what the structural determinants that explain the costs, efficiency, and effectiveness of the war on drugs are. To an important extent, the strategy used to achieve this (the building of a model and its estimation, employing the available data on the war on drugs) enables us to monitor the indicators of the costs and effectiveness of these policies over time. In fact, once the latest data available for 2007 and 2008 are incorporated into the estimates of the model,[8] the results suggest that the effectiveness of the war against production has been increasing. In particular, the data up to 2008 available from the United Nations (UNODC) show that while the number of hectares devoted to coca has not significantly fallen during the past three or four years (remaining at about 85,000 hectares), the potential production of cocaine did in fact significantly fall in the year 2008 (UNODC 2009). Some experts suggest that this was because with the intensification of the eradication campaigns, the average age of the coca plots has fallen, and with it their productivity, which in turn has counteracted the strategic responses of the cocaine producers, which center around increasing the productivity of the land. Another effect of the intensification of the campaigns to eradicate the coca fields is that they have become increasingly smaller and more isolated, which once again increases production costs and reduces the observed productivity of the land used for coca cultivation.

It is worth noting, nevertheless, that we still lack more recent data that might verify whether the results seen in 2008 are sustainable and thus indicate a permanent fall in the production and trafficking of cocaine in Colombia. Another aspect that should be taken into account when analyzing the results seen in Colombia are occurrences in other producer countries in the region, particularly Peru and Bolivia.

The (Other) Role of Consumer Countries in the Effectiveness of Anti-Drug Policies in Producer Countries

The effectiveness of anti-drug policies in producer countries particularly depends on the kind of anti-drug policies that are implemented in consumer countries. Or, to be more precise, consumer countries can try to reduce the demand for drugs through policies of treatment and prevention and with the use of education campaigns aimed at reducing the consumption of illegal drugs, or they can reduce supply by attacking the distribution networks (what is known as the microtrafficking of drugs) and by punishing the consumers of illegal drugs. The effectiveness of the policies in the producer countries will depend on the emphasis given to different kinds of anti-drug policies by consumer countries. This is an aspect of potential importance that is often ignored by the governments that implement these policies and those who analyze them. For example, the United States channels about 60 percent of federal spending on the fight against drugs into measures to reduce supply, while only 40 percent goes on reducing demand (Aguilar and Castañeda 2009). That being so, the emphasis on reducing the internal supply through punitive measures against microtrafficking and consumption pushes the prices of illegal drugs upwards, making the activities of production and trafficking in the producer countries more profitable. If, on the other hand, anti-drug policies in consumer countries were to focus more on reducing demand, through educational campaigns for example, the lower demand would reduce prices and act as a negative stimulus for the activities of producing and trafficking drugs and thus would reduce the costs and increase the effectiveness of anti-drug policies in producer countries. In order to detect and quantify this effect, Mejía and Restrepo (2011) have extended the basic framework they laid down in 2010 to incorporate the dilemma faced by consumer countries when they choose between policies aimed at reducing the supply of drugs and those aimed at reducing demand. The novelty of this refinement of the model is that it covers a crucial question for the governments in consumer countries: whether resources for the fight against drugs should be allocated to policies aimed at reducing supply in producer countries or those aimed at reducing their own internal demand.

When we estimate this extension of the basic framework, several interesting results emerge once again. Although in theory policies for the reduction of demand seem to be effective, in practice they are not a panacea. Our estimates indicate that the elasticity of demand in the face of increases in the resources allocated to prevention and treatment policies is approximately –0.15, which means that a 1 percent increase in the federal resources allocated to prevention and treatment policies would reduce the aggregate demand for cocaine by approximately 0.15 percent. What is more, the estimates available on a microeconomic scale show an even smaller elasticity, no higher than 0.10 percent. With the estimate of the effectiveness of policies aimed at reducing demand and that of other parameters like the price elasticity of the wholesale demand for cocaine (–0.66), very close to the estimate obtained in Mejía and Restrepo (2010), and the relative efficiency of the Colombian government's expenditures on policies for reducing the supply (0.61), it is possible to estimate the optimal distribution of resources between policies aimed at reducing the demand for drugs and policies aimed at reducing the supply of drugs originating in producer countries. In particular, in Mejía and Restrepo (2011), we show how the higher the effectiveness of the policies for reducing demand

and the lower the price elasticity of demand and the effectiveness of anti-drug policies in the producer countries, the higher should be the allocation of resources to policies of treatment and prevention policies aimed at reducing drug consumption.

In short, the objective of this extension of the basic model developed in Mejía and Restrepo (2011) is to show how the specific kind of anti-drug policies implemented in the consumer countries interacts with the measurements of the effectiveness and costs of the anti-drug policies implemented in producer countries. This refinement shows that while the policies of prevention and treatment are not as effective as one would like them to be in reducing demand in the consumer countries, they cause a positive and not insignificant collateral effect in reducing the costs and increasing the effectiveness of the policies for reducing supply implemented in producer countries.

The "Carrots" Versus the "Sticks" of Anti-Drug Policies in Producer Countries

The other natural extension to the basic framework in Mejia and Restrepo (2010) is to incorporate the "carrots" component found in anti-drug policies in producer countries: programs for alternative development. The main objective of these programs is to encourage the peasant-farmer who grows coca to abandon the crop and turn to legal crops for which he will receive support, training, monetary incentives, and help in commercializing those products. With the incorporation of this possibility into a model for the war on drugs in producer countries, we cover practically the whole range of strategies employed in the war on drugs in such countries, that is, on the one hand the policies that seek to reduce supply through the eradication of crops, the confiscation of products, and the blocking of transport routes, and on the other hand, the policies that try to reduce the growing of coca by subsidizing legal alternatives for the peasant-farmers. This refinement is presented in Mejía, Restrepo, and Uribe (2010), where the original model is extended to the first link in the chain of producing and trafficking cocaine: the peasant-farmer's decision to grow coca or turn to legal crops. The dilemma the peasant-farmer faces in this case is whether to choose coca, the price of which is higher than that of legal crops but presents the risk that his coca will be destroyed by the eradication campaigns, or opt for legal crops, which, while they have a lower price, will not be eradicated and for which he may receive technical or monetary assistance. More precisely, those incentives are incorporated into the model as increases in the productivity of the legal crops. A crucial element in understanding this dilemma is that the peasant farmer who chooses coca is largely free of the problem of selling it, since the local producers of cocaine directly buy the leaves at the farmers' plots. The commercialization of legal products, on the other hand, requires a minimum infrastructure to place them in local markets. With this in mind, the enlarged model incorporates a condition that is indispensable to the success of the programs for alternative development: that access to markets is viable and, in turn, that the technical support given to the farmers is not lost if and when the farmers cannot send their products to the markets.

This refinement seeks to establish the local conditions that are needed to make alternative programs viable, efficient, and sustainable in the medium term as a mechanism to reduce the cultivation of coca. Another important aspect that should be taken into account is what is known as the "balloon effect," the possibility that the illegal crops do not disappear but are just shifted to zones where there are no programs for alternative development. That is, an unintentional effect of these programs may be that when the peasant-farmers who have entered into alternative development programs in one region can no longer meet the producers' demand for coca leaves, this will lead peasant-farmers in more marginal or remote regions to take up the slack. While it is true that the producers' profit margins fall as coca plots move to ever more marginal areas, it is likewise true that the business of producing cocaine still counts on a very high margin that allows it to pay higher prices for coca leaves and still make enormous profits. The purpose of this observation is to call attention to the possibility that the programs for crop substitution may unleash a rat race as the government and the drug producers compete to offer the best deal to the peasant-farmers.

In short, just as it happens with programs for reducing demand in the consumer countries, crop substitution programs in producer countries sound fine in theory. But in order for them to work in practice, they need to be adequately implemented, coordinated with other anti-drug strategies, and, of critical importance, regarded as programs for regional development. Such programs should not only provide short-term technical assistance to the small farmers (which makes them unsustainable in the medium term), but also an infrastructure that allows for the following: first, the commercialization of legal products; second, local institutions that guarantee compliance with contracts and respect for property rights (especially those to do with land holdings); and last and on a more general level, specific reminders of the "presence of the state," such as education and health programs. These kinds of programs are being tried in a pilot program in La Macarena, a region in southeast Colombia, with important results in areas like the reduction of illegal crops, improvements in the indicators of violence, outstanding social indicators, and a stronger presence of Colombian state institutions (DeShazo, McLean, and Mendelson 2009; Isaacson and Poe 2009; USAID 2009).

CONCLUDING REMARKS AND POLICY RECOMMENDATIONS

The studies that form part of the above-mentioned research agenda yield recommendations that should serve as a guide to the formulation of more effective and less costly antinarcotics strategies. Some of the main recommendations are as follows:

1. Focus more on the detection and destruction of laboratories, *cristalizaderos*, and the networks for distributing chemical inputs and less on the campaigns for eradicating illegal crops. There are several fundamental reasons for this recommendation. First, land is not the most important factor in the production of cocaine, and, as the available evidence shows, the producers have come up with strategies to counteract these policies, making them relatively ineffective at reducing the potential production of cocaine. Second, when anti-drug policies focus on the crops, they are attacking the link in the chain that least benefits from the cocaine business (the peasant-farmer growers). While they are involved in an illegal activity, there is no firm evidence that allows us to declare that the money they earn from growing coca is being used to attack the Colombian state and its institutions, as happens in other links of the cocaine production chain. Third, when a laboratory

is discovered, this not only reduces the operative capacity of the groups of producers but it also blocks the market potential of many hectares of coca grown near that laboratory. Fourth, while it is true that it is easier to detect a hectare sown with coca than a laboratory or *cristalizadero* for the processing of cocaine, the first option means a loss of approximately US$400 to US$500 for the producers (the value of the harvested coca leaves), whereas the detection of a laboratory may mean a loss for them of more than US$700,000 (the average cost of establishing a production laboratory, not counting the value of the cocaine stored there). Finally, although there are few independent studies about the collateral effects of the aerial eradication campaigns against illegal crops (for example, on human health and the environment), focusing its anti-drug policies on those links where the least negative collateral effects are caused is more sustainable in the medium term for the Colombian state.

To sum up, while it is true that the Colombian state has sound reasons for focusing the fight against drugs on the war against production, there are more efficient and less costly ways to do it than the campaigns to eradicate illegal crops.

2. With regard to reducing the trafficking of cocaine, efforts must be focused on intelligence work that facilitates the detection of the routes and networks used by drug traffickers to transport the drugs to foreign countries. As the shipments are of low volume but high value, the work of detection must not only focus on improving radar systems and other technologies but also use intelligence to infiltrate the narcotics trafficking networks and anticipate the methods these groups use to transport drugs to the consumer countries.
3. The Colombian government should center its attention on the positive effects of reducing demand in the consumer countries on the anti-drug policies implemented in Colombia. There are substantial reasons to believe that the major long-term benefit for Colombia's internal anti-drug policy will come from these programs of prevention and treatment and educational campaigns aimed at reducing the consumption of drugs. While Colombia has made an enormous effort to obtain funding for the different fronts of the war on drugs, in the medium term the only solution to the problem of narcotics trafficking in Colombia is to permanently reduce the incentives to get involved in this illegal business. If they are implemented in an effective way, campaigns focused on reducing demand may relieve the pressure on the prices of illegal drugs, lower the profit margins of this business, and act as a negative incentive for involvement in these activities by local producers and traffickers.
4. Regarding alternative development, our main recommendation is the need for better planning and interinstitutional coordination. Or, to put it more precisely, many conditions have to be met for these campaigns to be successful, but if their coordination is achieved, it is possible that these campaigns will have the double effect of reducing illegality and increasing economic development on a local level in marginal zones. The conditions needed to make these programs work in the medium term have to do with facilitating access to markets (that is, infrastructure), providing guarantees for property rights (especially those relating to the secure tenure of lands for the adequate exploitation of legal agricultural activities), monitoring the possible shift of illegal crops toward marginal zones not covered by these

programs, and guaranteeing minimum conditions of security for those peasant-farmers who enter into programs for the substitution of illegal crops.

NOTES

1. Plan Colombia is the official name of the program that, among other aims, provides the institutional framework for the military alliance between the United States and Colombia in the war against the production and illegal trafficking of drugs and against the criminal organizations associated with these illegal activities.
2. The original article takes, as a reference, the results for 1999 and 2000 as the base years before Plan Colombia, and the results for 2005 and 2006 as the base years after Plan Colombia. It is done that way because the goals of the plan were originally set for six years, that is, with the reference years used in the study. Some preliminary results of the estimates that incorporate more recent years (2007 and 2008) will be briefly discussed below.
3. If the elasticity is less than 1 as an absolute value, the demand is called *inelastic*, while if it is greater than 1 as an absolute value, it is called *elastic*.
4. The average total aid for the military component of Plan Colombia between 2000 and 2006 was US$465 million annually. That is, by raising it to 1.5 billion we are making an estimate of what might happen in the war on drugs in Colombia if the military aid of the United States were tripled.
5. It is worth noting that these simulations are made on the assumption that the respective allocation of subsidies to Plan Colombia for the two fronts of the war on drugs is the most efficient one possible (from the viewpoint of the United States), that is, an allocation in which all the US military aid to Plan Colombia is aimed at the fight against the trafficking of cocaine.
6. Although this reduction is apparently small, given the large increase in aid, in this case the cost the United States pays (US$1 billion) for reducing the amount of cocaine that passes its frontiers by 20 percent (in the form of subsidies for the war against drugs in the producer countries) would have to be compared to the costs of reducing, by the same percentage, the amount of cocaine traded by employing prevention and treatment policies to reduce the demand or policies that strengthen internal enforcement in the United States to decrease the domestic supply.
7. If the simulations were made with the observed distribution of subsidies allocated to the two fronts of the war on drugs, the cost would be much higher.
8. These estimates based on the latest available figures are still in progress and for that reason this chapter places an emphasis on the estimates that use the figures up to 2006.

REFERENCES

Aguilar, R., and J. G. Castañeda. 2009. *El narco: La guerra fallida*. México: Santillana Ediciones Generales.

Becker, G., K. Murphy, and M. Grossman. 2006. "The Market for Illegal Goods: The Case of Drugs." *Journal of Political Economy* 114, no. 1: 38–60.

DeShazo, P., P. McLean, and J. Mendelson. 2009. *Colombia's Plan de Consolidación Integral de La Macarena, an Assessment*. Center for Strategic and International Studies (CSIS) Americas Program, Washington, DC, June.

DNP (Departamento Nacional de Planeación). 2006. *Plan Colombia Progress Report: 1999–2005*. Bogotá: Departamento Nacional de Planeación (DNP) and Departamento de Justicia y Seguridad (DJS), September.

GAO (Government Accountability Office). 2008. "Plan Colombia Drug Reduction Goals Were Not Fully Met, But Security Has Improved; U.S. Agencies Need More Detailed Plans for Reducing Assistance," GAO 00-71, October.

Isaacson, A., and A. Poe. 2009. "After Plan Colombia, Evaluating 'Integrated Action,' the Next Phase of U.S. Assistance," Center for International Policy, November.

Mejía, D. 2009a. "Evaluación del Plan Colombia." Fedesarrollo: *Cuadernos de Fedesarrollo*, no. 29.

———. 2009b. "The War on Illegal Drugs: The Interaction of Anti-Drug Policies in Producer and Consumer Countries." Cesifo working paper no. 2459, November.

Mejía, D. 2010. "Evaluating Plan Colombia." In *Innocent Bystander: Developing Countries and the War on Drugs*, edited by P. Keefer and N. Loayza. Washington, DC: Macmillan/Palgrave. Retrieved from *www-wds.worldbank.org/external/default/WDSContentServer/IW3P/IB/2010/03/25/000333037_20100325005015/Rendered/PDF/536410PUB0Inn01010fficia10Use00nly1.pdf*, accessed May 12, 2015.

Mejía, D., and P. Restrepo. 2010. "The War on Illegal Drug Production and Trafficking: An Economic Evaluation of Plan Colombia." Documento CEDE no. 19, Universidad de los Andes, October.

———. 2011 "The War on Illegal Drugs in Producer and Consumer Countries: A Simple Analytical Framework." Documento CEDE 2011-2, February, Facultad de Economía, Universidad de los Andes.

Mejía, D., P. Restrepo, and M. J. Uribe. 2010. "The 'Sticks' vs. the 'Carrots' of Anti-Drug Policy in Producer Countries: The Case of Colombia." Forthcoming.

UNODC (UN Office on Drugs and Crime). 2009. Coca Cultivation Surveys for Bolivia, Peru and Colombia. Vienna: United Nations Office. Retrieved from *www.unodc.org/unodc/en/crop-monitoring/index.html*, accessed May 12, 2015.

USAID. 2009. *Assessment of the Implementation of the United States Government's Support for Plan Colombia's Illicit Crop Reduction Components*. Washington, DC: Management Systems International (MSI), April.

4 Alternative Development Policies in Colombia (1982–2009)

Carlos Zorro-Sánchez

Nowadays the fight against illegal drugs is a fundamental although profoundly controversial component of international policy. As the world's largest producer of cocaine and its basic input, coca paste, Colombia has necessarily been immersed in the vicissitudes of that policy, which has traditionally been characterized by two components: repression, including forced eradication of illegal crops and interdiction, which seek to check the different links in the narcotics trafficking chain in a coercive way; and encouragement, which tackles the first link of this chain by providing incentives to replace illegal crops with legal ones.

It must be taken into account that most of the peasant-farmers who grow illegal crops in Colombia belong to the classes with the lowest incomes and fewest economic and social opportunities. For that reason, different authors and international bodies have thought that the expected crop substitution will only be sustainable in the long term if those peasant-farmers are furnished with a set of tools that not only allow them to abandon the banned crops but also set out on the path to a better quality of life. Thus the original idea of the "substitution of illegal crops" has been replaced by the concept of "alternative development."

The present chapter examines the second component mentioned in the first paragraph of this introduction and analyzes the policies of alternative development that have been adopted and at least partially carried out in Colombia since 1982. This chapter begins with a reflection on the concept of alternative development and the way it has been approached by Colombian policies in the fight against drugs. It then goes on to characterize the different phases of these policies, and finally, on the basis of the analysis, points to some conclusions and recommendations.

SUBSTITUTION OF ILLEGAL CROPS OR ALTERNATIVE DEVELOPMENT: THE DILEMMA AND ITS EXPRESSION IN COLOMBIAN POLICIES

"Alternative development" is an expression that has been used in very different senses, ranging from the simple substitution of illegal crops to complex processes of economic and social development. According to the United Nations, alternative development is "a process to prevent and eliminate the illegal growing of plants which contain narcotic and

---

Carlos Zorro-Sánchez: Associate professor, CIDER, Universidad de los Andes. Written with the collaboration of economist Carlos Caicedo, political scientist Carolina Peña, and economist Diego Andrade.

psychotropic substances through measures of rural development specifically designed for that aim" (UN 1998, 20) (Presidencia de la República n.d., 42). For the United Nations Development Program in Colombia (UNDP), it is an "integrated rural development in regions with the presence of illegal crops" (UNDP 2000). Plan Colombia, the framework for the activities of the Uribe administration in this field, also adheres to this broad vision of alternative development.

The Inter-American Drug Abuse Control Commission (CICAD) cites three objectives of this policy: "to pacify and stabilize . . . the areas subject to the domination and violence of narcotics traffickers"; "offer real alternatives for subsistence to the producers of illegal drugs"; and "honor the commitment to the collaboration between the consumer countries and those which produce such crops." The second of these principles is the main driving force of alternative development (CICAD 2009).

Nevertheless, as already indicated, there is a semantic problem: in practice, the above definitions are challenged by the idea that alternative development is only a program for substituting illegal crops (Cabieses 1999, 38), and it turns out to be paradoxical that while the latter meaning has tended to be weakened in the political discourse, it tends in practice to prevail in the decisions of governments. According to de Rementería (2001), this is due in part to the complexity of applying the more ambitious logic.

Granted, at bottom these policies are not contradictory; both seek to eliminate illegal crops. But while that is the main aim in substitution, in alternative development it is barely a condition for improving the situation of the small farmers. Alternative development requires actions broader and deeper but also more functional than substitution, as they must heighten the costs of illegality and the benefits of the legal activity, which would tend to close the profit gap that makes illegal crops attractive.

The tension between the two logics has become evident in Colombian policies. The alternative development programs in Colombia arose from the clear mission to substitute illegal crops, and their initial problem was agricultural and financial. What crops would replace coca? How much would this substitution cost? It was later that the idea came to the fore that substitution would fail if there was not a social and economic change in the communities affected by such crops. But this idea, which has been incorporated since then into the formulations of policies of alternative development, has not managed to consolidate itself in strategic and operational terms, as has been shown by the numerous changes of emphasis in the programs designed and implemented for that end in different presidential administrations.

These changes can be appreciated in the development of Colombian alternative development policies, which show three relatively well-differentiated phases:

A. Formation, where the initial strategy of concentrating on the forced eradication of illegal crops, almost always by fumigation, was complemented by a strategy of substituting such crops.
B. Consolidation, where the state directly assumed responsibility for guiding alternative development by means of an institutional framework designed for that end.
C. A shift in direction, which, gathering some aspects of the accumulated experience, and on the basis of the logic of Plan Colombia, maintains the discourse of development but simplifies it in the effort to make its actions more efficient.

Certainly, there are external and internal pressures behind these policies that promote the fight against drugs, pressures that the Colombian state has had to deal with in especially difficult conditions, insofar as narcotics trafficking has meshed with the armed conflict and become the main source of resources for the irregular armed groups.

"The State's inability to end this situation has meant a loss of legitimacy, which transmits within and outside of the country the image of a weak State, which has lost its legitimate monopoly of force" (Orjuela 1998, 2), and that is internationally questioned for being the country that places the largest amount of narcotics on the world market. Thus the strength of its reaction is not surprising, aimed as it is at recovering the full control of its territory and restoring its reputation as a state able to honor its international commitments. That is why Colombia has resorted to alternative development, forced eradication, and interdiction (Torres 2006, 8–11).

CHARACTERISTICS OF THE DIFFERENT PHASES OF ALTERNATIVE DEVELOPMENT IN COLOMBIA

The characteristics of the three phases in question will be briefly set forth, with an emphasis on the third, which was in force until the end of Alvaro Uribe's government (2010), and a mention of some of their common elements.

The Formative Phase: The Shift from Fumigation as a Strategy of Eradication to the Substitution of Illegal Crops as a Complementary Strategy (1982–1993)

The first actions to substitute illegal crops in Colombia were undertaken on the initiative of the United Nations in 1985 and were only directly assumed by Colombian public institutions in 1993. The effort to confront the drug traffic with the purely repressive focus that had characterized the fight came in 1973 with the issuance of decree 1206, which created the National Narcotics Council (CNE).

During the presidency of Belisario Betancur (1982–1986), the country's economic backwardness, weak state presence, and poverty were emphasized as the "objective" conditions for the emergence and persistence of violence and illegality. Seeking solutions for the regions most affected by these conditions, programs for economic recuperation and reconciliation were promoted, among them the National Rehabilitation Plan (PNR), the actions of which included the substitution of illegal crops, and which later, for a short time, led the Program for Alternative Development (Programa Presidencial para la Convivencia 1994).

At the same time, the United Nations International Drug Control Program (UNDCP), now the United Nations Office on Drugs and Crime (UNODC), which has operated in Colombia since 1985, undertook its first important action: the program for the substitution of illegal crops in the south of Cauca, extended to Nariño in 1989. In reality, it was a set of isolated projects that supported the gradual replacement of coca crops grown by small farmers in order to prevent their expansion (ODCCP 2001).

This simple model of crop substitution began to be reformulated in 1987, when it was linked with processes of rural development that encouraged the participation of farmers and their organizations, the identification and opening of commercialization channels, and the construction of agro-industrial plants and a variety of related infrastructures. Despite that change, the projects continued to be seen as a complement to forced eradication, aimed at assuring the temporary survival of the small producers, peasant-farmers, and indigenous persons who agreed to substitution, through individual credits for development and technical assistance (Tocancipá 1997, 2; ODCCP 2001, 18). For that reason, the resources were not generally applied to substitution and were not paid back in accordance with the agreements, and there were no sustainable results.

Most of these activities took place during the administration of President Virgilio Barco (1986–1990), the period in which the United Nations Convention against Illicit Traffic in Narcotics Drugs and Psychotropic Substances (signed in 1988) "introduced the concept of alternative development . . . to balance and reduce the impact of the forced eradications and criminal prosecution of small farmers" (Franco 2008, 6).

The 1990s began with the sending of contradictory signals: on the one hand, under pressure from the US government, president César Gaviria (1990–1994) intensified the spraying of illegal crops, which had declined toward the end of the previous administration, but on the other hand, in 1990, within the framework of the 1988 convention, the UNDCP began a program for the substitution of illegal crops in Caquetá, Putumayo, and Guaviare through integral processes of rural development (Tocancipá 1997, 3).

The Colombian state then began to interest itself in alternative development and apply for funding from international cooperation agreements. For that reason, the PNR registered, among its achievements for the period of 1985–1993, the substitution of 3,476 hectares of coca (96 percent of them in Cauca) and the voluntary eradication of nearly 1,000 hectares of poppy destined for heroin (Programa Presidencial para la Convivencia 1994, 32). Compared to the 42,000 hectares sown with coca in 1989 (Ortiz 2000), the first figure shows how limited that achievement was, and even more so considering there that were no follow-ups to guarantee that the substitution would last.

Phase of Consolidation

Two stages may be distinguished in this phase. The first was the formation of a public institutional framework, and the second was a peak and crisis in alternative development.

The Formation of a Public Institutional Framework: Programs of Alternative Development (1993–1998)

In 1993, the PNR, administered by the Administrative Department of the Presidency of the Republic (DAPR), became responsible for coordinating alternative development (under decree 2707), and a document issued by the National Council of Economic and Social Policy (CONPES, no. 2734) adopted the National Program of Alternative Development (PNDA) as part of the anti-drug strategies and as a response to rural development. The duality of crop substitution/alternative development is glimpsed in this decision.

To begin with, the PNDA undertook projects in three departments. These projects, forerunners of the current agreements, were based on agreements with the communities in which the state committed itself to improve their presence in the markets "by means of investments in the development of the region, the financing of regional projects, and the implementation of revolving funds" (Iglesias 2003, 19) and the communities committed themselves to the voluntary eradication of their illegal crops.

With the first international credits for alternative development, the government sought to remedy the wants of the regions affected by these crops. There is no doubt that the most important credit up to the year 2000 was the one provided by the International Development Bank (IDB, BID in Spanish), which financed a large part of the respective programs until the beginning of this century (CONPES 2734, 1994, 1). With the direct participation of the municipalities through municipal operational plans and a partial monitoring by the Interdisciplinary Center of Regional Studies (CIDER) of the University of los Andes in Bogotá, its resources could be channeled toward five basic components: institutional and community development, technical and productive development, support for indigenous peoples, recuperation and conservation of environmentally fragile areas, and infrastructure for development. The last one captured the most resources.

The same period marked the beginning of the growing role of nongovernmental organizations for development, as interlocutors in the rehabilitation councils and administrators of projects agreed on or coadministered with public entities (Dorantes 1991, 81)

The implementation of the PNDA did not stop the intensification of the fumigations in 1994. In accordance with a decision of the National Narcotics Council, these fumigations had to be complemented by civic/policing actions to deal with the humanitarian crises caused by the crop spraying and to dissuade the affected population from resuming illegal activities. A link was thus established between eradication and alternative development (Iglesias 2003, 19), which, in practice, led people to confuse one program with the other and frequently led the communities that rejected fumigation to oppose alternative development.

To begin with, the government of Ernesto Samper (1994–1998) subordinated alternative development to an essentially repressive policy based on forced eradication; alternative development was a palliative for the negative effects of eradication on the affected population. Paradoxically, the CONPES (in document 2799/1995) reorganized the program, giving it a broader vision. From then on the actions of this program were incorporated into the PNDA, which, under decree 0472/1996, became known as the "Plante." The plan sought to provide "an economic alternative, within the law, for the 300,000 small farmers who grow illegal crops" and carry out a "preventive program in other areas of the country which, because of their neglected conditions, are susceptible to becoming zones of expansion for new [plantations of illegal] crops."

The Operational Municipal Plans, POMs, were maintained in this model of intervention, which included components similar to those of the programs financed by the IDB credit. To implement it, Colombia won the support of the United States Agency for International Development (USAID), and two tools were designed that would later be of great importance: Support for Associative and Community Groups (IAGAC) and Capitalization of Business Enterprises (ICE).

The ICE, carried out through the Incubadora Empresarial de Producción y Comercialización Agropecuaria (INCUAGRO, roughly translated as the Managerial Incubator for the Production and Commercialization of Agricultural and Stock-Rearing Products), sought to capitalize companies and productive projects through the formation of limited companies made up of small farmers' organizations and businessmen from the private sector interested in the proposed programs (CONPES 2734/1994, 9). The IAGAC, for its part, was oriented toward "financing small productive projects through the organizations of peasant-farmer and indigenous producers" (Restrepo n.d., 2).

The protest marches undertaken in el Guaviare in 1995 to demand that the small farmers who grew coca be treated differently from the large producers made evident not only the territorial nuances of the problem but the widespread dissatisfaction with the policy. In fact, the simultaneous realization of the fumigations and the Plante programs set off the protests of the peasant-farmers, who demanded above all that the areas where they had subsistence crops should not be sprayed, which was happening, because the fumigations were destroying the products of the substitution projects. The government did not yield, and the breach between the Plante and the growers widened.

Partly as a result of the protests, decree 2586/1997 ordered that from then on the productive projects would be realized within the framework of the Regional Plans of Alternative Development (PRDA), which had replaced the POMs (Plante-CIDER 1998),[1] and they should result from a joint agreement between the civil society and the regional institutions on the creation of options with an economic dynamic capable of counteracting the growing of illegal crops.

This decision was a turning point in the priorities of the government. Whereas alternative development had been initially subordinated to the eradication of those crops, the idea was to give it the leading role again, but without impairing the fumigations. It is worth noting that the reforms contemplated by the Samper administration were ambitious, and while barely applied at that time, they were later perfected and served as the basis of a large part of subsequent actions.

Application and the Crisis of the Model of Alternative Development (1998–2002)

The government of Andrés Pastrana (1998–2002) initially adopted the institutional apparatus of the Plante and accelerated its activities,[2] especially through three measures: pacts between the government and the communities, the ICE, and the IAGAC.

To implement the social pacts for alternative development and manual eradication, the beneficiary communities signed contracts that, in contrast to the previous ones, were of a collective nature. In them, the government committed itself to pay two million pesos to each family for food security, carry out studies for the commercialization of alternative crops, support productive projects, provide technical assistance, and finance infrastructures, education, health, and electricity. In exchange, the community was obliged to eradicate coca within the twelve months following the payment for food security, replace the illegal economy with legal activities, and not sow more coca. The pacts were relevant in the Putumayo: thirty-five, covering 35,000 families, were signed in 2001, but despite a promising start, each party accused the other of noncompliance. The government resumed the fumigations and suspended the program a few weeks before the end of its term, after paying 70 percent of the subsidies for food security and without any great progress in the projects (Comunicado de prensa 2001).[3]

Nor were the twenty-six PRDAs designed at that time successful. In fact, they were merely diagnostic, without a strategic vision or resources, and they eventually were dropped.

The ICE and IAGAC, for their part, remained the framework of the productive projects for nearly a decade. As the IDB, the main source of funding in the first years of the Pastrana government, did not allow the funds from its credit to be used for direct loans to the producers, two mechanisms were created, known as windows, whereby the intermediaries, who it was assumed had the capacity to transfer technology to the producers, received the resources to spread them among the producers as a complement to their transference of technology.

Window 1, capitalization of businesses, promoted strategic alliances between peasant-farmer associations and businessmen with a broad experience and operative capacity in the agricultural and stock-rearing sector, in accordance with the above-mentioned scheme.

Window 2, reserved for the IAGAC, allocated resources from revolving funds to second-tier organizations formed by associations of small producers. The resources were used for the projects of their affiliates, who were urged to substitute illegal crops. CIDER's monitoring found strong support from the beneficiaries of this tool, for three reasons: it inspired trust, it provided practical training for the peasant-farmers and their associations, and, on occasions, it showed considerable yields (Plante-CIDER 2001, chap. 2; Plante, BID, CIDER 2004, chap. 1).[4]

Between 2000 and 2004 the IAGAC cofinanced twenty-one projects for the benefit of 3,142 families linked to thirty-four organizations and established 5,723 hectares of legal crops (Restrepo n.d., 2). Although these figures are not insignificant in absolute terms, they were a long way from providing the counterweight needed to deal with such an enormous problem. For the rest, most of the projects did not benefit from rigorous feasibility studies, which became one of the main flaws in their implementation.[5] In 2001 CIDER did an ex post facto assessment of the projects of several associations, among them ASOHECA (rubber) and ACUICA (fish farming) in Caquetá, which yielded a positive net present value. The subsequent development of ASOHECA, which is now the country's biggest producer of rubber, confirms the conclusion of that assessment.

When asked about the projects, the producers surveyed by CIDER within the framework of its monitoring were emphatic in rejecting those that implied a return to subsistence activities. In addition, their responses showed an important change of attitude toward illegal crops. Illegal crops were no longer regarded as a panacea; at best, they were seen as a necessary evil that had to be overcome, and for that reason, producers no longer proposed projects with a similar profitability as a condition for eradicating them. But producers did demand solutions that would provide the producers and their families with acceptable living conditions in the countryside. Despite the limitations of the program, and especially the failure to achieve a good dialogue with its beneficiaries, most of those who were polled greatly appreciated its work and its support for the culture of legality (Plante CIDER 2001, chaps. 3 and 6; 2004, chap. 6).

1999 marked the adoption of Plan Colombia for "peace, prosperity and the strengthening of the State."[6] Among its ten strategies were alternative development, to "promote agricultural and stock-rearing schemes and other profitable economic activities for the peasant-farmers and their families" (Presidencia de la República, n.d.), and to stop the expansion of illegal crops. In a certain manner, its objective 6—"To strengthen and enlarge the plans for alternative development"—assumed the functions of the Plante (16).

Always in coordination with the DAPR, the plan introduced a new institutional framework, which included, among other things, a Fund of Investments for Peace (Fondo de Inversiones para la Paz, FIP), charged with setting the guidelines of the PNDA—which absorbed but did not eliminate the Plante—and adopting criteria of focalization, geographical priorities, and lines of action.

The plan maintained the major strategy lines of alternative development: It reaffirmed that its focus would be based on "productive participatory projects," and it emphasized work with productive chains, the organizing of small producers, institutional strengthening, and physical and social infrastructure. It maintained the ICE and IAGAC and designed other tools, like the "countryside in action" program, kept up by the following administration.

Plan Colombia turned the United States into the main cofinancer of the fight against drugs and restored the priority and coverage of fumigations, including the areas where there were "fragmented or mixed crops" (that is, a mixture of alternative and illegal ones). This harmed the subsistence crops (Torres 2006, 23) and caused great uncertainty about the program because, in the popular imagination, the plan, including the alternative development and other components, became synonymous with fumigation.

Shift of Direction Phase: Alternative Development Programs (2002–2010)

The Plante continued to operate during the first year of the first term of president Álvaro Uribe (Contraloría General de la Nación 2002, 33). After that, alternative development was redefined and set in the framework of the Presidential Campaign against Illegal Crops (Gestión Presidencial contra Cultivos Ilícitos, PCI), based on the same principles as its predecessors.[7] An outline of its main activities follows.

Decree 100/2004 abolished the Plante and gave rise to the PDA, formalized in 2003 under the CONPES document no. 3218, as a component of the second phase of Plan Colombia, linked to the strategy of democratic security and subject to the guidance of the PCI. The purpose was to concentrate on strengthening the state in the zones devoted to growing illegal crops, with a focus on regional development aimed at promoting legal alternatives for employment and income in the communities that would commit themselves to keeping the previously eradicated zones free of illegal crops. Its guidelines emphasize the importance of the communities and their organizations, and give priority to the "strengthening of local capacities of governability . . . with the aim of consolidating democratic security in areas . . . 'free of illegal crops'" (CONPES 3218, 2003, 6).

Toward these ends, three programs have been adopted: the forest ranger families ("*familias guardabosques*," FRP); productive and income-generating projects (PPP); and institutional strengthening, social development, and monitoring. The first two linked to the strategy of voluntary manual eradication (UNODC 2007),[8] which does not exclude forced mechanical eradication. The third supports "the commitments to not plant or replant undertaken between the State and the communities," provides "social and management accompaniment to rural organizations which participate in the two main components," and "includes the verification and certification of nuclei free of illegal crops" (CONPES 3218, 2003, 11), since the programs within the "rural districts free of illegal crops" policy require previous eradication and keeping the whole district free of illegal crops (Acción Social, PCI, PDA 2009).

Forest Rangers Program (FRP)

Description The FRP seeks to check the advance of illegal crops in zones on the agricultural frontier and eradicate them in areas where they are already established, while also protecting ecosystems that are socially and environmentally strategic. To achieve this, it aims to associate itself with other public and private entities. The areas are selected in accordance with the presence or threat of illegal crops, the strategic character of the eco-regions, and the collective will of a community (a rural district, for example) to make three commitments: (a) keep its district free of illegal crops; (b) save between 40 and 50 percent of the conditioned subsidy it receives to cofinance productive projects or buy land; and (c) undertake activities of environmental protection (Acción Social, UNODC, 2008, 18).

On the basis of these commitments, the families receive money (conditioned incentive) and technical support (social, productive, and environmental) for three years. The subsidy must be used to facilitate the participation of the families in the program of productive projects.

The activities of the FRP follow three stages: (a) selection of and approach to the communities, which ends with the signing of a contract, which is collective but is signed by representatives of each family in the rural district or community that wishes to be included in the program; (b) fulfillment of the commitments (eradication of illegal crops, signing of the individual contract, and first payment) and (c) accompaniment, follow-up, and evaluation. In contrast with the strictly collective pacts of the previous period, the commitments thus acquired are now individual ones, but they are managed collectively: if a single person breaks his or her promise, all the beneficiaries are excluded from the program. Compliance is verified by the UNODC and the Community Committees for Verification and Social Control (CCVCS), made up of leaders elected by the families and the FRP.

This has had five phases.[9] Each has included nine municipalities; the amount and term of the incentive may differ in each phase and in fact it was decreasing in the period between 2003 and 2008 (Table 4.1).[10] From its start to the 2009 budget year, the FRP had operated in 23 departments and 121 municipalities and has linked 107,081 families (individual contracts signed). In March 2009, 60,267 families were active in it[11] and had had received subsidies of some 668 billion pesos[12] (64 percent of the investment in the PCI in that period).

Some Results *Voluntary eradication.* By 2008, the FRP had eliminated, in a manual and voluntary way, 14,557 hectares of illegal crops; replanting was 5 percent (UNODC, Acción Social, 2008, 24).

Use of the conditioned incentive. The conditioned incentive, which in the name of gender equality is given to the women involved (Ibid., 29), has been crucial to the substitution of illegal crops, and it is further assumed that it can also support sustainable processes. This is shown both by the use of the incentive, according to the follow-up done by the UNODC (Ibid., 15–17)[13] (Table 4.2), and by the fact that while it was essential as a source of income for 75 percent of the families at the start of the program

TABLE 4.1. Phases of Forest Ranger Families Program

Phase	Incentive*	Duration of program	Number of municipalities	Start of phase
I	$833.000–$600.000	36 months	13	2003 and 2004
II	$ 600.000	36 months	22	2004
III	$ 600.000	36 months	25	2005
IV	$ 408.000	18 months	40	2007
V	$ 408.000	18 months	21	2008
Total			121	

* Calculated in pesos of the initial year of the programming of each phase. As the text indicates, the program is implemented in phases, each of which has a specific programming whose basic components are restated in the columns of this table. *Source:* Acción Social. Information System of the PCI (SIPCI 2009).

TABLE 4.2. Use of the conditioned incentive (2005–2008)

Phase	Time of recording	Family Expenditure	Savings	Agricultural/ stock-rearing activities	Others
Phase I and II	Final line	36.50%	7.60%	26.90%	29.00%
Phase III	Follow-up	55.90%	16.50%	15.40%	12.20%
Phase IV	Baseline	27.60%	46.70%	12.10%	13.60%

Source: Acción Social and UNODC. Survey cited in "Executive Report" (2008, 28).

(phases I and II), it was gradually replaced by other sources in the course of the process and at the end of these phases it was only fundamental for 16.4 percent of these families (Ibid., 28). Nevertheless, while, in accordance with the expectations of the program, the proportion of families linked to the productive projects reached 79 percent for those who participated in phases I and II, it tended to fall in phase III and, above all, in phase IV (23).[14] One important reason for it may have been the reduction of the incentive, shown in Table 4.1.

According to UNODC, Acción Social (2007a, 10),[15] the beneficiaries of the PDA were relatively satisfied in 2006. More than 80 percent said it was not only the public entity with the strongest presence in their communities but also met its requests (63.9 percent) and had managed to strengthen their trust in the state, their autonomy, and their capacity to organize themselves: 57.1 percent of the families belonged to productive organizations and of these, 85.6 percent were legally recognized entities, which is important for the aim of legality (UNODC, Acción Social 2007b, 47–52).

Apart from that, of the 36.3 percent of the families who owned plots devoted to illegal crops and eradicated them to qualify for the FRP, only 1.4 percent regretted their decision, while 34.5 percent did not (Ibid., 26). Unfortunately, it is not known whether this favorable attitude was due to the success of the FRP or to fear of the fumigations.

Program for Productive and Income-Generating Projects (PPP)

The aim of this program is to establish a regional and local economic base that offers stable sources of legal employment and income and helps to improve the food security of the peasant-farmers and communities on the basis of the sustainable use of natural resources (CONPES 1996, 2318, 8). It is thus divided into two components (Ibid., 6):

Food security and cash flows, subsistence crops in unproductive periods

Medium and long-term productive projects for which priority has been given to six lines: cacao, coffee, rubber, oil palm, cattle, and sugar cane.

The PPP, which incorporated elements from previous programs,[16] provides support for the formulation and implementation of productive projects to peasant-farmer organizations or cooperatives that work within the agricultural frontier. The program gives priority to initiatives that are economically, financially, and environmentally viable in areas that depend on or are at risk of depending on illegal markets. It includes technical, social-managerial, and commercialization assistance and helps gain access to fair trade, organic, and other niche markets (Acción Social, UNOCD, 2008, 36). It also promotes the acquisition of lands for the beneficiaries, on the assumption that ownership of such land is one of the most effective tools for stabilizing them in the region and encouraging activities other than growing illegal crops.

Between 2003 and 2007, the PPP applied two models of intervention: a joint tender and a risk capital fund, both of which were reformulated. In the first, the PCI and international cooperation agencies established agreements to support projects chosen by the program and linked to the plans of each region (UNODC, Acción Social, 2008, 36). The projects, chosen in a competition following a bidding offer, received a nonrepayable disbursement of up to 40 percent of the investment. The second model, the capitalization of businesses (INCUAGRO) described above, functioned in a similar way to the joint tender,[17] but the choice of organizations and projects was not made in open competitions but through analyses and agreements between the entities responsible for their implementation (Ibid., 6).

The investment of the program in the period 2003–2008 reached 74,768 million pesos[18] (7.1 percent of the total investment of the presidential campaign against illegal drugs, PCI, during that period), which leveraged 171,491 million pesos from diverse codonors and allowed for the establishment of 441,871 hectares devoted to projects which benefit a total of 630,647 families.[19] This amounts to a per-family investment no higher than 500,000 pesos during the period.

According to the UNODC (Acción Social, UNODC 2008, 36 and 39),[20] the sales in 2007 and up to September 2008 from twenty-five projects (22 percent of the total) that had advanced to the stage of production and commercialization represented nearly 0.1 percent of the agricultural and stock-rearing GDP, despite insufficient marketing studies.[21] This suggests that their products have potential. The inclusion of aggregate value is still lacking—76 percent of the projects sell their goods to the wholesale market (Ibid., 40–41)—but the proportion of projects with ex-ante feasibility studies is higher than in the previous phases (53 percent of the 126 projects reviewed had these studies) and the average projected internal rate of financial return (TIR) was 45 percent (Ibid., 42). An earlier evaluation indicated that of the eighty-two organizations that were analyzed, 82.5 percent had net profits in 2006, although only 19.6 percent surpassed 10 million pesos[22] (Ibid., 9 and 37). That meager margin illustrates the risk faced by many of the projects now underway.

At first sight, an assessment of this phase of alternative development would lead to the conclusion that the incoming government modified the institutional arrangements in order to make the eradication and substitution of illegal crops more effective, at the cost of lessening the comprehensiveness of its actions, limiting the initiative of the peasant-farmers and their organizations, and simplifying the basic philosophy of the projects. In practice, the institutional scheme that emerged supported most of the projects already under way and framed them in the logic of prior total eradication, which, despite the inevitable traumas, did not hold back the program's advance.

The new strategy shows undeniable operational strengths: the certainty of eradication; the transparency of the commitments assumed by the parties; and the clarity of the activities administered by projects set in a territorial context, although without great pretensions about the short-term progress of regional development. Nevertheless, within those same strengths are some of the limitations of the strategy: a weakening of the logic of human development; the relative isolation of the projects, which are rarely integrated into productive or value chains and relevant regional or local processes; a simplification that tends to focus the projects on mere subsistence and limits the dynamics of individual and associative management attained by the beneficiaries in the previous stage.

Some Additional Considerations Derived from the Experience as a Whole

The above account does not cover all the relevant aspects of the alternative development policies adopted in Colombia. For that reason, it would be pertinent to go over some key points emphasized by diverse authors and entities about the experience as a whole or some of its specific stages.

In the first place, the program did not reduce in a sustainable manner the area sown with coca in any of the producer departments during the first two phases of the policy—although the incentives in the third phase seem to be having a stronger impact—and its effect on the totality of the country's coca crops is not clear. Even so, experiences like that of Thailand show that alternative development may be effective on a national level, but only if it is a long-term policy capable of mobilizing different social and political forces (Acción Social, Uniandes, Universidad de los Andes 2004).

Alternative crops confront agricultural and economic factors that reduce the probability of their success compared to illegal ones. The latter are transitory crops, easy to grow, the processing and marketing of which are controlled by mafias that are able to overcome the defects of infrastructure in the affected regions and who pay higher prices than those of most legal crops. It is possible to augment that probability, but it requires investments and actions that must be sustained for relatively long periods, even in the case of crops with a short life cycle. Without those actions, an improved infrastructure, and a social and cultural change that would close the gap in profitability between legal and illegal activities, the former will not be able to maintain themselves.

This would require a state policy with clear concepts, objectives, and strategies; a meticulous institutional design; sufficient amounts of investment; and reasonable periods for the desired results to become sustainable. The total amount invested by the Colombian state and international entities in the period 1986–2008 totaled some US$971 million (in 2008 values), a bit more than $42 million annually, an insufficient amount to counteract the power of narcotics trafficking. Furthermore, in the final phase (2003–2009), this investment—which fluctuated highly (Figure 4.1[23])—represented on

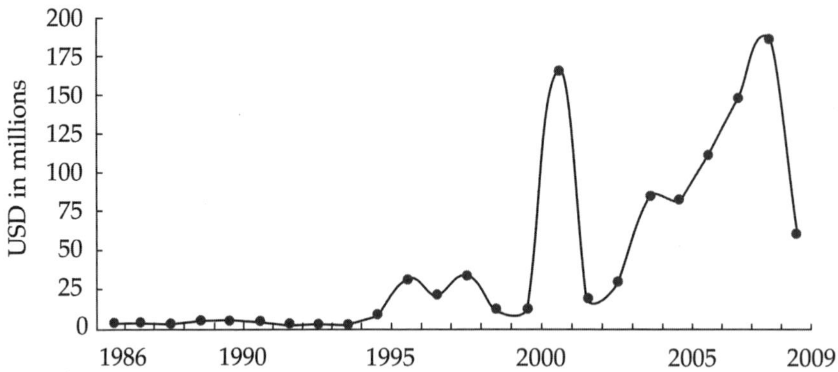

FIGURE 4.1. Investments in alternative development (1986–2009). Source: UNODC (1986–2003), Acción Social, PCI (2004–2009)

average only 2.3 percent of Colombia's annual public investment budget, which shows that it is not a state policy.[24]

It is worth making two final observations about the dominant practice in this field:

1. The policies continue to be formulated in terms of products: hectares to be eradicated, families to be attended and investments to be made, but not of transformations in the conditions of the beneficiaries or strategies leading to that end.
2. The institutional arrangements of the program have been detached from both the main national policies that are related to it—peace, agricultural development, international trade, and the fight against drugs, for example—and from other institutional and social agents involved in the promotion of alternative development.

CONCLUSIONS AND RECOMMENDATIONS

This section sets forth some conclusions and recommendations about future actions.

Conclusions Derived from the Colombian Experience

A. With regard to the conception and implementation of alternative development, some notable changes from one government to the next are noted. Despite that, after a time, each policy tends to retrieve some of the lessons of the previous experiences, although in a partial, insufficient, and at times dilatory way.

The strategies follow a pendular movement between crop substitution and alternative development: the initial aim of substitution gave way to a more ambitious one of development but has now returned to substitution. There may be several explanations for this.

- The absence of a clear idea about alternative development and its implications.
- The commitments acquired by the government in the global fight against drugs
- The complexity of applying alternative development policies.
- Institutional and funding limitations.

At certain times, the policy of alternative development has been conceived of and applied in a way parallel to eradication strategies, and at others it has been subordinated to the latter. For that reason, its essential aim of helping peasant-farmers affected by illegal crops has not been evident. In fact, it has faced the greatest problems when it has been most closely linked to the fumigations, since the rejection of the latter extends to the former.

B. In the economic field, and from a strategic point of view, there is the risk of falling into a logic, opposite to the rationality of the market and rejected by the population, where the alternative solutions not only ignore the channels that tend to add value to the products, but also assume that the small farmers—who despite the illegality of their activity are already integrated into the marketplace, even the international one—are willing to return to their traditional, peasant-style economy, focused at times on self-subsistence.

From another angle, the lack of follow-ups and records and, above all, the almost complete absence of ex post facto studies that evaluate the impact of the agreements and the projects make it difficult to estimate the proportion of failures and successes in these initiatives. Nevertheless, it is clear that practically none of those undertaken in the first phase was sustainable. The situation has been improving, and according to the feasibility studies, at least half of the current projects have a real possibility of success. Many of them, however, still lack these kinds of studies and have still not resolved weaknesses like the absence of productive linkages, an overly short-term view, and formulations that do not fit into the due social and territorial context.

C. On the sociocultural front, probably the most notable aspect has been the change in the attitude of many communities toward illegal crops, due in part to the opening of other opportunities by the initiatives on alternative development. They have been creating conditions for substitution, reflected in the growing trust of the peasant-farmers and their willingness to enter or remain "legal" (UNODC, Acción Social 2007a, 44–48; 2007b, 26–27; 2008, 33–35).

For the rest, although the dynamism of community participation has been uneven and has tended to decline in the final phase, two positive aspects are worth emphasizing:

- The decision to make the first- and second-tier peasant-farmer organizations responsible for the management of the resources.
- The conception and implementation of the state-community pacts, which are the culmination of the positive development of this tool linked to productive projects.

D. Finally, it must be emphasized that the institutional framework's tendency to operate as a closed system has limited its strategic capacity and the scope of its actions.

Recommendations

Many recommendations set forth in different studies have been derived from the experience described. Here we highlight the importance of a few.

A. There is a need to unify the concept of alternative development with its policies, and not just among the different public institutions but among the population of the affected zones as well. This would give more clarity and stability to the policies and strategies and facilitate coordination among the diverse agents.

Whatever that concept may be, however, the programs cannot limit themselves to setting forth goals for funding and crop substitution. They should indicate the transformations that will allow the population to become legal, exercise their rights, and improve their lives. The study of these transformations requires the availability of both baselines for those aspects that one expects to change and a system for evaluating impacts that allows for the assessment of the changes attributable to the projects.

In line with the philosophy of the UNODC, the fight against illegal crops cannot be based on their mere eradication. It must integrate growth and development, guarantee economic progress, improve the quality of life of the peasant-farmers, and acknowledge the environmental and regional/political problems. Without that, the achievements of this fight may be valuable in a particular territorial or social ambit, but they will not have an impact on a national level.

A new reflection on the strategy of alternative development is required. Promoting a process of development that leads to the substitution of illegal crops is not the same as making their eradication the starting point of development. Although the former option seems to offer more of a guarantee of long-term sustainability, the experiences of the FRP and the PPP show that the latter may be viable if it is based on eradication agreements.

From an economic standpoint, it is essential to identify and attack the factors that tend to widen the breach between the profitability of illegal crops and the possible alternatives. To progressively close it, it is necessary to raise the costs of the former, which requires institutional and social actions (interdiction, social control), and reduce those of the latter through, on the one hand, efficient and productive systems, access to attractive markets, and actions to improve technology, management and infrastructures of distribution, and on the other hand to transform the social environment so that it makes the processes endogenous and sustainable.

It is worth underlining that substitution cannot be seen as part of a military project (fumigation). Those responsible for alternative development, a key factor in the anti-drug fight, must work in close coordination with those responsible for interdiction, but it is indispensable that the community distinguish one program from the other.

Finally, and to complement the above, the policy, strategies, and programs must be defined autonomously and jointly by the state and society of Colombia; external supports must be adjusted to these definitions, and not the reverse.

B. It must be stressed that the institutional arrangements of alternative development should be a state policy that transcends the framework of any particular government and may be extended beyond immediate political concerns and the ups and downs of elections. In other words, its success cannot depend on a single entity but on an open, interconnected, and coordinated institutional scheme in line with the commitment of the state and society. From an administrative point of view, this requires, on the one hand, reformulating the strategic framework, including action lines, priorities, functions, and responsibilities, and on the other hand strengthening the scope of the program as an interinstitutional promoter and coordinator of the policy on diverse functional and territorial levels.

C. We call attention to two aspects of the social focus of the policies.
   - The peasant-farmer and the indigenous person no longer fit into the traditional patterns. They are people hardened by war and immersed in globalization and markets, and they demand solutions that are suitable to their new relationship with the world.
   - The experience of the IAGAC with regard to the responsibility of the peasant-farmer associations deserves to be used and adjusted to the new lessons learned, and efforts to consolidate such associations should take into account their heterogeneity.

As mentioned above, these recommendations are those that most directly arise from the contents of this chapter. Nevertheless, the results of studies undertaken from other vantage points, including the monitoring done by CIDER, enable one to make a more integral reflection that could enrich the ideas proposed here.

NOTES

1. Which failed, to a large extent, because of the municipalities' operative weaknesses.
2. In the third year of this period, the highest levels of investment of the two early phases analyzed here were reached (Figure 4.1).
3. See also *www.colectivodeabogados.org/Reporte-al-congreso-sobre*.
4. The CIDER monitoring program surveyed the agents linked to projects of alternative development. Although the samples were not representative, they covered all of the associations that executed the main projects. In phase three, 129 producers were surveyed in four Plante-BID departments and there were seven workshops with these producers. In phase four, 129 peasant-farmers and 47 indigenous beneficiaries and 17 non-beneficiaries in five departments.
5. This has been gradually rectified in the final period, as will be seen below.
6. Subtitle of Plan Colombia.
7. *www.accionsocial.gov.co/contenido/contenido.aspx?catID=217&conID=965*, retrieved Feb. 2010.
8. This strategy involves physically uprooting the illegal crops. This makes the results more lasting, since it prevents the recovery of the harvest, which frequently occurs after fumigations.
9. They are different from the phases that group together the policies discussed in this chapter.
10. Decline attributed to budget factors (author's interview of PCI officials, February, 2010).
11. *www.accionsocial.gov.co/contenido/contenido.aspx?catID=217&conID=167*, retrieved 2010.
12. But the figure that appears there is inconsistent, since it does not show that the figure is in thousands of pesos. (The approximate exchange rate during this period was US$1 = 2,300 Colombian pesos.)
13. National "*Guardabosques*" survey, phases I, II, III, and IV of the FRP, carried out by UNODC between December 2005 and September 2008, with a representative sample of 82,981 families who are active in the program (nearly 80 percent of those linked to it in November 2008): 29,460 for phases I and II, 18,592 for phase III, and 34,929 for phase IV.
14. This statement depends on more recent results that may corroborate or invalidate it.

15. A survey different from the one above, based on a simple random sampling between December 1, 2005, and February 3, 2006, of 4,190 "*Guardabosque*" families out of a total of 29,460 from phases I and II.
16. *www.accionsocial.gov.co/contenido/contenido.aspx?catID=170*, retrieved Jan. 2010.
17. From an interview by the author to the person in charge of the program at the Corporación Colombia Internacional.
18. The following amounts in pesos, except when the opposite is indicated, correspond to the sum total, in the current pesos for each year, of annual investments made in the period in question. (The average exchange rate during this period was about US$1 = 2,300 Colombian pesos.)
19. *www.accionsocial.gov.co/contenido/contenido.aspx?catID=217&con ID=170*, retrieved Feb. 2010.
20. Information gathered between August and September of 2008 during visits to 71 implementers who operate 126 projects located in 19 departments and 75 municipalities, to which are added surveys of 261 productive organizations. The projects involve 26,529 families, which amounts to 211 families per project.
21. Programs official of the UNODC, interview carried out in February 2011.
22. In 2006, US$1 represented about 2,600 Colombian pesos.
23. While the statistics seen in the figure correspond to two different series, constructed respectively by the UNOCD (1986–2003) and Acción Social (2004–2009), they are methodologically compatible, and the sharp fluctuations are corroborated by other sources for the respective years.
24. Figures on investment in alternative development provided by Acción Social.

REFERENCES

Acción Social, PCI, PDA. 2009. Informe de Acción Social. In a CD-ROM given to CIDER in November 2009.

Acción Social, UNODC. 2008. "Informe Ejecutivo Encuentro Nacional del Programa Presidencial contra Cultivos Ilícitos (PCI), erradicación, prevención y sustitución de cultivos." In Sistema de Seguimiento y Evaluación SS/E UNODC. Bogotá.

Acción Social, Universidad de los Andes, IICA. 2004. *La política de desarrollo alternativo y su modelo institucional—Retos y Desafíos—Memorias de Seminario Internacional.*" Edited by L. F. Restrepo, C. Zorro, et al., Bogotá: Universidad de los Andes.

Cabieses, H., ed. 1999. *Desarrollo alternativo y desarrollo rural: Debate sobre sus límites y posibilidades*. Lima: IICA.

Caicedo, C. 2006. "Expectativas racionales y persistencia de los cultivos ilícitos de coca en Colombia 1986–2003." In Trabajos de grado CIDER, Bogotá.

Cano, G. 1998. *Un proyecto de desarrollo agroempresarial, sustitución de cultivos ilícitos y reforma agraria para la paz.* Bogotá: IICA.

Comunicado de prensa del gobernador y de los alcaldes del Putumayo. 2001. November 15.

Comunidad Andina. 2005. Estrategia Andina de Desarrollo Alternativo Integral y Sostenible. Working paper SG/dt 307, Comunidad Andina, Secretaría general.

CONPES. Documents 2734, 1994; 2799, 1995; 2835, 1996; 3218, 2003.

Contraloría General de la Nación (CGN). 2002. Plan Colombia (2002), Informe de Evaluación.

Contraloría General de la Nación. 2004. Plan Colombia (2004), Informe de Evaluación.

Defensoría del Pueblo. 2000. *Los cultivos ilícitos. Política mundial y realidad en Colombia.* Bogotá: Imprenta Nacional de Colombia.

Dorantes, C. 1991. *Importancia de la vinculación de las ong con el pnr dentro del proceso de democratización en Colombia.* Bogotá: Universidad de los Andes.

Fonseca, D., Ó. Gutiérrez, and A. Rudovist. 2005. *Cultivos de uso ilícito en el sur de Bolívar: Aproximación desde la economía política.* UNDP-ASDI. Bogotá: Lito Camargo Ltda.

Franco, D. 2008. *Historia de las ideas en 'vuelo': el caso del prohibicionismo y el desarrollo alternativo en la política colombiana de erradicación de cultivos ilícitos.* Bogotá: Universidad de los Andes.

Iglesias, J. 2003. "Los efectos de las fumigaciones sobre el desarrollo alternativo (1994–2002)." CESO document no. 55 Bogotá: Universidad de los Andes.

Ministerio de Agricultura, Departamento Nacional de Planeación (DNP). 1993. *Proyecto de desarrollo alternativo en áreas de economías campesinas productoras de cultivos ilícitos en la Serranía del Perijá.* Primera fase 1993, Bogotá.

Orjuela, L. J. 1998. "El Estado colombiano en los noventa: Entre la legitimidad y la eficacia." *Revista Estudios Sociales* no. 1. Bogotá: Universidad de los Andes.

Ortiz, C. 2000. "La evolución de la política de desarrollo alternativo en Colombia." In *Universidad Javeriana, Seminario Internacional.* Bogotá: Universidad Javeriana. Retrieved from *biblioteca.clacso.edu.ar/ar/libros/rjave/mesa7/ortiz.pdf*, accessed May 15, 2015.

Plante. 2000. Informe de gestión y otros documentos no publicados, suministrados por la subgerencia de planeación del Plante.

Plante, bid, CIDER. 2004. *Última fase auditoría técnica crédito externo Plante-*bid *984 OC/CO.* Unpublished photocopied report, Bogotá.

Plante-CIDER. 1998. *Monitoreo-Auditoría técnica al pnda-bid.* Primera fase, unpublished photocopied report, Bogotá.

———. 2001. *Sistema de Monitoreo Auditoría Técnica al Programa Nacional de Desarrollo Alternativo-bid.* Tercera fase, unpublished photocopied report, Bogotá.

PNDA, CIDER. 1999. *Monitoreo-auditoría técnica al pnda-bid.* Segunda fase, unpublished photocopied edition, Bogotá.

Presidencia de la República. N.d. *Plan Colombia. Plan para la paz, la prosperidad y el fortalecimiento del Estado.* Bogotá.

Programa Presidencial para la Convivencia. 1994. *Plan Nacional de Rehabilitación, Memorias del pnr, 1982–1994.* Bogotá: Presidencia de la República.

Rementería, I. de. 2001. *La guerra de las drogas: Cultivos ilícitos y desarrollo alternativo.* Bogotá: Editorial Planeta.

Thoumi, E. 2009. *Sociedades vulnerables al desarrollo del narcotráfico, el fracaso de las políticas contra las drogas y los problemas estructurales, institucionales, culturales y morales de Colombia.* Working Paper. Austin: University of Texas.

Tocancipá, J. 1997. "Coca, campesinos y desarrollo en los Andes colombianos." Guadalajara: 49º Congreso Internacional de Estudios Latinoamericanos, LASA97.

Torres, E. A. 2006. *Posibilidades de cambio en la estrategia de la lucha contra las drogas en Colombia: El desarrollo alternativo, una opción.* Bogotá: Universidad de los Andes.

UNODC, Oficina de las Naciones Unidas contra la Droga y el Delito. 2007. *Desarrollo alternativo en el Área Andina.* Guía Técnica.

UNODC, Acción Social. 2007a. "Descifrando las familias guardabosques, indicadores año 2006." Municipios fases II y III, Bogotá.

———. 2007b. *Informe Ejecutivo sobre el Seguimiento a los Programas de Familias Guardabosques y Proyectos Productivos.* Bogotá.

———. 2008. *Organizaciones productivas que hacen posible el desarrollo alternativo en Colombia.* Bogotá.

UNDP, Grupo Temático sobre Desarrollo Alternativo. 2000. *Desarrollo alternativo en Colombia,* photocopied edition.

Vargas, R. 1999. *Drogas, máscaras y juegos. Narcotráfico y conflicto armado en Colombia.* Bogotá: TM editores, TNI-Acción Andina.

Zorro, C. 2005. "Algunos desafíos del desarrollo alternativo en Colombia." *Pensamiento y Cultura* 8, no. 1: 105–32.

WEB PAGES

CICAD (Comisión Interamericana para el Control del Abuso de Drogas). 2009. Retrieved from *www.cicad.oas.org/Desarrollo_Alternativo/ESP/Projects.asp*, accessed November 2009.

Colectivo de Abogados José Alvear Restrepo. 2005. "Reporte al Congreso sobre Fumigaciones, Violaciones de la Ley Colombiana y las Condiciones de la Ayuda norteamericana." Retrieved from *www.colectivodeabogados.org/Reporte-al-congreso-sobre*, accessed Nov. 2009.

Ley 558/1999. 1999. "Plan nacional de desarrollo: cambio para construir la paz." Retrieved from *www.secretariasenado.gov.co/senado/basedoc/ley/1999/ley_0508_1999.html*, accessed May 12, 2015.

ODCCP. 2001. Studies on Drugs and Crime. Alternative Development in the Andean Area: The UNDCP Experience. Naciones Unidas, Oficina para el Control y Prevención de las Drogas y el Delito, New York. Retrieved from *www.unodc.org/pdf/publications/alt-development_andean.pdf*, accessed May 12, 2015.

Ramírez, M. C. 2002. "Balance sobre el componente social del Plan Colombia." Retrieved from *www.mamacoca.org/separata_nov_2002/art_ramirez_balanc_%20social__plan_colombia.htm*, accessed May 12, 2015.

Restrepo, J. A. 2005. "Reporte al Congreso sobre fumigaciones, violaciones de la ley colombiana y las condiciones de la ayuda norteamericana." Retrieved from *www.javeriana.edu.co/fear/m_des_rur/documents/Restrepo-ponencia-mesa4.pdf*, accessed May 12, 2015.

Restrepo, L. F. N.d. "El instrumento de apoyo a grupos asociativos y comunitarios: Modelo participativo de gestión del Plan Nacional de Desarrollo Alternativo." Retrieved from *www.javeriana.edu.co/fear/m_des_rur/documents/Restrepo-ponencia-mesa4.pdf*, accessed May 12, 2015.

UN. 1998. Documentos Oficiales A/S-20/PV.2. Vigésimo Período Extraordinario de Sesiones, Segunda Sesión Plenaria, New York. Retrieved from *www.un.org/spanish/aboutun/organs/ga/63/sessions/special.shtml*, accessed May 12, 2015.

Vargas, R. 2005. "Drogas y conflictos: Desarrollo alternativo y conflicto en Colombia." In *Futuros, Revista Trimestral Latinoamericana y del Caribe de Desarrollo Sostenible.* Retrieved from *www.revistafuturos.info/futuros_9/drogas_1.htm*, accessed May 12, 2015.

www.accionsocial.gov.co/contenido/contenido.aspx?catID=170, accessed July 2010.

www.accionsocial.gov.co/contenido/contenido.aspx?catID=217&conID=965, accessed July 2010.

www.accionsocial.gov.co/contenido/contenido.aspx?catID=217&conID=167, accessed July 2010.

www.accionsocial.gov.co/contenido/contenido.aspx?catID=217&conID=170, accessed July 2010.

www.mamacoca.org/separata_nov_2002/art_ramirez_balanc_%20social__plan_colombia.htm, accessed July 2010.

www.presidencia.gov.co/planacio/cap4.htm#1, accessed July 2010.

www.revistafuturos.info/futuros_9/drogas_1.htm, accessed January 2010.

APPENDIX

CHRONOLOGY: ALTERNATIVE DEVELOPMENT POLICIES IN COLOMBIA

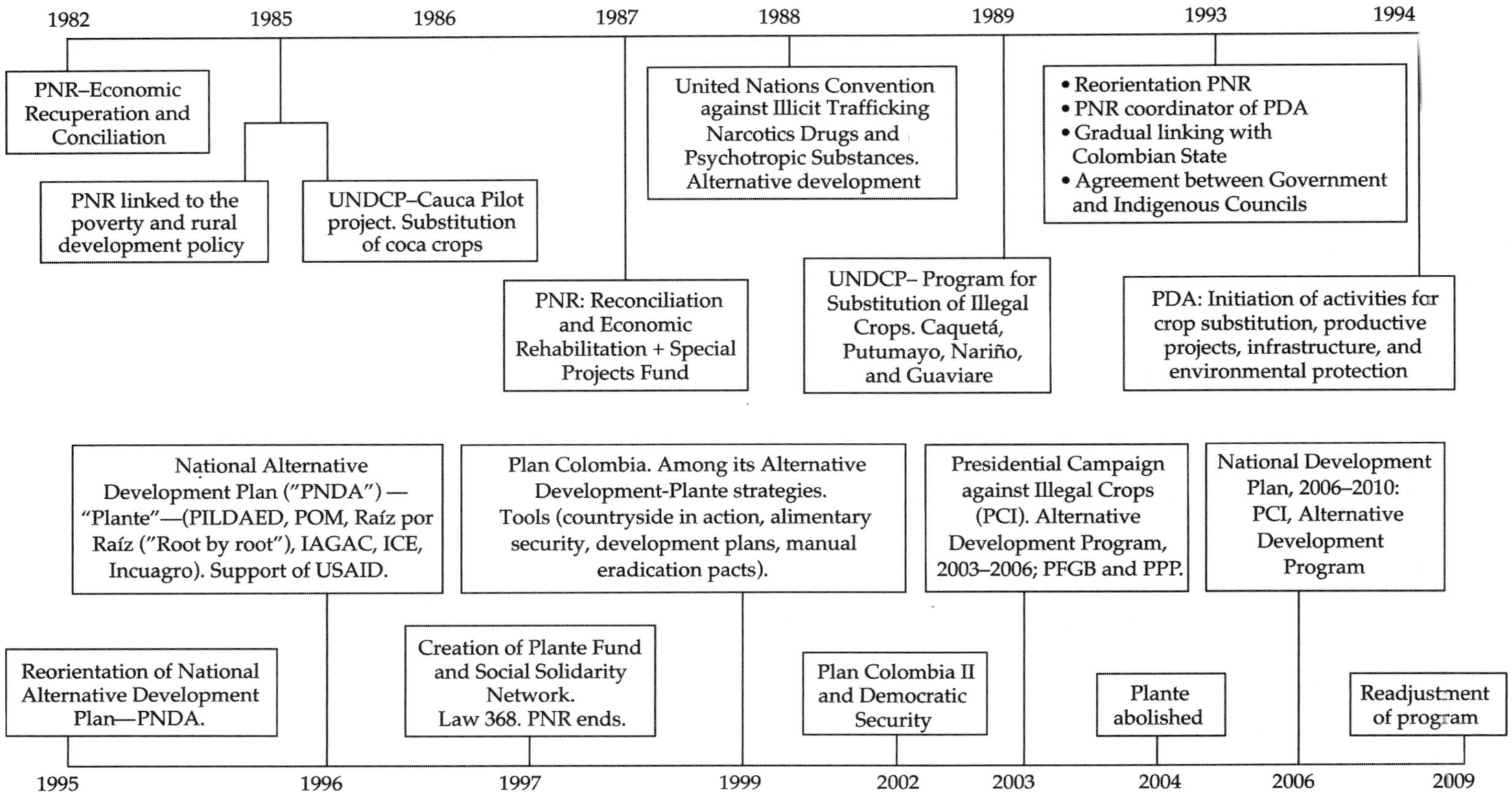

5 Demand as a Drama

The Prevention and Treatment of Drug Use in Colombia

Jorge Larreamendy-Joerns and María Fernanda Vence

INTRODUCTION

In the uproar of implementing strategies to reduce the supply of illegal drugs, one forgets that drug use is in the first place a personal reality, a human drama. According the latest national health study (Ministerio de la Protección Social and Fundación FES Social 2003), problems associated with the use of psychoactive substances[1] represent the third largest set of disorders among the general population (10.6 percent), after anxiety disorders (19.3 percent) and mood disorders (15 percent), and they are in first place in the male population (20.8 percent). The study also notes that one out of a hundred people suffers from substance abuse and approximately one out of two hundred from dependence, a situation that is even more critical in the case of men. The personal, family, and social costs of drug use are enormous.

To the suffering and dependence must also be added the consequences of drug use on the productivity of work and health (Xie et al. 1996). Despite their obvious importance, policies for the reduction of demand have gone relatively unnoticed on a national level. There are no ongoing national or local prevention programs in places as obvious as the school curriculum, the family, the communities, and the mass media. The absence of therapeutic interventions that may be and have been evaluated is also notorious.

With the exception of the Programa Presidencial Rumbos (The "Directions" Presidential Program, of the administration of Andrés Pastrana), there has been no place in the higher spheres of government for reflections on the strategies of reducing demand. Despite including some efforts toward reducing the demand for drugs in their mission, agencies like the Dirección Nacional de Estupefacientes (National Narcotics Administration, DNE) have concentrated almost exclusively on actions to eliminate supply. In this context, one understands why one of the objectives of the recent policy for reducing drug consumption (Ministerio de Protección Social 2007) is precisely giving more visibility to the phenomenon of consumption.

There are many reasons for this absence of strategic thinking and significant advances in the field of prevention and treatment of drug use. In the first place, we should recognize that the problem of how to prevent drug consumption is a challenge that has only recently become a concern of public policy and the academic world (and

Jorge Larreamendy-Joerns: Director and associate professor, Department of Psychology, Universidad de los Andes. Prof. Larreamendy-Joerns unfortunately passed away.

María Fernanda Vence: Supervisor of professional practices, Department of Psychology, Universidad de los Andes.

consequently scientific research), both on a national and international level. One is dealing with a spectacularly complex and dynamic problem, about which we understandably only have a sketchy knowledge so far.

A second reason, which applies to Colombia, has to do with our persistent and of course mistaken self-image as a producer country, not a consumer one. It is a self-satisfying image that has wound up hiding a reality that has been ours for decades. A third reason is that the political, economic, and moral resonances of the drug problems have meant that discussions of prevention and treatment frequently derive from ideological debates. This is naturally aggravated by the precarious data about consumption and the treatment of addiction. As the Ministry of Social Protection itself states in its latest document on policies for reducing demand, periodical or methodologically comparable evaluations have not been carried out in Colombia (Ministerio de la Protección Social 1996; Programa Presidencial Rumbos 2001; Ministerio de la Protección Social and Fundación FES Social 2003; Ministerio de la Protección Social and CICAD/OAS 2004; Ministerio de la Protección Social 2009). Nor does the country have a centralized system of information about initiatives on the prevention and treatment of drug consumption (comparable, for example, with the National Registry of Evidence-Based Programs and Practices of the substance abuse and mental health administration of the US Department of Health and Human Services). Finally, as we mentioned above, we are facing a singularly complex phenomenon.

Consumption and addiction depend on pharmacological, genetic, cognitive, attitudinal, social, personal, and developmental determinants (Botvin et al. 2003). The explanation and prediction of cases do not follow a straight line. By way of example, although a transition in the consumption of certain drugs is documented (Kandel 1975; Pérez 2007), a high proportion of adolescents consume alcohol or illegal drugs at some point without turning into frequent or dependent consumers.[2] Paglia and Room (1999) even speak of a cultural myth in the sense that alcohol, tobacco, and marijuana inevitably lead to the consumption of hard drugs. That myth seems to be linked to the ideology of the nineteenth-century temperance movement in the United States and Europe, which equated prevention with abstinence and consumption with moral weakness.

The purpose of this chapter is to propose recommendations for the formulation in Colombia of public policies related to the prevention and treatment of drug use. Toward that end, we start with a brief account of public policies on the prevention of consumption and treatment of drug addiction. We then present a characterization of the panoramas of prevention and treatment, mentioning both the sound practices documented in the technical literature and the state of the discussion of the subject in Colombia. The chapter finishes with some general recommendations about the reduction of demand.

EVOLUTION OF POLICIES FOR THE REDUCTION OF DEMAND IN COLOMBIA

The results of the recent National Study of Drugs Consumption undertaken by the Ministry of Social Protection (Ministerio de la Protección Social 2009) shows a disturbing consumption of illegal drugs in Colombia. According to the study, while Colombia does not have comparatively high levels of marijuana consumption, the proportion of dependence is alarming (nearly one out of two consumers). Taking into account the set of indicators of consumption, Colombia is in an intermediate position in the ambit of Latin America, with lower levels of consumption than in Argentina, Chile, and Uruguay, but higher levels than in Ecuador and Peru (see Chapter 2). In the context of these results it is thus clear that Colombia's self-perception that it is essentially a producer country and not a consumer one must be reformulated.

Colombia has traditionally been a basic reference point for the efforts to reduce supply. Within the framework of the so-called "war on drugs," Colombia has been regarded as a producer nation and a leader in the illegal trade of substances such as marijuana and heroin (more recently) and the world's biggest producer of cocaine. It is not surprising that during the last two decades of the twentieth century and the first decade of the twenty-first, the state has devoted its greatest efforts toward the internal fight against narcotics trafficking.

The emphasis on the reduction of the supply of Colombian drugs on the international markets has eclipsed the initiatives to reduce both the internal supply of drugs and the national demand for them. This tendency to control demand through the control of supply has not appeared in isolation. The public policies of the Colombian state to reduce demand during the past twenty years have been influenced by the policies of institutions such as the United Nations, the Organization of American States, and the Andean Community of Nations. Moreover, successive administrations of the United States have made the anti-drug policy a matter of priority for national security, and this has influenced Colombian public policies as well. Giving priority to the fight against drugs to the detriment of actions to reduce demand is evident in fairly early legislative measures, as in the case of law 30/1986, the National Narcotics Statute. That law is especially prolific in defining violations and categorizing crimes, but it is sparing about matters of prevention, rehabilitation, and treatment, to the point where the discussion of them is nearly a formalism. This continued to be the tendency of the national development plans of the governments of César Gaviria (1990–1994) and Ernesto Samper (1994–1998), where one notes meager references to public policies for reducing drug consumption.

Those policies, discussed in a generic way in the guidelines on health and education, were in any case secondary in the scenario of an escalation of violence caused by narcotics trafficking and the scandals about the infiltration of drug money into the 1994 presidential campaign. There was an exceptional advance in that period, however: the Constitutional Court's decision to decriminalize the personal dose of certain illegal drugs.

It was president Andrés Pastrana, during his 1998–2002 administration, who, despite the implementation of Plan Colombia, gave more priority to the consumption of drugs in line with similar initiatives during his time as mayor of Bogotá (1988–1990). While his government's National Development Plan did not give a prominent place to the need for reducing demand, Pastrana proposed the National Plan: An Integral Drugs Policy for Peace, one of the aims of which was to "control the consumption of illegal drugs, the growing trend of the unwarranted use of legal ones, and provide alternatives of treatment, rehabilitation and social reinsertion for those dependent on drugs" (Dirección Nacional de Estupefacientes 1999).

One of the first results of this plan was the creation of the presidential program for confronting drug consumption, Rumbos (Directions). One of the purposes of the Rumbos program was to assist the president of Colombia and the national government to design governmental policies for the prevention and treatment of drug consumption. It is worth underlining that the program operated independently of the National Narcotics Administration, a circumstance that undoubtedly gave the problem of consumption a prominence not previously seen.

The Programa Presidencial Rumbos, run by the then Universidad de los Andes professor Augusto Pérez, was meant to coordinate policies for reducing demand on a local, regional, and national level, as well as facilitate the work of the network of governmental institutions and nongovernmental organizations. Rumbos promoted the participation of the relevant government agencies in the policies and guidelines for programs for the prevention of the consumption of psychoactive substances, among them the Ministry of Social Protection, the Ministry of Education, and the regional secretaries of education and health. To achieve that, Rumbos recommended winning a commitment from society as a whole, that is, youngsters, families, the educational system, and community organizations, among others.

In our opinion, Rumbos represented two fundamental advances over previous initiatives: First, it granted the status of state policy to the programs for reducing demand and helped put the problem of consumption on the political agenda. Second, Rumbos made scientific research the foundation of decision making. In particular, Rumbos was instrumental in promoting evaluative research into models and protocols for prevention and treatment, as well as in strengthening the System for the Epidemiological Monitoring of Psychoactive Substances (VESPA), the initial purpose of which was to provide unified information about internal consumption. This spur to investigation bore fruit in studies on subjects of obvious relevance, such as the phenomenon of codependence, the relation between teenage gangs and violence, intrafamily violence and drugs, and the problems arising from injecting drugs and the risks of being infected by HIV and other sexually transmitted diseases.

The Rumbos program was canceled at the beginning of the first presidential term of Álvaro Uribe Vélez. The responsibility for the problem of drug consumption was then transferred to the Ministry of Social Protection in the context of a state policy centered on sanctioning the personal dose. Despite that, president Uribe's policy for reducing drug consumption led to important advances, particularly by encouraging the realization of diagnostic studies on consumption, investigating institutions that provided treatment and rehabilitation services, and establishing public policies based on empirical studies.

Among the results worth noting were an assessment of institutions for the treatment, rehabilitation, and social reincorporation of consumers of psychoactive substances in Colombia (2004); a study done in 2007 by the Corporación Nuevos Rumbos and financed by the National Narcotics Administration on transitions in drug consumption in Colombia (Pérez 2007); and the National Study of Drug Consumption, undertaken in 2008. Advances in the regulation and control of the health services that offer treatment for drug consumption gave rise to regulatory decrees, as in the case of resolution 4750 (December 20, 2005) of the Ministry of Social Protection. Finally, we should single out the official presentation of the National Plan for Reducing Demand (2009–2010), which established a general framework for policies on consumption and ideas about treatment.

Unfortunately, as often happens in Colombia, advances in regulations are not always turned into effective practices. Today we have a set of measures and regulations that are, in a certain sense, exemplary in their conceptions and aims, but we lack the resources and organization needed for their effective enforcement. Going against the trend toward the systematization of experiences and the creation of an organizational infrastructure, the passing of legislative act no. 2/2009, which prohibited the possession of the personal dose of narcotics and established mandatory treatment, represents a reverse in the internal policy of reducing the demand for drugs. In our opinion, the prohibition of the personal dose is nonviable, not only from the point of view of judicial implementation, but also in ignoring that the health services lack the infrastructure and specialized personnel to carry out its aims.

Additionally, the criminalization of the personal dose marks a backward step in what we might call a sophisticated and complex conception of the consumer. Instead of acknowledging the diversity of consumption profiles and consumers, penalization winds up reducing that diversity to a single profile, or, as the US sociologist Howard Becker (1963) might have put it, to the idea of consumption as aberration and addiction, and addiction itself as delinquency.

Thus seen, the panorama of prevention and treatment in Colombia includes recent advances, but they are in any case sociohistorical processes. The reduction of supply has been the focus of public and academic discussion, and the reduction of demand has been a supplementary matter that is often discarded. The panorama has slightly changed under the past two governments (of Pastrana and Uribe), first with the inclusion of the subject of demand in the higher spheres of government, and then with the formulation of policies that promise to bring order to a scenario that has been dispersed up to now, although the policies lack adequate foundations in terms of their approach to the problem.

PREVENTION: FROM THE DISSEMINATION OF INFORMATION TO THE EPIDEMIOLOGICAL MODEL

The story of the prevention of drug consumption in Colombia has been one of marginality if it is compared with the notoriety and centrality of the fight against supply. There have been few systematic initiatives, with the notable exception of the Rumbos presidential program and the recent creation of the National Commission for the Reduction of the Demand for Drugs (CNRDD), which acts in an advisory capacity under the National Narcotics Council and which in 2007, on the basis of a broad consensus, proposed guidelines for preventing, mitigating, and overcoming the consumption of psychoactive substances.

The ultimate goal of the policy proposed by the CNRDD is to "reduce the frequency and prevalence of the consumption of psychoactive substances in Colombia and mitigate the negative impact of consumption on the individual, the family, the community and society." To achieve that, the policy defines prevention as one of its operational axes, the aim of which is to "avoid/prevent the start [of consumption] and the unwarranted use of psychoactive substances at any point of the life cycle." The emphasis on preventive actions involves reducing the probability that consumption may occur, and when it does occur, ensuring that it does not become a habit or grow in intensity.

In that sense, prevention strategies, in the original meaning of the term, are in line with the operational axes for prevention and mitigation proposed by the CRNDD. We must emphasize that the purpose of prevention programs is not to deter those who already consume or are dependent on drugs (that is dealt with by treatment) but to keep potential consumers from the occasional consumption of or dependence on drugs. How do you prevent the consumption of psychoactive substances? In the past twenty years the answers to this question have moved from the realm of personal ingenuity to that of evidence, particularly due to the emergence of what is becoming known as the science of prevention (Botvin 2004). Empirical assessment studies now provide a relatively clear panorama of the characteristics that effective prevention programs should have.

An initial strategy, perhaps the oldest and probably the least effective, has been limited to divulging information about the effects and damages done by drugs to potential consumers at different stages of life. This viewpoint, which is consistent with traditional pedagogical premises, presupposes that consuming drugs is an irrational act, resulting from the absence of knowledge about its effects. It also assumes that the potential consumers are rational beings who seek to maximize the utility of their decisions on the basis of the relevant knowledge. Preventive programs based on the dissemination of information have been especially frequent in the ambit of education and the mass media.

Studies show that programs based on the model of the rational consumer and the dissemination of information are not effective (Botvin and Griffin 2003; Paglia and Room 1999) and ignore the fact that consuming drugs may be a functional (and on occasion symbolic) conduct, as in the case of consumption by adolescents, who, by means of drugs and other risk-seeking behavior, bolster their autonomy in opposition to authority figures and strengthen their identity as they interact with their peers. Although their ineffectiveness at modifying the prevalence of consumption has been documented, the dissemination programs may be useful, however, at calling attention to the phenomenon, generating knowledge that can be used as the basis of other strategies (for example, peer-group discussions) or modifying attitudes.

A variation of the informative approach, just as ineffective and anchored to a conception of the consumer as a rational being, are the preventive programs based on provoking fear or dread. These essentially dwell on the negative consequences of consumption in a way that touches on basic emotional states. One that is well remembered was a TV commercial, sponsored by the Banco Cafetero in the 1980s, with the slogan "drugs destroy your brain," which showed, in a particularly graphic manner, the physical deterioration associated with chronic drug consumption. Other examples are the recent television campaign *La tengo viva* (roughly, "She's still alive!"), which, while it had an initial impact on the public, shortly turned into a joke among consumers, and the most recent, *La mata que mata* ("The plant that kills"), which was widely criticized by diverse sectors of public opinion.

The prevention programs employing dissemination, based on a schoolmasterly idea of prevention and the rational consumer, have recently given way to prevention strategies based on an epidemiological model. As Brown and Hawkins (2007) point out, the logic is simple. If you want to prevent a certain conduct, you have to modify the variables that predict it (i.e., risk factors) and the variables that moderate it (i.e., protective factors). It is not surprising that predictive and moderating variables work on diverse levels: of the individual (genetic vulnerability, traits of risk seeking, self-esteem); the family (strategies of child rearing, levels of conflict, permissiveness of norms); the school (academic performance, attendance); peers (rejection or acceptance by peers, the conduct of model peers themselves); the community (existence of interdiction, obeisance of laws). We should note, as Paglia and Room (1999) indicate, that the variables that explain early experimentation with drugs (peer pressure, availability of drugs) may not be the same as those responsible for chronic use and dependence (biological or psychological factors).

Among the strategies based on the model of risk and protective factors, as well as solid psychological theories, there is the model of social influence. This model of prevention is based on Albert Bandura's theory of social learning and in its different versions proposes encouraging psychological, cognitive, and attitudinal factors associated with avoiding the consumption of psychoactive substances. One strategy that has been particularly successful in the United States is the Life Skills Program, designed by Botvin and his collaborators.

Life Skills is a program that provides children and adolescents with activities and scenarios that enable them to develop self-management skills (to improve their self-esteem, solve problems creatively, reduce stress and anxiety, and manage anger) and skills of resistance (to develop defenses against the pressures and influence of peers).

As can be seen, it is a program the logic of which lies in promoting psychosocial skills that empirical research has shown are absent in cases of drug consumption and present in cases of drug avoidance. As may be inferred, the panorama of prevention today is anchored to empirical evaluations, solid psychological theories, and an understanding of the predictive and protective factors on diverse levels associated with drug consumption and with the psychosocial characteristics of the target populations.

An essential aspect of the epidemiological model is an acknowledgment of the diverse levels on which prevention should operate. There is an emerging consensus about the need to develop universal, selective, and indicated programs (Kumpfer and Baxley 1997); that is, programs aimed at the general population; others tailored to particular segments of the population (e.g., adolescents, communities at risk); and still others that aim at populations that are already affected by the problem of consumption. In the same way, it is to be hoped that the planned range of the programs' effects (near or distal) will be perceptible. These distinctions naturally complement some of the more traditional ones, like the differences between the primary, secondary, and tertiary levels of prevention.

With a similar logic, research has shown the need to deploy preventive efforts in diverse scenarios: the school, community, mass media, and peer networks. An enormous majority of the effective programs have been implemented in school or, more generally, educational settings, either as part of the regular curriculum or in situations where there is access to the school population.

As we noted above, the most effective programs to date are those that emphasize the development of resistance skills (to confront group pressures and influences) and general social skills (to allow youngsters to establish interpersonal relationships and participate in sociocultural practices that offer alternatives to consumption). Equally, some typical characteristics of the effective programs have been the interacting and participation of peers.

Although, as we have said, most of the programs have been designed to be implemented in schools (by virtue of the psychosocial risks associated with childhood and adolescence), a growing number of documented programs (Brown and Hawkins 2007; Hawkins et al. 2009; Kibel and Holder 2003) have been implemented in the domain of the community. One possibility that has always been obvious to a degree is the promotion of activities that serve as alternatives to drug consumption, as in the case of recreational and sports activities. In this category we also find programs that promote family skills, support groups, and family counseling.

Finally, there is the scenario of the mass media. As might be expected, and despite the difficulty of empirically evaluating their effects, the media have the potential to become a platform for prevention, in particular due to their strong penetration among youngsters and their ample coverage. Palmgreen and Donohew (2003) insist on the need to develop formative evaluations in the design phase of the messages, produce messages of professional quality (which compete with high-impact commercial messages), segment the audience adequately, and incorporate proven strategies of persuasion. Naturally, like the prevention programs in other scenarios, the interventions in the media must be frequent and prolonged.

Of course, prevention in the school, community, and media has the aim of preventing possible consumers from consuming. Nevertheless, as Paglia and Room (1999) indicate, complete prevention is a difficult and rarely achieved goal. That is why prevention programs must be supplemented by programs for the reduction of harm, which assume that abstinence may not be a reasonable or attainable goal for those who are already consumers but that it may be possible to reduce harm or confine the use of drugs within certain parameters. Examples of campaigns for the reduction of harm are the distribution of syringes to heroin or morphine addicts in Europe (to reduce the incidence of HIV) and the national campaign "If you are going to drink, don't drive," which modifies the consumption of alcohol with the aim of preventing traffic accidents.

As might be expected, prevention programs act or should act in the context of legal and normative measures that restrict access to illegal drugs or regulate the consumption of legal drugs (such as alcohol and tobacco) in certain settings or by minors. Hence regulations like the minimum age of consumption imposed on legal drugs (alcohol and tobacco), which have been shown to be steps in the patterns of transition toward illegal drugs, are also part of prevention.

The research carried out in the past two decades has consistently pointed out sound prevention practices. We now know with a reasonable certainty that in the first place the programs must be adjusted to the diversity of drugs (not all drugs are created equal) and patterns of consumption (not all consumers fit into a single profile). We also know that the programs must be adapted to the particular culture (hence the simple importation of foreign programs is a doubtful strategy) and adjusted to the age of the public (a message that gets through to an adolescent is not the same as one that gets through to an adult).

We know that interactive programs, where a discussion with peers is possible instead of a torrent of unanswerable information, are more effective. Finally, the literature agrees that whatever the case, the programs must be persistent (that is, one or two activities will hardly be effective) and open to evaluation (without evaluation, there is no way to improve effectiveness).

TREATMENT: ADVANCES AND CHALLENGES

If the Colombian panorama of prevention is precarious, the panorama of treatment is no more encouraging, and in our opinion, there are two fundamental reasons for this: first, in common with prevention, treatment suffers from adverse circumstances, like its marginal place in public policies. Second, the question of whether therapeutic interventions (for addiction and other disorders) are effective has inherited the uncertainties of nearly a century of debate in psychiatry and psychology.

What does rehabilitation mean? What is an addict? What does a cure imply? These questions are still discussed with the same vehemence as they were decades ago. Given the vagueness of therapeutic goals and the diversity of theoretical perspectives, it is not surprising that there are a considerable number of therapeutic approaches to addiction, which include, among many others, cognitive-behavioral therapies, theo-therapy, pharmacological interventions, and the eclectic approaches based on the anecdotal experience of the therapist who is a recovered addict.

As we might expect, the approaches to treatment are closely linked to the same conceptions of addiction, which may be arranged in a continuum of modifiability ranging from those based on willpower (which regard addiction as a drama wholly modifiable by self-will) to genetic conceptions (which highlight hereditary predisposition as a risk factor). In the same way, treatment and prevention share ideas and ontologies about the process of learning and change, as well as about the learner or the patient. In that sense, and as one may suppose, the two phenomena and literatures are not independent.

One of the most influential approaches to addiction and understandably one of the earliest is that associated with the very origin of the word. Holman and Howatt (2005) remind us that the term "addiction" comes from the Latin word *addicere*, which means to "worship or surrender oneself to a master." In a certain sense, the etymology of the term anticipates the moral idea of addiction, which conceives of the addict (and by extension, the abuser) as someone with doubtful moral credentials. The addict is thus considered to be an individual without willpower, who is irresponsible, criminal, dangerous, violent, manipulative, and deceitful. For its part, consumption is seen as a slippery slope to an inevitable deterioration.

Given the closeness of this state of things to the beliefs of the nineteenth century temperance movement (Gately 2008), it is not surprising that cure is seen as a spiritual or specifically religious experience that implies a moral shift. This model persists, in a sense, in the theo-therapeutic approaches, which, as Inés Elvira Mejía notes in her *Diagnosis of the situation of institutions for treatment, rehabilitation and reincorporation*, base their interventions "on religious beliefs, Bible reading, group reflections which are called 'devotional' and religious cults" (Ministerio de la Protección Social 2004, 6).

Although, as we shall see below, the moral model continues in force today and forms part of the social imaginary about addiction, in recent decades there have emerged conceptions that, to a greater or lesser extent, incorporate biopsychosocial elements in their causal explanations. We are speaking of approaches that grant the biochemistry of psychoactive substances their due place in the processes of dependence, but in the same manner acknowledge the behavioral, social (as in the case of codependence [Pérez and Delgado 2003]), and cultural dimensions of addiction.

At the current time, the latest edition of the *Diagnostic and Statistical Manual of Mental Disorders* (DSM-IV-TR), the most frequently employed diagnostic tool in the international mental health sector, avoids using the term "addiction" and prefers to use the terms "substance abuse" (for a repeated use which does not imply addiction or symptoms) and "substance dependence" (for a compulsive and repetitive use of substances that may cause tolerance and symptoms of abstinence) (American Psychiatric Association

2000). Seen in that way, dependence is a variety of substance abuse. The definition of the DSM-IV-TR is important because it recognizes, on the one hand, that both abuse and dependence are disorders that are relative to the kind of drug (i.e., to its addictive power) and, on the other, that dependence involves both biological and psychosocial processes. It is the biopsychosocial nature of abuse and dependence that, in a certain manner, explains the variety of treatments and, as has been recently demonstrated, their complementariness in many cases. The modalities of treatment differ in their specific strategies, the focuses that inspire them, and their goals. The goals may vary from detoxification to the achievement of total abstinence, or, on the contrary, a functional consumption. For their part, the specific strategies may imply the use of drugs to moderate abstinence symptoms, the use of cognitive-behavioral techniques (such as skills of confrontation, training in the management of stress, training in social and communication skills, feedback, training in assertiveness, and anger management), the participation of the patient in therapeutic communities or support groups, and the intervention of spouses, relatives, and even communities. The effectiveness of these strategies, which may be developed in residential or ambulatory modalities or mixed models (as in the case of overnight shelters for addicts), depends on their adaptation to the characteristics and needs of the patient and his or her environment, as well as the specific kind of drug in question (alcohol, marijuana, cocaine, synthetic drugs).

In the United States in particular, there is a growing consensus about some kinds of treatment that have proven to be effective in well-designed clinical experiments. Some of them, in the ambit of nonpharmacological treatments, are systemic therapy, cognitive-behavioral therapy (CBT), motivational improvement therapy, the twelve steps self-help groups (like Alcoholics Anonymous) and multidimensional family therapy in the case of adolescent consumers. Some of the principles underlying these and other effective interventions include the idea that no therapy is universally effective, the need to provide long and easily accessible treatments, the convenience of combining behavioral therapies and medication, and the need to make frequent evaluations of the changing needs of the patient.

One principle that should be added, so obvious it is often unnoticed, is that not every consumer needs treatment, and spontaneous remissions without intervention often occur (particularly in the consumption of certain drugs) (Cunningham 1999). Naturally, certain reservations apply to these sound practices, which should be regarded not as dogmas but as working hypotheses, which in any case must stand the test of cultural adaptation.

An essential aspect of sound practices, the importance of which deserves a special mention, is the role of the family. Drug addiction represents suffering and destabilization not only for the affected individuals, but also for their families. The scientific literature agrees on the influence of the family in recuperation, the prevention of relapses, and the social reinsertion of the drug addict (Frances, Millar, and Mack 2005; Ministerio de la Protección Social 2004; Ministerio de la Protección Social, Fundación Procrear 2007). In fact, the involvement of families in the treatment is a predictor of their effectiveness. The intervention of the families has multiple aims: it may help to counteract the risk factors that favor the establishment of the addiction and may define the dynamics and patterns of family interaction that act to prolong addiction and orient the family group, with the aim of preventing relapses and offering support.

In our opinion, what has allowed these emerging but still preliminary consensuses to come about is the combination of three factors: first, the undertaking of valid empirical research into the relative effectiveness of treatments (for example, through experimental designs); second, the creation and promotion of platforms for disseminating information about effective interventions, as in the case of some initiatives by the National Institute on Drug Abuse in the United States (2001); and finally, the participation of duly trained professionals in the development and realization of therapeutic protocols. What is the situation of treatment in Colombia? As we noted above, the inclusion of treatment in state policies goes back to, among other measures, law 30/1986, which ordered the then Ministry of Health to include in its programs the "provision of prevention, treatment, and rehabilitation services for drug-dependents" and take charge of authorizing and inspecting the institutions dedicated to those aims.

Ten years later the Luis Amigó University Foundation, together with the National Narcotics Administration, carried out a diagnostic study of the modalities of treatment and rehabilitation. In 2004, the Ministry of Social Protection and the General Administration of the Quality of Services (Dirección General de la Calidad de Servicios) published the study by Inés Elvira Mejía, *Diagnosis of the situation of institutions for the treatment, rehabilitation, and social reincorporation of the consumers of psychoactive substances in Colombia*, in our opinion the most complete analysis of the current panorama of treatment in Colombia (which is not to say that it offers an in-depth view of what is actually done in Colombia).

Among the findings of this diagnosis, we would like to single out three, which in our opinion are particularly consistent with the perceptions of the professionals of psychology and psychiatry who work in the field of addictions. The first is related to the increase in recent years and prevalence in Colombia of programs based on theo-therapy, programs without much structure and with precarious (sometimes nonexistent) theoretical foundations. This state of things goes against the current of the growing empirical evidence about the effectiveness of treatments such as behavioral therapy, systemic interventions, programs based on the twelve steps and combined therapies (i.e., the use of drugs to treat abstinence symptoms and cognitive-behavioral counseling). In fact, the diagnosis found that the treatments based on such evidence are a minority on a national level. The marginal position of treatments in the ambit of what is, strictly speaking, clinical psychology and psychiatry is also consistent with the limited availability of services for the management of overdoses, the abstinence syndrome, and detoxification.

The second finding we would like to single out is the marginal nature of treatments aimed at reducing harm, that is, therapeutic goals that do not imply total abstinence. This circumstance is particularly worrying in the context of chronic dependencies, as is the case of the one associated with the use of heroin, a drug in which the reduction of harm is in many cases the only alternative to the loss of lives.

Finally, it is worth stressing the financial precariousness of most institutions, which has a negative effect on the quality of their professionals, strategies for keeping up to date with the latest studies, and in general the quality of the services they offer (which, for example, in most cases do not include integral evaluations of their clients or care for women or minority groups). The lack of qualified professionals, added to the implementation of intervention strategies of doubtful (or at least unproven) effectiveness, mean that, taken as a whole, the treatments are not up to the challenges they face.

That being so, the panorama of treatment is one of information that is barely beginning to be consolidated, general regulations that are loosely enforced, and interventions that, in the absence of professionals with the due training and experience to support them, diverge from what is recommended by the emerging literature on evidence-based treatments. It is a panorama in which institutions, often without due qualifications and certifications, provide services inspired by professions of faith or personal, anecdotal ideas about rehabilitation. There is no doubt that this scene contrasts with more integral models for addictions and their treatments, as in the case of the biopsychosocial model.

GENERAL RECOMMENDATIONS

The reduction of the demand for drugs (legal or illegal) should be a priority of state policies. It is a matter of debate whether the state itself (as opposed to nongovernment organizations) should provide programs of prevention and treatment, from the stage of design to the different levels and modalities of implementation. The creation and provision of such programs by the state may eventually disseminate more quickly knowledge and the adoption of homogenous criteria for the design and evaluation of initiatives. Nevertheless, at the same time, centralizing actions in the state may have the undesirable effect of reducing the diversity of prevention and treatment programs and thus restrict innovation in their conception and adaptation to local needs.

In any case, positioning prevention as an action of special urgency must be a priority for the state. The state must thus exercise rigorous control over the private institutions that specialize in the treatment of substance addiction and must make decisions about the demand for illegal drugs based on scientific studies. The lack of systematic and comparable studies in the past twenty years has created fundamental gaps in the information about the nature, evolution, and effectiveness of prevention programs and activities in the field of treatment and rehabilitation.

This, in turn, has led to a lack of definition in the relevant public policies, in accordance with a phenomenon that shows signs of change over the years. We single out the achievements reached by the Pastrana government (with the Rumbos program) and the progress in the past eight years in the research and guidelines found in state policies on this matter. For that reason, we recommend that the strengthening of information systems continue so they may be systematic and long-lasting. Such systems must be the repositories of sound practices and programs of prevention and treatment that have undergone rigorous evaluations. Up-to-date information will enable public policies to be adjusted to the changing needs and priorities of the reduction of the demand for drugs in the country.

The need to centralize information and undertake rigorous evaluative research is in reality an aspect of the broader need to make the phenomenon of drug consumption a subject of academic inquiry and analysis. This, in our judgment, implies that consumption must stop being the exclusive or preferred concern of psychology and be an object of study by disciplines like anthropology, history, economy, political science, and sociology, to name only a few.

Policies for reducing demand must address two specific aspects. In the first place, they should be based on the type of substance: whether its characteristics, the social perception of its harm, or its legal or illegal nature. In the second, they must be guided by the needs of citizens involved in the use and abuse of drugs. For that reason, it is imperative to break down prevention programs into universal, selective, and indicated ones, taking into account the sector of the population to be intervened with in terms of age, gender, or specific characteristics (e.g., educational level, social marginality, vulnerability).

Along the same lines, national and international studies suggest that there are trajectories or transitions, of a probabilistic nature of course, in the use of psychoactive substances, beginning with legal drugs and ending with the use of illegal drugs. In Colombia the transitions beginning with the use and abuse of alcohol (which is consumed at an ever earlier age, with a recent increase in the female population) have been especially documented. From that arises the need to prevent alcohol abuse, especially among the younger generations. As a strategy for the prevention of alcohol use, the reduction of harm, while it may not be the only response, should in our opinion be a concern of governmental policy in order reduce the collateral damages of consumption (traffic accidents, homicides, intrafamiliar and marital violence, social violence, sexual violence, and suicides).

For the same purpose, additional state efforts are required (through stricter regulations and bolder and less tolerant and contradictory publicity campaigns) to reduce the consumption of tobacco, which has reached alarming levels, especially among the younger segments of the population.

With regard to the prevention of illegal drugs, the specialized literature shows that marijuana is the most widely consumed illegal substance, with a perception of low risk among the general population. For that reason, preventing its use must be regarded as a priority, with truthful information about its possible effects without exaggerating the harms it causes. In the case of Colombia, the prevention of the abuse of cocaine must also be seen as a priority, due to our status as the world leader in its production and trafficking, a circumstance which facilitates the internal trafficking of production surpluses and its availability at very low prices.

It is also necessary to implement strategies to prevent heroin consumption, especially in the regions of the country where the production of this substance is focused, and to strengthen strategies for the recuperation of current consumers. Due to the particular characteristics of heroin, users may require pharmacological substitutes to help them and may require strategies for the reduction of harm, aimed at, among other things, the control and treatment of illnesses like HIV/AIDS and hepatitis B and C.

Finally, in the field of prevention we must address, as a matter of utmost urgency, the increase of the consumption of substances used by youngsters during the "rumba" (partying), among which we find legal inhalants and synthetic drugs like ecstasy, among others. The use of synthetic drugs by young people in the context of normal social activities has wound up transforming the social insularity of consumption, turning it into a cultural practice accepted by the majority. Synthetic drugs also present the aggravating circumstance that they are easy to produce and are massively distributed. Hence the need to directly confront their use.

In our opinion, the programs for preventing drug consumption must be required at the different levels of the educational system, from basic primary education to higher education. As the literature suggests, the programs must begin at an early age, focused on the teaching of self-control, self-care, and civic ethics, with the direct participation and commitment of parents. In that sense, the prevention of drug abuse (legal and illegal) must count on the commitment and shared responsibility of society in general, the educational system, the private sector, and the communications media.

The recent literature on the effectiveness of prevention programs offers results that are sufficiently solid for certain advances in the science of prevention to become the basis for the design of programs and policies for reducing demand. The epidemiological model distinguishes between the risk factors and protection factors that must become the pillars of prevention efforts, along with robust theories about what leads people to consume drugs (like Albert Bandura's theory of social learning and Jean Lave's sociocultural theory).

We optimistically welcomed the National Plan for the Reduction of Psychoactive Substances and their Impact, 2009–2010, presented by the Uribe government, which evidences an intention to systematize and update policies. The effects of the policies set out in the plan should become a matter of analysis and discussion based on the result of evaluation exercises. In that sense, we hope the great conflicts and social problems the country faces will not again be an excuse for the government to abandon or only partly develop established reforms.

Although we insist that the prohibition of the personal dose represents a needless backward step, or at least a decision not backed by a consensus of educated opinion, we must highlight the advances seen during these past eight years, not so much in the implementation of effective treatments or the development of the required material and human infrastructure, but in the obtaining of reliable information about the state of the institutions that provide services to consumers and addicts. The precarious situation of Colombian rehabilitation centers documented in the above-mentioned diagnosis suggests that, given a context where urban violence is increasing and the presence of narcotics trafficking persists, the legal measures aimed at those found with a personal dose and their supplementary treatment will become a dead letter. In fact, we believe that the possibility of the state being able to offer adequate rehabilitation to those offenders who ask for it is remote, especially in view of the large number of those who would need treatment.

But while the panorama is unclear and the goals seem too distant, given the important advances represented by the 2009 National Study of Consumption and the 2004 diagnosis, it would be contradictory for the state not to give priority to the need to guarantee that the regulations decreed under the Uribe administration be rigorously enforced for the benefit of addicts and their families.

Once the most common and critical problems have been identified, it only remains for the state to demand that the institutions comply with the law and maintain a constant and long-term control over them, thus guaranteeing that addicts receive effective treatments focused on their needs and personal characteristics, the kind and degree of consumption, and their age, gender, and degree of social vulnerability. Of special importance, we believe, is that the state must guarantee that the personnel in charge of such institutions have adequate professional training (in areas like clinical psychology or psychiatry) and the required experience, in line with what is prescribed by the regulations in force and independent of the methodologies implemented.

The technical literature suggests that an effective intervention for the treatment of addiction must take into account the nature of the drug and the affectation or severity of the clinical profile; the age, gender, and singularities of the personality and history of the patient; his or her spiritual dimensions and the social and cultural factors that give meaning to the patient's actions.

Although it is not possible to define a type of intervention that will be effective for all affected individuals, we acknowledge that the biopsychosocial model is the most complete, integral, and fully supported by evidence. In that sense, intervention programs should to some extent take into account all the suggested dimensions of the problem of addiction. Thus the treatments should be open to pharmacological aids when they are required, that is, in cases where they help to overcome the abstinence syndrome or for patients who show comorbidities, whose treatments should include medication as well as counseling, strategies of social reinsertion, family intervention, and follow-ups over time to prevent relapses.

As we said at the beginning of this chapter, the problem of drugs is, in the first and last instance, a human drama. It is the drama of youngsters and adults, men and women, who, with their urgent needs and search for altered states and extreme experiences, foster a demand that in turn is able to nourish a whole series of actions in the field of supply. Consumption and addiction are phenomena of relatively recent study in the social and health sciences. Even so, in recent decades there have been crucial advances in explaining them, quite distant from the forms of understanding (and on occasions of justification) based on moral, religious, or discriminatory discourses.

The challenge for the Colombian state, like that of modern states in general, is to delineate policies based on systematic research and academic debate and, by means of valid periodic evaluations, watch over the quality of the programs and interventions that are carried out. This, of course, requires that the reduction of demand for drugs should be as much a priority as the efforts to control the supply of drugs.

NOTES

1. A psychoactive substance is a chemical substance, whether legal or illegal or natural or synthetic, which acts on the central nervous system and alters perception, emotional states, awareness, and conduct. In this chapter we use the term drugs as a synonym for psychoactive substances, whether legal (such as tobacco and alcohol) or illegal (such as marijuana, cocaine, and synthetic drugs).
2. The differences between an occasional consumer, habitual consumer, abuser, and dependent are still a matter of debate in both the specialized and nontechnical literature. The elusiveness of these categories derives, in part, from the close relationship that exists between consumption as a problem and the nature of the drug that is used, as well as between consumption and the evaluation or cultural and social perception of the consumer.

REFERENCES

American Psychiatric Association. 2000. *Diagnostic and Statistical Manual of Mental Disorders* (DSM-IV-TR). Washington, DC: American Psychiatric Publishing.

Becker, H. 1963. *Outsiders: Studies in the Sociology of Deviance*. New York: The Free Press.

Botvin, G. J. 2004. "Advancing Prevention Science and Practices: Challenges, Critical Issues and Future Directions." *Prevention Science* 5: 69–72.

Botvin, G. J., and K. W. Griffin. 2003. "Drug Abuse Prevention in School Curricula." In *Handbook of Drug Abuse Prevention: Theory, Science and Practice*, edited by Z. Sloboda and W. J. Bukoski, 45–76. New York: Kluwer/Plen.

Botvin, G. J., et al. 2003. "Preventing Tobacco and Alcohol Use Among Elementary School Students Through Life Skills Training." *Journal of Child and Adolescent Substance Abuse* 12: 1–17.

Brown, E. C., and J. D. Hawkins. 2007. "Communities that Care: A Science-Based Approach to Prevention in Communities." Paper presented at the seminar *Prevención basada en la evidencia: Comunidad y drogas*. Organized by the Alianza para el Avance de la Investigación Sobre Sustancias Psicoactivas (AVISPA). Bogotá, March 15–16.

Cunningham, J. A. 1999. "Untreated Remissions From Drug Use: The Predominant Pathway." *Addictive Behaviors* 24, no. 2: 267–70.

Dirección Nacional de Estupefacientes. 1999. *Plan nacional: Una política integral de drogas para la paz*: Bogotá.

Dreier, O. 2008. *Psychotherapy in Everyday Life*. New York: Cambridge University Press.

Frances, R. J., S. I. Millar, and A. H. Mack. 2005. *Clinical Textbook of Addictive Disorders*. New York: Guilford Press.

Gately, I. 2008. *Drink: A Cultural History of Alcohol*. London: Gotham.

Hawkins, J. D. et al. 2009. "Results of a Type 2 Translational Research Trial to Prevent Adolescent Drug use and Delinquency: A Test of Communities that Care." *Archives of Pediatric and Adolescent Medicine* 163, no. 9: 789–98.

Holman, R., and W. A. Howatt. 2005. *The Addiction Counselor's Desk Reference*. New York: John Wiley.

Kandel, D. 1975. "Stages in Adolescent Involvement in Drug Use," *Science* 190: 912–14.

Kibel, B. M., and H. D. Holder. 2003. "Community-Focused Drug Abuse Prevention." In *Handbook of Drug Abuse Prevention: Theory, Science and Practice*, edited by Z. Sloboda and W. J. Bukoski, 145–56. New York: Kluwer/Plen.

Kumpfer, K. L., and G. B. Baxley. 1997. *Drug Abuse Prevention: What Works?* Rockville, MD: National Institute on Drug Abuse.

Ministerio de la Protección Social. 1996. *Estudio nacional de consumo de drogas*. Bogotá.

———. 2004. *Diagnóstico situacional. Instituciones de tratamiento, rehabilitación y reincorporación social a consumidores de spa en Colombia*. Bogotá.

———. 2007. *Política nacional para la reducción del consumo de sustancias psicoactivas y su impacto*. Bogotá.

———. 2009. *Estudio nacional de consumo de drogas*. Bogotá.

Ministerio de la Protección Social and CICAD/OAS. 2004. *Encuesta nacional sobre consumo de sustancias psicoactivas en jóvenes escolares entre 12 y 17 años*. Bogotá.

Ministerio de la Protección Social and Fundación FES Social. 2003. *Estudio nacional de salud mental*. Bogotá. Retrieved from *onsm.ces.edu.co/uploads/files/1243030_EstudioNacionalSM2003.pdf*, accessed May 12, 2015.

Ministerio de la Protección Social and Procrear. 2007. *Hacia un modelo de inclusión social para personas consumidoras de sustancias psicoactivas*. Bogotá.

National Institute on Drug Abuse. 2001. *Principios de tratamientos para la drogadicción: Una guía basada en investigaciones*. National Institutes of Health, no. 01-4180(S).

Paglia, A., and R. Room. 1999. "Preventing Substance Use Problems Among Youth: A Literature Review and Recommendations." *Journal of Primary Prevention* 20, no. 1: 3–50.

Palmgreen, P., and L. Donohew. 2003. "Effective Mass Media Strategies for Drug Abuse Prevention Campaigns." In *Handbook of Drug Abuse Prevention: Theory, Science and Practice*, edited by Z. Sloboda and W. J. Bukoski, 27–43. New York: Kluwer/Plenum.

Pérez, A. 2007. *Transiciones en el consumo de drogas en Colombia*. Bogotá: Dirección Nacional de Estupefacientes.

Pérez, A., and D. Delgado. 2003. *La codependencia en familias de consumidores y no consumidores de drogas: Estado del arte y construcción de un instrumento*. Programa Presidencial Rumbos.

Programa Presidencial Rumbos. 2001. *Encuesta nacional sobre consumo de sustancias psicoactivas en jóvenes 10 a 24 años*. Bogotá.

Xie, X., et al. 1996. *The Economic Costs of Alcohol, Tobacco and Illicit Drug Abuse in Ontario: 1992*. Research Document No. 127. Toronto: Addiction Research Foundation.

PART III: INTERNATIONAL RELATIONS AND ANTI-DRUG POLICIES IN COLOMBIA

6 Colombia's Multilateral Drug Policy during the Two Uribe Administrations

Toward Prohibitionist Activism in an Era of Détente

Sandra Borda

INTRODUCTION

In this chapter, I intend to show that the most important objective Colombia has pursued in multilateral forums[1] has been to obtain material support and logistical, military, and economic cooperation to wage its war against drugs. Accordingly, concepts like *shared responsibility, integrality, multilateralism, equilibrium, and international cooperation* precisely point in that direction; the problem of the production, trafficking, and consumption of illegal drugs concerns everyone in the international system and must be fought jointly.

Nevertheless, in the international system of today, transfixed by the global war against terrorism unleashed by the September 11th attacks in the United States, the subject is far from being a priority. The lack of interest and absence of international political will have made the Colombian government's search for this support more difficult, and likewise the winning of a more tangible commitment and a more focused attention from the international community. In the face of this adverse scenario, the strategy of the Colombian government has thus been to highlight the links between illegal drugs and other matters that do form part of the priorities of the international agenda, like terrorism, the environment, and, more recently, the defense of human rights.

The Colombian state has taken up its participation in international organizations as an additional way to advance its internal political agenda. This trend is not exclusive to Colombia and much less to the administrations of president Álvaro Uribe, to which the analysis in this chapter is devoted. Nor is it a trend that only applies to the subject of the

Sandra Borda: Associate professor, Department of Political Science, Universidad de los Andes.

illegal drug trafficking. In fact, and speaking more theoretically, the relations between states and international organizations are a two-way street, and just as international institutions try at times to transform the behavior and modify the interests of states, states equally try to advance their particular interests in the international arena by making use of international organizations (Hasenclever et al. 1997; Barnett and Finnemore 2004).

In this chapter I will analyze the way the Colombian government links these subjects on the international stage, and I will suggest that doing so causes more problems than opportunities. Furthermore, while it is assumed that such linkage politics normally leads to positive results for the states that design and implement it, my argument is that its deployment may help to stimulate a circumstantial international attention but produce a kind of entrapment in the future and place Colombia in a scenario of greater vulnerability, where the international community will exert higher levels of conditioning and a greater pressure.

Thus, as Keohane suggests (1984, 91), although governments organize and construct their foreign policy in accordance with the way matters are set forth and formulated on an international level, "linking affairs which pertain to different regimes will always be difficult." In this chapter I will try to explain the nature of these difficulties.

Insofar as I analyze Colombian strategies with regard to the international anti-drug regime here (of which international organizations, among others, form a part), I use Stephen Krasner's definition of an international regime. According to Krasner, regimes are the principles, norms, rules, or procedures for decision making, whether explicit or implicit, around which converge the expectations of the agents in a given area of international relations. Regimes are thus specialized arrangements that correspond to well-defined activities, resources, or geographical areas that often involve the same subgroup of members of the international society (Krasner 1982).

In other words, the international regime on illegal drugs in which Colombia is immersed comprises the global rules of the game by which the international community as a whole, and states in particular, wage their fight against this problem.

In addition to identifying the difficulties of this particular deployment of "linkage politics," I also suggest that one of the fundamental and noteworthy features of Colombian strategy during the two presidential administrations of Álvaro Uribe was its largely uncritical adherence to the *prohibitionist* version of the fight against drugs. In other words, during the Uribe administrations the Colombian government did not try—at least through its diplomacy in multilateral forums—to change the rules of the game of the international anti-illegal-drugs regime, which in its current form is mainly prohibitionist (although, as I will suggest below, with strong tendencies toward change) (Galán and Guerrero 2008; Thoumi and Jelsma 2008).

Colombia has focused its strategies on implementing the dictates of that regime, but it has not adopted a *revisionist* or *critical* attitude toward it. Instead, it has been the opposite: one of the most notorious characteristics of the current Colombian position on the subject of drugs, internationally speaking, has precisely been its support for the position of zero tolerance and a franker and harsher criminalization of consumption.

The arguments the government used to support this change of position mainly rested on the level of criminality and corruption produced by the increased consumption of narcotics in Colombia (due to the legalization of the personal dose, so the argument goes), the difficulty of distinguishing between a retail dealer and a bearer of the personal dose, and the inconsistency of prohibiting production and trafficking while legalizing consumption.

In this sense, the most important recommendation that arises from this study is precisely that it is a favorable moment, internally and internationally, for the country to lead the move toward what may become an important turning point in the global fight against illegal drugs. The reputation Colombia has won as a solid partner in the fight against the production and trafficking of narcotics and the way it has secured relatively stable results in that battle have even enabled the country to boost itself on an international level as the possessor of unequaled know-how in this field.

Its international status as a loyal soldier in the antinarcotics battle allows Colombia to adopt a relatively critical and of course constructive position, which may eventually help to bring about a gradual change in the international anti-drug regime.

In this undertaking, the country might even be accompanied by the United States, a nation that, after promoting a staunch prohibitionism, now seems to be gradually moving toward a less criminalized and more flexible perception of this subject.[2]

In terms of methodology and to be able to precisely identify the guidelines of Colombia's diplomatic activity in multilateral forums, the ideal would be to compile a record of the country's voting in the most important organizations. In the case of the United Nations, however, the annual session of the Commission on Narcotic Drugs makes a series of decisions and recommendations that are generally adopted by the consensus of its members. The purpose of the negotiations that take place before and during the session is to arrive at language acceptable to all the parties. These decisions and recommendations are then passed to the United Nations Economics and Social Council (ECOSOC), of which the commission is a subsidiary body, which then adopts them using the same mechanism. As for the General Assembly, the themes that come from the ECOSOC are consolidated into an "omnibus resolution," which is also passed by consensus.

The OAS functions in a similar way. The record of the activities, decisions, and recommendations of the Inter-American Drug Abuse Control Commission (CICAD) is published in its annual report, which is then submitted to the General Assembly of the hemispheric organization, and its opinion is also arrived at by consensus. As a result, the practice of voting on the subjects on the multilateral drugs agenda is usually exceptional.[3] For that reason, any attempt to work out the general trends of the Colombian position on drugs in these international forums requires a review of the speeches given by the country's representatives and the heads of the Colombian missions at these institutions, and of the official documents which have been published where the government's position on the specific themes discussed in these forums is stated.

Having given this clarification, I return to my central argument about the position of Colombia in these scenarios and during the two administrations of president Álvaro Uribe. That position has been characterized by a definition of the problem that has been constantly linked to other subjects that are priorities on the global agenda; a now traditional discourse of Colombian diplomacy that emphasizes the shared responsibility for and integral nature of the problem, although it denounces the international community's lack of support for and interest in the nearly solitary struggle Colombia carries on; and a militant prohibitionism the aim of which has already surpassed the former strategic purpose of aligning the fight against Colombian drugs with the global fight against narcotics trafficking that the United States has been waging and leading since the beginning of the 1970s.

In this chapter, I set forth my ideas in the following order: First, I describe the nature of the principle of a common and shared responsibility Colombia has proclaimed since the 1990s at these multilateral organizations and was an integral part of the Uribe government's multilateral policy. I then evaluate the nature of the three links this government forged and promoted in the international scenario (drugs/terrorism, drugs/environment, drugs/human rights).

In the analysis of these three links I show how prohibitionism and the absence of a critical position toward the international anti-drug regime cut across Colombia's multilateral strategy. Finally, I end with a section of conclusions and recommendations that presents a general summary of the current multilateral policy on this subject and gives some suggestions on transforming the Colombian position into a tool that will be internally useful and will favor and improve the country's participation in the international scenario.

THE PRINCIPLE OF COMMON AND SHARED RESPONSIBILITY

The principle of shared and common responsibility was incorporated into the international lexicon of the war on drugs during the Twentieth Special Session of the United Nations General Assembly in 1998, to an important extent due to the international activism of the Colombian government, initially complemented by the proposals of the British government and later by those of the Mexican government. In that way, the convergence of proposals by Latin American and European countries was what led to the incorporation of this principle into the international anti-drug regime in 1998.

Although in the past that principle had mainly referred to the reduction of demand, it has now been extended to and has incorporated joint activities and commitments for the control of precursor chemicals, the laundering of assets, arms trafficking, and other criminal activities related to the illegal trafficking of narcotics. Shared responsibility may thus be called the fundamental pillar and "umbrella" principle that guides the work of the Colombian government in multilateral forums.

It is important to note that the principle of shared responsibility is a long way from international solidarity. In fact, the Colombian government has refused to use the latter term, insofar as it does not wish the commitment of the states to be thought of as altruistic or charitable help for Colombia and its fight against this problem, but instead simply as an obligation of each country to assume its corresponding share in a problem that requires the commitment of the whole international community. In the words of the minister-counselor of the Colombian Mission at the United Nations:

> [U]nder the criterion of shared responsibility we must balance the asymmetries which arise in the fight against this scourge. We have to redouble the efforts to reduce consumption, control production and the diverting of precursor chemicals, and intensify cooperation in order to prevent illegal financial resources from being "laundered" through their entrance into the global banking system. (Dávila 2003)

This common and shared responsibility is directly associated with the promotion of decisions and evaluations of a multilateral character (over and above unilateral coercion and determinations); a full perception of the integral nature of the problem, including the need to control production and chemical substances and to strengthen judicial systems and interdiction systems; controlling the laundering of assets and arms trafficking and reducing demand; and finally, the need to balance the emphasis of the fight against illegal drugs, applying equal effort and resources to the attacks against all the stages or links of the problem. The application of these principles to the global policy for checking illegal drugs implied an important task of redesigning the framework of international institutions[4] and transforming and refining the international regime in this field. In this process Colombia has played an active role at the heart of the UN.

For example, and in line with the above-mentioned principles, particularly as applied to the subject of alternative development during the past two administrations, in 2005 Colombia actively participated in the proposal that led to the Narcotics Commission's passing of the resolution on the "strengthening of alternative development as an important strategy for the prosecution of drugs and declaration that alternative development is a matter of intersectorial scope" (Ministerio de Relaciones Exteriores 2006).

On the subject of precursor chemicals, Colombia promoted (also in the Narcotics Commission) mechanisms for the exchange of information and the strengthening of vigilance, winning in that same year the approval of a project for the "strengthening of international cooperation to prevent the illegal manufacture and trafficking of narcotics and psychotropic substances, by stopping the diversion and smuggling of precursors and essential equipment, in the context of Project Prism, Operation Purple, and Operation Topaz" (Ministerio de Relaciones Exteriores 2006). Finally, during the negotiations on the UN General Assembly's resolution 60/288 in 2006, the Colombian delegation proposed the following text, which was later adopted by that body:

> To strengthen the legislative measures against the laundering of assets, trafficking of illegal drugs, illegal trafficking of arms, munitions, and explosives, kidnapping and other manifestations of the organized crime used by terrorist organizations to finance and facilitate their activities, and provide the necessary international cooperation and judicial assistance to locate, detect, freeze and confiscate the funds that finance terrorism. (Ministerio de Relaciones Exteriores 2007, 113)

As I will explain below, this proposal by the Colombian delegation reflects a skillful strategy that seeks to align Washington's concern with terrorism following the 9/11 attacks with the aim of obtaining funding for the fight against narcotics and the illegal groups that benefit from that trade. But for the moment it is important to emphasize that the Colombian government has been relatively successful in its aim of promoting, at least from a purely normative point of view, a broader vision and understanding of illegal drugs, and it has collaborated in the design of mechanisms in harmony with this principle. In this sense, the Colombian position, in contrast with what happens, for example, with the subject of human rights, has gone beyond simply reacting and defending itself and tried to be more proactive and constructive.

Thus this principle of common and shared responsibility also helped the Uribe government to formulate a strategy of linking the policies[5] it presented to the international community. The linchpin of that strategy was the existence of the sharp interdependence of the production, trafficking, and consumption of illegal drugs on the one hand, and the strengthening of terrorism, degradation of the environment, and violation of human rights on the other. In the following sections, I describe the nature of those links and explain the problems they pose.

LINK 1: ILLEGAL DRUGS AND TERRORISM

The link between illegal drugs and terrorism has been a constant feature of Colombian politics and domestic strategy, but it is more frequently seen in the positions Colombian delegations have adopted in multilateral forums following the 9/11 attacks: narcotics trafficking, as in Afghanistan, is portrayed[6] as the fuel that powers the machinery of international terrorist organizations (among which, of course, are included Colombian subversive and paramilitary groups). The Colombian version of this last link between the 9/11 attacks and so-called terrorism was built during the final year of the Pastrana administration (Moreno 2002) but was considerably reinforced in the early years of the Uribe administration.

President Uribe began his speech at the beginning of the fifty-seventh ordinary session of the United Nations by saying, "Not far from this place, on that fateful September 11, two thousand eight hundred and one citizens of the world died. In Colombia violence causes as many deaths every month" (Uribe 2002). In the same speech, given six months before the Bush government began its military invasion of Iraq, President Uribe tried to create an additional link that clearly sought to win the attention of Washington:

> There is concern about weapons of mass destruction in the United Nations forum, and we share this anguish. Please, we must understand that drugs have the capability for mass destruction equivalent to that of the most feared chemical weapon.

Two months after President Uribe's declaration, the Colombian minister of foreign affairs, Carolina Barco, continued to insist on this association in her speech before the Permanent Council of the OAS, but this time less ambiguously and more clearly suggesting how organized crime can be a mechanism for facilitating international terrorism:

> For a time stretching back to several five-year periods, we have fought with tenacity and perseverance to get the concept of shared responsibility accepted, in the first place, as a facet of the world problem of drugs. But, now, with much more reason, in the face of the terrible threat of terrorism and the criminal activities of an international character which nourish it, among them: organized global crime, in its different manifestations; the illegal trafficking of arms, munitions and explosives, and the laundering of assets. (Barco 2002, 3–4)

To corroborate the role this kind of association may have in Colombia's search for international support in its fight against illegal drugs, and with the clear aim of keeping the country at the center of a negative international agenda, Ambassador María Ángela Holguín, in a speech delivered three years later, emphasized the following point:

> We would like to reiterate that for the Colombian government there is only one kind of terrorism. Therefore, the international community's commitment to fighting it must be unequivocal. There cannot be a terrorism of first and second rank when their effects on societies are similar. Terrorism has no justification whatsoever and cannot be utilized as a tool to defend demands of any kind. (Holguín 2005)

Thus the construction of this drugs-terrorism axis has two different but complementary dimensions. In the first place, there is an appeal of a normative character to the international community; in the second, there is another appeal based on empirical evidence about the existence of this link. In the first sense, the Colombian government presents the fight against illegal drugs (the ones associated with terrorism) as a *duty* of the international community, which implies an attitude of zero tolerance toward consumption and the complete elimination of the conditions that make the drug trade possible.

According to this interpretation, a world absolutely free of drugs is possible and desirable and will lead almost inevitably to a world at least partly free of terrorism. In the second meaning, and as a complement of the first, the government constantly presents evidence of the use of money from narcotics trafficking for the financing of so-called terrorism. The Colombian ambassador to the United Nations articulated this double purpose in an eloquent way:

> In sound logic, if an internal conflict is financed by narcotics trafficking, the consumers of illegal drugs would be co-responsible for that conflict and the violations of human rights and international humanitarian law that occur. For that reason the international community is overdue in initiating an effective cooperation in that matter. (Giraldo 2003)

One cannot help but finding it interesting that at this juncture and on this precise occasion the recurrent use of the term "terrorism" had been replaced by the use of the term "conflict" and also that the norms of international humanitarian law were mentioned, which are applied par excellence precisely to situations of conflict. The point here, though, is that the Colombian government was trying to create an international sense of moral responsibility that rests on the premise that the money from narcotics trafficking, or, more precisely, from the consumers of narcotics, finances the "internal conflict" in Colombia.

The trend is toward a greater and more profound *securitization* of the drug problem, to use a term of Ole Waever, who defines it as the process by which a state declares a certain matter to be a problem of security and through the use of this strategy manages to claim a special and exceptional right to control that problem (Waever 1995, 54). This semantic exercise, which nevertheless has strong political implications, is clear in a variety of official declarations by the Colombian government. The following is but one of many recent examples:

> The world drug problem has transcended the ambit of public health and policing and turned into a matter of *national security*, because of its grave influence on the social, economic, and political stability of nations. (Giraldo 2003)

President Uribe's tone was similar, which suggests a strategic line created by the government: "Our problem is an international menace. . . . If Colombia does not check terrorism, it will cause difficulties for the democracies of the region" (Uribe 2003).

Nevertheless, it is not a new trend in Colombian foreign policy (Borda 2002a). The attempt to turn the drug problem into one of international security has been frequent and has sought to simultaneously fulfill two key aims. On the one hand, it has tried to make the subject a priority of the international agenda and achieve, as a result, a stronger international cooperation for Colombia. On the other, it has sought to convince the international community that the priority of the Colombian government is its unconditional commitment to the war against illegal drugs and that it will not accept weak versions of that commitment. In other words, it is a matter of what we might call a *symbolic securitization*, where the government tries to give the impression of an active and wholehearted participation in the fight against drugs, even though the concrete results of that participation have usually been meager and highly questionable.[7]

To this traditional strategy a relatively new component was added during the two Uribe administrations: a strong emphasis on the criminalization of the use of narcotics, the result of the extension of a domestic agenda that sought to revoke the Constitutional Court's legalization of the possession of a personal dose.

Instead, the government proposed the creation of treatment panels, made up of judicial officials (judges and prosecutors) jointly working with health professionals, to deal with both occasional consumers and those whose dependence on drugs may even lead them to commit crimes (*El Tiempo* 2009). Thus, thanks to the Uribe administration, not only the production and trafficking of narcotics is considered to be a threat to security, but consumption has also become part of the securitization process.

This governmental activism, which seeks the recriminalization of drug consumption, was accompanied and supported by an international strategy that advocates a zero tolerance of the consumption of narcotics. These positions go beyond the now traditional insistence on the need of the consumer countries to reinforce their policies to check demand. Once again, to promote the criminalization of consumption now fulfills the additional objective of strengthening and supporting an internal policy that seeks to end the legalization of the personal dose.

On several occasions, the Colombian delegations at these multilateral forums openly and unambiguously condemned the consumption of illegal drugs:

> Each gram of cocaine consumed by addicts is a gram that turns into financial resources for illegal armed groups that recruit and use children in Colombia. Each gram that is consumed is a potential cause of death and mutilation. Each gram consumed is transformed into the laying of antipersonnel mines that leave hundreds of victims. The drugs consumed by addicts and the money paid for them are transformed into illegal arms trafficking, forced displacement, the

> violation of the rights of indigenous peoples, and the destruction of our forests. Vulnerable groups and children in particular directly suffer these consequences. (Blum 2006)

The coincidence of this discourse of zero tolerance toward drug consumption and the practical disappearance of "harm reduction" from the vocabulary of Colombian diplomacy is reminiscent of Nancy Reagan in the 1980s and the message of her Just Say No program:

> Drugs steal away so much. They take and take, until finally every time a drug goes into a child, something else is forced out—like love and hope and trust and confidence. Drugs take away the dream from every child's heart and replace it with a nightmare. . . . Each of us has to put our principles and consciences on the line, whether in social settings or in the workplace, to set forth solid standards and stick to them. There's no moral middle ground. Indifference is not an option. We want you to help us create an outspoken intolerance for drug use. For the sake of our children, I implore each of you to be unyielding and inflexible in your opposition to drugs. (Reagan 1986)

In other words, the Colombian discourse on drug consumption during the Uribe administrations clearly resembled that of the Reagan administration of the 1980s and adopted a more radical, proselytizing, and internationally vocal tone. This discourse is not compatible with the adoption of a more progressive position on illegal drugs. On the contrary, it is a *pro statu quo* discourse that has deepened the securitization (whether symbolic or not) of the subject, its criminalization, and even its *terrorization*, but has contributed little to the search for a rigorous evaluation of the results of the anti-drug policy in its current form. In fact, it is a position unsupported by the empirical evidence found in studies like those of the World Health Organization (WHO) on the true effect of drug consumption (WHO 1995), but a moralistic rejection of the consumption of these substances.

Additionally, and as will be argued in the analysis of the following two links, while the Colombian government has the autonomy to construct and promote these thematic linkages to achieve the objectives of its domestic policy, it does not have the same control over the effects these linkages may produce in the international scenario. In the specific case of the link between drugs and terrorism, one of its (not entirely unexpected) consequences is the criminalization of those individuals who are linked to or benefit from the business of illegal drugs.

In particular, the inclusion of armed insurgent groups in the category of "terrorists" may be an obstacle to the eventual holding of peace negotiations to end the armed conflict in Colombia and, even worse, to the participation of those international agents who have already been persuaded by the Colombian government to label those groups as "terrorists" and would doubtlessly be able to play an important role in bringing about a political solution to the conflict. This is the case, for example, of powerful countries and international organizations that may be able to exert a much more effective influence in bringing the parties to the negotiating table and, in the future, make them responsible for honoring their pledges.

LINK 2: THE ENVIRONMENT AND DRUGS

During the second administration of President Uribe an international strategy was created that was mainly promoted by Vice President Santos and revolved around the argument that the impact of illegal drugs on the environment was a problem of shared international responsibility.

In 2006, the vice presidency formally launched, in London, a search for resources to support initiatives for the prevention of consumption by using arguments about the environmental damage and violence produced by the illegal trafficking of drugs. On one of his tours, Vice President Santos insisted on the links between illegal drugs, terrorism, the environment, and human rights:

> Drugs cause violence and death in Colombia because they finance illegal armed groups, the same who destroy lives with their terrorist acts. The wealth and diversity of the Colombian environment is under threat. More than 174,000 hectares of tropical forest have been devastated since the year 2000 by the production of cocaine. Likewise, one out of a half million [*sic*] Colombians is being displaced from his or her home by the illegal armed groups backed by cocaine trafficking. Thousands more have been victims of terrorist acts committed by these groups. (Santos 2006)

In 2008, the Colombian vice presidency ran an anti-drug campaign in Europe titled Shared Responsibility. Through the use of photographs that showed the impact of coca production on the environment, the government sought to create a sense of responsibility in European consumers.

The message of that campaign insisted that habitual consumption and even recreational use came at the cost of the loss of hectares of Colombian forests. The photo exhibition was shown in Austria, England, Italy, Sweden, Norway, the Netherlands, Belgium, and Portugal.[8]

In that way, the government linked the subject of illegal crops with the deforestation of the jungle and the tropical mist forest, but of course did not mention the environmental cost of eradication or fumigation with glyphosate. At the Fifteenth Summit on Climate Change, held in Copenhagen in December 2009, the Colombian government explained the relationship between the problem of illegal drugs and the environment in the following way:

> Fifty-two percent of Colombian territory is made up of jungle, more than 460,000 square kilometers of the Amazon jungle. Narcotics trafficking has destroyed more than two million hectares of our jungle. Narcotics trafficking destroys the jungle, it begins to cause environmental imbalances. When precursor chemicals are used to transform coca leaves into cocaine, the soil is contaminated, along with small and large rivers; the fauna is murdered, the flora is murdered and finally this criminal trade murders human beings. Narcotics trafficking is the murderer of human beings in every way, because it murders people and also murders the environment. Every time a citizen of an industrialized country consumes cocaine, he is killing the lungs of mankind,

> which is our Amazonian jungle. Every time a citizen of an industrialized country consumes narcotics he is causing a twofold spilling of blood in a country like Colombia: the spilling of blood caused by the murder of a citizen and the spilling of blood caused by the impoverishment of a nation which sees its environment being destroyed. We need to understand that narcotics trafficking is an effective cause of deforestation, climate change, environmental disorder, the killing of life, and poverty. For that reason we ask for a big commitment from everyone to oppose the production, trade, and consumption of illegal drugs. (Uribe 2009)

Thus, this process of building international awareness of the damages done to the environment by consumption is compatible with and nourishes the even stronger and more radical discourse that criminalizes consumption. In fact, it is probably an extension of an approach that returns to the prohibitionist language used in the United States in the 1980s and blocks more flexible perceptions that are not necessarily less effective.

Additionally,

> [I]n reality, the campaign winds up blaming the environmental tragedy—what is called an ecocide—on the peasant-farmer producer, the weakest link in the drugs chain, while it completely ignores the complexity of the subject and the unfortunate consequences (this ecocide, among them) which derive directly or indirectly from the absurd drugs policies that are applied in Colombia. (Armenta 2008)

The government's Shared Responsibility website states that "the main source of pollution in the Colombian jungle is the smoke from the trees burnt in order to plant coca," which, as Germán Quimbayo writes, "from the start, and without the least prior analysis, lays most of the blame for the catastrophe on the peasant-farmer who grows coca" (Quimbayo 2008, 1). As the same author points out, the FAO states, on the contrary, that the main cause of deforestation in Colombia is the growth of cattle farming and that the forced eradication of coca, mainly through the use of fumigation, has worsened ecosystemic contamination, destroyed ecological niches, and affected the gene pool of local biodiversity (Ibid., 9).

Finally, he presents an argument that fundamentally weakens the logic of linking environmental conservation to the consumption of illegal drugs. Referring to the vice presidency's campaign, he states that

> [I]t sets out to leap over the logic of the consumption of a product in high demand like cocaine with a moralizing argument. Since when have people stopped consuming something because they discover that it comes from a "bad" source? Western society massively consumes all kinds of illegal products that, in many cases, are known to have harmful effects on the environment or represent an assault of nature. . . . What we do know, on the other hand, is that the consumer hopes that things are produced in a clean way. Meanwhile, he continues to consume them in the form that they are put on the market. The most horrifying pictures of the ecocide caused by coca are not what will stop

> a drug user, be he an occasional or habitual one. On the other hand, it will be a reassurance for him to know that the cocaine he is [consuming] has been produced in a healthy way, without causing negative effects on the place where it is produced or the people who produce it. (Ibid., 2)

To sum up, the discourse that links environmental problems to illegal drugs weakens the Colombian government's interpretation of the subject, which is that the problem must be dealt with in terms of coresponsibility and integrality.

Here the responsibility is clearly focused on the first link in the chain (production), which puts Colombia at the center of the problem again and lays the whole weight of responsibility for it on the country and its farmers. And what is worse, if Quimbayo's analysis is correct, this campaign aimed at dissuading First World consumers may eventually have no effect.

LINK 3: HUMAN RIGHTS AND DRUGS

Finally, the Uribe government began to set forth a direct relationship between drug trafficking and the human rights situation in Colombia. In this realm, the links were established in a varied way and the message was occasionally confusing. At the opening of the regional conference of the UNESCO in Cartagena (September 2008), President Uribe publicly presented an initial approach. To begin, he suggested that "it is a time to think very seriously about a battle against consumption, a path which is starting to affect human rights." Then he complemented the point by arguing that "for that reason we cannot separate the fight against drugs from the fight for human rights." He finished by insisting on the "need to fight against drugs, a factor in the violation of human rights" (EFE 2008).

The vice presidency, the institution in charge of the subject of human rights in the Uribe administration, also spoke internationally about the link between the problem of narcotics trafficking and violations of human rights. The essential argument is that the money derived from the illegal trafficking of narcotics helps to strengthen illegal armed groups that systematically violate the human rights of the civilian population through murder, kidnapping, and displacement. The central idea is that illegal drug money interposes itself between the state and its objective of guaranteeing the security and human rights of its citizens. As in the previous cases, the building of this link leads to the creation of a wrong interpretation of the human rights situation in the country.

In the first place, it completely diverts attention from the role the state has historically played, by action or omission, in the worrying internal situation of human rights. Additionally, the argument gives the impression that the only manner in which human rights have been affected is through the use of money from narcotics trafficking by illegal groups. It omits that these rights have been equally violated by the penetration of the same monies into the Colombian political class and the very apparatus of the state.

If there is a place where it is necessary to begin reforms leading to the guarantee of human rights in Colombia, it is precisely the state, the agent whose function and main obligation is to guarantee those rights.

In fact, the same government on occasions allowed us a glimpse of the tension between the demands for ending violations of human rights in the country and the antiterrorist fight (closely linked, as is already known, with the antinarcotics fight), and even more important, it openly told the international community what its priorities were. Ambassador Holguín eloquently expressed the Uribe administration's frustration in a speech at the General Assembly in 2005:

> Human rights keep us awake at night. Why don't we feel the same when it is a matter of terrorism? Why are we not able to clearly condemn the terrorist groups that affect the civilian population, instead of finding excuses and claims that are very difficult to justify when what is happening is that the possibility that each individual may freely enjoy the right to a life with security and without fear is ignored? (Holguín 2005)

In this interpretation, the defense of human rights is clearly placed on a secondary plane, after the so-called fight against terrorism. In fact, if one follows the arguments presented in the sections on links 1 and 2, it becomes clear that the aim of guaranteeing the rights of the civilian population in a context of armed conflict seems to be a byproduct or even an unexpected consequence of an eventual success in the fight against drugs: if the fight against drugs is successful, the fight against terrorism will also be, and as a result there will be no more violations of human rights. In the view of any unaware observer, the order of these stages is definitely reversed, insofar as guaranteeing human rights is and must be the main priority, in a period now known as the "age of rights" (Simmons 2009).

In addition, it is necessary to point out that there is a certain inconsistency in the strategy advanced by the government in that the growing securitization and criminalization of the problem are strategies that tend to emphasize the military and policing dimension of the fight against illegal drugs. The Uribe government sought aid from the international community to strengthen and consolidate its apparatus of repression (the military and the police, once again) and increase its control over the civilian population and its territory. As is to be expected, obtaining these resources would make the Colombian state more inclined, or at least provide it with more tools, to violate or turn a blind eye to violations of human rights.

In a number of countries, including Colombia, the escalation of the war on drugs in its more militarized version has caused nearly permanent insecurity and the death of civilians; produced extrajudicial killings of both those suspected to be traffickers as well as innocent civilians; facilitated practices like imprisonment without the promise of an eventual trial and without respect for due process; and violated the right to health of poorer sectors of the population who remain in hiding thanks to the same prohibition (Human Rights Watch 2008; Salgado 2004).[9]

Thus, contrary to what this new strategy of the Colombian government suggested, a greater securitization and militarization of the antinarcotics fight, combined with a radical prohibitionist position, are not even remotely complementary to or compatible with an improvement of the situation of human rights in the country.

Finally, and as an extension of the previous argument, the success of the fight against drugs and subversion in Colombia might be taking place (at least partly) at an enormous cost in the field of promoting and respecting human rights. In fact, the high levels of displacement, the extrajudicial executions carried out by the armed forces and locally known as "false positives," and even illegal governmental wiretapping ("*chuzadas*") are all—to a greater or lesser extent—effects of the implementation of the Uribe government's policy of "democratic security." This phenomenon would thus reveal one of the main difficulties that arise as a result of implementing this specific kind of linkage of narcotics trafficking and human rights: the inconsistency and virtual contradiction between the management and achievements in one field and the other make the linkage less credible and therefore less acceptable to the international community.

Taken together, these three forms of framing the problem of drugs lead to Colombia's being presented at international forums as a place where all the problems that are a priority for the international system converge. In presenting Colombia as a problematic case, the idea is not only to direct the attention of the international community to the country, but also channel its resources toward the anti-drug fight. According to Thoumi, a position has always been taken that tends to portray the country as a victim in need of international help in order to wage its always solitary fight against illegal drugs (Thoumi and Jelsma 2008, 200). The strategy is to present itself as the "eye of the hurricane," the place where, thanks to the production and trafficking of drugs, all the other key problems of the international system converge.

Additionally, the Colombian discourse constantly denounces the lack of commitment to the anti-drug campaign on the part of a large sector of the international community, and the Uribe government used the emphasis on this problem to secure another crucial aim of its foreign policy: to justify what some considered to be its excessive closeness to Washington.

At a public hearing in July 2009, the Colombian minister of foreign affairs announced the signing of an agreement with the United States that authorizes the presence of US armed forces on Colombian bases with the aim of consolidating the war on drugs (among other ends) and explained that despite the storm it caused in several countries of the region, the decision was legitimate by virtue of the traditional and historic nature of the Colombian–United States alliance in the fight against narcotics trafficking, and for the generalized international indifference toward the sacrifices made by Colombia. To an important extent, the failure of the Colombian multilateral strategy nourishes and consolidates the most important international component of the country's fight against drugs: its alliance with the United States.

CONCLUSIONS AND RECOMMENDATIONS

In the current situation of the international system, the subject of illegal drugs is not considered to be a priority. This lack of interest means there is a constant lack of commitment by the members of the community of nations that forces the Colombian government to create different diplomatic strategies to obtain the political, logistic, and economic support the country needs to fight against the problem of the production and trafficking of illegal drugs.

The strategy has two facets that became even more visible during the Uribe administration: on the one hand, it has sought to link drugs with subjects that have risen to the top of the international agenda (e.g., terrorism, the environment, and human rights), and on the other hand, it has advanced a version of the problem that is even more prohibitionist than the one the United States originated long ago and now serves as the foundation of the international regime against drugs.

The argument in this chapter is precisely that both strategies are wrong and counterproductive, and that in view of the declining importance of the subject and serious indications that a move toward a more flexible policy may be imminent—above all in the United States—the government should be promoting the opposite strategy. Colombia should be taking the lead in a more "scientific" and less politicized approach to the problem, one based more on the results of a serious and pragmatic evaluation of the achievements so far and less on ideological and moral commitments, and based more on a realistic calculation of what is and is not possible to achieve in this field and less on the relatively useless ideal of wiping the drug problems off the face of the earth.

In fact, there are signs that point to at least the beginning of a gradual but decisive transformation of the international anti-drug regime. The new Democratic administration in the United States and other pertinent sectors of the international community seem to have initiated a transition toward a less prohibitionist regime, with a strong interest in the human health aspects of the subject. But in the face of this process of transformation (which is still a long way from being consolidated and the final outcome of which is difficult to determine), Colombian diplomacy has put itself on the side of those who defend the status quo and who even encourage an intensification of the harshest versions of prohibitionism, a group from which the United States seems to be distancing itself. In that way, Colombia has taken its place in the radical prohibitionist faction of the international community, alongside the Islamic world, Sub-Saharan Africa, Russia, Eastern Europe, Cuba, and China, among others. This, I insist, is a counterproductive strategy.

In the field of consumption, for example, the Colombian position should on the contrary draw closer to what it was in the 1990s, when, along with countries like Australia, Bolivia, and Canada, the country promoted the study "of a series of possibilities to legalize and decriminalize the use or personal possession of cocaine and similar products" (Thoumi and Jelsma 2008, 189). In fact, Colombia should support Bolivia's proposal in this area instead of continuing with a strategy that punishes minimum consumption on an internal level and tries to promote this criminalization of consumption on an international level.

In March 2009, the Bolivian government requested the opening of a process of consultations and discussions that would last eighteen months and decriminalize the chewing of coca leaves. The administration of Evo Morales has undertaken a campaign at the United Nations to remove coca leaves from the list of illegal substances (List 1) in its Convention on Narcotics Drugs and convince the international community that the chewing of such leaves is a tradition of the Andean people that has nothing to do with the modern process of producing cocaine. In addition, at a meeting of the CICAD and the Commission on Narcotic Drugs, Bolivia, citing the principle of shared responsibility, called on the countries with high indexes of consumption to draft public policies for prevention with the aim of reducing the demand for illegal drugs. Once again, Colombia should be thinking about forging regional alliances to strengthen this type of approach.

Naturally, a change in this sense or in the fields of production and trafficking will imply amending the 1961 United Nations Single Convention on Narcotic Drugs and other agreements that form the complicated international regime on the so-called "war on drugs." The path, in this sense, is tortuous and hard and

> requires convincing the world of the need to do it. To marginally alter a convention takes between five and ten years. For the process to be successful, the Colombian government needs to present specific proposals. . . . In other words, it needs to take the position of an active agent and not a victim. (Thoumi and Jelsma 2008, 224)

But the process of changing the international regime on narcotics may be relatively simpler if, in formulating its multilateral position, Colombia manages to surpass the traditional dichotomy of "prohibitionism vs. legalization." These are far from being the only alternatives available for reducing the negative impacts of the illegal drug business (Borda 2002b). To be clear about it, to suggest a change in the Colombian position does not necessarily imply a radical shift toward the other extreme of the debate, legalization. For reasons that have already been explained to the point of saturation (Thoumi and Jelsma 2008), legalization is not an option for Colombia, either domestically or internationally.

But to start with, changing a discourse of zero tolerance and total eradication for one of reducing harm would not only be a more realistic alternative for Colombia's international diplomacy, but also more in harmony with current international interests. The adoption of a diplomacy of this nature would not only make it easier for Colombia to attain a more prominent and credible place on the international stage, it would also allow for a more rational approach to the changing nature of the global fight against narcotics.

Colombia's commitment to the so-called "war on drugs" means that it has nothing to be ashamed of. On the contrary, it has not spared any resources in waging a frontal battle against the problem, and this has meant large costs for its population, the strength of its state, its rule of law, and the consolidation of its democratic regime. In this sense, Colombia's participation in multilateral forums has cemented its undeniable authority in this field and highlighted the experience it has acquired in formulating and implementing policies to fight against the whole problem of drugs.

In fact, Colombia's position is even stronger insofar as it is on the way to consolidating itself as an exporter of know-how in the field of the anti-drug fight. The country has begun a transition toward a scheme of South-South cooperation in which it offers help and does not just receive it. In other words, the Colombian government may present itself as a participant in the fight against drugs and terrorism that is *expert* and able to provide advice about the development of key operational capacities in the fight against drugs, such as training, the handling of equipment, intelligence, sea and river interdiction, and about the adaptation of juridical frameworks to the fight against narcotics (Ministerio de Relaciones Exteriores 2009, 18).

In these forums the government presents an image of Colombia as a country with the capacity to advise other countries in the midst of the most difficult part of their battle against criminal organizations. As the Colombian minister of foreign affairs during the Uribe administration announced, Colombian personnel are, in fact, already working in Mexico, Guatemala, Panama, Haiti, and Afghanistan (in the latter case through NATO, removing land mines and fighting against drugs). But this kind of multilateral and international political capital can no longer be used to promote a prohibitionist policy that is not only radical but that goes against a strong trend among another group of countries (including a large part of Western Europe) toward establishing an international anti-drug policy that is much more rational and productive and less emotional and inefficient.

NOTES

I would like to especially thank Nicolás Mejía for his help as a research assistant in the writing of this chapter; several officials of the Ministry of Foreign Relations in Bogotá, New York, and Washington, who diligently provided crucial information for this analysis; Juan Tokatlian, Ralf Leiteritz, Muriel Laurent, Arlene Tickner, Álvaro Camacho, and the editor's of this book for their comments and suggestions; and María Paz Berger for her careful and patient editing and copyediting.

1. I must point out that I place a special emphasis in this chapter on Colombian participation in the United Nations (UN) and the Organization of American States (OAS). Consequently, I leave aside the country's participation in multilateral bodies of lesser scope like the Andean Community of Nations, Unsasur, and the Coordination and Cooperation Mechanism on Drugs between the European Union and Latin America and the Caribbean. I place emphasis on the UN and OAS because of restrictions of time and space, but any enlargement of this analysis would have to deal with Colombian strategy in the just mentioned forums of lesser reach.
2. Some examples that illustrate the eventual change in the US position are the Obama administration's proposal to stop using the language of the "war on drugs" as incompatible with its new approach to the subject; the executive branch's decision to stop the federal government's prosecution of patients who use medical marijuana and their suppliers in states where this practice is allowed; and the setting in motion in the US Congress of an independent commission sponsored by both parties that will evaluate, in the course of a year, the government's policy to reduce the supply and demand of illegal drugs. All these recent decisions seem to point toward a gradual but important change in the US policy on narcotics.

   Nevertheless, the limitations on this change were shown in the position the federal government assumed toward proposition 19, voted on in the California elections of November 2, 2010, which proposed the legalization of marijuana: the Department of Homeland Security emphatically stated that it would continue to implement the antimarijuana laws in the state of California, even if the proposition was passed, which implies a position still inspired by prohibitionism. Although the proposition was defeated, the results do show a substantial change in the attitude of the average California voter; 45 percent voted in favor of it and 55 percent against. A decade ago, such a relatively narrow result would have been unthinkable. It is also worth noting that these changes of attitude are not clearly reflected in the current federal budget allocations either, nor in the US government's position in multilateral forums (I would like to thank Daniel Mejía for calling my attention to the latter point).
3. I would like to thank several officials of the Chancellery (Ministry of Foreign Relations) for their help in explaining the nature of the decision-making process in these organizations.
4. To cite only one example: as the principle of multilateralism became stronger, the community of the American states saw the need to create a mechanism of evaluation (MEM) at the heart of the OAS, which would replace (at least partially) the traditional and very unilateral US certification process.

5. In speaking of the "formulation of a strategy" I suggest that the building of these links fulfills a specific political purpose. It is necessary, however, to clarify that when I use the term "built" or "created" I am not suggesting that these links are unreal or merely invented by the Colombian government. I am simply identifying them.
6. To return to the same point: when I suggest that the link is "portrayed" to the international community in this form, I am not trying to weaken the argument that the illegal armed groups are in fact linked to the drug business. But, once again, the nature and dimension of these links are questions that necessarily require additional studies.
7. I would like to thank Juan Tokatlian for calling my attention to this fundamental point.
8. All the information on the campaign undertaken by the vice presidency may be found at *www.sharedresponsibility.gov.co/en*.
9. For additional versions of the impact of the drug war on human rights, see Salgado 2004 and Llorenti n.d.

REFERENCES

Araújo, F. 2007. *Memoria al Congreso Nacional 2007*. Bogotá: Fondo Editorial Cancillería de San Carlos.

———. 2008. *Memoria al Congreso Nacional 2008*. Bogotá: Fondo Editorial Cancillería de San Carlos.

Armenta, A. 2008. *¿La responsabilidad de quién? Drogas y conflicto en Colombia*. T. Institute. Retrieved from *colombiadrogas.wordpress.com/2008/05/27/%C2%BFla-responsabilidad-de-quien*, accessed May 12, 2015.

Barco, C. 2002. Speech by Carolina Barco, minister of foreign affairs to the Permanent Council of the Organization of American States, December 11, Washington. Retrieved from *www.oas.org/es/centro_noticias/discurso.asp?sCodigo=03-0026*, accessed May 12, 2015.

Barnett, M. and Finnemore, M. 2004. *Rules for the World, International Organizations in Global Politics*. Ithaca, NY: Cornell University Press.

Blum, C. 2006. Statement by Ambassador Claudia Blum, permanent representative of Colombia to the United Nations, president, Public Security Council Debate on Children and Armed Conflict in Colombia, Permanent Mission to the United Nations, November 28, New York. Retrieved from *www.colombiaun.org/consejo_seguridad/Actuaciones-2006/Ni%F10s%20y%20Conflictos%20Armados%2011-28-06.htm*, accessed May 12, 2015.

Borda, S. 2002a. "La política exterior colombiana antidrogas o cómo se reproduce el ritual realista desde el Tercer Mundo." In *Prioridades y desafíos de la política exterior colombiana*, edited by A. B. Tickner, M. Ardila, and D. Cardona, 283–314. Bogotá: Fundación Hanns Seidel Stiftung, Friedrich Ebert Stiftung en Colombia-Fescol.

———. 2002b. "Una aproximación constructivista a la guerra en contra de las drogas." *Colombia Internacional* 54: 73–102.

Dávila, P. 2003. Statement by Deputy Chief Patricia Dávila de Navas at the General Debate of the Second Committee, Economic and Financial Affairs, Permanent Mission of Colombia to the United Nations, October 7, New York. Retrieved from *www.colombiaun.org/discursos/AG-58/AG58%202DebateGeneral-10-07-03.htm*, accessed May 12, 2015.

EFE. 2008. "Uribe insta al mundo a que lance batalla contra el consumo de drogas."

El Tiempo. 2009. "Tribunal para tratamiento de drogas," presented to the UN by the interior minister and foreign minister, March 8. Retrieved from *www.eltiempo.com/archivo/documento/CMS-4864888*, accessed May 12, 2015.

Galán, J. M., and L. J. Guerrero. 2008. "La legalización de las drogas ilícitas en Colombia: Elementos para una discusión." In *La batalla perdida contra las drogas: ¿Legalizar es la opción?*, ed. J. M. Galán, F. Thoumi, W. Ramírez, and R. Vargas, 23–149. Bogotá: Intermedio Editores.

Giraldo, L. G. 2003. Statement by Ambassador Luis Guillermo Giraldo, permanent representative of Colombia at the Open Debate on the Role of the Security Council in the peaceful settlement of disputes, Permanent Mission of Colombia to the United Nations, May 13, New York. Retrieved from *www.colombiaun.org/consejo_seguridad.htm*, accessed May 12, 2015.

Hasenclever, A., et al. 1997. *Theories of International Regimes.* Cambridge: Cambridge University Press.

Holguín, M. A. 2005. Statement of the representative of the Mission of Colombia to the United Nations in the discussions of the General Assembly on the group of topics, II: Freedom from Fear, M. d. C. a.1. United Nations. New York: Mission of Colombia to the United Nations.

Human Rights Watch. 2008. "UN: War on Drugs Does Not Justify Rights Violations." Human Rights Watch, March 10.

Keohane, R. O. 1984. *After Hegemony. Cooperation and Discord in the World Political Economy.* Princeton, NJ: Princeton University Press.

Krasner, S. 1982. "Structural Causes and Regime Consequences: Regimes as Intervening Variables." *International Organization* 36, no. 2: 1–21.

Llorenti, S. S. N.d. *La guerra contra las drogas en Bolivia: Más vino viejo y odres viejos.* Retrieved from *www.noticias.nl/*, accessed May 12, 2015.

Ministerio de Relaciones Exteriores. 2006. *Memoria al Congreso Nacional 2005–2006.* Bogotá: Fondo Editorial Cancillería de San Carlos.

———. 2007. *Memoria al Congreso Nacional 2007.* Bogotá: Fondo Editorial Cancillería de San Carlos.

———. 2009. *Memoria al Congreso Nacional 2009.* Bogotá: Fondo Editorial Cancillería de San Carlos.

Moreno, L. A. 2002. "Aiding Colombia's War on Terrorism." *New York Times*, May 3. Retrieved from *www.nytimes.com/2002/05/03/opinion/aiding-colombia-s-war-on-terrorism.html*, accessed May 12, 2015.

Quimbayo, G. A. 2008. "Cultivos de uso ilícito y ecocidio ¿Es realmente el cultivo ilícito el principal responsable del daño ecosistémico en Colombia?" *Informe sobre políticas de drogas,* no. 28, T. Institute, Amsterdam.

Reagan, N. 1986. Address to the Nation "Just Say No." CNN speeches archive, September 14. Retrieved from *edition.cnn.com/SPECIALS/2004/reagan/stories/speech.archive/just.say.no.html*, accessed May 12, 2015.

Salgado, H. 2004. "Plan Colombia: ¿Guerra contra las drogas o contra las poblaciones amazónicas?" *Bajo el Volcán—Benemérita Universidad Autónoma de Puebla* 4, no. 7: 77–103. Retrieved from *www.colectivodeabogados.org/CINEP-Plan-Colombia-guerra-contra*, accessed May 12, 2015.

Santos, F. 2006. "Países europeos comprometidos en la lucha contra la maldición de la cocaína. Colombia logra total respaldo internacional para la campaña de responsabilidad compartida." *Noticias,* November 2. Vice president of the Republic of Colombia. Retrieved from *www.vicepresidencia.gov.co*, accessed July 12, 2007.

Simmons, B. 2009. *Mobilizing for Human Rights: International Law in Domestic Politics.* New York: Cambridge University Press.

Thoumi, F., and M. Jelsma. 2008. "La normatividad internacional: Soporte del paradigma prohibicionista." In *La batalla perdida contra las drogas: ¿Legalizar es la opción?*, ed. J. M. Galán, R. Vargas, F. Thoumi, and W. Ramírez, 153–231. Bogotá: Intermedio Editores.

Uribe, Á. 2002. Statement of the president of the Republic of Colombia in the 57th Ordinary Session of the United Nations, M. d. C. a.1. United Nations. New York: Mission of Colombia to the United Nations.

———. 2003. Speech by president of Colombia, Álvaro Uribe, to the General Assembly of the United Nations, Permanent Mission of Colombia to the United Nations, September 30, New York. Available from *www.colombiaun.org/consejo_seguridad.htm.*

———. 2009. Speech by President Uribe at the closing of the XV Summit on Climate Change. Presidency of the Republic of Colombia, Copenhagen.

Waever, O. 1995. "Securitization and Desecuritization." In *On Security*, edited by R. D. Lipschutz. New York: Columbia University Press.

WHO (World Health Organization). 1995. "Publicación del estudio global más amplio que se haya realizado sobre el uso de la cocaína." WHO Press release no. 20, March 14.

7 Colombia and Europe Face the Drug Problem

Disagreement Yet Cooperation

Muriel Laurent

In the course of the Pastrana and Uribe administrations, the relations between Colombia and Europe[1] in the field of the fight against drugs were marked by a certain discord that nevertheless has not prevented the development of different axes of cooperation. The disagreement is explained by the divergent approaches to the anti-drug policy of the two actors, as well as by their respective interpretation of the situation in Colombia and the role of drugs in it. On the one hand, whereas Colombia emphasizes a fundamentally repressive policy toward drugs, which it shares with the United States, the European Union has focused on a perspective where the reduction of harm and public health have the priority. On the other hand, while the EU places human rights above the problem of drugs, Colombia regards the fight against narcotics trafficking to be the priority, for being the driving force of the conflict.

To this it is worth adding three other factors: (1) the marked leaning toward the United States of Colombian foreign policy (Ardila, Cardona, and Tickner 2002, 29–30), whereas the EU is seen as an agent of lesser importance; (2) the low priority given to Colombia—and Latin America in general—in European foreign policy, concerned as the EU is with regions that are nearer, less stable, and more strategic for it (Ramírez 2006, 73–74); (3) the preference for promoting regional integration in the rest of the world found in the EU's foreign policy (Europa 2008), whose correlative is establishing relations with integrated blocks rather than individual countries (Sanín et al. 2004, 3).

The above has led European cooperation to follow a specific line in the fight against drugs in Colombia, different from that of the United States and from what Colombia has expected. For the rest, there isn't sufficient knowledge, on a domestic level, of the relations between the EU and Colombia in the field of drugs, as academic studies have warned (Sanín et al. 2004, 1; Ramírez 2006, 97). Below, we try to correct this fault, explaining the disagreement between the respective policies of the two actors (point 1) and offering an assessment of the cooperation that has nevertheless taken place (point 2).

DISCORD

The European Union's Anti-Drug Policy and the European View of Colombia

In this section, we present the main guiding principles of the European Union's anti-drug policy, its action lines in this field, an assessment of the criticisms that have been

Muriel Laurent: Associate professor, History Department, Faculty of Social Sciences, Universidad de los Andes.

made of the European anti-drug fight, and finally a diagnosis of the Colombian situation and the priorities of the EU's cooperation with this country.

Guiding Principles

Three considerations form the basis of the EU's policy in the fight against drugs: (1) its principles and values,[2] social welfare, public health, public security, and a balanced and integrated approach to the drug problem;[3] (2) the relevant agreements of the United Nations; and (3) the juridical framework of the EU and EC and the respective responsibilities of the union, the community, and the member states in this field (Consejo 2004b, 2).[4]

As an interior market, without frontiers and ruled by the free circulation of goods, persons, services, and capital and thus a place where illegal products, agents, and monies can freely circulate, the EU faces multiples concerns, insofar as it considers illegal drugs "a serious threat to the security and health of European society" (Conseil 2008, 7). These concerns are internal consumption and its impact on health, the diversion of chemical products within and outside of its territory, the laundering of capital, the shipment to and trafficking of drugs in its territories, and relations with the countries where drugs are produced or transported (Consejo 2004b). In most of these areas the European institutions[5] have exclusive jurisdiction or one shared with the member states, but they are not responsible for defining the penalization of consumption, which is left to its member nations. This explains the coexistence of states prone to decriminalization, such as the Netherlands and Portugal, and punitive states such as France. The EC believes that these divergent approaches are transcended by the concerns of the political leaders of the EU (Conseil 2008, 7), which are seen, for example, in the priority given to activities aimed at suppressing supply as compared to those aimed at consumption (OEDT 2009, 11).

As the premise and reason for its actions, "the EU acknowledges its share of responsibility for the problem of drugs on a world level, both as a consumer of narcotics and psychotropic substances which originate in third-party countries and in its condition of being a producer and exporter of synthetic drugs in particular; and it is determined to confront these problems" (Consejo 2004b, 5). This commitment to coresponsibility is complemented, as we have noted, by an integrated, multidisciplinary, and balanced approach, with the aim of working in favor of the reduction of consumption in its territory, cooperating with the producer countries by funding projects to support their fight against drug production, acting in accordance with agreements to prevent the diversion of precursor chemicals and the laundering of monies from narcotics trafficking, and promoting cooperation among European police, customs, and judicial authorities (Consejo 2004b, 3; European Commission 2009).

Lines of Action

In harmony with the above, the European Union's three main action lines are the reduction of demand, the reduction of supply, and international cooperation.

With regard to the *reduction of demand*, the EU seeks a considerable reduction of consumption, dependence, and risks for health and society through prevention and access to treatment programs (Consejo 2004b). The assessment of consumption—lower in the EU than the United States—is that cannabis is the most widely used illegal drug; the second most widely used one is cocaine along with other stimulants like amphetamines and ecstasy; the consumption of heroin is on a relatively small scale, but its social and health cost—though lower than in the United States—is high (European Commission 2009). Consumption continues to be high and is characterized by a stabilization or decrease in the consumption of heroin, cannabis, and synthetic drugs, compared to an increase in the consumption of cocaine in certain member states, an increase associated with the fact that the EU has been the target of a vast trade in this product in recent years (Conseil 2008, 8). Among recent concerns is an increase of polytoxicomania, the combined consumption of different substances (OEDT 2009, 15). In this field, the EMCDDA works to consolidate a better knowledge of the reality of consumption in the EU, while the commission finances three programs for health and prevention.[6]

With regard to the *reduction of supply*, the EU seeks a substantial improvement in actions aimed at the production and illegal trafficking of drugs, precursor chemicals, and capital, that is, against the organized crime devoted to the drug trade, which implies intensifying police, customs, and judicial cooperation (Consejo 2004b). To achieve that, the EU combines its legislation on the diversion of precursor chemicals and the prevention of money laundering—both internally and externally, as well as law enforcement initiatives—with cooperation agreements, projects, and intelligence operations with third-party countries (European Commission 2009, 9). Insofar as this has implications for the security of its citizens, the EU thinks it is important to focus its intelligence work on "the suppliers responsible for the greatest harms or who represent the biggest threats" (Conseil 2008, 9).

With regard to *international cooperation*, the EU seeks to reduce the production of drugs and their availability in Europe, as well as assist third-party countries in their fight and promote a balanced approach to the problem in international forums, one that combines the reduction of demand and of supply. This is done by:

- helping those countries to become more effective in reducing demand and supply by including the subject in the general dialogue of the Foreign and Security Policy and in cooperation for development.
- integrating the subject of drugs into cooperation for development (Comisión 2007) to help increase the sustainability of efforts to reduce supply—the encouragement of alternative means of subsistence—and the consequences of consumption.
- facilitating international police and customs cooperation to improve the effectiveness of the fight against trafficking and production and thus reduce supply (Consejo 2004b; European Commission 2009).

The EU has several areas of concern about the producer countries and drug shipments toward European territory due to the arrival of heroin, cocaine, and cannabis resin (European Commission 2009; Consejo 2004b). The above explains its logic for allocating resources to cooperation for development. By way of example, for projects financed throughout the world (European 2009), in 2006 the commission gave some 666 million euros to those related to drugs in third-party countries. Most of these funds went toward alternative development projects focused on preventing the growing of opium and coca, since the EU regards illegal crops as an important component of drugs supply. Nearly two-thirds of these funds went for projects in Afghanistan and nearly a third to Colombia, Bolivia, and Peru. More than three-quarters (76 percent) went on alternative development and of the projects it financed sixty-two were in Afghanistan, forty-one in the three Andean countries, thirty-six in other countries of Latin America and the Caribbean, two in the Andean Community, and the rest in other regions[7] (European Commission 2009). Although there is no doubt about the relative weight of aid to the Andean countries, the projects in Afghanistan (against heroin) have a clear priority, and the importance given to supply routes is notable.

Assessment and Criticisms

The EU has to confront the multiple facets of the problem in its own territory, which is not only a market for Colombian cocaine. To achieve that, the EU does not accept the scenario of a "war on drugs," since it believes that prohibition has caused important unintentional but partly predictable harms, nor does the EU include any military component in its action lines (Labrousse 2006, 47–48), which, in any case, is beyond its powers, since this area continues to be the responsibility of the member states and they do not agree on the validity of using that resource in the fight against drugs. The subject of drugs is handled from the standpoint of public health, prevention, and the reduction of harm, without neglecting aspects of security and law enforcement and taking into consideration that drugs are a "complex phenomenon which requires a long-term approach to bring about changes" (Conseil 2008, 9).

It is not superfluous to underline a series of criticisms the EU has received about the political, economic, and bureaucratic difficulties of its fight. In political terms, (1) it has not been sufficiently emphatic in defending its policy in the international arena, although that would force it to clash with the United States, (2) it tends to set forth objectives that are so ambitious and so long-term that it does not wind up achieving them, and (3) it has still failed to unify its legislation on the punishment of consumption. As for its economic difficulties, its financial resources are usually not enough to support its anti-drug policy and, in the end, its international cooperation. Among its bureaucratic or institutional deficiencies are the following: (1) there is a lack of knowledge and reliable data about the availability of illegal drugs in Europe and the impact of the projects it finances in third-party countries; (2) it has to improve the institutional coordination among the multiplicity of agencies and responsibilities it has in the field; (3) with regard to international cooperation, its officials lack the requisite expertise, the process of evaluating aid projects is faulty, and the European Commission's slowness in disbursing aid is notable (Estievenart 2006, 26–27; Labrousse 2006, 40 and 57–59; Ramírez 2006, 96; Conseil 2008, 8).

Analysis of the European Commission's Handling of the Colombian Situation

The European Commission publishes a *Country Strategy Paper* on its policy for third-party countries, which in the case of Colombia was put out in 2007 (Comisión 2007). The document provides a diagnosis of the situation of that country and on that basis decides on the kind of cooperation for development that would be relevant for that country. Its central points are:

- The country suffers from an internal armed conflict where guerrilla groups, government forces, and paramilitary groups are fighting each other. The government is trying to re-establish the authority of the state in regions traditionally abandoned by it. The conflict has caused the forced displacement of between 1.5 to 3 million people and nearly three thousand persons have been kidnapped during its course. There are high rates of violations of human rights and international humanitarian law and they are usually the work of illegal armed agents (the FARC and AUC), but sometimes are the responsibility of the military.
- It is the world's biggest producer of cocaine (57 percent). The illegal economy deriving from that is both a result and a cause of the conflict. Most of the coca plots (70 percent) belong to small producers. Opium poppy is also grown (the main source of heroin on the US market).
- There are great economic and social inequalities. Poverty and the trend toward the concentration of property in the hands of big landowners, narcotics traffickers, and illegal armed groups nourish the armed conflict.
- The basic needs of the indigenous and Afro-Colombian populations are unmet, they suffer from a higher rate of poverty and illiteracy than the rest of the population, and they are victimized by the armed conflict in a scenario of forced displacement, the production of illegal crops, and fumigations.
- The country has 10 percent of world biodiversity, which suffers from the harmful impact of poverty, the illegal extraction of timber, the extension of the agricultural frontier, and illegal crops.

On the basis of this assessment, the EC has decided that its priorities in Colombia are the negotiated solution of the conflict, the promotion of peace, care for the victims of violence, respect for human rights, the fight against drugs, the reduction of poverty, and sustainable economic and social development. To achieve that, it has concentrated its cooperation efforts since 2001 on the establishment of peace, arguing that there is not a single solution to attaining it and one needs to simultaneously attack the different aspects of the conflict, the interrelationship of which is noted in the diagnosis. This approach has been evidenced in its political support for negotiations with the FARC before February 2002, the establishment and financing of the Peace Laboratories, and its participation in the meetings of the "donor" countries.

In accordance with this view, the fight against drugs is an effort aimed, above all, at the medium term; the promotion of peace includes cooperating with the government "to attack the scourge of drugs, whose production and trafficking directly nourish the conflict" (Comisión 2007), and acknowledging its coresponsibility, supporting initiatives for alternative development, fighting against consumption in Europe, and working to dismantle the networks of traffickers. The short-term action of the EU is focused on providing aid to the victims, its medium-term aim is to promote peace on a local and national level, and its long-term aim is to secure a permanent solution to the conflict by promoting development for all sectors of the population and thus attacking the root of the armed conflict. All this implies that the current orientation of the EU gives more priority to ending the conflict and securing peace than the fight against drugs that characterized the EU's policy in the 1990s. In that regard, the change is attributable to the work of Colombian foreign policy, which began to emphasize the subject of drugs during the Barco administration, and then, starting under the Pastrana administration, shifted the emphasis to the armed conflict, with violations of human rights always a special concern (Consejo 2004a; 2004c; 2007; 2009).

Colombian Foreign Policy: In the Fight Against Drugs and Toward the EU

The Pastrana and Uribe governments converged in their aim of eliminating the production and trafficking of drugs, making them central areas of their programs and asking for help from the international community for those ends. Despite this continuity, the differences between the respective focuses of each administration are notorious. Before turning to an assessment of those years, however, we should first look at their respective proposals and the European reaction to each.

The Pastrana Administration

If on the domestic level Pastrana's most important initiative was the search for a negotiated settlement with the FARC, his most important foreign policy initiative was Plan Colombia (PC). PC emphasized the use of a repressive and militarist strategy to attack narcotics trafficking and asked the United States to finance it, with an additional component of social and economic development presented to Europe in the hope that it would finance it. The difference between the implementation of one strategy and the other led to criticisms of the Colombian government, since while a strong lobby was mounted in the United States, the approach to Europe was slow and haphazard (Mendiluce 2000, 28–29; Ramírez 2006, 81).

In the European response, the rejection of PC by the European Parliament, European Commission, and most of the member states was emphatic, given their conviction that (1) a greater militarization of the fight against drugs would carry the risk of an escalation of the conflict in the region, (2) the repressive and militarist nature of the plan contradicted the aims of the projects the EC was financing in the country (Mendiluce 2000, 28), and (3) it did not coincide with the EU's support for the peace negotiations and belief that a negotiated solution was the only way to secure a lasting peace (Ramírez 2006; Labrousse 2006; Roy 2001; European Parliament 2001). The EU nevertheless chose to strengthen its cooperation by financing projects that were related to what it had already been doing;[8] in particular, it enlarged the Peace Laboratories.

Despite this concerted position on the part of the EU, some of its member states chose to exercise their freedom to diverge from the common response and maintain relations with Colombia in accordance with their own interests. Spain and the United Kingdom, whose respective leaders—Aznar and Blair—were close to the US government, supported PC (Labrousse 2006, 51; Ramírez 2006, 83). The military aid offered by those two countries[9] caused a sharp reaction from the other member states, given that it did not fit in with their guiding principles (Molano 2009, 109). The reaction to PC showed that with the exception of this minority response, the EU was opposed to the dominant policies of the "war on drugs." But, as Labrousse pointed out (2006, 52),

> the dissemination of this position was very discreet. The EU never publicly criticized Plan Colombia, with the pretext that the problem exclusively

concerned Colombia and United States. It did not propose an independent study of the effects of the fumigations.

The EU offered its support for the peace negotiations with the FARC and allowed some of the commanders of that guerrilla group to visit Europe (Ramírez 2006, 79; Roy 2001, 5–27). When the Colombian government broke off the negotiations in February 2002, its decision was supported by the EU. After the terrorist attacks of September 11, 2001, in the United States, the Pastrana government asked the EU to put the Colombian armed groups on its list of terrorists, which it did by including them in the Common Position 2004/309/CFSD, which allows it to take measures against the laundering of assets derived from narcotics trafficking (Ramírez 2006, 87; Consejo 2004d).

The Uribe Administrations

The two Uribe administrations focused their handling of the conflict, seen as the terrorism of illegal actors allied with narcotics traffickers, on the policy of "democratic security" and the continuation of PC. This policy included an important program for alternative development, and the government sought external financing for part of it. In 2004, the president's European tour was criticized by some members of the European Parliament because certain sectors in Europe thought he favored the paramilitaries. When the Uribe government asked for support for its alternative development program, the EU was in favor of continuing with the projects begun under the previous government (Molano 2009, 105–21), despite the inconsistencies between the Colombian focus on national security and the European one on development and the EC's requisites for authorizing such aid. The EU, however, did not accept Colombia's request to study the possibility of military aid for the rescue of those kidnapped by the FARC, made by president Uribe during his visit to Europe in 2004 (BBC 2004; Molano 2007, 60).

Beginning in 2006, the Colombian Chancellery, through its embassy in Brussels, undertook an information campaign to increase the visibility of Colombia by publicizing the achievements of the "democratic security" policy and counteracting the positive image of the guerrilla groups among certain sectors in Europe (Castañeda 2009, 176). Likewise, Vice President Francisco Santos, working from London, promoted the Shared Responsibility (Responsabilidad Compartida) campaign, which sought to strengthen "awareness about the ecocide [caused by] cocaine in Colombia" and "share the responsibility [of the problem of illegal drugs] in order to find solutions,"[10] with an emphasis, hitherto little seen in the international arena, on the environmental damage caused by the growing of coca and trafficking of narcotics.

Thus, even though the United States remained the main focal point of Colombian foreign relations, in those eight years an increasing attention was given to the EU as Colombia tried to counteract its low visibility and win more cooperation from Europe. Noticeable, however, was the government's repeated tendency to make declarations that went down well on a domestic level and clearly obeyed its aims, but failed to take into account the reality of the relations between Europe and Colombia. The following two examples illustrate this trend.

The first happened when Vice President Francisco Santos said that the EU is "a very important vein [*veta*]" to mine to strengthen the fight against drugs (Comunidad 2008a), doubtlessly with the aim of obtaining more financial support. But it was said in a way that implied that there was not a sharp difference of views between the parties on the problem, and it gave the Colombian public the impression that European cooperation was null. Thus the European perception was that, as Colombia showed little concern for being inconsistent and/or uninformed, it had consciously set out to take advantage of European resources.

On another occasion, Francisco Santos stated that Peru and Colombia hoped to "sensitize" Europe about narcotics trafficking (Comunidad 2008b). In addition to that surprising appeal, useful for portraying themselves as "abandoned" in the fight against drugs, the Andean countries also underlined their interest in getting more collaboration from Europe. Although the Colombian strategy clearly included the demand for international funding, it was not really clear if it also referred to other kinds of cooperation. This model of asking for the financing of projects, which was already open to criticism in 1999–2000 with Plan Colombia because it repeated the scheme used by Barco in 1990, continued to be the order of the day for Colombia in 2003–2005 and again in 2008. This habit of asking for funds caused Colombia to lose the "opportunity to link itself more politically to the European Union" for the peaceful solution of the conflict (Mendiluce 2000, 27), a link that might have positive effects on reducing the production of drugs. In other words, instead of taking advantage of the opportunities offered by the EU, the Colombian tendency to appeal for financing, combined with its lack of interest in the European view of the situation, makes its opportunity to enjoy the real support the EU might offer it even more remote.

Balance Sheet

Pastrana's idea that peace was necessary to combat drugs was closer to European views than Uribe's denial of the armed conflict, emphasis on fighting narco-terrorism, and attitude of "zero tolerance" toward drugs (see Chapter 8). While it is true that both governments thought that international, and thus European, cooperation was needed to confront the drug problem, they did it through strategies that were only partly in line with European interests.

First, the search for military support, both through PC and for the liberation of kidnapping victims, was either rejected or ignored. While the Colombian attempt to secure both military and social assistance from the international community roughly worked, insofar as it got US financing for the former and EU financing for the latter, the result was counterproductive since it caused the EU to be skeptical about Colombia's attempt to combine two incompatible strategies. Second, Pastrana's attempt to link the EU to a negotiated ending of the conflict coincided with European interests and was thus successful, while, on the contrary, Uribe's attempt to get Europe committed to the idea of narco-terrorism and the absence of an armed conflict did not work. While successive Colombian administrations and the EU have agreed on the need to strengthen the Colombian state, the EU gives priority to the strengthening of institutions like the judicial system and the implementation of economic and social reforms, while Colombia has emphasized the strengthening of its armed forces. Third, both administrations' attempts to seek more aid for development worked, although Europe thinks this strategy is repetitive and could be much more effective if there were a stronger Colombian commitment to the search for a negotiated settlement.

Fourth, the Colombian strategy of internationalizing the conflict (under Pastrana) or defining the problem as narco-terrorism (under Uribe) has doubtlessly borne fruit, in the sense of helping Europe to attain a better knowledge of the Colombian situation and sending more missions to Colombia.

COOPERATION

The Place of the Anti-Drug Fight in the Political Dialogue and Cooperation Agreements

One of the basic aspects of cooperation between the EU and Colombia are the spaces for political dialogue where the parties discuss matters of joint interest, and the agreements that have been signed over the years. These two kinds of mechanisms, which have the merit of already being in place and of evidencing some mutual priorities—above all in the case of the agreements—nevertheless run into difficulties when they are applied.

Coresponsibility is the focus of the two spaces for political dialogue that exist in the field of drugs. In 1998 the EU, Latin America, and the Caribbean began holding an annual, high-level political dialogue on illegal drugs. Twice every six months, their representatives meet for more technical discussions about cooperation and coordination. As a complement to this activity, the EU is currently beginning to allocate a budget for projects to analyze the national anti-drug policies of the producer countries (Molano 2007, 48; Arenas 2010). Since 1995 there has been a specialized, high-level dialogue on drugs between the EU and the Andean Community of Nations (CAN), where information is exchanged, national and regional programs are presented, and cooperation projects are discussed (Molano 2007, 40 and 49; Arenas 2010; Kurtenbach 2005, 8). Although it is worth noting that the EU does not engage in this kind of dialogue with any other region of the world, which is evidence of a special interest, it should be underlined that the initiative has suffered from the institutional and political weakness of the CAN. In fact, the meeting of the joint CAN-EU Commission in March 2010, which also deals with the subject of drugs and is crucial to the dialogue, was its first in two years (Kurtenbach 2005, 8; Arenas 2010).

The framework for cooperation continues to be governed by the Framework Agreement on Cooperation between the European Economic Community and the Cartagena Agreement and its member countries (Bolivia, Colombia, Ecuador, Peru, and Venezuela, which was signed in 1993 and came into force in May 1998. In fact, the Political Dialogue and Cooperation Agreement between the CAN and its member states and the EU and its member states, signed in 2003, has still not been implemented due to its pending ratification by Colombia and Greece (Delegación de la Comisión Europea en Bogotá 2004; Pauwels 2010). It is important that the parties on both side of the Atlantic finish the ratification processes, given that the general legal framework for cooperation was established in the first half of the 1990s and another agreement more suited to the current context was convened seven years ago but has not been ratified yet.

Another two agreements, of a thematic nature, should be mentioned above all in reference to the control of precursor chemicals and policing, matters of vigilance and security of interest to both parties, and reasons for an alliance in the fight against narcotics trafficking.

In December 1995 Colombia and the EC signed a bilateral agreement to control the supply of precursor chemicals used in the manufacture of illegal drugs (the same treaty was signed by other countries of the CAN). Its purpose is to allow for mutual assistance in supervising the trade of these products, through consultation and the exchange of information when there is a suspicion of diversion, but without prejudice to the legitimate interests of trade and industry. Its annex A lists a series of products (like potassium permanganate, acetone, and ethyl ether), which require the presentation of an export permit to the country of destination. The agreement, in force since January 1997, laid down the establishment of a Joint Follow-up Group to administer it (Molano 2007, 49–50; "Acuerdo . . ." 1995, 11–17; Treaties Office Database n.d.). Our request for information about its application, functioning, and results over the past twelve years[11] received no response from the National Narcotics Administration or the EU delegation in Colombia. Nevertheless, on the basis of the meager knowledge in Colombia of an initiative begun some years ago under the Pastrana administration, the results have been far from encouraging.

In April 1999 the newspaper *El Tiempo*, reporting on the seizure of twelve tons of potassium permanganate, denounced the lack of control and cooperation in the export of chemical substances from Europe to Colombia. The attorney general (*fiscal general*) and the director of the police expressed their strong concern: "We feel alone in the fight against drugs," "we feel abandoned in this fight," and "the European Union should collaborate by neutralizing the trafficking of the inputs they produce." These expressions of lack of support for Colombia in the drug fight led the author of the article to speak of the need for at least some help "to control the trafficking of chemical inputs," since the European authorities "do little or nothing to stop their exports to organizations of narcotics traffickers" (Bustos 1999, 1A and 9A). These statements reveal a lack of knowledge about the existence of an agreement on precursor chemicals that had already been in force for three years and would have enabled the attorney general and police chief to make a protest that would have been diplomatically valuable for Colombia, though essentially groundless. This ignorance is surprising and is difficult to explain. If the restrictions under the agreement were not being adequately enforced, the Colombian authorities could have criticized its weak implementation, instead of speaking as if the treaty did not exist, or pointed out that such chemical products are also of legal industrial use and it is difficult to prohibit their trade.

Under the Uribe government, Europol (the European Police Office) and the Colombian police signed an agreement, in force since the end of 1994, on the fight against narcotics trafficking, money laundering, terrorism, the white slave trade, and illegal migration. To prevent, detect, eliminate, and investigate the activities of international organized crime, this agreement facilitates the exchange of technical and strategic information such as policing methods, training, and information on trafficking routes. Thanks to the presence of two liaison officers from the Colombian police at the headquarters of Europol, the resulting cooperation has already shown some successes in operations against narcotics trafficking and the FARC (Council 2004; Europol 2009, 23; Europol 2008, 45; Europol 2004; Presidencia 2005). In 2009, negotiations began for an agreement of an operational kind to strengthen the pact, with the possibility of exchanging personal data as well. Before this new agreement was signed in September 2010, Colombia had to provide guarantees that it would sufficiently protect internal data (Celare 2009; ABC 2010; *El Espectador* 2009).

The Anti-Drug Fight and Trade Preferences

When, at the end of the 1980s, Colombian president Virgilio Barco called for the international coresponsibility needed for the fight against drugs, the then European Economic Community (EEC) responded by offering Colombia, among other things, a system of tariff reductions for the agricultural and industrial goods coming from the Andean countries that were producers of narcotics. This system, established in 1991 and known as the Andean Drugs' Generalized System of Preferences, allowed a series of legal products from the Andean countries to enter the Common Market without tariffs or with very low tariffs, in recognition of the high cost they paid in the drug fight and their condition as developing nations. The basic idea was that reduced import tariffs would boost their exports and thus motivate the peasant-farmers responsible for illegal crops to turn to legal produce. It also sought to diversify their exports and reduce their dependence on raw materials. Although the list of products was ample, a product as important for Colombia as bananas was excluded due to Europe's interest in benefiting African, Caribbean, and Pacific countries. Its periodical renewal, which always occurred, was conditioned to advances in the fight against narcotics trafficking (Laurent 1997, 426–40; Ramírez 2006, 75 and 77). In commercial terms, the results of this tariff privilege were undeniable: "the exporters saved a total of 120 million dollars per year thanks to the GSP" (Mendiluce 2000, 27), and according to the Secretariat of the CAN,

> during the period of its strongest increase (1993–1996), the GSP represented 983 million USD and has generated a gross product of 1.8 billion USD and 120,000 jobs. The GSP has allowed for the diversification of Andean exports to the European market. In fact, between 1991 and 2000, the number of products rose from 1,554 to 1,923. In the case of Colombia, 95% of its products enter the Union without paying customs duties, and it is the country that has taken the greatest advantage of the GSP. (Labrousse 2006, 43)

As a tool in the anti-drug fight, on the other hand, it cannot be said that the GSP has achieved its purpose (Sanín et al. 2004, 4) insofar as it has not had the expected result of reducing the illegal crops grown by small farmers.

In 2005, this Andean drugs GSP was replaced by the GSP Plus, which focuses on developing countries, on the condition that they comply with the main international conventions on labor rights, sustainable development and environmental protection, human rights, governance, and the fight against drugs (Comisión 2007; Molano 2007, 51–54). With this modification, the aspect of drugs originally included in it has become much less visible, but the logic of reducing tariffs is maintained and now covers 7,200 products (bananas continue to be excluded). According to figures published in 2007, the GSP Plus benefits 20 percent of Colombian exports to the EU, and, given that 64 percent of Colombian exports to the EU are already completely exempt from tariffs under its most favored nation status, the result is that 84 percent of Colombian products sold in Europe are exempt from customs duties (Comisión 2007, 18). The positive result for Colombia is maintained, but the EC has insisted that it should take more advantage of the concessions (Koetsenruijter 2005; *Euronotas* 2005, 6).

With the aim of obtaining even greater access to the European market, Colombia and the EU negotiated and signed a Multipartite Trade Agreement (the name used by the EU) or, as Colombia calls it, a Free Trade Treaty. In 2007 an Agreement of Association with the CAN was proposed, but its trade aspect had to be restricted with the subsequent withdrawal of Bolivia and Ecuador from the negotiations. According to an estimate made by Vice President Santos in 2008, this agreement will help the strategy for fighting against narcotics trafficking by opening up a market of alternative products of particular benefit to peasant-farmers (Comunidad 2008a). His assertion sounds like mere politics, insofar as he seemed to forget that the GSP Plus and a number of cooperation projects have already been seeking this objective and their impact on small farmers remains to be seen. Santos should have focused instead on Colombia's efforts to enlarge the list to include products currently excluded from the GSP Plus and open the European market for agricultural ones.[12] In any case, the negotiations for the trade agreement have obtained more benefits than the current ones, for example for bananas and sugar, but it won't come into force for ten years. It will have the advantage of not being unilateral nor subject to a conditioned renewal and thus more democratic than the previous ones. Nevertheless, none of the parties now justifies it as a tool for fighting against narcotics trafficking.

The Role of the Anti-Drug Fight in Cooperation for Development

Another response of the then EEC to President Barco's call for it to assume its part of the responsibility for waging the anti-drug fight was its financing of a package of projects. When this funding was set into motion through the Special Cooperation Program, the EEC already counted on a North-South budget line to help the developing countries fight against drugs.[13] The money under this budget item was always modest, and its disbursement ended in 2003 (Estievenart 2006, 29; Labrousse 2006, 40 and 48–49). When this option of financing was canceled, in the same period when the GSP changed, the projects mainly aimed at the fight against drugs tended to become much less prominent.

For more than a decade now, the main focus of the EU's projects in Colombia has been peace, which is complemented by other aims like justice, human rights, displaced persons, and drugs. In the period from 2001 to 2006, the cooperation amounted to 105 million euros in programmable aid (in concert with the Colombian government) and 170 million euros in nonprogrammable aid.[14] For the period from 2007 to 2013, programmable aid amounted to 160 million euros, distributed as follows: 70 percent for peace and stability, including alternative development; 20 percent for the state of law, justice, and human rights; and 10 percent for productivity, competitiveness, and trade (Comisión 2007, 30–34). The fight against drugs is included in both the first and last categories, as explained below.

In the first category are included the Peace Laboratories, which aim to reduce illegal activities, one of which is the production and trafficking of drugs. This aspect sets out to strengthen "actions for alternative development so that they will turn into an important

TABLE 7.1.

Peace Laboratories	Area covered	Duration	Budget
I	Magdalena Medio – 30 municipalities in the departments of Cesar, Bolívar, Antioquia, and Santander	Eight years 2002–2010	42.22 million euros (UE: 34.8, Col.: 7.42)
II	62 municipalities of eastern Antioquia, Norte de Santander and Alto Patía, Colombian Massif	Eight years 2003–2011	41.40 million euros (UE: 33, Col.: 8.4)
III	Part of the department of Meta and Montes de María in the departments of Bolívar and Sucre	Four years 2006–2010	30.25 million euros (UE: 24.2, Col.: 6.05)

Source: Compiled on the basis of Sig/Web Delcol.

part of the initiatives for peace and economic development" (Ibid., 31). As shown in Table 7.1, the three laboratories are cofinanced by the Colombian government. These resources support a multitude of small initiatives that arise from grassroots social organizations, and their general objective is to deactivate the causes that set off the conflict, encourage dialogue and peaceful coexistence through the use of mechanisms of peaceful resistance and protection of the civilian population, and favor a sustainable socioeconomic development (Castañeda 2009, 164; Delegación 2004; Labrousse 2006, 56).

The chosen regions are characterized by a worsening of the armed conflict and high levels of violence, marginality, and poverty accelerated by the presence of armed groups and their financing by illegal crops. Let us look at the economic causes of these situations (the other causes are institutional and social), since the funds for the fight against drugs are focused on them: "lack of viable economic alternatives; the non-sustainable and inadequate use of natural resources and environmental deterioration; low productivity and the volatile prices of traditional crops; the disintegration of the rural economy" (Delegación 2004). Among its specific objectives and as one of its components is the fight against drugs, in the following terms: reorientation of the course of economic activities, productive activities and alternative development, productive and environmental processes for equity and sustainable development, a sustainable socioeconomic development that improves the conditions of life of the target population in harmony with environment, actions for territorial and alternative development, reduction of illegal economies (Sig/Web Delcol n.d.). Thus the alternative development proposed for the laboratories aims at eliminating the peasant-farmers' dependence on coca, allowing coca growers to replace it with other sources of income, and discouraging poor persons from migrating to regions where coca is grown. Since this alternative development includes voluntary manual eradication, a willingness to give up the growing of coca is seen as an aspect of a culture of peace (Labrousse 2006, 54 and 56; Molano 2009, 103). With regard to these objectives, the fact that the three Peace Laboratories are programmed for long periods, in contrast with cooperation projects, is a positive factor.

One of the conditions the EU requested for the sound development of the laboratories was to suspend the fumigation of illegal crops (Castañeda 2009, 164; Vincenti et al. 2005, 20). But even when the Colombian government was fumigating in the department of Meta, the European position was not clear, since it did not exert any pressure on

Colombia to honor this condition (Molano 2009, 113–14). Our inability to obtain data on the percentage of the above-mentioned funds that are devoted to alternative development is regrettable for the purposes of this study and makes it difficult to estimate the impact of the Peace Laboratories and of cooperation for development in general. The significant fact is that the funds from the European budget assigned to Colombia have increased (though they are still less than those assigned to Afghanistan), an achievement that is due to Colombia's insistence on obtaining international aid, the mutual interest in alternative development, and the European focus on peace. We make a final observation about European aid in general and the Peace Laboratories in particular. If one accepts Thoumí's argument (2009, 60–82) about the central role played in the phenomenon of narcotics trafficking in Colombia by the breach between legal and social norms, and the resulting need to develop policies to close that breach, then Colombian demands to the EU might be usefully centered on this problem. The laboratories, which focus on a culture of peaceful coexistence, are working toward this ideal and could be given a larger role in its attainment.

The general objective of productivity, competitiveness, and trade is to strengthen Colombia's capacity to integrate itself into the globalized economy, and one of its specific objectives is to find outlets for products that provide an alternative to illegal crops in regions where there are alternative development projects (Comisión 2007, 33–34). In this category two projects were carried out. The one for local economic development and trade (development of small and medium businesses) had a European funding of 6 million euros and a Colombian counterpart funding of 1.56 million euros for the period from 2008 to 2011. It took place in the departments of Valle del Cauca, Boyacá, Santander, Cesar, and Bolívar. Its general objective was to "to promote an equitable and sustainable local economic development in the country, as well as decent employment for its population." The one for technical assistance to trade (support for trade) had an EU funding of 4.4 million euros and a Colombian one of 1.01 million euros and a national coverage (2008–2012). Its general objective was to "promote Colombian exports by strengthening internal competitiveness and productive investments through the institutional strengthening of the system of foreign trade" (Sig/Web Delcol n.d.).

Finally, in collaboration with the Andean Community, the EU runs an anti-drug project known as the Program to fight illegal drugs in the Andean Community (Pradi-Can), which seeks to strengthen the national drug-monitoring centers and link them into a network, as well as develop regional activities for controlling precursor chemicals in the CAN and improve the capacity of those countries to undertake analyses of illegal drugs. The budget for 2007–2013 is 4 million euros, of which 3.25 million come from the Commission (Europa 2008). This is the only community project operating in Colombia whose heading specifically refers to the fight against drugs.

RECOMMENDATIONS

To understand the substance of the EU's relations with Colombia in the fight against drugs, one has to take into account the EU's preference for approaching the subject from the standpoint of public health and cooperation for development, and not of militarized repression. Europe's interpretation of the Colombian situation emphasizes a negotiated solution to the armed conflict, while it regards drug production and narcotics trafficking as aspects, not the main cause, of such a conflict—something we pointed at when we discussed how the drug problem has been conflated with the issue of peace. Europe also gives a central importance to human rights. This is a consensus policy of the EU, which offers an opportunity Colombia could exploit. In the midst of the disagreements over procedures between Colombia and Europe, there is a shared wish for results and this has led the EU to cooperate with Colombia in several matters, by increasing its budget and political support for programs in the country, among other efforts. These may grow even more if Colombia were to have a better understanding of the European policy on drugs and know how to take advantage of it to promote programs aimed at reducing illegal crops.

The EU has assumed its coresponsibility by fighting in its own territory against consumption and the circulation of the money of the narcotics traffickers, and also by signing agreements with the producing states giving them a favorable access to its market and funding for projects. By contrast, Colombia has consistently claimed that Europe's role in the fight against drugs is not sufficient. In part, this is because it does not have the same objectives as certain sectors in Colombia. But it is not always clear what the Colombian government expects the EU to do, taking into account the limits on its actions. It is clear that the Colombian government would like a type of cooperation—military—that the EU is not willing or authorized to provide. In this sense, we recommend that Colombia revise its focus on the anti-drug fight, which would allow for a convergence between the two parties and increase the possibilities of European cooperation.

In any case, the EU and its member countries have a variety of budget lines that might be taken better advantage of, since it is up to the third parties (their governments and NGOs in particular) to present the projects to be considered. Colombia has recently placed much more weight on coresponsibility in the environmental field. The funding allocated for the environment in the EC's budget could be made use of and approaches could made to the member states who are interested in funding such projects. Beyond that, in view of the current activities to end the conflict and narcotics trafficking on the part of the Peace Laboratories, the length of such programs could be extended, remembering that the structural problems they are tackling require a long-term effort. Another channel for development aid that might be better exploited is the budget line for the fight against demand in third-party countries, which, if Colombia requests its reactivation, might allow it to better deal with drug consumption and addiction within the country (see Chapter 5). There is also the possibility of cooperation with the EMCDDA, which has expertise in measuring consumption and related information.

Additionally, Colombia needs to improve its knowledge of and to take into better account the responsibilities of the different institutions and agencies of the EU, the levels on which they operate, the mechanisms which pertain to each, and the officials to be approached (*El Tiempo* 2005a, 1 and 4; 2005b, 7). This means the country must strengthen its institutional capacity to correct the current situation, where the implementation of its foreign policy on narcotics trafficking is dispersed among different entities (Puyo 2002, 423–25). And it would be worth treating the problem of narcotics trafficking as a matter of regional interest that crosses borders and is common to the Andean countries. Although it is not yet the right moment for that, a joint approach with neighboring countries, preferably through the CAN, would be highly advantageous.

NOTES

I would like to thank Diana Mejía and Victoria Pauwels (of the Colombian Chancellery in Bogotá) and Héctor Arenas (of the embassy in Brussels) for the help they gave me.

1. By Europe I mean the European Union (EU), as the entity mainly responsible for many aspects of foreign relations (I only mention some of its member states in specific cases where their policies were different from that of the EU). The EU is made up of twenty-seven member states that have delegated their respective sovereignty to the EU in certain fields. These supra-national policies are handled by the European Community (EC). In the case of foreign relations, commercial policy is an exclusive concern of the EC and cooperation for development is a shared responsibility of the member states and the EC. Other policies, like the Common Foreign and Security Policy (CFSP) and the policy for penalizing consumption, are intergovernmental, without yielding sovereignty.
2. Human dignity, freedom, democracy, equality, solidarity, the state of law, and human rights.
3. This combines the reduction of supply and the reduction of demand, with a priority on the reduction of harm.
4. The documents of the main European institutions (Council of the European Union, European Commission, European Parliament), whether in Spanish, English, or French, are cited in parentheses under the first word of the name of the institution responsible for the authorship of the document.
5. The council establishes the general policy guidelines and, in its ministerial version, participates in the legislative process with the European Parliament. The latter also encourages political debate, while the commission manages policies, particularly its Directorate-General of Public Health and its Directorate-General of Foreign Relations. Several specialized agencies complement this activity, particularly the European Monitoring Centre for Drugs and Drug Addiction (EMCDDA) and Europol (Consejo 2004b). The mission of the EMCDDA is to provide the EU and its member states with an objective view of the drug problem in Europe and a solid basis for it to discuss the subject. Europol is the police agency of the EU, the objective of which is to make Europe a safer place by helping the national police agencies fight against serious kinds of crime and international terrorism (see the websites of these agencies).
6. The Public Health program (2008–2013, 321.5 million euros) seeks to strengthen the health and safety of citizens, promote health and reduce health inequalities, and produce and disseminate information and knowledge about health. The Drugs Prevention and Information program (2007–2013, 21.35 million euros) works to prevent and reduce the use of drugs and drugs dependence and harm.
7. Twenty-eight in the Balkans and the Mediterranean, twenty in Central and Eastern Europe, forty-nine in Asia, thirty-three in Africa, eleven in Russia, one in the South Caucasus, seven in Iran, and forty-two in other countries and regions.
8. Two donors meetings were held in the year 2000—one in Madrid in July and another in Bogotá in October—which defined the European contributions for cooperation in structural fields like violence, economic and social development, institutional strengthening, and respect for human rights (*Euronotas* 2000a, 7; *Euronotas* 2000b, 5).
9. In 2003 and 2004, the delivery of military aid by Spain for the fight against narco-terrorism was established (Molano 2009, 105). The military aid of the United Kingdom had been supplied since the beginning of the 1990s ("UK Ends Bilateral Military Aid" 2009).

10. Cf. *www.sharedresponsibility.gov.co.*
11. We would have liked to determine, for example, how many seizures are made with the aid of this agreement, how many chemicals are prevented from reaching their destination, and whether the exchange of information foreseen in the agreement takes place.
12. Agricultural protectionism on the part of Europe has been criticized by the developing countries in the framework of the World Trade Organization.
13. Between 1987 and 1995, nineteen projects were financed in Colombia. Most were for the reduction of demand—ten for the prevention of consumption and five for the treatment of drug addictions—and the rest for the reduction of supply—three for crop reconversion or substitution and one for repression. The latter was for a satellite information system for detecting and controlling illegal coca and poppy crops (Laurent 1977, 399 and appendix 11).
14. The aid was distributed in the following way: 46% to support the peace process; 16% for displaced persons; 16% for the environment, ethnic groups, and rural development; 13% for the consolidation of the state of law, human rights, and justice; and 9% for economic and social development (Comisión 2007, 17).

REFERENCES

ABC. 2010. "Policía colombiana y Europol firman acuerdo para combatir crimen trasnacional." Retrieved from *www.abc.es/agencias/noticia.asp?noticia=524133*, accessed September 27, 2010.

"Acuerdo entre la Comunidad Europea y la República de Colombia relativo a los precursores y sustancias químicas utilizados con frecuencia en la fabricación ilícita de estupefacientes o de sustancias psicotrópicas." 1995. *Diario Oficial*, no. L 324 December 30, 11–17.

Ardila, M., D. Cardona, and A. Tickner. 2002. "Prólogo. El análisis de la política exterior colombiana: Lugares comunes y grandes silencios." In *Prioridades y desafíos de la política exterior colombiana*, edited by M. Ardila, D. Cardona, and A. Tickner, 17–44. Bogotá: Fescol-Hanns Seidel Stiftung.

Arenas, H. 2010. Ministro plenipotenciario, Embajada de Colombia en Brussels, Belgica. Telephone interview, February 26, 2010.

BBC. 2004 "Uribe pide ayuda militar a la UE." Retrieved from *news.BBC.co.uk/hi/spanish/latin_america/newsid_34 80000/ 3480951.stm*, accessed February 19, 2010.

Bustos, A. F. 1999. "Fiscalía y Policía critican falta de apoyo de UE—Duro reclamo de Colombia a UE." *El Tiempo* (Bogotá), April 16, 1999, 1A and 9A.

Castañeda, D. 2009. "¿Qué significan los laboratorios de paz para la Unión Europea?" *Colombia Internacional* 69 (Jan.–June): 162–79.

Celare. 2009. "Unión Europea retrasa aprobación de negociación de nuevo acuerdo entre Europol y Colombia." In "Centro Latinoamericano para las relaciones con Europa." Retrieved from *www.celare.org/index.php?option=com_contentandtask=viewandid=5900andItemid=28*, accessed February 12, 2010.

Comisión Europea. 2007. Colombia. Documento de Estrategia País 2007–2013, March 28 (E/2007/484).

Comunidad Andina. 2008a. "Vicepresidente de Colombia opina que firma de TLC entre CAN y UE ayudará a lucha antidrogas." Retrieved from *www.comunidadandina.org/prensa/noticias/30-7-08.htm*, accessed October 22, 2009.

———. 2008b. "Perú y Colombia buscarán obtener mayor ayuda de Europa en lucha antidrogas." Retrieved from *www.comunidadandina.org/prensa/noticias/30-7-08.htm*, accessed October 22, 2009.

Conseil de l'Union européenne. 2008. "Plan d'action drogue de l'Union européenne (2009–2012), 2008/C 326/09." *Journal officiel de l'Union européenne* C326, December 20.

Consejo de la Unión Europea. 2004a. "Conclusiones del Consejo de Asuntos Generales y Relaciones Exteriores de la Unión Europea." January 26.

———. 2004b. "Estrategia europea en materia de lucha contra la droga 2005–2012." Brussels, November 22, 15074/04.

———. 2004c. "Conclusiones del Consejo sobre Colombia." December 13.

———. 2004d. "Posición Común 2004/309/PESC del Consejo 2 Apr. 2004 por la que se actualiza la Posición Común 2001/931/PESC sobre la aplicación de medidas específicas de lucha contra el terrorismo y se deroga la Posición Común 2003/906/PESC."

———. 2007. "Conclusiones del Consejo–Colombia." November 19.

Consejo Europeo. 2009. "Conclusiones sobre Colombia." November. Retrieved from *ec.europa.eu/delegations/colombia/eu_colombia/political_relations/index_es.htm*, accessed September 27, 2010.

Council of the EU. 2004. Press information S0034/04, Press Office, Secretary General, High representative for CFSP. Brussels, February 6.

Delegación de la Comisión Europea en Bogotá. 2004. "Laboratorios de paz: La apuesta de la UE en la búsqueda de soluciones al conflicto." DB/AMM, January 15.

Delegación de la Comisión Europea en Bogotá. *Acuerdos*. Retrieved from *eeas.europa.eu/delegations/colombia/eu_colombia/political_relations/agreements/index_es.htm*, accessed May 12, 2015.

El Espectador. 2009 "Cooperación Europol y Colombia buscará cercar rutas a narcotráfico y FARC." September 17, 2009, judicial section. Retrieved from *www.elespectador.com/noticias/judicial/articul0161886-cooperacion-europol-y-colombia-buscara-cercar-rutas-narcotrafico-y-*, accessed 12 Feb. 2010.

El Tiempo. 2005a. "UE decidió apoyar la reinserción." December 23, 2005, 1 and 4.

———. 2005b. "Víctimas, énfasis de ayuda de UE." December 24, 2005, 7.

Estievenart, G. 2006. "La estrategia antidrogas de la Unión Europea y América Latina." in *Narcotráfico: Europa, Estados Unidos, América Latina*, edited by A. Camacho, 13–38. Bogotá: Universidad de los Andes.

Euronotas. 2000a. July–September, 23.

———. 2000b. October–December, 24.

———. 2005. April–June, 33.

Europa. 2008. "Asistencia a la Comunidad Andina: La Comisión Europea apoya la integración económica regional y la lucha contra las drogas ilícitas." Press release, Brussels, July 28, IP/08/1213. Retrieved from *europa.eu/rapid/pressReleasesAction.do?reference=IP/08/1213andformat=HTMLandaged=0andlanguage=ESandguiLanguage=en*, accessed October 22, 2009.

European Commission. 2009. *Illicit Drugs, a Major Concern for Europe*. Directorate General Justice, Freedom and Security.

European Parliament. 2001. European Parliament resolution on Plan Colombia and support for the peace process in Colombia. B5–0087/2001.

Europol. 2004. "Colombian Vice President Visits Europol." Press release, Public Relations Unit, The Hague, March 18.

———. 2008. *Annual Report 2008*. Retrieved from *www.europol.europa.eu/publications/Annual_Reports/Annual%20Report%202008.pdf*, accessed March 2, 2010.

———. 2009. *Ten Years of Europol 1999–2009*. The Hague. Retrieved from *www.europol.europa.eu/publications/Anniversary_Publication/Anniversary_publication.pdf*, accessed March 2, 2010.

Koetsenruijter, A. 2005. Comments made at the seminar "El Sistema Generalizado de Preferencia de la Unión Europea: Herramienta para mejorar el acceso de los productos colombianos al mercado comunitario." Bogotá, August 2.

Kurtenbach, S. 2005. "Europe and the Colombian Conflict." Working Paper, Inter-American Dialogue, June.

Labrousse, A. 2006. "La cooperación en materia de drogas entre la Unión Europea y América Latina." In *Narcotráfico: Europa, Estados Unidos, América Latina*, edited by Á. Camacho, 39–59. Bogotá: Universidad de los Andes.

Laurent, M. 1997. "La lucha contra el narcotráfico en Colombia: La cooperación de la Unión Europea entre 1980 y 1995," Universidad Complutense de Madrid. Published as a CD-ROM in the Colección Tesis Doctorales—Ciencias Sociales—Universidad Complutense de Madrid.

Mendiluce, F. de. 2000. "La mesa está servida." *Credencial* (Bogotá), June 2000, 26–29.

Molano, G. 2007. "El diálogo entre la Comunidad Andina y la Unión Europea sobre drogas ilícitas." *Colombia Internacional* 65 (Jan.–June 2007): 38–65.

———. 2009. "El apoyo de la Unión Europea a los programas de desarrollo alternativo en Colombia. Cooperación para el combate contra el terrorismo y el tráfico ilícito de estupefacientes." *Análisis Político*, no. 66 (May–Aug.): 100–22.

OEDT. 2009. *Informe anual 2009, El problema de la drogodependencia en Europa*. Luxemburg. Oficina de Publicaciones de la UE.

Pauwels, V. 2010. Director of the Bureau for Europe, Ministry of Foreign Affairs of Colombia. Telephone interview, March 4.

Presidencia de la República. 2005. "Policía colombiana y Europol firmaron convenio contra crimen internacional." Bogotá. Presidencia de la República, February 12. Retrieved from *www.presidencia.gov.co/uribe%20europa/europa12.htm*, accessed February 12, 2010.

Puyo, G. 2002. "La política exterior colombiana frente a la Unión Europea en la década 1990." In *Prioridades y desafíos de la política exterior colombiana*, edited by M. Ardila, D. Cardona, and A. Tickner, 399–429. Bogotá: Fescol-Hanns Seidel Stiftung.

Ramírez, S. 2006. "Actores europeos ante el conflicto colombiano." In *Nuestra guerra sin nombre. Transformaciones del conflicto en Colombia*. Bogotá: IEPRI-Norma, 71–120.

Roy, J. 2001. "La asistencia europea a Colombia: ¿Una contribución virtual a un plan virtual de paz?" *Colombia Internacional* 51 (Jan.–April): 5–27.

Sanín, J. et al. 2004. *Relaciones Colombia-Unión Europea: De la incertidumbre política al posicionamiento estratégico*. Policy Paper 4—La inserción de Colombia en el sistema internacional cambiante, Unión Europea, Bogotá, Fescol—Fundación Hanns Seidel; Cepei; Academia Diplomática de la Cancillería; CEI Universidad de los Andes; CEPI Universidad del Rosario; CEESEDEN-Facultad Ciencias Políticas, Universidad Javeriana; Facultad Finanzas, Gobierno y Relaciones Internacionales Universidad Externado de Colombia; IEPRI, Universidad Nacional de Colombia, January.

Sig/Web Delcol. N.d. Georeferenced information system of cooperative projects supported by the Delegation of the European Commission in Colombia. Retrieved from *customers.gkudos.com/delcol/sigweb/flex/bin/#*, accessed February 12, 2010.

Thoumi, F. E. 2009 "Políticas antidrogas y la necesidad de enfrentar las vulnerabilidades de Colombia." *Análisis Político*, no. 67 (Sept.–Dec. 2009): 60–82.

Treaties Office Database, European Commission. N.d. Summary of Treaty (Agreement between the European Community and the Republic of Colombia on precursors and chemical substances frequently used in the illicit manufacture of narcotic drugs or psychotropic substances). Retrieved from *ec.europa.eu/world/agreements/prepareCreateTreatiesWorkspace/treatiesGeneralData.do?step=0andredirect=trueandtreatyId=425*, accessed March 5, 2010.

"UK Ends Bilateral Military Aid to Colombia." 2009. *The Guardian*, April 29. Retrieved from *www.guardian.co.uk/world/2009/apr/29/colombia-uk-military-aid*, accessed February 18, 2010.

Vincenti, F., et al. 2005. "Tercer Laboratorio de Paz en Colombia. Análisis y reflexiones sobre el proceso de preparación." Retrieved from *www.kus.uu.se/pdf/publications/Colombia/Informe_final_Tercer_Laboratorio.pdf*, accessed February 18, 2010.

8 The Role of Illegal Drugs in Colombia–US Relations

Arlene Beth Tickner and Carolina Cepeda

After ten years and more than seven billion dollars of investment, Plan Colombia (PC) has been singled out as a successful model of bilateral cooperation. Although it was originally formulated as an expanded and improved version of the counternarcotics cooperation between Bogotá and Washington already in force since the 1980s, in practice and above all since the rupture of the peace negotiations with the FARC in 2002, PC has functioned as a counterinsurgency strategy and tool to strengthen the state in which the "war on drugs" has occupied a central role.

Although there is a consensus among the defenders and critics of PC that the climate of domestic security in Colombia has gone through an important transformation since 2000, the conclusions about its effect on illegal drugs are less clear. The reduction in the area of land devoted to growing coca leaves in Colombia and its productive potential, following gradual increases since 2004, has given rise to assertions that Colombia is winning the "war on drugs," which is considered fundamental to also winning the "war on terrorism," given the links between illegal armed groups in Colombia and narcotics trafficking. By contrast, the fact that the total area devoted to illegal crops in 2008 was comparable to the level reported in 1999, according to US statistics, as well as the marginal effect of PC on the availability, price, and purity of cocaine on the streets of the United States and collateral effects (like the "balloon effect"[1]), have been cited as conclusive proof of its failure.

While the Uribe government insisted on maintaining a policy of zero tolerance toward all manifestations of illegal drugs, including the growing of coca (and poppies, for heroin) and the consumption of personal doses of narcotics, a different trend is observable in the United States. Fourteen states and the District of Colombia have legalized the medical use of marijuana, and a growing number of its inhabitants believe that this substance should be regulated and taxed like alcohol and tobacco.[2] The country's economic crisis has highlighted the cost of punitive policies: the US prison population has grown by 400 percent since 1980 and its courts are jammed with minor cases of drug possession. Although the subject of illegal drugs continues to be a victim of bureaucratic inertia in Washington, there are signs that both the administration of Barack Obama and the Congress have begun to revise official policy, which has resisted substantial modifications for nearly forty years. Among these, the appointment as the anti-drug czar of Gil Kerlikowske, who has called for an end to the "war on drugs"; the

Arlene Beth Tickner: Full professor, Department of Political Science, Universidad de los Andes.

Carolina Cepeda: Doctoral student in political science, associate professor, Department of Political Science and adjunct investigator of the Center for International Studies (CEI), Universidad de los Andes.

change of position on strategies like the eradication of illegal drugs in countries like Colombia and Afghanistan; and a bill, drafted by congressman Eliot Engel, that calls for a revision of the anti-drug policy in the Western hemisphere, stand out.

The fact that the tenth anniversary of PC coincided with a change of government in Colombia and a climate of relative re-evaluation and open-mindedness in the United States provides an opportunity to undertake a retrospective analysis of the bilateral relations surrounding this subject and set forth possible scenarios for the future. The main emphasis of the following part of our chapter is on illegal drugs and only touches in a secondary way on other components of PC, like counterinsurgency and the strengthening of the armed forces, even though we are aware that these have been of equal or greater importance from the standpoint of the Colombian government.

In the first section of this chapter we speak of the basic premises of the "war on drugs." Although this has been analyzed by other authors (Bagley and Tokatlian 1992; Tokatlian 1995; Zirnite 1997), it is important to situate its origins in the complementary tendencies of "American exceptionalism" and *securitization* in order to understand the kind of policies the United States has historically adopted to fight against illegal drugs, as well as the obstacles to modifying them. The second part briefly examines the development of the relations between Colombia and the United States during the governments of Andrés Pastrana and Álvaro Uribe. Although the bilateral relation has been "narcotized" since the 1980s, we explore the period previous to Plan Colombia to show how and why it went through a transformation the most significant result of which was the expansion of the bilateral agenda and a greater US involvement in the country's internal conflict.

After that, we present a general balance sheet on the anti-drug strategy in both countries, as well as the "unexpected" consequences that have been detected.[3] While it is difficult to separate an analysis of the "war on drugs" from the other objectives of this bilateral cooperation, that this has had a leading role in PC merits a focus on it. Finally, we discuss the debates on illegal drugs that have recently taken place in the United States, a mention of which is indispensable when it comes to understanding the current course of bilateral relations as well as their future scenarios. The chapter ends with a series of recommendations.

THE "WAR ON DRUGS": PRINCIPLES AND PREMISES

Interpreting illegal drugs as a threat and danger has a long history in the political and social imaginary of the United States (Campbell 1992; Bewley-Taylor 2001). While it was not until 1971 that President Richard Nixon declared that they represented "public enemy number one" against which a "war" needed to be waged—an interpretation that was radicalized under the administration of Ronald Reagan—since the beginning of the twentieth century US policy has been based on two different but complementary premises. On is that drugs are a moral evil, and the other is that they represent a security threat. Among the traits that have given rise to the notion of "American exceptionalism," the moralism mainly derived from the Protestant work ethic occupies a leading place in the national and international policy of the United States (Lipset 1997; Schuck and Wilson 2008). To a large extent, the religious origin of US attitudes toward subjects like drugs, sexuality, crime, and punishment explains the nature of public debates on them (Kennedy 2007, 178–81).

As well as being portrayed as an evil that the United States has a moral duty to act against, drug consumption has historically been understood as a depraved behavior that lies beyond the normal limits of society (Bewley-Taylor 2001, 6). This explains why the problem of illegal drugs, as well as the policies that have been developed to combat it, have been based on the premise that its origins lie beyond the United States, in the producer countries, and within the United States in undesirable social groups, typically racial and ethnic minorities (Campbell 1992, 169–89). That drugs are seen as a universal evil that threatens moral purity also exerts a restrictive influence on public debate. This is not only set forth in rigid and dichotomous terms (good/bad, prohibition/legalization), but tends to ignore and deny the validity of an endless number of studies in different disciplines which suggest that the war on drugs has not worked, since such studies do not give a central role to the moral imperative underlying the problem.

At what is apparently the opposite pole to such moralism, the anti-drug policy of the United States is also based on the idea that illegal drugs are a security threat. The concept of securitization puts an emphasis on the discourses employed by states when the time comes to justify their policies (Waever 1995). Especially through the use of such discourses, state actors come up with specific interpretations of different public problems, which are not the result of objective evaluations but a set of historical, political, and social factors (Lipschutz 1995). In the case of security, when a specific theme is labeled a threat or securitized, that action produces important political effects (Waever 1995). Declaring that *x* represents a security threat allows the representatives of the state to invoke a condition of emergency and the right to use any strategy needed to deal with it, including the use of force. As a consequence, securitization empowers the state to monopolize the handling of certain problems and at the same remove them from the public sphere, where they may be subject to the dynamics of democratic debate and the consideration of alternative policies.

Taken as a whole, the religiosity that has influenced an understanding of the drug phenomenon, as well as its securitization, explain the perdurability of the current policies. What is commonly known as the punitive or prohibitionist paradigm offers a specific interpretation of illegal drugs ("they are bad and have to be destroyed"); identifies the source of the problem ("drugs are too cheap and easy to obtain"); and offers its possible solutions ("punishment, coercion and prohibition") (Bertram et al. 1996). In doing that, the paradigm establishes the limits within which the debate on the subject may take place, as well as the policies that must be adopted. These consist of a combination of interdiction, eradication, and attacks on the organizations of narcotics traffickers in the producing countries, and criminalization and imprisonment within the United States to deal with the problem of demand, with little emphasis on treatment and education. "If the war against supply seeks to discourage consumption by increasing the economic cost of drugs use, the war against consumers seeks to increase the risk associated with consumption by imposing punitive measures" (Bertram et al. 1996, 4). Given that it is thought of as a security threat, the war on drugs also presupposes an important military component, the yielding of society's right to express opinions about the handling of the subject, and "collateral damages" that are included in the formulation of policies to fight against the phenomenon.

Apart from the factors just mentioned, there is a political and bureaucratic inertia in Washington that strengthens the opposition to change, despite the ever-growing recognition that the war on drugs has been a failure. Although a growing number of people in the United States think the current policy is not working, only a small percentage believe the punitive paradigm should be dropped, except in the case of marijuana (Naim 2009). For that reason, the political risk associated with the formulation of alternative strategies is high, especially in the case of the House of Representatives, where elections are held every two years.[4] Likewise, the high degree of bureaucratic institutionalization resulting from decades of implementing the same policy represents a further obstacle.

The Terrorization of the War on Drugs

One repercussion of the terrorist attacks on September 11, 2001, was to change the nature of the war on drugs. That is, the "global war against terrorism" became a new strategy of securitization for the United States, which linked, in a single analytical framework, a group of world threats, including the illegal trafficking of drugs and arms, and weapons of mass destruction. The link between terrorism and drugs, symbolized by a new concept—"narco-terrorism"[5]—enabled securitization to be tied to those two problems (Buzan 2006, 1104). Additionally, and as happened in the case of drugs, terrorism began to be seen through a moralistic lens, as seen in the use of the terms like "axis of evil," "zero tolerance," and "infinite justice" applied to this new threat.

The terrorization of the war on drugs had important repercussions for the US anti-drug policy in Colombia, where the ending of the peace negotiations with the FARC by President Andrés Pastrana gave rise to their classification as terrorists.[6] As will be discussed in the following section, the Colombian government's insertion of its internal conflict into the international war against terrorism had a strong influence on the bilateral relation between Colombia and the United States insofar as it broadened its main axes. A narcotized relation, where the only thing occurring in Colombia of interest to the United States was related to drugs, gave way to one where the strengthening of the coercive apparatus of the state, basically for counterinsurgency efforts, became the fundamental objective.

COLOMBIA–UNITED STATES: A NARCOTIZED RELATION

In the mid-1980s the bilateral relations began to get narcotized as a result of the expansion of organizations of narcotics traffickers in Colombia, as well as the growing concern in the United States about the consumption of illegal drugs and the crime associated with them (Tokatlian 1995; Crandall 2002). The Andean Initiative, created by the first Bush government in 1989 at the end of the Cold War, gave Colombia a definite place on the US foreign policy agenda due to its concern with narcotics trafficking. Since then, the way the war on drugs has been carried out in Colombia has depended to a large extent on the US approach to the problem.[7]

The role played by drugs in the bilateral relations went through an important change after the government of Ernesto Samper, above all because of the mutation of the political economy of narcotics trafficking in the country, as well as its increasing synergy with the armed conflict (Tokatlian 2000; Tickner, 2007a). When Samper took office in 1994, the division of labor in the cocaine business was such that Peru and Bolivia produced most of the raw material (coca paste) and the Colombian cartels processed and exported it. This productive infrastructure changed in the mid-1990s, insofar as the coca plots began to shift to Colombia, largely due to successful eradication and interdiction campaigns in Peru and Bolivia and the blocking of aerial transport routes between those two countries and Colombia, efforts that caused a balloon effect. Thus, between 1996 and 1998, the production of coca in Colombia rose by approximately 50 percent (GAO 2008, 10), which turned the country into the main grower of coca leaves in the Andean region and the world. In addition, more than 50 percent of the coca was grown in the Putumayo, a department controlled by the FARC. Furthermore, the dismantling of the Cali and Medellín cartels in the middle of the decade caused a power void, which was filled not only by minicartels but also by illegal armed groups, especially the paramilitaries and the FARC. In both cases, their participation in different links of the productive chain provided them with a crucial source of income that allowed for their territorial expansion.

When Andrés Pastrana was elected president in June 1998, Colombia supplied 90 percent of the cocaine that entered the United States, as well as a large part of the heroin sold on its east coast. He thus took over the leadership of a country on the edge of collapse: "a convergence of destabilizing factors—among them, drugs, illegal armed groups, weak public security, official corruption, growing violence and a severe economic recession—pointed to the dramatic loss of State authority" (DeShazo, Primiami and McLean 2007, 6). For the incoming government, a "Marshall Plan for Colombia"—as Pastrana himself frequently referred to it because it aimed at a reconstruction of the country through international cooperation—was fundamental for the attainment of peace. In this plan, the fight against narcotics trafficking was one of several aspects. In the initial version of what would become Plan Colombia, presented by Pastrana in October 1998, alternative development was chosen as the first of six objectives, among which were the reduction of supply (where eradication had a secondary place), the strengthening of justice, the reduction of demand, environmental protection, and international cooperation. For his part, the Colombian president, in several visits to the White House in the same year, tried to convince his counterpart, Bill Clinton, that the ending of the armed conflict was an essential prerequisite for attacking narcotics trafficking more effectively (Tickner 2007a).

Despite its efforts to distance itself from the US interpretation of the problem, the Pastrana government saw clearly that the success or failure of its "diplomacy for peace" depended, to a large extent, on the support of the United States, given the lack of commitment by other international donors, and that Washington's main interest in Colombia continued to be the war on drugs (Arnson and Tickner 2010). Thus it sought to ensure the participation of the United States by invoking that war.[8] The version of PC that was presented in the United States incorporated a broad range of problems considered to be important—among them economic recovery, the reform of justice, development, and human rights—and illegal drugs occupied a central place in its strategy (Presidencia de la República 1999, 9).

While in its original version, PC was meant to be a policy complementary to the peace process with the FARC, it wound up with a heavy leaning toward its military component and the problem of illegal crops in the south of the country, where the presence of the FARC made it difficult for the Colombian police to implement antinarcotics measures. As a consequence, 80 percent of the first package of US aid—the largest source of external financing of PC, amounting to $1.6 billion in 2000 and 2001—went to the

Colombian army and consisted of the supply of helicopters, the training of antinarcotics battalions, and military support for activities of eradication and interdiction. Much less went to the Colombian police.

Despite that, seeing Plan Colombia as simply more of the same of the war on drugs would be a mistake. The argument set forth by the Pastrana government in its "Plan for peace, prosperity and the strengthening of the state" (Presidencia de la República 1999) was that illegal drugs represented a threat to Colombian national security, basically because they fueled the armed conflict, and that the state was too weak to deal with the problem on its own. This precariousness of the state was associated with its failure to control its own territory and exert a monopoly of force, which, among other things, prevented the Colombian police from effectively implementing its anti-drug policies in those regions of southern Colombia where the growing of coca leaves was concentrated, precisely the regions controlled by the guerrillas. Thus, from the Colombian standpoint, PC fulfilled a twin purpose: to strengthen the state by improving its military capacities and attack one of the FARC's main sources of income in southern Colombia, specifically in the Putumayo, where the coca plots had grown exponentially (Presidencia de la República 1999).

Independently of the virtues of PC as an antinarcotics strategy—a problem we will discuss in the following section—it managed to satisfy the interests of the two countries, which were not necessarily the same: in the case of the United States, to show its determination in the war on drugs, and in Colombia to ensure the support of Washington to strengthen the army and begin to attack the FARC's territorial control of the coca-growing zones. Nevertheless, as the terms of the bilateral debate began to change with PC, the main US objective in Colombia—to reduce the amount of narcotics that might enter its territory—was circumscribed by the strengthening of the Colombian state and the stabilization of the country (Wallace-Wells 2007; Arnson and Tickner 2010).

The terrorist attacks on September 11, 2001, and the consequent shift in the foreign policy of the United States were another factor that had an impact on bilateral relations. In addition to the inclusion of the FARC, ELN, and AUC on the State Department's list of terrorists, to a large extent the war on drugs became an appendix of the global war against terrorism, especially in those cases where the two phenomena converged. While some US officials began to refer to Colombia's problems as a case of "narco-terrorism," it wasn't until February 20, 2002, when President Pastrana made the decision to break off the peace negotiations with the FARC, that the Colombian government accepted that definition.[9] It later began to spread the idea that the Colombian conflict represented the biggest terrorist threat in the Western hemisphere (Moreno 2002, 23A), which firmly put the country on the new map of US priorities.

A nearly immediate effect of the change in the language used in both countries was the ending of the restrictions on the use of US military aid provided under PC. In March 2002, President George W. Bush asked the Congress to authorize the use of such aid in the fight against terrorism, which completely erased the tenuous distinction between anti-drug and counterinsurgency activities Washington had tried to maintain till then.

This trend continued and became more pronounced after Álvaro Uribe won the Colombian presidential elections in May 2002. From the beginning, the backbone of that government's strategy was to draft and implement a policy of security the main focuses of which included the war against illegal armed groups and narcotics trafficking. Despite the marked differences between the Pastrana and Uribe administrations—the former's emphasis on peace and the latter's insistence that there was no armed conflict in Colombia—the "policy of defense and democratic security" was based on a diagnosis of the Colombian crisis similar to the one advanced by the Pastrana government when it designed PC with the United States. This diagnosis was that the weakness of the Colombian state created conditions that allowed for the growth of the armed groups and narcotics trafficking, and that an indispensable condition for guaranteeing the state of law and strengthening democratic authority was to secure the state's control of its national territory (Presidencia de la República and Ministerio de Defensa Nacional 2003, 12).

The convergence of the definitions of the problem, as well as of some of the policies needed to solve it, especially the process of professionalizing and modernizing the armed forces begun under Pastrana, helped to conserve a significant degree of continuity in Colombia's relations with the United States (Tickner and Pardo 2003). Given that Washington was regarded as a crucial partner for the implementation of the policy of democratic security, the cultivation of a "special" bilateral relationship and the broadening of the US role in the internal conflict became the main aim of Colombian foreign policy (Borda 2007; Tickner 2007b). The hardening of the anti-drug and antiterrorism discourse of the Uribe government facilitated this process by causing the viewpoints, strategies, and goals of the two countries to coincide more than they had under the Pastrana administration.

On the specific subject of drugs, while Pastrana had basically regarded the problem as a means to guarantee Washington's collaboration in strengthening the state and thus bring about conditions suitable for the attainment of peace, the war against narco-terrorism turned into one of the main aims Uribe set for his government, both within and outside of the country.[10] It was based on a different interpretation of the Colombian crisis and the role played by narcotics trafficking, as president Uribe reiterated: "Colombia still suffers from violence because it has illegal drugs"; that is, there would have been no terrorism if drugs hadn't existed.[11] The energetic application of a policy of zero tolerance toward any expression of the drug problem, including consumption, can be basically attributed to this change of focus.

The hardening of the war on drugs was reflected in, among other things, the Uribe government's lifting of all restrictions on the aerial fumigation of illegal crops, the exponential increase in the areas fumigated, the increase in seizures of coca paste and cocaine and the destruction of laboratories, and the intensification of extraditions of Colombian citizens to the United States, a topic dealt with in the following section.

The beginning of the Plan Patriot in 2003 furnished a more intense level of military cooperation between Colombia and the United States, with the aim of increasing the offensive capacity of the armed forces. This stage coincided with the first of three phases of the strategy for consolidating the policy of democratic security, designed in collaboration with the US government and consisting of (1) clearing the FARC out of different regions of Colombian territory in order to establish the control of the state, (2) stabilizing the areas thus controlled with the permanent presence of the armed forces, and (3) consolidating the state presence through a plan for integrated action that coordinated the counterinsurgency efforts of the military and the anti-drug fight with civil activities, among them economic development and the administration of justice.[12] Beginning in 2006, the strategy was fully adopted by the Uribe government when it created the Center for the Coordination of Integrated Action (CCAI), followed by the implementation of plans for integral consolidation in different regional centers, among them La Macarena and the Montes de María (Ministerio de Defensa Nacional 2007).

As will be discussed later, one of the lessons left by the implementation of the integrated action doctrine in Colombia—above all for USAID, which administers US funding for alternative development—and which suggests a shift in the focus of the United States, is that the traditional emphasis on the eradication of illegal crops has to be replaced with a more flexible policy (USAID 2009). This trend was also strengthened by the modifications given to US aid to Colombia since 2008, which consist of cuts in military aid, mainly for fumigation, and an increase of activities like alternative development and judicial reform.

GENERAL BALANCE SHEET OF THE ROLE OF THE WAR ON DRUGS IN THE BILATERAL RELATION

Various evaluations have been made of the achievements and failures of Plan Colombia (GAO 2008; Acevedo, Bewley-Taylor and Youngers 2008; Mejía and Restrepo 2010; DeShazo, Mendelson and McLean 2009; Isacson and Poe 2009; Felbab-Brown et al. 2009). While most emphasize both security and drugs, they serve as input for drawing up a balance sheet on the role of the war drugs in the bilateral relation between Colombia and United States.[13] For that aim, it is also important to take into account the different objectives of the two countries in the field of illegal drugs and analyze the available statistics on those subjects. For the United States, the main aim has been to minimize the amount of cocaine that reaches its shores in order to affect its purity and price and thus reduce consumption (which is also deterred by punitive measures); whereas Colombia has sought to reduce production in order to attack the sources of financing of the illegal armed groups. Although the nature of narcotics trafficking makes it difficult to compile precise information about prices, earnings, and levels of purity, and the two entities that gather statistics about drugs—the US government and the UNODC—use different methodologies and tools of measurement (Thoumi 2009; Mejía and Posada 2010), we will try, as far as possible, to draw some conclusions from the data of both.[14]

Colombia

For Colombia, especially during the two administrations of Álvaro Uribe, the main focus of the war on drugs was the policy of zero tolerance toward the production of cocaine, which includes reducing the growing of coca leaves; dismantling the cocaine laboratories; seizing coca base and paste, cocaine, and precursor chemicals; and extradition. Nevertheless, as we have said, its interest in US aid and military cooperation for the realization of counterinsurgency measures was the same or greater. While PC did help to improve the situation of internal security in Colombia, there is a consensus that its achievements with regard to reducing coca crops and the production of cocaine fall relatively short of the proposed goals (GAO 2008; Acevedo, Bewley-Taylor, and Youngers, 2008; DeShazo, Mendelson, and McLean 2009; Isacson and Poe 2009; USAID 2009).

There was a general reduction in the area of coca leaf plots in Colombia between 1999 and 2008 (see Figure 1.1 in Chapter 1), although there is no agreement about its size in the reports of the State Department and the UNODC.[15] According to the State Department, the number of hectares devoted to coca in 2008 (119,000) was nearly the same as in 1999 (122,500), the year before the start of PC. By contrast, the statistics of the UNODC suggest that the area of crops was halved in the same period, falling from 160,100 to 81,000 hectares. Independently of the discrepancies between the two sets of figures (Thoumi 2009; Mejía and Posada 2010), both sources show a pendulum-like movement of ups and downs in the area of coca crops, with the rises being much more pronounced in the estimates of the State Department. Nevertheless, the estimates of both entities suggest that there is little correspondence between the rates of reduction of illegal crops and the exponential increase in the eradication campaigns begun in 2000. Coca crops have declined much more slowly than the increase in eradication, which since 2006 has risen two or three times as much as the total area under cultivation, while there are periods in which the illegal crops have grown despite substantial increases in eradication. This suggests not only a strong capacity for adaptation by the growers and the cocaine trade in general but also the limited effectiveness of eradication as a leading strategy in the fight against drugs (Thoumi 2009).

From 2005 onwards, the aerial fumigation of illegal crops began to be complemented by manual eradication, which progressively grew until it reached a maximum level in 2008, when 95,620 of the 229,117 hectares devoted to coca were manually eradicated. This peak in manual eradication coincided with the first reduction of the total area of coca crops reported by the United States since 2003, which led many to believe that it was a much more effective strategy than aerial fumigation. According to the operative balance sheet of the Anti-Narcotics Administration of the Colombian Police, however, in 2009 manual eradication fell to 60,557 hectares out of the total of 165,329 eradicated, not only because it is a slower and more expensive procedure,[16] but also because the cuts in US aid had affected the eradication program.

Felbab-Brown et al. (2009) single out three factors that have allowed for the recuperation of coca in Colombia after the initial success at reducing it between 2001 and 2003: the adaptation of strategies by the peasant growers and narcotics traffickers, such as the use of more resistant plants, the increased density of the plots, their smaller size and techniques, which minimize the effects of fumigation; the existence of structural obstacles that prevent the growers and ex-growers from gaining access to viable legal alternatives; and the Uribe government's policy of zero tolerance toward the illegal crops, which denies official aid to those regions of the country where there are still illegal crops. As a consequence, both this and analyses undertaken by Acevedo, Bewley-Taylor, and Youngers (2008) and the International Crisis Group (2008a) speak of the need to formulate a renewed focus that attacks the structural causes of growing coca leaves, and meanwhile integrates and synchronizes all the elements of the anti-drug policy.

Despite the reduction of the hectares where coca is grown in Colombia (slightly according to the State Department, and almost by half according to the UNODC), this has not led to a proportional reduction of the production of cocaine, nor of its availability on the streets of the United States (see Chapter 1). The data suggest that there has been a reduction in the potential production of cocaine during the past ten years, but there is no direct or constant relation between the reduction of the plots of coca leaf and the potential of cocaine production. According to the US government, while the illegal crops only fell by 2.8 percent between 1998 and 2008, the potential of production of cocaine fell by 44.3 percent. By contrast, the UNODC found that the reduction in crops was greater than that of the potential cocaine production, 49.4 percent and 36.8 percent respectively.

The asymmetrical relation between the reduction of crops and the potential production of cocaine leads one to think that technological innovations in the narcotics industry have allowed the traffickers to produce more cocaine with fewer coca leaves (Mejía and Restrepo 2010). Nevertheless, in view of the divergence between the State Department and UNODC, there is no consensus on this point. While the UNODC reported 81,000 hectares of coca in Colombia in 2008 compared to the 119,000 reported by the State Department, UNODC believes that the potential production of cocaine in Colombia (estimated at 430 tons) is higher than the estimate of the State Department (only 295 tons). In both cases, the correspondence between the crops and the potential of cocaine varies a great deal in the course of this period. Between 2001 and 2002, both sources reported that both the crops and the potential of cocaine had fallen, while between 2006 and 2007 the area devoted to coca growing rose but the potential production fell.[17]

The data also indicate that seizures of cocaine have gradually increased in Colombia, with a slight fall in 2006. A trend that is even more noteworthy is seen in the case of the destruction of laboratories that produce coca base and cocaine, which rose from 347 in the year 2000 to 1,751 in 2008. One feature of the seizures that deserves notice is that the number of tons of cocaine seized, especially in 2008 (199 tons) tends to approach the potential production of cocaine (295 tons), which suggests that there shouldn't be so much cocaine in Colombia.[18]

Another cornerstone of anti-drug policy in Colombia, above all during the two governments of Álvaro Uribe, has been extradition. According to the Drugs Monitoring Office of the National Narcotics Administration, 913 Colombian citizens (including thirteen paramilitary leaders) have been extradited to the United States since extradition was re-established in 1997, of which 849 correspond to the period 2002–2009, which suggests that extradition stopped being an exceptional practice and turned into a central deterrent of the policy of zero tolerance. While the immediate effect of this strategy is to remove some of the capos and middle-rank traffickers from the business, their places in the productive chain are rapidly filled, so that the measure does not affect the economic possibilities of narcotics trafficking as such (FIP 2010). Likewise, the extradition of paramilitary leaders has had a negative impact on the amnesty negotiations (guided by the principle of "peace, justice, and reparation") with the demobilized members of paramilitary groups in Colombia.[19]

The United States

The main objective of the United States in the war on drugs has been to prevent large amounts of cocaine from entering the country, by means of such strategies as interdiction and eradication, the aim of which is to affect the availability, prices, and purity of cocaine (National Drug Intelligence Center 2007, 2008). Between 2002 and 2006, one observes a clear trend toward falling or stable prices and increases in the purity of cocaine, which raises doubts about whether the war on drugs has achieved the results it hoped for.[20] In the first half of 2008 this trend was slightly reversed; according to the data of the National Drug Intelligence Center, the purity of cocaine declined from 63 percent in 2007 to 56 percent, while a minimum increase in its price was reported, from US$121 to US$124. From another angle, a significant scarcity of cocaine in the thirty-six main markets in the United States was reported in 2007, which did not have a visible impact on prices (which should have risen), purity (which should have fallen), or retail distribution (National Drug Intelligence Center 2008, 1). This suggests that the blocking of cocaine imports, either because of increased seizures or reduced production, does not have an immediate or direct effect on purity or prices.[21]

Despite the above, the Bush administration was optimistic about the data for 2007 and 2008, interpreting the slight increase in prices and fall in purity as proofs of the success of the interdiction and eradication policies. This supposed achievement was questioned by different US organizations, which pointed out that it was no more than a passing change in the cocaine market, similar to other cycles (like those from 1999 to 2001) and in no way contradicted the clear trend toward falling prices and increasing purity, despite breaks from time to time (Walsh 2009, 2). These fluctuations should be regarded as cyclical moments of readjustment in the structure of narcotics trafficking itself, which, after being hit by law enforcement measures, rapidly adapts to new conditions and reorganizes itself in order to carry on with the business.

Nor does the pattern of cocaine consumption in the United States follow the predictions of the punitive paradigm. Even when there has been a greater availability of cocaine at lower prices on the streets of the United States in the past few years, there have been no significant changes in general consumption, which suggests that the relation between the availability of cocaine and demand/consumption is not a direct one. In fact, the National Drug Intelligence Center's reports for 2008 and 2009 suggest that the consumption of cocaine has remained stable during the past six years, despite the fall in prices and rise in purity.

The problem of consumption is being dealt with through prevention and treatment programs, but above all through the pursuit and imprisonment of dealers, traffickers, and consumers. The punitive aspect of the drug fight has been problematic for several reasons, among them the severity of the jail sentences, the large prison population, the high financial costs for the prison system, and the racial slant of convictions for drug crimes (International Crisis Group 2008b; Bewley-Taylor, Hallam, and Allen 2009). If one compares the inverse relation between the investment in education and prevention on the one hand and imprisonment for drugs-related crimes on the other—US$12.3 billion for the upkeep of prisoners in 2006 compared to US$4.6 billion for education in 2008 (International Crisis Group 2008, 8)—there is evidence of a strong imbalance that raises questions about the need to redesign the anti-drug policy and tip the scales more toward education and prevention.

"Collateral" Effects

In general, the assessments made of the role of the war on drugs in the bilateral relation agree that the major achievements of Plan Colombia do not have to do with a reduction of coca growing and cocaine production in Colombia or the weakening of consumption in the United States, but the improvement of security, weakening of the illegal armed groups, modernization of justice, and reduction in the growing of poppies for heroin, an activity that behaves differently than that of coca (Acevedo, Bewley-Taylor, and Youngers 2008; Felbab-Brown et al. 2009; DeShazo, Mendelson, and McLean 2009). In addition to its failure to achieve positive results in solving the problem that partly brought it into being, it is an enormously costly policy in terms of the benefits it brings. Mejía and Restrepo (2010) find, for example, that it is hardly justifiable in terms of the ratio between the resources invested in Plan Colombia by the governments of Colombia and the United States and the results in reducing coca crops and the potential production and price of cocaine.[22]

The anti-drug fight in Colombia has also had negative repercussions on the growing of coca and the production of cocaine in the other two producer countries, Peru and Bolivia, which have shown increases during the past three years as a result of the balloon effect (see Chapter 3).[23] The area devoted to coca growing in the Andean region as a whole showed slight falls between 1999 and 2008, although the State Department figures suggest they have remained nearly the same. Nevertheless, the UNODC's information about the potential production of cocaine indicates that there has only been a slight fall during the same period, from 925 to 845 tons.

The other "collateral" harms reported have to do with the environment, human rights, democracy, and violence. The environmental, economic, political, and social effects of eradication by fumigation have included damages to vegetation, human health, animals and, waters;[24] the loss or reduction of legal crops; the displacement of the population in the fumigated areas; and a sharpening of the armed conflict (Sicard et al. 2005; CODHES 2004). For its part, the militarization of the anti-drug policies has had negative effects on respect for human rights and democracy (Youngers and Rosin 2005; International Crisis Group 2008a).

Even in the area of security, where there is a stronger consensus on the positive impact of PC, the correlation between US cooperation and the improvement of civic security in Colombia is not entirely clear. In particular, the success of the civic security component of the integrated strategy currently being implemented depends on strengthening the presence of the civil aspect of the state and implementing socioeconomic projects in order to minimize the risk of weakening its legitimacy in the areas where control has been recovered from the illegal armed groups (Isacson and Poe 2009; USAID 2009).

THE INTERNAL DEBATE IN THE UNITED STATES: A GRADUAL LEARNING PROCESS?

Ever since the 1990s, the prohibitionist paradigm in the United States has begun to weaken, a process in which the decriminalization of marijuana use, its legalization for medical purposes, and opposition to prison policies have played a central role. In fourteen states and the District of Columbia, the use of medical marijuana has been legalized, while in 2009 Jim Webb, a Democratic senator, proposed a reform of criminal justice.[25] No less telling is that the Obama government has dropped its predecessor's policy of pursuing marijuana consumers in those states where its medicinal use is legal or consumption has been decriminalized.

There are signs that this trend may become stronger. Among these, the appointment of the former chief of the Seattle police, Gil Kerlikowske, as anti-drug czar and the changes seen in the anti-drug policy in countries like Afghanistan and Colombia are the ones most relevant to our study.[26] In May 2009 the new czar called for an end to the war on drugs ("White House Czar" 2009), the invocation of which has played a fundamental role in the securitization of the antinarcotics fight. This has been interpreted as a change in the way the Obama government regards the problem. In particular, it suggests that instead of being a threat to security, it is a matter of public health in which treatment and harm reduction must be more of a priority than imprisonment. That the deputy director of the Office of National Drug Control Policy (ONDCP), A. Thomas McLellan, has been a pioneer in the investigation of addiction and rehabilitation supports this idea. As a result of the above, the hope is that the priorities of the ONDCP will begin to change, as Kerlikowske himself has stated (2009).

Furthermore, the transformation of the public debate on drugs in the United States has begun to have an influence on its Congress, which has been characterized up to now by its inertia on the problem. In particular, in 2009 Democratic congressman Eliot Engel proposed the Western Hemisphere Drug Policy Commission Act, the aim of which would be to revise and evaluate the anti-drug policy of the United States, especially in the Western hemisphere, as well as set forth alternatives to improve the present policy (US House of Representatives 2009, 4).[27]

As well as the changes glimpsed in the general guidelines of the US anti-drug policy, in both Afghanistan and Colombia the Obama government has shown signs of a greater willingness to learn from the failures of the measures used up to now and to develop an alternative strategy. In Afghanistan, which Felbab-Brown (2010, 178) cites as a test case for the new antinarcotics policy of the United States, the conventional interpretation of narco-terrorism—that the main objective of the dual war against drugs and terrorism must be to attack the sources of income of the armed groups—has been dropped in favor of a priority given to civic security and alternative development, rather than the eradication of opium poppy. This is a reflection of the argument that the conditions of insecurity in different regions of that country are the reason why there are poppy crops and not vice versa (Nordland 2010). As a consequence, US armed forces no longer participate in or sponsor eradication campaigns in Afghanistan.[28]

In the case of Colombia, USAID (2009) has argued that the Uribe government's policy of zero tolerance toward coca restricted the state's capacity to work with local communities and bring about the transition toward a legal economy. It thus insists on making the current policy more flexible as well as changing its focus so that the eradication of coca would be replaced by a concern for a stronger institutional presence of the state and providing economic opportunities other than the growing of coca. In the same sense, Stepanova (2010) believes that the armed conflicts and narcotics trafficking should not be regarded as purely military problems that can be solved simultaneously, but as long-term phenomena that should be dealt with through broader strategies for the building of democratic states, such as development and the integration of marginal populations and geographical areas.

RECOMMENDATIONS

The growing consensus among diverse governmental and societal sectors in Colombia and the United States that the war on drugs has been a failure opens a substantial window of opportunity for its reformulation, in political terms. As we have indicated, the securitization of drugs, especially by the use of terms like "narco-terrorism," has had its repercussions in the militarization of the antinarcotics fight in countries like Colombia, and has meanwhile thwarted a more open public discussion of the problem by establishing a false dichotomy of alternatives, such as legalization versus prohibition or repression versus permissiveness. By insisting on that, the Uribe government widened the distance between Colombia and the United States (and Europe, but not necessarily other countries) and lost the opportunity to lead the bilateral debate on illegal drugs, an opportunity president Juan Manuel Santos should not waste.

At the present time there are favorable conditions for the country to lead this discussion. It not only has extensive experience on the subject as well as the moral authority to propose a frank debate about the war on drugs, but it can do it at a time when the results of the drug war are being questioned on a hemispheric level (Comisión de Drogas y Democracia para América Latina 2009).

As we have argued, the terms of the debate have also become more flexible in the United States, among other reasons because of the high economic and social costs associated with the current policy.[29] The opening in October 2010 of a high-level dialogue between Colombia and the United States on human rights; democracy and sound government; and energy, science, and technology, the main aim of which is to redefine the terms of bilateral interaction and broaden the agenda, could be exploited to promote a parallel binational discussion of anti-drug policies.[30]

It is a situation very different from the one the Colombia–United States Commission analyzed at the end of 1990s, when it was created to analyze the bilateral relation, and drugs occupied a leading place on the agenda. Now, thirteen years after the publication of its findings (Comisión Colombia–Estados Unidos 1998), it is interesting to observe that while most of its proposals were never implemented by the two governments, they continue to be critical aspects of any alternative approach to the problem of illegal drugs: a permanent evaluation of anti-drug legislation to determine its effectiveness; an objective analysis of the costs and benefits of the fumigations policy; paying more attention to links in the productive chain other than growing and dealing; a systematic follow-up of the debate about drugs in the consumer countries; and a rejection of a military slant in the solution of the problem.

On the basis of the analysis in this chapter, as well as the current political situation, we conclude with the following recommendations

- Taking advantage of its current circumstances, Colombia should promote a broad revision of the role drugs have played in hemispheric and bilateral relations, as well as of the costs, results, and negative effects of securitization, with the participation of representative sectors of the two countries, along with those from other countries strongly affected by narcotics trafficking, like Mexico and Brazil. While the UN Security Council would not be an appropriate forum for holding this discussion—precisely because it would strengthen the undesirable association between drugs and security—the seat held by Colombia may be positively used to interest other member countries in such a proposal.
- Colombia should diversify its current strategy for diplomacy with the United States, which is centered on the relation between Bogotá and Washington, in order to establish direct dialogues with states that have adopted policies distinct from prohibition and penalization, learn from their experiences, and create

strategic alliances with them in getting its message across to the US Congress. This approach should also include the local governments of the regions most affected by the narcotics trafficking phenomenon in Colombia.

- Along the same lines, the Colombian government should encourage NGOs and universities investigating the effects of prohibition to participate in the discussion, both in Colombia and the United States, so it can obtain better analytical tools when the time comes to consider alternative strategies for the anti-drug fight.
- Following the recommendations of USAID, as well as the experience of the coalition in Afghanistan, the governments of Colombia and the United States should channel more resources from bilateral cooperation toward strategies that promise to be more effective than military ones, such as alternative development and strengthening the civic aspect of the state. In order for them to be self-sustainable in the long term, it is indispensable that they result from negotiations and consensuses with the local governments and communities affected by the problem and that they range from a definition of the problem to be solved to the design and implementation of policies.
- The Colombian government must be guided by the awareness that despite the significant interdependence of illegal drugs and the armed conflict, narcotics trafficking does not exclusively depend on the conflict, nor vice versa, and it should thus adopt different policies for each aspect and deal not only with their tangible effects but their deeper causes as well. By the same token and given that the militarization of the anti-drug fight may worsen the situation of human rights in the country, any new strategy for combating narcotics trafficking in the country should include an explicit proposal for overcoming this discordance.

NOTES

1. The balloon effect refers to the tendency of illegal crops and other phases of the drugs production chain, like trafficking, to shift to other zones in response to local campaigns of control.
2. Different surveys of public opinion, among them Zogby, Gallup, and the Pew Research Center for the People and the Press, suggest that around 75 percent of Americans are in favor of the sale and use of marijuana for medical purposes, while between 40 and 50 percent think that consumption should be completely legalized.
3. For a more detailed analysis of the main indicators of the phenomenon of illegal drugs in Colombia, see Chapter 3.
4. Such a risk is not limited to the legislative sphere, as was shown during the administration of Bill Clinton. Following an exhaustive review of the country's anti-drug policy, Clinton introduced substantial modifications, but they had to be withdrawn due to pressures from Congress.
5. See, for example, the testimony of Rand Beers, assistant secretary of state for international narcotic and law enforcement affairs, "Narco-Terror: The Worldwide Connection between Drugs and Terror," presented to the Senate on March 13, 2002.
6. While the FARC, as well as the ELN and the AUC, had been classified as terrorist organizations before February 20, 2002, it was only then that the Colombian government began using that term in its public references to them.
7. Despite that, the violence unleashed by the drug cartels at the end of the 1980s to prevent their extradition led President Gaviria to design a different strategy, the main axis of which

was the policy of their negotiated surrender to the judiciary. When Pablo Escobar escaped from La Catedral prison, however, the US government pressured Colombia to return to the anti-drug orthodoxy.

8. Jaime Ruíz, ex-director of the National Planning Department (Departamento Nacional de Planeación), personal interview, Bogotá, June 4, 2009.
9. In his televised speech, Pastrana declared that "No longer can anyone doubt that, between politics and terrorism, the FARC chose terrorism."
10. For an analysis of Colombia's multilateral policy on the theme of drugs, see Chapter 6.
11. Speech by Álvaro Uribe at the UN General Assembly, September 24, 2008.
12. The "doctrine of integrated action" reflects the current thinking of the US military sector on counterinsurgency operations and emphasizes the importance of coordinating those operations with antinarcotics activities and the civil presence of the state, as well as strengthening engagement with the civilian population (Marcella 2008, 433-36).
13. Since the 1990s many analyses have been made of the prohibitionist model applied by the United States and copied in producer countries like Colombia, and also of its main defects. See Clawson and Rensselaer (1996); Bertman et al. (1996); Thoumi et al. (1997); Vellinga (2004); Youngers and Rosin (2005), and Tokatlian (2009) for some representative discussions of this topic.
14. The statistics on illegal drugs are published every year and may be consulted in the following reports: US State Department, International Narcotics Control Strategy Report; UN Office on Drugs and Crime (UNODC), Colombia Coca Cultivation Survey; and UNODC, World Drug Report.
15. According to the data of the UNODC, in 2009 the area devoted to growing coca leaves in Colombia fell from 81,000 to 68,000 hectares. As happened between 2005 and 2008, however, a significant part of this reduction is due to the drought the country suffered and not the eradication policy. Cf. Chapter 1 for a more detailed analysis.
16. According to the Anti-Narcotics Administration (Dirección de Antinarcóticos), the manual eradication of one thousand hectares of coca leaves may take an average of two months, whereas the same area can be fumigated in one day, although that does not imply the definitive eradication of the fumigated plants. Personal interview, Bogotá, January 6, 2009.
17. The fall in productivity is partly explained by the intensification of spraying, which has reduced the average age of the plantations.
18. The double counting of seizures—which are simultaneously recorded as paste and base and as cocaine chlorhydrate—may partly explain this trend.
19. The exaggerated use of this tool has been questioned by the Supreme Court of Justice since 2009 and it has denied several requests for extradition on the grounds that crimes of lese-humanity are above those of narcotics trafficking.
20. In a similar way, the prices of heroin fell by 30 percent between 1997 and 2007.
21. By contrast, the fact that consumption in Europe has increased since 2004 may explain the periods of scarcity in the US market.
22. Cf. Chapter 3.
23. In Colombia the plots of coca leaves have also become scattered and atomized as a result of the balloon effect. Between 1999 and 2008 they spread from twelve to twenty-four departments (Observatorio de Drogas, Dirección Nacional de Estupefacientes).
24. It is worth noting that the environmental effects of cocaine production are equally negative.
25. While it only has 5 percent of the world's population, the United States has 25 percent of its prison population, a fifth of which is linked to nonviolent, drug-related crimes.

26. Although Proposition 19, which proposed the total legalization of marijuana in California, was not passed in the elections held on November 2, 2010, it represents an important landmark in the public debate of the subject
27. It is still too early to measure the real impact that this revision may have on US policy. The law that will authorize it has still not been ratified by the Senate, while the current Republican majority in the House of Representatives since the elections of November 2, 2010, may lead to a new hardening of anti-drug measures, or least the rhetoric around it.
28. This policy has not been free of polemics, especially on the part of Russia, the world's leading consumer of heroin, which has accused the United States and NATO of being tolerant of the poppy growers in Afghanistan.
29. In an additional way, the violence associated with the Mexican cartels of narcotics traffickers has created a favorable climate for the consideration of alternative strategies, especially in the frontier zones.
30. Independently of the polemics surrounding the treaty that authorized the United States to establish seven military bases in Colombia in mid-2009, which did not enter into force due to a ruling by the Constitutional Court, this suggests that despite the differences between the two countries on subjects like human rights, "false positives," and the Free Trade Treaty, Colombia is regarded as an important ally, with the potential influence that implies.

REFERENCES

Acevedo, B., D. Bewley-Taylor, and C. Youngers. 2008. *Ten Years of Plan Colombia: An Analytical Assessment*. Beckley Foundation Drug Policy Programme.

Arnson, C. J., and A. B. Tickner. 2010. "Colombia and the United States: Strategic Partners or Uncertain Allies?" In *Contemporary U.S.-Latin American Relations: Cooperation or Conflict in the Twenty-First Century?*, edited by J. I. Domínguez and R. Fernández de Castro, 164–96. New York and London: Routledge.

Bagley, B., and J. Tokatlian. 1992. "Dope and Dogma: Explaining the Failure of U.S.-Latin America Drug Policies." In *The United States and Latin America in the 1990s. Beyond the Cold War*, edited by J. Hartlyn, J., L. Schoulz, L., and A. Varas, 214–34. Chapel Hill: University of North Carolina Press.

Bertman, E., et al. 1996. *Drug War Politics. The Price of Denial*. Los Angeles: University of California Press.

Bewley-Taylor, D. 2001. *The United States and International Drug Control*. New York: Continuum.

Bewley-Taylor, D., C. Hallam, and R. Allen. 2009. *The Incarceration of Drug Offenders: An Overview*. Beckley Foundation Drug Policy Program.

Borda, S. 2007. "La internacionalización del conflicto armado después 11 Sept." *Colombia Internacional* (Jan.–June): 66–89.

Buzan, B. 2006. "Will the 'Global War on Terrorism' Be the New Cold War?" *International Affairs* 82, no. 6: 1101–18.

Campbell, D. 1992. *Writing Security*. Minneapolis: University of Minnesota Press.

Clawson, P., and L. Rensselaer. 1996. *The Andean Cocaine Industry*. New York: St. Martin's Press.

CODHES (Consultoría para los Derechos Humanos y el Desplazamiento). 2004. "Fumigación de los cultivos de uso ilícito y vulneración de los derechos humanos en la frontera colombo-ecuatoriana." July 23.

Comisión Colombia–Estados Unidos. 1998. *Informe de la Comisión*. Bogotá: Tercer Mundo Editores.

Comisión de Drogas y Democracia para América Latina. 2009. *Democracy: Toward a Paradigm Shift*. Statement by the Latin American Commission on Drugs and Democracy.

Crandall, R. 2002. *Driven by Drugs: United States Policy toward Colombia*. Boulder, CO: Lynne Rienner Publishers.

DeShazo, P., J. Mendelson, and P. McLean. 2009. *Countering Threats to Security and Stability in a Failing State. Lessons from Colombia*. Americas Program, Center for Strategic and International Studies. Washington: CSIS Press. Retrieved from *csis.org/files/publication/090930_DeShazo_CounteringThreats_Web.pdf*, accessed May 12, 2015.

DeShazo, P., T. Primiani, T., and P. McLean. 2007. *Back from the Brink. Evaluating Progress in Colombia, 1999–2007*. Americas Program, Center for Strategic and International Studies (CSIS). Washington: CSIS Press. Retrieved from *csis.org/files/media/csis/pubs/071112-backfromthebrink-web.pdf*, accessed May 12, 2015.

Felbab-Brown, V. 2010. *Shooting Up. Counterinsurgency and the War on Drugs*. Washington, DC: Brookings Institution Press.

Felbab-Brown, V., et al. 2009. *Assessment of the Implementation of the United States Government's Support for Plan Colombia's Illicit Crop Reduction Components*. Washington, DC: Management Systems International–USAID.

FIP (Fundación Ideas para la Paz). 2010. "Corte Suprema de Justicia: Haciendo justicia rescatando a la justicia." Investigation into the uses and abuses of extradition in the fight against drugs. Policy brief, no. 16. March 15, Bogotá.

GAO (Government Accountability Office). 2008. *Plan Colombia*. Washington, DC, Government Accountability Office, October, GAO-9-71.

Hauguard, L. et al. 2008. *A Compass for Colombia Policy*. Washington, DC: Latin American Working Group. Retrieved from *www.lawg.org/storage/documents/compass.pdf*, accessed May 12, 2015.

International Crisis Group. 2008a. "La droga en América Latina I: Perdiendo la lucha." *Informe sobre América Latina*, no. 25.

———. 2008b. "La droga en América Latina II: Optimizar las políticas y reducir los daños." *Informe sobre América Latina*, no. 26.

Isacson, A., and A. Poe. 2009. *After Plan Colombia. Evaluating 'Integrated Action,' The Next Phase of U.S. Assistance*. Washington, DC: Center for International Policy, December. Retrieved from *ccai-colombia.org/files/primarydocs/091203_col.pdf*, accessed May 12, 2015.

Kennedy, S. 2007. *God and Country. America in Red and Blue*. Waco, TX: Baylor University Press.

Kerlikowske, G. 2009. Remarks at the Release of the 2009 *World Drug Report*, June 24.

Lipschutz, R. D. 1995 "On Security." In *On Security*, edited by R. D. Lipschutz, 1–23. New York: Columbia University Press.

Lipset, S. M. 1997. *American Exceptionalism: A Double-Edged Sword*. New York: W. W. Norton and Company.

Marcella, G. 2008. *Affairs of State: The Interagency and National Security*. Washington, DC: Strategic Studies Institute, US Army War College.

Matthiesen, T. 2000. *El arte político de conciliar. El tema de las drogas en las relaciones entre Colombia y Estados Unidos, 1986–1994*. Bogotá: Fescol-Cerec-Fedesarrollo.

Mejía, D., and C. Posada. 2010. "Cocaine Production and Trafficking: What Do We Know?" In *Innocent Bystander: Developing Countries and the War in Drugs*, edited by The World Bank. New York: McMillan/Palgrave.

Mejía, D., and P. Restrepo. 2010. "The War on Illegal Drug Production and Trafficking: An Economic Evaluation of Plan Colombia." Documento CEDE 2008-19, Facultad de Economía, Universidad de los Andes, October.

Ministerio de Defensa Nacional. 2007. "Política de Consolidación de la Seguridad Democrática (PCSD)." Bogotá: Ministry of Defense. Retrieved from *pdba.georgetown.edu/Security/citizensecurity/Colombia/politicas/consolidacion.pdf*, accessed May 12, 2015.

Moreno, L. A. 2002. "Aiding Colombia's War on Terrorism." *New York Times*, May 3, 23A.

Naim, M. 2009. "Wasted." *Foreign Policy*, April 15. Retrieved from *www.foreignpolicy.com/articles/2009/04/15/wasted-0*, accessed March 1, 2010.

National Drug Intelligence Center. 2007. *National Drug Threat Assessment 2008*. Washington, DC: National Drug Intelligence Center. Retrieved from *www.justice.gov/archive/ndic/pubs25/25921/25921p.pdf*, accessed May 12, 2015.

———. 2008. *National Drug Threat Assessment 2009*. Washington, DC: National Drug Intelligence Center. Retrieved from *www.justice.gov/archive/ndic/pubs31/31379/31379p.pdf*, accessed May 12, 2015.

Nordland, R. 2010. "U.S. Turns a Blind Eye to Opium in Afghan Town." *New York Times*, March 20. Retrieved from *www.nytimes.com/2010/03/21/world/asia/21marja.html*.

Presidencia de la República de Colombia. 1999. *Plan Colombia. Plan for Peace, Prosperity and the Strengthening of the State*. Bogotá: Presidencia de la República. Retrieved from *www.usip.org/sites/default/files/plan_colombia_101999.pdf*, accessed May 12, 2015.

Presidencia de la República de Colombia y Ministerio de Defensa Nacional. 2003. Política de defensa y seguridad democrática. Retrieved from *www.mindefensa.gov.co*.

Ruiz, J. 2009. Interviewed by A. Tickner, June 4, Bogotá.

Schuck, P. H., and J. Q. Wilson, eds. 2008. *Understanding America: The Anatomy of an Exceptional Nation*. New York: PublicAffairs/Perseus Books.

Shifter, M. 1999 "Colombia on the Brink." *Foreign Affairs* 78, no. 4: 14–20.

Sicard, T. L., et al. 2005. "Observaciones al 'Estudio de los efectos en el programa de Erradicación de Cultivos Ilícitos mediante la aspersión con el herbicida glifosato y de los cultivos ilícitos en la salud humana y en el medio ambiente.'" Instituto de Estudios Ambientales, Universidad Nacional de Colombia, May 11.

Stepanova, E. 2010. "El negocio de las drogas ilícitas y los conflictos armados: Alcances y límites de sus vínculos." In J. G. Tokatlian, *Drogas y prohibición. Una vieja guerra, un nuevo debate*. Buenos Aires: El Zorzal, 313–43.

Thoumi, F. 2009. "Las drogas ilegales, el fracaso de la política antinarcóticos y la necesidad de reformas institucionales en Colombia." In *La guerra contra las drogas en el mundo andino: Hacia un cambio de paradigma*, edited by J. G. Tokatlian, 51–123. Buenos Aires: Libros del Zorzal.

Thoumi, F., et al. 1997. *Drogas ilícitas en Colombia. Su impacto económico, político y social*. Bogotá: PNUD, DNE, and Editorial Planeta.

Tickner, A. B. 2007a. "U.S. Foreign Policy in Colombia: Bizarre Side-Effects of the 'War on Drugs,'" In *Democracy, Human Rights and Peace in Colombia*, edited by G. Gallón and C. Welna, 309–52. Notre Dame, IN: University of Notre Dame Press.

———. 2007b. "Intervención por invitación. Claves de la política exterior colombiana y de sus debilidades principales." *Colombia Internacional*, no. 65 (Jan.–June): 90–111.

Tickner, A. B., and R. Pardo. 2003. "En busca de aliados para la 'seguridad democrática': La política exterior del primer año de la administración Uribe." *Colombia Internacional*, no. 56–57 (Sept. 2002–June): 64–81.

Tokatlian, J. G. 1995. *Drogas, dilemas y dogmas*. Bogotá: TM Editores, CEI.

———. 2000. "La polémica sobre la legalización de drogas en Colombia, el presidente Samper y los Estados Unidos." *Latin American Research Review* 35, no. 1: 37–83.

———. 2009. "Conclusión: La urgencia de una eventual opción realista ante la equívoca lógica de la 'guerra contra las drogas.'" In *La guerra contra las drogas en el mundo andino: Hacia un cambio de paradigma*, compiled by J. G. Tokatlian, 313–44. Buenos Aires: Libros El Zorzal.

United States House of Representatives. 2009. *An Act to Establish the Western Hemisphere Drug Policy.* 111th Congress, 1st Session, H.R. 2134. Retrieved from *www.gpo.gov/fdsys/pkg/BILLS-111hr2134rfs/html/BILLS-111hr2134rfs.htm*, accessed May 12, 2015.

USAID. 2009. "Lessons Learned from the Integrated Consolidation Plan for La Macarena (PCIM)." Working Paper, July. Retrieved from *www.fbo/gov*, accessed March 10, 2010.

Vellinga, M., ed. 2004. *The Political Economy of the Drug Industry*. Gainesville: University Press of Florida.

Waever, O. 1995 "Securitization and Desecuritization." In *On Security*, edited by R. D. Lipschutz, 46–86. New York: Columbia University Press.

Wallace-Wells, B. 2007. "How America Lost the War on Drugs." *Rolling Stone*. Retrieved from *www.rollingstone.com/politics/story/17438347/how_america_lost_the_war_on_drugs.*

Walsh, J. M. 2009. *Lowering Expectations, Supply Control and the Resilient Cocaine Market.* Washington, DC: Washington Office on Latin America (WOLA).

"White House Czar Calls for End to 'War on Drugs.'" 2009. *Wall Street Journal*, May 14.

Youngers, C., and E. Rosin, eds. 2005. *Drogas y democracia en América Latina. El impacto de la política de Estados Unidos*. Buenos Aires: Biblos.

Zirnite, P. 1997. "Reluctant Recruits: The U.S. Military and the War on Drugs." Washington, DC, Washington Office on Latin America (WOLA).

PART IV: LEGAL AND INSTITUTIONAL ASPECTS OF THE WAR ON DRUGS

9 The Consumer's Right to a "Personal Dose" and the War on Drugs

A Study of the Policing of Drug Consumption in Bogotá, Colombia

Julieta Lemaitre and Mauricio Albarracín

In 1994, the Colombian Constitutional Court ruled that criminalizing the possession and use of small amounts of narcotics violated the constitutional right to the free development of personality.[1] The decision, controversial from the start, gave rise to a conservative backlash that culminated in December 2009 with the constitutional reform that prohibits the possession and consumption of narcotics, without specifying the nature of the prohibition. Even before this reform, however, the police habitually arrested people for the possession and consumption of drugs. This arrest, which is transitory, usually affects homeless people and young men from the poorer classes who smoke marijuana and *bazuco*, a cheap by-product of cocaine, in parks and plazas.

It is well-known that the life of the law does not only rest on its enactment but its daily enforcement. Citizens may massively disobey laws with impunity, which turns them into mere "paper" laws (García 2009). Also, public officials may or may not enforce the law, or may enforce only part of it, or enforce it only in certain circumstances, or may have different opinions of how it should be enforced. Furthermore, the implementation of laws may differ from their written content and have unforeseen effects, either because of the existence of other rules or because they affect different social groups differently. The conduct of both citizens and the state as well as the unforeseen consequences of the law causes a gap between the law on the books and the law in action, a breach that has been the object of much US literature on the relation between law and society and that is now responsible for a growing Colombian literature on the

Julieta Lemaitre: Associate professor, Faculty of Law, Universidad de los Andes.

Mauricio Albarracín: Doctoral student in political science, associate professor, Department of Political Science and adjunct investigator of the Center for International Studies (CEI), Universidad de los Andes.

same issues (Jaramillo and Alfonso 2008; García 2009; Lemaitre 2009; Rodríguez and Rodríguez 2010).

This chapter explores the breach between the right to the possession and consumption of a personal dose, established by the Constitutional Court in 1994, and daily practice. The questions we seek to answer are: How is the right to the personal dose applied? That is, does the freedom decreed by the Constitutional Court really exist? If so, how can that freedom coexist with the repression of consumption in public places, which is also ordered by law? What is happening with the constitutional reform? What meanings are given to the personal dose on the streets and in public forums? The answers to these questions are based on a study both of the norms and the political context in which decriminalization and the reaction against it took place. Once this analysis is set forth, we present a study of the daily practice of enforcement by the Bogotá police, the conclusion of which is that in certain circumstances, the police have not stopped repressing the possession and consumption of the personal dose, regardless of the right to the free development of one's personality. This repression is focused, and will probably continue to be focused in coming years, on certain sectors of the population: the homeless as well as poor young men who smoke marijuana and *bazuco* in public spaces.

THE CONSTITUTIONAL COURT'S DECRIMINALIZATION OF CONSUMPTION

From its inception the Colombian Constitutional Court advanced a liberal and progressive interpretation of the 1991 Constitution, broadening the concept of constitutional rights and freedoms.[2] One of the court's most controversial decisions is C-221/1994, which decriminalized the possession and consumption of small doses of illegal drugs by declaring unconstitutional articles 51 and 87 of the National Narcotics Statute (law 30/1986). These articles established minor punishments for the possession and use of small doses of narcotics, which the law called the "personal dose."[3] The court thus said that those amounts and lesser ones are personal doses, meant for consumption, and that larger amounts did entail the crime of trafficking.

The court argued that the criminalization of the personal dose violated, among others, the recently created right to the free development of one's personality (art. 16 of the Constitution). With that decision, it adopted a strong definition of that right in prioritizing personal autonomy over the state's interest in preserving the right to health. This autonomy includes the right to make decisions about one's own life and the state's duty to respect them. The court argued that the use and abuse of drugs, like the use and abuse of alcohol, fell within this sphere of autonomy granted to each individual, so long as the individual did not cause harm to third parties. Therefore, their criminalization represented an undue interference on the part of the state. The court stated, "Regarding a person as autonomous has its inevitable and inexorable consequences and the first and most important of all is that matters which exclusively pertain to a person must only be decided by that person."

It is important to clarify that while the court did not uphold the criminalization of the personal dose, that did not mean that it regarded the consumption of drugs to be a harmless activity that should be of no concern to the state. What the court objected to was the use of criminal law to establish imprisonment as punishment for an activity that does not harm third parties. In other sections of the decision it insisted that the state has the duty to prevent and deal with the abuse of drugs, which, like alcohol abuse, is a serious problem of public health. Nevertheless, given the constitutional protection of the free development of one's personality, the main solution available to the state is education. This does not exclude policing measures when the rights of third parties are affected. In those cases, the state may resort to administrative or punitive measures to regulate or repress consumption. These measures may be similar to those that control the use of alcohol in public establishments, its public consumption, sale to minors, etc.

The decision was strongly contested within the court itself: the majority opinion presented by Justice Carlos Gaviria passed by a five to four vote. The dissenting opinion, argued at length by the minority, adopted a different definition of the meaning of autonomy, one closer to the Catholic tradition than the liberal one, which currently dominates constitutional jurisprudence. Thus, for the minority, individual autonomy is linked to the transcendental purpose of human life: the search for perfection. In this view, human autonomy excludes decisions that harm the individual who makes them. These decisions are irrational, since reason itself tells us which decisions are harmful and which beneficial.

The decision exemplified the tension between the two concepts of autonomy. The debate it sparked outside the court, however, was not about these concepts but about its impact on the international political situation, particularly because it occurred during an intense stage of the war on drugs. Neither the majority nor the minority commented much on the possible contradiction between decriminalizing consumption while trafficking was being fiercely attacked. The majority opinion limited itself to a reference to the fact that the country's international commitments were related to the repression of trafficking, not consumption. Nevertheless, successive governments faced a problem with the decriminalization of the personal dose, one mainly thought of in terms of the tension between the decriminalization of consumption and the international war against drugs.[4]

DECRIMINALIZATION OF CONSUMPTION AND THE COLOMBIAN GOVERNMENT: THE PROBLEM OF THE WAR ON DRUGS

The decision of the Constitutional Court appeared at an inopportune political moment for the government of that time. In the previous years, Colombia had been worn down by a war between the narcotics trafficking cartels and between the cartels and the state, a war that became a national obsession. President César Gaviria (1990–1994) had been elected under the banner of the fight against narcotics trafficking, inherited from Luis Carlos Galán, the candidate assassinated by the drug mafias, and in 1994 Gaviria was still plagued by Pablo Escobar's escape from jail. And in the midst of the violence and uncertainty of the nation, the United States was also exerting a strong pressure on the country to show concrete results. It is not surprising, then, that when the government learned of the decision it threatened to call a referendum to revoke the decision of the court (a threat it never carried out), which it regarded as a grave mistake, given the war against the Medellín cartel in those years (*El Tiempo* 1994a, 1994b, 1995). The following government of Ernesto Samper (1994–1998), also from the Liberal Party, maintained this opposition to the decriminalization of consumption. As is well-known, Samper's administration was severely hampered by the investigation (known as the Proceso 8,000) into charges that money from the Cali cartel had financed his campaign. In those circumstances, Samper had to take a strong position against drugs even though in the late 1970s as president of the National Association of Financial Institutions he had famously called for the legalization of marijuana and criticized the United States for promoting the war on drugs (Samper 1980). In the 1990s, in the face of intense pressure from the United States, Samper rejected the decriminalization of the personal dose and likewise threatened to reform the Constitution to revoke the court's decision, though that threat was never carried out either (*El Tiempo* 1994d, 1995).

Both Gaviria and Samper asserted that the decriminalization of the personal dose went against the country's commitment to the war on drugs. Paradoxically, however, under his successor, the conservative Andrés Pastrana (1998–2002), closer to the United States than his Liberal Party counterparts, the subject of the personal dose seemed to have disappeared from the public agenda. There were several reasons for this. In the first place, the passage of time had showed that that there was little relation, at least in the military sense, between narcotics trafficking and domestic consumption. Decriminalization had taken place without a noticeably adverse effect on the war on drugs. In the second place, the war against the cartels was no longer the main concern; it was replaced by peace negotiations with the guerrillas. In the third place, the change of government in the United States, when Democrat Bill Clinton succeeded two Republican presidents, Ronald Reagan (1981–1989) and George H. W. Bush (1989–1993), meant that the promotion of the war on drugs and its foreign policy implications was less intense. Finally, and doubtlessly the most decisive factor, were the good relations between the government of Clinton and the government of Pastrana, and the alliance, justified as a war against narcotics trafficking, that was behind Plan Colombia. While Plan Colombia had several social aspects, it emphasized the strengthening of the military capacity of the Colombian state in its fight against international trafficking and showed little or no interest in domestic consumption (see Chapter 3).

The decriminalization of the personal dose became a matter of public debate again under the administration of Álvaro Uribe Vélez (2002–2010). Beginning with his presidential campaign in 2002, Uribe had insisted on the need to again sanction the "personal dose," a stance that seems to have had more to do with his conservative personal convictions than any political calculations (*El Tiempo* 2002b, 2009a, 2009e, 2010; Valencia 2002; Ochoa 2009; Uprimny 2009). In 2003 his administration submitted a series of constitutional reforms to popular vote, under the figure of a national referendum. It included an amendment that limited the right of personal autonomy (article 16, the free development of personality) to explicitly exclude drug consumption and to recriminalize it. The Constitutional Court, however, ruled the inclusion of this issue in the referendum unconstitutional, along with others, for procedural reasons (decision C-551/2003). In the 2006 elections Uribe's main opponent was Carlos Gaviria, the judge who had written the majority opinion for the 1994 decision that decriminalized consumption. That brought the subject back to life and turned it into one of Uribe's campaign pledges: to recriminalize consumption. Uribe fulfilled his campaign promise with five attempts at constitutional reform between 2006 and 2009.[5]

Initially, his proposals had little support in the Congress, in spite of the government's decriminalization of a Congress led by Uribe supporters. But even some of his more ardent supporters, as well as many outspoken members of the opposition (both the Liberal Party and the left Polo Democrático Party) objected to the different attempts at reform. The national press, liberal-minded on the whole, also denounced the measure in editorials and opinion columns.[6] Finally, in December 2009, the government's insistence and its good relations with the Congress bore fruit with the passage of a bill to amend article 49 (the right to health) to include the prohibition of consumption. Nevertheless, the final result was a moderate version of the government's proposal for criminalization of consumption. The new version reflected the transformation of the government's arguments in the different attempts at reform, from ones about traditional values and street crime in the failed bills to others about public health, the environment, and consistency in the war on drugs in the successful amendment.[7] The article that was finally approved prohibited the possession and consumption of narcotics but did not criminalize them nor clarify what the prohibition implies. In fact, the provision in the Criminal Code (article 376) that excludes the personal dose from the crime of narcotics trafficking remains in force. The only consequences of the reform are the provision of voluntary medical treatment for addicts and the state's assumption of all its costs.[8] The Uribe government nevertheless insisted that the reform implied, at the least, the obligatory confiscation of the personal dose by the police (Caracol Radio 2010; *El Tiempo* 2010). Also, before the end of his second term, the president presented a regulatory bill that established noncriminal sanctions, particularly the treatment of addicts with criminal offenses and the mandatory treatment of others.[9]

Despite calling for a consolidation of the achievements of the Uribe administration, his successor, Juan Manuel Santos (2010–2014), has not supported this regulatory bill. On the contrary, it has publicly stated that the financial costs of such a law would be difficult to assume, especially since the costs of treating addicts would put a further strain on the already exhausted health system.[10] At the same time, the Santos government has drafted a domestic security bill that would recriminalize consumption again by modifying the article that differentiates possession for consumption from trafficking.[11]

In this review of the history of the decriminalization of consumption, from the 1994 decision of the Constitutional Court to the recent declarations of the Santos government, one thing shines by its absence. In all the official declarations, the existence of the provision is regarded as an end itself, and apart from the costs for the health system, there is a notorious lack of knowledge of and concern for the way that the provisions are applied in daily life. The following section addresses this void, pointing to the importance of what the prohibition of the personal dose means on the streets of Colombian cities, regardless of the rationality of prohibition.

THE EVERYDAY LIFE OF THE DECRIMINALIZATION OF CONSUMPTION IN BOGOTÁ

The Laws Currently in Force

Once decision C-221/1994 came into force, the criminalization of the personal dose effectively ended, that is, from then on it was no longer valid to investigate, arrest, or imprison someone for the crime of possessing or consuming a personal dose of narcotics. In principle, this means that the public prosecutor (*fiscalía*) cannot accuse or try people for mere consumption. The Penal Code (CP) was even modified in the year 2000 to specify that the personal dose is excluded from the crime of narcotics trafficking (CP, art. 375) and this norm is still in force.[12]

Additionally, the Supreme Court of Justice, in a 2008 decision, limited the possibility of criminalizing possession for personal consumption, even when the dose is larger than that mentioned in law 30.[13] The Court referred to this as a question of possessing a "supply dose" (*dosis de aprovisionamiento*) and not only a personal dose, since it is natural that a consumer may buy an amount larger than a personal dose to be used over a long period. As a consequence, the criterion for deciding whether the crime of narcotics trafficking applies must be whether the possessor does or does not intend to sell and distribute the drugs, and not the amount possessed.[14] This criterion is currently used, for example, when the public prosecutor (*fiscalía*) sends the person who has been arrested to a medical examiner to determine whether the person is or is not just a consumer but a dealer.

The Supreme Court decision is consistent with current norms that grant a special importance to intent when establishing the crime of narcotics trafficking. Thus law 30/1986 (art. 2, heading j) states that the crime of narcotics trafficking arises with the intention to sell or distribute, so that in these cases the amount does not matter, even if it is less than the personal dose. As a consequence, dealers caught with small amounts cannot cite the amount as a defense if the intent to sell or distribute is proved. Therefore, at the present time in Colombia both jurisprudence and law agree that neither the consumption nor possession of illegal drugs is a crime, so long as their purpose is personal consumption. In an inverse manner, the possession of narcotics with the intent to sell or distribute is always a crime, regardless of the amount.[15]

That consumption or possession for consumption are not crimes does not mean that there are no restrictions on consumption: the same decision C-221/1994 establishes limits on consumption in public places, as have successive laws and municipal decrees. Thus law 745/2002 prohibited consumption in public spaces, places open to the public, commercial recreational establishments, educational centers and nearby places, and in front of boys and girls. There are, however, currently no procedures for this law and as such it cannot be applied.[16] At present only a later law is applicable, law 1098/2006, which established similar restrictions with regard to consumption by minor boys and girls, restrictions that also apply to alcohol and tobacco. In Bogotá, mayoralty decree 411/2008 is also applicable: it restricts the consumption of narcotics, alcohol, and tobacco in a number of public spaces and has noncriminal sanctions such as confiscation of the drug and mandatory attendance at talks on drugs abuse.[17]

It is important to highlight that in no case do the norms in force up to 2010 authorize the arrest of a person who consumes drugs in a public place. In the first place, since it is not a crime, arrest and the transfer of the case to the *fiscalía* are not permissible. In the second place, while a transitory arrest by the police is possible, this arrest is limited both by law and jurisprudence to a few circumstances, which do not include public consumption or the possession of a personal dose.[18] The general criterion for a temporary arrest is when there are strong suspicions that the arrested person committed a crime and it is necessary to establish his identity, or when there are reasons to think, from the person's highly altered state, that he or she is a danger to himself or herself or to others.

These are the applicable norms at the time of writing this article, since the above-mentioned reform of article 49 of the Constitution is not yet regulated and thus is not yet applicable. Nevertheless, an examination of the norms does not present a complete picture of the law as a living force. Public officials as well as ordinary people tend to interpret and apply the law in different ways, resulting in a conflict between the law on the books and the law in action. Having explained the applicable legislation and the debates surrounding its reform, we now have to answer the question: How are these norms applied in real life? To answer it, we designed and undertook a study of the personal dose in Bogotá in 2009.

The Personal Dose in Bogotá

The Reason for the Study, and Its Design

There has been a growing interest in the effects of the decriminalization of consumption, which has been particularly strong at certain points, especially during the Uribe government (2002–2010). There is very little information, however, about the implementation of and compliance with the decision, or of the constitutional reform passed at the end of 2009. In 2009, in the absence of such data, we designed and carried out a study of how the Bogotá police apply the norms on the personal dose, based on interviews with the very patrol officers who are responsible for enforcing the legal restrictions on consumption in public spaces.[19] Between September and December 2009, we interviewed thirty-four police officers.[20] Twenty-four were patrol officers (who do basic patrol work on motorbikes),[21] six were community police (whose focus is prevention and community relations),[22] and four were high-ranking officers at police stations, including two station heads, one noncommissioned officer, and a detective assigned to the narcotics intelligence division (CIPOL).[23] Later, during the first six months of 2010, we did ten interviews of patrol officers from five Rapid Response Posts (Centros de Atención Inmediata, CAI), to get a preliminary assessment of the impact of the constitutional reform of the prohibition of the consumption of the personal dose, which came into force on December 17, 2009. In addition to these interviews, we made four extensive visits in December 2009 to the Permanent Justice Unit (Unidad Permanente de Justicia, UPJ), the center for the temporary detention of persons arrested for violations of the law related to the consumption and possession of the personal dose.[24] These visits, along with the interviews, provided us with important information about the application of the norms now in force. We present the conclusions, as follows.

Consumption of Drugs in Public Spaces Is Frequent in the City and Is Handled in Accordance with the Profiles of the Consumers

The problem of the consumption of drugs in public spaces is part of the daily routine of the patrol officers we interviewed. In almost all districts, the patrol officers who work out of the Rapid Response Posts reported encounters with five to ten people consuming drugs on each shift, mainly marijuana and crack (*bazuco*). The exception to this rule were the CAIs located downtown, near a well-known *olla*, that is, a crack house or similar place where illegal drugs are sold, where twenty to thirty cases per shift were reported. In most of these cases, all the police officer did was confiscate the drugs and order the consumer or possessor to leave the public area; on occasions those caught with the drugs were taken for a short time to the CAI.[25] What the police officers report is that it is unusual to arrest people for the consumption of narcotics, but they do do it in certain circumstances and with a certain frequency. The persons are usually not detained for consumption alone, but for the consumption associated with certain categories of people who, in accordance with the informal profiles used by the patrol officers, lead the latter to think that they are likely to rob, mug, get into fights, or cause complaints by members of the community. They tend to be young men from poor backgrounds or homeless people. In some cases the police officer already knows them, because they have been previously arrested for petty crimes.

The arrests have to do with the patrol officers' conception of their work of vigilance and of their authority; in the interviews their work was often described as one of control and they even used the word "cleanse" to describe what they do in their districts. This includes not only a response to reports of crimes but also the prevention of them through the control of persons identified as real or potential delinquents, mainly young men from the poorer classes and street people.[26]

The Patrol Officers Would Like the Personal Dose to be Criminalized

For most (31) of the police officers who were interviewed, the decriminalization of the personal dose is a limitation on their capacity to arrest the people they should arrest, either because they think they are criminals as well as consumers or because it is important to check consumption among youngsters through prohibition. In the interviews the patrol officers often refer to certain consumers as presumed thieves, small-time drug dealers, and habitual muggers. They assume that these crimes are associated with the consumption of drugs, since those who consume marijuana and crack in parks and plazas are "the same" as those who commit the crimes. A common explanation among them for this link between drug consumption and crime is that those persons rob in order to "smoke" and "smoke" to get up the nerve to rob, and also that the dealers recruit habitual consumers as small-time dealers in exchange for drugs. Another common explanation in the interviews is that the dealers do not carry more than the personal dose, which due to decriminalization makes it very difficult to capture them. In the interviews the officers agree that there are other limitations on the policing aimed at controlling street crime, including ones of logistics and intelligence, but also the meager cooperation of the victims. According to the police officers, the best time to capture these delinquents is when they are smoking marijuana or crack in a public place or when, on being searched, they are found to be carrying illegal drugs, even though they may be small amounts. Nevertheless, the law does not allow the police officers to detain people for the above reasons. The solution, at least the temporary one, is their transitory arrest: people with "suspicious" profiles are sent to the UPJ for twenty-four hours, the "degree of arousal" being left to the discretion of the police.[27]

With the exception of three, the police officers who were interviewed believe that their work of vigilance and security would be easier if there were no decriminalization. Only three of the thirty-four said they agreed with decriminalization, mainly because criminalization does not solve the problem of addiction and the jails are already overcrowded. One high-level police officer stated that the only reasonable solution would be to legalize the sale of drugs, at least of marijuana, instead of putting the police in the impossible situation of capturing the sellers and letting the buyers go. But the majority of those interviewed (thirty-one) who confront the daily work of control and vigilance in specific districts believed that the norms on the personal dose were a threat to their effectiveness and authority as agents of the law.

The Patrol Officers Feel Pressure from the Community to Arrest Consumers

The patrol officers report pressure from the community to remove young men who smoke marijuana and remove street people from public spaces. People call the CAIs to complain or call the city's emergency phone line (123), which informs the CAIs.[28] In meetings between the police and the community, the police also hear complaints that they are not doing enough about the threat from youngsters and street people who use drugs in public spaces. Several of the police officers complained that the members of the community "do not know the law" and expect such people to be arrested. A few of them said that the community expected them to use illegal measures, perhaps the use of force as a form of dissuasion.

The consumers with "dangerous" profiles present a further problem for the patrol officers. While some individuals are recognized by the community and the police as persons who regularly commit crimes in their district, the victims do not bring charges, usually out of fear or a lack of trust in the judicial system. This makes it difficult to arrest those persons for the crimes they have committed, which tend to be minor offenses like muggings that require the testimony of the victims. By contrast, possession of the personal dose does not require a victim's report and allows police officers to detain those suspected of the crime, a reason why they support criminalization.

Community complaints take on an even more threatening meaning when they are related to "social cleansing," the systematic murder of "undesirables," among whom street people and those who use drugs in public are usually included. Thus, for example, in 2009 the media reported that several flyers containing threats by paramilitary groups were circulating in a number of neighborhoods in Bogotá. These anonymous announcements, which were photocopied and stuck onto lampposts and notice boards, were death threats aimed at members of the guerrilla groups, prostitutes, persons with HIV/AIDS, street people, drugs dealers, drug addicts, and youngsters found on the streets after 10 p.m. There is little data, however, about whether or not there have been serial murders related to drugs selling or use.[29] Despite the absence of concrete information, it is necessary to point out that there is a similarity between the language used in the flyers and that used by the police to describe the complaints they receive from the community and the dilemma the personal dose puts them in. Thus, for example, they speak of the same sectors of the population as undesirables and use the word and the concept of "cleansing" a district.

Apart from these interviews with police officers, we have little data about the communities' reaction to the decriminalization of the personal dose. Some surveys and press reports furnish some additional information. Thus, in different cities, including Bogotá, there was a perception of greater insecurity in 2008 and 2009, one that has to do with a stronger presence of criminals, but the informants thought that this increase in crime had more to do with poverty and gangs than the use of narcotics.[30] Another survey, taken in August 2009 by a civic monitoring program sponsored by the Mayoralty, *Bogotá cómo vamos* (Bogotá: How are we doing?), reported that 66 percent of those surveyed said that street assaults are the main threat to security, followed by drug dealing (38 percent), the presence of gangs (37 percent), and robberies of houses (20 percent). The survey did not directly inquire into the consumption of narcotics, however, only about narcotics trafficking. According to these surveys, it does not seem that the use of drugs in public is a main concern of the communities. What does concern them is the presence of known criminals and gang members in public spaces.

Nevertheless, other sources confirm that there is pressure from the community to control the use of drugs in public spaces, especially among youngsters who smoke marijuana in parks and plazas. In 2008, when the Mayoralty of Bogotá regulated the personal dose of narcotics (D. 411/2008), as well as alcohol and tobacco, prohibiting their use in different public spaces, it justified the measure as a response to repeated complaints and requests from the community in Citizen Security Councils (Consejos de Seguridad Ciudadana).[31] Likewise, at the beginning of 2010, the Bogotá councilman Felipe Ríos was cited in several communications media as a spokesman for the communities complaining about drug dealers and consumers who, according to Ríos, controlled 40 percent of the parks in Bogotá (*El Espectador* 2010a; City TV 2010).

Without further information, it is difficult to determine whether the community is intolerant of the personal dose per se or if its complaints are related to the feeling of insecurity caused by the link, whether real or perceived, between street crime and the public consumption of marijuana and *bazuco*.[32] Nevertheless, from the available data it is plausible to think that the community's hostility to the consumption of narcotics is related to the fear of crimes (assaults and robberies) that both the communities and the police associate with the public consumption of marijuana and *bazuco*.

Police Reaction to Consumption Depends on Consumer Profiling

The police officers who patrol the city on a daily basis use their discretion when making decisions about what measures to apply to the personal dose, which range from a warning to the consumer to a transitory arrest and confiscation of the drugs. Arrest, the most severe measure, is especially applied to marginal sectors of the population. These sectors are, first, young men from poor backgrounds who gather in groups in public spaces to smoke marijuana, and second, street people. Both for the police officers and the community, these persons increase the insecurity of the neighborhood.

When consumers are from the middle or upper classes, the situation is different. In upper-class neighborhoods the police restrict themselves to reporting on the public consumption of marijuana, asking the person to move on, and, on occasion, seizing the drug. The reasons for this are, first, that they regard those who are well off as "decent people" (*personas de bien*) whom they describe as parents or youngsters who live with their parents, and second, for the perception the police officers have that arresting a middle- or upper-class person may cause them problems with their superiors on the force.

To that extent, we may conclude that the first-level norms (those that refer to the personal dose) are applied in conjunction with second-level ones (those of transitory arrest) in a context where the police officers are given discretion in their interpretation.[33]

The result is that the recognition of the constitutional rights protected by the court in decision C-221/1994 is closely linked with social class, gender and age.[34]

When Patrol Officers Find the Personal Dose on Homeless People and Poor Young Men They Tend to Resort to a Transitory Detention at the UPJ

According to current norms and jurisprudence, transitory detention must only be applied in exceptional situations and limited to those cases where it is the only way to prevent harm to third parties or the detained person.[35] The police who were interviewed, however, interpret these norms differently from the Constitutional Court and assume that the discretion given to the police has a stronger role. Thus, the police officers cited articles 146 and 147 of the Bogotá Police Code, which allows for detention when a person shows a "high degree of arousal."[36] The police officers used the term in relation to particular contexts and profiles, showing the discretion they have in interpreting the norm, which in practice is broad. According to the police, street people tend "to get aroused when their drugs are confiscated," or they think this is the normal state of the street person, because of mental problems or his tendency to assault other people or the police. These circumstances of arousal are also linked to "representing a threat to him/herself and others," another legal justification for temporary detention. In addition to street people, young men who fit the profile of potential or presumed thieves and muggers also tend to show "a high degree of arousal" and are thought to be a threat. On occasions, it seems that the police regard the very fact of being under the influence of drugs as "being aroused." In sum, the interpretation of a "high degree of arousal" and of being a threat owes much to the discretion of the police, and the convenience of arresting such persons depends on the interpretation of the patrol officers.[37]

The persons who are temporarily detained under these criteria are sent to the Permanent Justice Unit (UPJ), a warehouse on Cra. 32 with Cll. 13 in downtown Bogotá, close to some of the city's most dangerous districts. The detained arrive with a remittance form that states that they have been informed of their rights and specifies their state of health and other conditions they are in when detained.[38] By day at least, when there are civilian personnel present at the UPJ (public officials and voluntaries), those detained are separated into four categories: women, street people, LGBT (lesbian, gay, bisexual, transgender, though they are usually transvestite prostitutes) and "other profiles." The latter category is mainly made up of young men from poor backgrounds whom the community and the police themselves regard as potential or actual assailants, thieves, gang members, drug dealers, etc. The "other profiles" categories occasionally includes youngsters from the lower middle class who are identified as students, as well as a few older men in a state of drunkenness.

Those detained remain in the UPJ from twelve to twenty-four hours, usually the whole night. In theory, those in each category are put into a separate holding pen. They must attend talks on drug abuse before being released.[39] In the course of this study, we attended four workshops for groups of between twenty and thirty detainees. The workshops cover such subjects as self-help techniques, "the parable of the prodigal son," the rights of the detained, the duties of citizenship, peaceful coexistence, and drug addiction. Those detained are usually apathetic, pay little attention or interest, and on occasion are hostile and threatening.

As with the patrol officers, the interviews with the staff of the UPJ show that social class is an important factor; those detained belong to the lowest social classes in Bogotá. The detention of a middle- or upper-class person is regarded as a problem by the authorities of the UPJ, since they recall past occasions when they were reprimanded, in person or over the phone, by high-ranking officers generically referred to as "the colonels," who regard the detention of someone of that profile as a mistake.

Those most frequently detained at the UPJ are street people. The woman director of the unit estimates that a bit more than half of the detained belong to that category. The other half are mostly young men with profiles that lead the police to regard them as potential delinquents, as well as male and female prostitutes. According to the director of the UPJ, the use of drugs is very common among the detainees: "nearly 80 percent of those who arrive here abuse the personal dose."[40]

In March 2009 we carried out an initial probe in some CAIs that led us to think that the situation has not changed since the passing of the constitutional reform earlier that year (legislative act 02/2009). While, as we explained above, the Uribe government insisted on several occasions that the article can be directly applied, at least through an immediate seizure of the drugs, such seizures were already being employed under the discretion exercised by the police officers. A preliminary survey of ten patrol officers from five CAIs in the city, chosen at random, revealed that there was little awareness of the constitutional reform and that while it has created a certain confusion about which norms are applicable, it has not changed the previous practices. In the opinion of some police officers, prohibition implies prosecution, even when the amount of drugs is smaller than the personal dose. For others, however, prohibition merely confirmed that drugs may not be consumed in public places and is an explicit authorization to seize the drugs and, at a minimum, detain the consumers in the UPJ. Nevertheless, in a few cases, it was clear that even when they were aware of a new duty to send the consumers to court, most of the patrol officers interviewed didn't want to "complicate their lives with paperwork and testimonies," the latter a necessary step for incriminating someone for trafficking, selling, or dealing narcotics. The police officers preferred to continue the practice of seizing the drugs and asking the consumer to leave the public space, and in the above-mentioned cases they continue to remit certain consumers to the UPJ.

Nevertheless, an article published in *lasillavacia.com* in November 2010 insists that the conditions have been changing. According to the reporter, the public prosecutor (*fiscalía*) is prosecuting cases for amounts less than the personal dose and sending the accused to the medical examiner (*medicina legal*) for an evaluation of their circumstances (Lewin 2010). If the experts decide that the person is an addict, there is no investigation, but if they believe that the person is a trafficker, an investigation is held, regardless of the amount seized. That, of course, is consistent with the norms currently in force, but it shows that the public prosecutor has a stronger interest in trying people who carry less than the personal dose than our interviews suggested. This may be the result of the press coverage of what is called the "the retail dealing of narcotics" (*narcomenudeo*) and the constitutional reform itself. There is a need for more research into the current situation.

CONCLUSIONS AND RECOMMENDATIONS

In the case of the personal dose, the breach between the law and practice is a complex matter. We have no hesitancy in stating that since there has been no prosecution of consumers, the Constitutional Court's decision is being applied. At the same time, we note how other laws and regulations come into play that lead to the repression of consumption in other ways. On the one hand, there are laws that prohibit consumption in certain places and circumstances, and on the other, there are norms and interpretations that turn transitory detention into an everyday practice in the case of certain groups of "suspicious" persons. These are applied by the police in the name of a social control of sectors of the population perceived as dangerous, particularly young men from the poorer classes and street people. Other consumers, particularly those of the more prosperous classes, are rarely repressed, even when they are caught consuming drugs in public spaces.

This leads us to single out three conclusions that are especially relevant to the design of public policies. The first conclusion is that the problem of the personal dose, in practice, is really about the repression and social control of poor sectors of the population whom police officers regard as dangerous, a subject on which there is an ample sociological literature (Waquant 2007, 2001; Garland 2001; Svampa 2006; Gargarella 2009; Zaffaroni 2003; Iturralde 2009; Dammert 2005; Briceño-León 2007). And as the literature also notes, the police exercise an important degree of discretion when they undertake their work, choosing when and when not to apply the law (Goldstein 1960; Davis 1969; LaFave 1965; Manning 1977; Lundman 1980; Kleinig 1996).

The second conclusion is that, the above-mentioned practice of social control aside, the discussions that take place in public forums mainly have a symbolic effect, that is, the creation of social meanings and the legitimization of the authorities. The main effect of the arguments wielded by the Constitutional Court, like those of the successive governments, is to legitimize themselves in the eyes of domestic and international public opinion as authorities who fulfill their constitutional task and whose defense of a political position (liberal or conservative) is coherent. The law legitimizes the authorities in the eyes of the public, but beyond eliminating criminalization, it is difficult to apply and there is not even much interest in understanding how its application really works.

The third conclusion is that there is a need for more information about the real life of the law in order to be able to design evidence-based public policies. This cannot be limited to evidence about consumption in general, but must also include evidence about how the authorities function and their relations with the consumers. In particular, we believe that a better understanding of the way the decriminalization of consumption is applied requires more ethnographic studies of the experience and perception of police officers, consumers of different profiles, and small-time drugs dealers. In addition, we need to know more about what happens in parts of the country other than Bogotá.

Despite the need for more studies, we believe that the available evidence allows for three major recommendations about public policy that are in line with our conclusions. The first recommendation is to acknowledge that the repression or liberalization of the personal dose has important effects on the way the police exert social control over marginal sectors of the population. To ignore it leads to a situation where repression may be the only public policy used for those groups or where it functions without being coordinated with other policies of social support.

The relation between consumption and marginal sectors of the population who are regarded as dangerous is not a strictly Colombian concern. Public policies on drugs in a number of European countries have specifically focused on this link, with programs and projects that should be known and evaluated. Thus, for example, there is talk of the need for an integral approach to consumption that includes other forms of rehabilitation and social integration and does not emphasize repression. Successful experiments in the legalization of the sale of certain substances, especially marijuana, for example, have caused consumption to be separated from different kinds of minor criminality and even shown, at least in the Portuguese reform, a tendency toward a general decrease in consumption (Greenwald 2009; Hughes and Stevens 2009; Jelsma 2009; Rodrigues 2009).

The second recommendation, which relates to a subject broader than the one in this study, is, as the introduction to this book proposes, the need for evidence-based drug policies that include evidence on the way laws are actually enforced. Debates both in the courts and the Congress reveal that policy design has been guided by principle rather than by evidence. A clear example is the supposition of a link between increased consumption and the need for prohibition that was behind the December 2009 amendment, which failed to address the question of whether there really was a link between criminalization/decriminalization and consumption.

The third recommendation follows from that one, and it is the importance of undertaking more empirical studies about the way laws are enforced in Colombia. As mentioned above, these studies are needed for the design of evidence-based public policies and to avoid making decisions based solely on principle without assessing the policies' actual scope in practice. In this case, the decriminalization of consumption serves to limit police harassment of street people and young men in poor neighborhoods, but it does not eliminate it.

NOTES

The authors would like to thank Jorge Alberto Rodríguez and Julián Martín Berrío for their valuable help with the research for this project.

1. We use the term decriminalization to refer to the elimination of the penal sanctions against consumption, and legalization to denote the elimination of penal sanctions against the sale of drugs and permitting it to take place.
2. Thus, for example, euthanasia with the consent of the passive subject (C-239/1997); the decriminalization of abortion in three exceptional cases (C355/2006); the recognition of a de facto marital union between partners of the same sex and almost all of its rights (C-075/2007 and C-029/2009); and the right to conscientious objection to obligatory military service (C-728/2009), among other decisions.
3. Before law 20, drug trafficking was penalized under decree 1188/1974, which included the personal dose. The term refers to a specific amount: 20 grams of marijuana, 5 grams of hashish, 1 gram of cocaine, 1 gram of crack (*bazuco*), and 2 grams of methaqualone. Since 1980 the Supreme Court of Justice had insisted that narcotics addicts and users required treatment and not a prison sentence. See Colombia, Corte Suprema de Justicia, Sala de Casación Penal (Appeals in Cassation Division), May 6, 1980.
4. The tension is political. In juridical terms, the state may well penalize only one aspect, which implies not that it considers the activity to be beneficial but that it does not believe that all the aspects related to it merit the strongest sanction (prison). A similar example is prostitution: engaging in it is not a crime, but benefiting from the prostitution of others is.
5. In the bill for reforming justice in 2006, the government, as it had done in the referendum proposition in 2003, proposed a reform of the article in the 1991 Constitution that

guarantees the right to the free development of one's personality in order to explicitly turn the possession and consumption of narcotics into a crime (legislative bill 133/2006). When two separate versions of this bill failed in 2007, the government proposed a new constitutional reform, this time of the article which guarantees the right to health (art. 49), aimed at establishing sanctions against consumption other than prison, such as the obligatory treatment of addicts (legislative bill 22/2007 and legislative bill 04/2007). In 2009 the government again drafted a legislative bill to reform the article guaranteeing the right to health, one that returned to the penalization of possession and consumption but allowed for a suspended decision if the person found guilty accepted a medical treatment supervised by specialized medical courts (bill for law 248/2010).

6. Even when the support of the main party that supported Uribe, the Partido de la U, favored the reform, some of its key figures, like senators Armando Benedetti and Gina Parody, voted against the measure on the grounds of conscientious objection (Benedetti 2002; *El Tiempo* 2007). On the opposition of liberals, see, for example, Arbeláez 2009; Arrieta 2009; Chinchilla 2009; D'Artagnan 1995, 2003; *El Espectador* 2008a, 2008c, 2009a, 2009b, 2009e, 2010b; Gómez 2009; Molano 2009; Pacheco 2009a, 2009b, 2010; Plata, 2009; *Semana*, 2002a, 2002b, 2002c; Samper Pizano, 2002; Santos 2009; Uprimny 2009; Valencia 2002.
7. In one of its first bills, the government insisted on the defense of traditional values and the harm drugs did to families, and it also linked the consumption of drugs to crime and the deterioration of security in neighborhoods (legislative bill 22/2007 and legislative bill 04/2007). In 2009 the government used other kinds of arguments to defeat the opposition. It linked decriminalization to an increase in consumption; an important factor was the publication in 2008 of the National Study of Drugs Consumption undertaken by the Ministry of the Interior and Justice and the National Narcotics Administration (Dirección Nacional de Estupefacientes). It also linked the decriminalization of consumption to the social costs of narcotics trafficking, including the economic costs of the war and the deterioration of the environment (bill for law 248/2010). And, as a reaction to the support for the legalization of marijuana and other changes in the war on drugs expressed by three former Latin American presidents (César Gaviria of Colombia, Ernesto Zedillo of Mexico, and Fernando Henrique Cardoso of Brazil), Uribe insisted that as a producer country, Colombia could not be soft on consumption.
8. Colombia, Political Constitution of 1991. The new article (legislative bill 02/2009) says, "Article 49. The possession and consumption of narcotic or psychoactive substances is prohibited, except by medical prescription. For the purposes of prevention and rehabilitation, the law will establish administrative measures and treatments of a pedagogical, prophylactic or therapeutic kind for the persons who consume such substances. Submission to these measures and treatments requires the informed consent of the addict. Likewise, the State will devote a special attention to the dependent or addicted patient and his or her family in order to strengthen their adherence to values and principles which help to prevent conducts which affect the integral health care of those persons, and, therefore, of the community, and it will undertake, in a permanent way, prevention campaigns aimed against the consumption of drugs or narcotic substances and in favor of the recuperation of the addicts."
9. This bill proposes two major changes in the current regime. In the first place, people who are discovered possessing or consuming the personal dose will be reported at the police station where they are held and must submit themselves to pedagogic, prophylactic, or therapeutic measures, according to their circumstances. Judges will decide on the measures,

independently of the person's will, with the accompaniment of doctors affiliated with drug addiction centers. These measures will be financed by the national health system (though it is not clear whether these people will be detained). In second place, the bill reforms the penal definitions of drugs trafficking, broadening the crime of trafficking and leaving it to the National Narcotics Council (CNE) to determine the amount of the drug that makes the person guilty of a crime. This implies the possibility of penalizing consumption through an administrative decision of the CNE, which would definitely overturn the decriminalization of the personal dose (Colombia, Congreso de la República, proyecto de ley 248/2010, Senado de la República).

10. Germán Vargas Lleras, minister of the interior, declared this in several communications media: "The prohibition of the possession and consumption of psychoactive substances would be unviable, according to the Minister of the Interior." Retrieved from *www.cmi.com.co/?nt=53049*, accessed on November 15, 2010.
11. Colombia, Congreso de la República, proyecto de ley 164/2010, Senado.
12. Colombia, Congreso de la República, Código Penal, ley 599/2000: Artículo 376.
13. The decision reviewed the case of a young man condemned for narcotics trafficking for possessing an amount of marijuana slightly greater than the personal dose; it ordered the young man to be freed, arguing that the personal dose should be interpreted in terms of the person's intention to consume, and not according to the exact amount (Sala de Casación Penal, decision of November 18, 2008).
14. This decision was reaffirmed in a 2009 decision, in which the court dealt with the case of a person who had been imprisoned for possessing an amount of cocaine 0.3 grams above the dose permitted for personal use (1 gram). In this case the court invoked the concept of a "supply dose" (*dosis de aprovisionamiento*) for personal use, and repeated that a person may not be sanctioned for possessing drugs exclusively for personal use, even when the amount exceeds the personal dose. Cf. Colombia, Corte Suprema de Justicia, Sala de Casación Penal (Appeals in Cassation Division) decisions of November 18, 2008, and July 8, 2009. This line of argument by the Supreme Court is consistent with the Appeals in Cassation Division's defense of the principle that penal law is the ultima ratio or last resort for dealing with social problems and may not replace nonrepressive public programs and policies for confronting the problems associated with marginalization or of citizens' security.
15. This reflects the Supreme Court's liberal position on reserving penal law for cases that are especially grave (like trafficking) and not for all the conducts society considers reproachable (like consumption).
16. The original procedure was declared unconstitutional by the Constitutional Court in 2004 on the grounds that it no longer respected certain procedural guarantees; therefore there would be no way to implement the sanctions established by the law so long as no norm was adopted to establish the procedures of the case (decision C-101/2004).
17. The Mayor's Office of Bogotá prohibited the personal dose in any of the following places or any area within two blocks from them: public plazas and parks of any kind, public and private educational establishments, child care establishments, and health institutions. The decree establishes educational and preventive sanctions, like inscription in a book of infractions and the obligation to attend talks on the effects of drugs abuse. Cf. Bogotá, municipal decree 411/2008.
18. Transitory arrest was established as a corrective measure by the National Police Code (art. 186, num. 80) and is aimed at two situations: the person who wanders around in a drunken state and does not agree to be led to his domicile, and the person who, due to a

state of extreme excitation, may commit an imminent infraction of penal law (art. 207, n. 2 and 3 of the National Police Code [Código Nacional de Policía]). The Constitutional Court established important restrictions on this measure in decision C-720/2007, where it ruled that "transitory arrest may only be applied when it is strictly necessary and respecting the following constitutional guarantees: i) a report, with the reason, must be immediately sent to the Office of the Attorney General (Ministerio Público), with a copy immediately given to the detained person; ii) the detained person may at any time be permitted to communicate with a person who may help him; iii) the detained person may not be held in the same place where those captured for infractions of the penal law are held and must be separated by reason of his or her gender; iv) the detention will end when the detained person overcomes the state of excitation or intoxication, or when a responsible person may assume the required protection, and in no case may it surpass a period of 24 hours; v) minors must be protected in accordance with the Code on Children and Adolescents; vi) subjects requiring special constitutional protection may only be taken to places where their condition is cared for" (Colombia, C. Const., sent. C-720/2007).

19. While the study's focus on Bogotá was made for reasons of convenience, it is important to highlight that the importance of Bogotá not only lies in its being the capital of the country, but also because its police force has been specially trained to respect the 1991 Constitution and human rights. In contrast with other police forces in the country, the Bogotá police are regulated by the Bogotá Police Code, decree 79/2003, which emphasizes the protection of and respect for human rights in harmony with the 1991 Constitution. In addition, the training police officers in Bogotá receive has important aspects of human rights and legal limits on the use of force. This leads us to think that respect for the decriminalization of the personal dose must be stronger in Bogotá than in the other cities of the country.
20. The total number of interviews reflects the attainment of a saturation point.
21. The study concentrates on the patrol officers responsible for public vigilance, since they are the ones who confront the problems related to the possession and consumption of small amounts of illegal drugs. The patrol officers work out of a police station, but they are usually assigned to shifts in one or another of the city's CAIs (rapid response centers). During these shifts the officers patrol the district they are assigned to on motorbikes and respond to incident calls sent from the station through the CAIs.
22. The community police, whose members are much fewer than the patrol officers, are responsible for undertaking preventive and proactive activities aimed at security problems, through mechanisms for coordination and participation with the community and different social actors. Each police station has a small force of community police officers, whose role is to create links with community leaders and undertake educational activities, like those of the DARE program for the prevention of drug addiction in schools.
23. These figures are a proportional representation of the composition of the Bogotá police. The choice was random insofar as the individuals who were interviewed but were stratified with regard to localities and neighborhoods: twelve were stationed in neighborhoods of strata 2 and 3, typical of most of Bogotá; eight in neighborhoods of stratum 1 (the lowest) or in districts with major illegal drug distribution centers (known as *ollas*, roughly "stewpots") and four in localities of strata 4, 5 and 6 (the highest). The community police officers were from the Suba station, a district with highly diverse strata.
24. But not for narcotics trafficking: when the dose is higher, the detained persons are sent to the respective office of the public prosecutor (*fiscalía*), where they are charged, that is, where the penal procedure is begun.

25. In any of these cases it may happen that bribes are offered or requested, but due to the limitations of this study (which focuses on information reported by the police), there are no data available for the frequency with which requests for bribes (popularly known as *mordidas*, roughly "bites") occur during these arrests, nor are there data about other kinds of corruption, like not reporting the real quantity of the seized drugs.
26. It is important to point out that the police do not regard street people in the same way as they do presumptive delinquents. Several of the police officers who were interviewed had a more tolerant attitude toward the former than toward the young men they associate with delinquency. In the case of street people, while the police officers say that many commit minor robberies and assaults, several defined them as people with mental problems or in desperate situations. Nevertheless, the patrol officers also say that the street people heighten the citizenry's perception of insecurity and cause problems in public spaces, for which reason they frequently remit them to the UPJs.
27. It is possible that there are other sanctions of an informal or illegal nature, like detaining persons in CAIs or other unsuitable places, or even beating, torturing, or extorting them, but for obvious reasons these were not reported by the officers who were interviewed.
28. The system, however, does not record these calls in a specific category. Nevertheless, a right-to-information request about the system revealed that it received 33,918 calls in 2010 that reported the "consumption, possession, sale, distribution or fabrication of substances which produce a psychotropic dependence." The records of the system do not distinguish between consumption and sale. Message from José Santos Cogua Morena, general coordinator of the Nuse system. File number N.20105510230471, June 15, 2010.
29. The phenomenon of pamphlets with collective threats was recently reported on in the annual report of the UN High Commissioner for Human Rights on the situation of human rights in Colombia (United Nations 2010).
30. A survey undertaken in December 2009 by the Bogotá Chamber of Commerce says that of those who report a perception of heightened insecurity (58 percent of the total), 47 percent related it to an increase in poverty and unemployment, and 29 percent to the presence of criminal gangs; only 4 percent of those surveyed related it to the use and sale of narcotics (Cámara de Comercio de Bogotá 2010).
31. The sanctions for these acts are of a pedagogic and preventive nature. Cf. Bogotá, municipal decree 411/2008.
32. A survey in 2008 reported that 80 percent of those surveyed rejected drug addicts and drugs sellers as equally undesirable neighbors, but it is not clear how they defined addicts and if they distinguished between consumers and addicts (Secretaría de Cultura de Bogotá 2008). The National Narcotics Survey of 2008 eliminated from its questionnaire the question, asked in the 1990s, about whether drug consumption should be prohibited. In the surveys of 1992 and 1996, 96 percent of those surveyed gave an affirmative answer.
33. By first-level norms we mean those that directly and substantially refer to the legal question, while second-level norms are those through which public officials exercise their powers; they are generally of a procedural nature and do not directly refer to the question in dispute (cf. Jaramillo and Alfonso 2008).
34. The patrol officers who were interviewed were aware of the limitations on their capacity to detain citizens from the higher strata, since it implies a number of problems. In the words of one, "he might end up being the son of a senator." This phenomenon has to do with the

resources at the command of people from the higher classes when it comes to defending their rights, including connections with top officials of the police and government and access to lawyers.

35. According to the law and jurisprudence, transitory detention is only justified for the protection of the detained person. Cf. Colombia, Corte Constitucional, decision C-720/2007. But reports on human rights note that transitory detention is used to the detriment of the marginal sectors of the population. For example, in 2008 the UN Working Group on Arbitrary Detention stated its concern about this matter in Colombia (United Nations 2009a, 2009b).
36. The National Police Code has a similar regulation in its articles 186, 192, and 207. Colombia, Código Nacional de Policía, decree 1355/1970.
37. The use of this norm is not unknown in the daily work of the police, as the police reported to the newspaper *El Espectador*: "The Metropolitan Police of Bogotá report that they daily arrest 17 persons for the consumption of narcotics in public thoroughfares, there are even days when 28 arrests for this cause are recorded" (*El Espectador* 2010a).
38. In the police detention report, the following characteristics of the person are noted: good state of health, infectious-contagious diseases, psychiatric complaints, state of pregnancy, street person, member of LGBT (lesbian, gay, transgender, or bisexual), minor, sixty years of age or older.
39. Street people also receive minimum social services; their wing has a cold-water hose for showers, and, depending on availability, they may receive a meal or medical visit or have their hair cut and even be given clean clothes. But all this depends on whether donations are available or if the Mayoralty's respective social program is present in the UPJ.
40. Director of the UPJ, interview, November 2009.

REFERENCES

Acevedo, D. 2009. "Dosis mínima, Libertad individual y chicharrón." *El Tiempo*, April 1.

Arbeláez, J. 2009. "Dosis mínima." *El Tiempo*, March 11.

Arrieta, L. 2009. "Dosis mínima ¿Error o acierto?" *El Espectador*, March 25.

Benedetti, A. 2002. "Un plan alucinado sobre alucinógenos." *El Tiempo*, November 18.

Bogotá cómo vamos. 2010. *Programa Bogotá cómo vamos. Informe de evaluación de la calidad de vida en Bogotá D.C. 2010.* Bogotá: Casa Editorial El Tiempo / Cámara de Comercio de Bogotá / Fundación Corona / Universidad Javeriana. Retrieved from *oab.ambientebogota.gov.co/apc-aa-files/57c59a889ca266ee6533c26f970cb14a/bogota_como_vamos_2010.pdf*, accessed May 15, 2015.

Briceño-León, R. 2007. *Sociología de la Violencia en América Latina.* Quito: Flacso y Municipio Metropolitano de Quito.

Cámara de Comercio de Bogotá. 2010. Bogotá: Encuesta de Percepción y Victimización 2009.

Caracol Radio. 2010. President Uribe ordered the seizure of the "minimum dose." Caracol Radio, March 21. Retrieved from *www.caracol.com.co/nota.aspx?id=973158*, accessed March 6, 2010.

Chinchilla, T. E. 2009. "Modernas inquisiciones." *El Espectador*, April 11.

City TV. 2010. District parks are used as "pots" to use drugs (video), available from City TV, March 6. Retrieved from *www.citytv.com.co/videos/56854/parques-distritales-son-usados-como-ollas-para-consumir-droga.*

Comisión Latinoamericana sobre Drogas y Democracia. 2009. "Drogas y Democracia: Hacia un Cambio de Paradigma." Retrieved from *www.plataformademocratica.org/Publicacoes/declaracao_espanhol_site.pdf*, accessed November 10, 2009.

Dammert, L. 2005. *Violencia criminal y seguridad ciudadana en Chile*. Santiago: Cepal.

D'Artagnan. 1995. "Polémica de nunca acabar." *El Tiempo*, June 18.

Davis, K. C. 1969. *Discretionary Justice*. Westport, CT: Greenwood Press.

———. 2003. "La afirmación del ministro." *El Tiempo*, November 19.

El Espectador. 2008a. "La penalización del consumo, sexta parte." June 6.

———. 2008b. "Gobierno volverá a insistir en penalización de dosis personal." December 4.

———. 2008c. "La moral y las drogas." December 5.

———. 2009a. "Del cultivo y el consumo al tráfico de drogas." February 23.

———. 2009b. "Tribunales de tratamiento de droga: Vuelve al ruedo la penalización de la dosis mínima." March 2.

———. 2009c. "Gobierno obligará a tratamiento médico a todos los drogadictos." March 20.

———. 2009d. "Marchas en tres ciudades para apoyar dosis mínima de drogas." March 26.

———. 2009e. "Dosis de personalidad." March 27.

———. 2009f. "Aprobado en tercer debate prohibición de porte y consumo de dosis mínima." June 2.

———. 2009g. "Senado aprueba prohibición de porte y consumo de dosis mínima." June 17.

———. 2009h. "Los días contados de la dosis mínima." October 2.

———. 2010a. "Policía de Bogotá arresta diariamente a 17 personas por consumo de droga." February 25.

———. 2010b. "Discriminación a consumidores." May 23.

El Tiempo. 1994a. "Despenalizan uso de drogas." May 7.

———. 1994b. "Rebelión política contra la Corte." May 12.

———. 1994c. "Gobierno dijo no al referendo." November 18.

———. 1994d. "Aplazan castigo por dosis mínima." December 18.

———. 1995. "Gobierno busca acabar la dosis personal." April 2.

———. 2000. "Uso de la dosis personal sería contravención." November 12.

———. 2002a. "Sanción a consumo de droga en público." May 15.

———. 2002b. "Revive debate por dosis personal." October 3.

———. 2003. "Víctimas, no criminales." July 11.

———. 2007. "Por aprobación de la penalización de la dosis personal de drogas, uribistas se dividieron." May 14.

———. 2008. "Una adicción peligrosa." August 5.

———. 2008a. "Prohibición de dosis mínima pasó sin sanción penal y tratamiento con aprobación previa del paciente," June 14.

———. 2008b. "Jóvenes hacen mercado de drogas en el norte de Bogotá." June 28.

———. 2008c. "Fallo de la Corte Suprema reabre polémica sobre tratamiento a personas adictas." November 28.

———. 2008d. "Dosis personal fue prohibida en plazas y parques por la alcaldía." December 8.

———. 2009a. "Por tema de dosis mínima, Álvaro Uribe recrimina fuertemente al fiscal general." February 24.

———. 2009b. "Consumo de droga como falta menor, con rehabilitación obligatoria al adicto, propone el Gobierno." March 26.

———. 2009c. "Jóvenes protestan contra proyecto de ley que penaliza el consumo de drogas." March 26.

———. 2009d. "Ataque y defensa de la dosis mínima." April 21.

———. 2009e. "Dosis: Vuelve y juega." May 19.

———. 2009f. "Senado dio vía libre a prohibición de la dosis mínima: La aprobó por 51 votos a favor y 16 en contra." July 23.

———. 2009g. "Anulada otra condena por porte de dosis mínima por la Corte Suprema." September 9.

———. 2010. "El Gobierno ordena a la Policía que inicie incautaciones de dosis mínima de droga." March 24.

García, M. 1993. *La eficacia simbólica del derecho*. Bogotá: Universidad de los Andes.

———. 2009. *Normas de papel*. Bogotá: Siglo del Hombre.

Gargarella, R. 2009. *De la injusticia penal a la justicia social*. Bogotá: Siglo del Hombre.

Garland, D. 2001. *Culture of Control. Crime and Social Order in Contemporary Society*. Chicago: University of Chicago Press.

Goldstein, J. 1960. "Police Discretion Not to Invoke the Criminal Law Process." *Yale Law Journal* 4, no. 69.

Greenwald, G. 2009. *Drug Decriminalization in Portugal, Lessons for Creating Fair and Successful Drug Policies*. Washington, DC: Cato Institute.

Guzmán, D., and R. Uprimny. 2010. *La prohibición como retroceso: La dosis personal en Colombia*. Washington, DC: Washington Office on Latin America and Transnational Institute, Series on Drug Reform Legislation, no. 4.

Hernández, S. 2009. "El debate de la dosis mínima." *El Tiempo*, March 30.

Hughes, C., and A. Stevens. 2009. "The Effects of Decriminalization of Drug Use in Portugal." The Beckley Foundation Drug Policy Programme—BFDPP. Retrieved from *www.idpc.net/php-bin/documents/BFDPP_BP_14_EffectsOfDecriminalisation_EN.pdf.pdf*, accessed on November 19, 2009.

Iturralde, M. 2009. *Castigo, liberalismo autoritario y justicia penal de excepción*. Bogotá: Siglo del Hombre, Uniandes e Instituto Pensar.

Jaramillo, I. C., and T. Alfonso. 2008. *Mujeres, cortes y medios: La reforma judicial del aborto*. Bogotá: Siglo del Hombre and Universidad de los Andes.

Jelsma, M. 2009. "Innovaciones legislativas en políticas de drogas. Iniciativa latinoamericana sobre drogas y democracia." Retrieved from *www.tni.org/sites/www.tni.org/files/download/innovacioneslegislativas.pdf*, accessed on November 10, 2009.

Kleinig, J., ed. 1996. *Handled with Discretion: Ethical Issues in Police Decision Making*, Lanham, MD: Rowman & Littlefield.

LaFave, W. 1965. *Arrest: The Decision to Take a Suspect into Custody*. Boston: Little Brown.

Lemaitre, J. 2009. *El derecho como conjuro: Fetichismo legal, violencia y movimientos sociales en Colombia*. Bogotá: Universidad de los Andes and Siglo del Hombre.

Lewin, J. E. 2010. "Con la prohibición de la dosis personal la trabada ahora es Medicina Legal." *lasillavacia.com*, October 25. Retrieved from *www.lasillavacia.com/historia/18949*, accessed October 25, 2010.

Lundman, R. 1980. *Police Behavior: A Sociological Perspective*. New York: Oxford University Press.

Manning, P. 1977. *Police Work: The Social Organization of Policing*. Cambridge, MA: Massachusetts Institute of Technology Press.

Molano, A. 2009. "Dosis máxima." *El Espectador*. June 6. Retrieved from *www.elespectador.com/columna144372-dosis-maxima*, accessed May 15, 2015.

Ochoa, L. N. 2009. "Las dosis políticas de Uribe." *El Tiempo*, March 27.

Pacheco, D. 2009a. "Porte su dosis de personalidad." *El Espectador*, March 9.
———. 2009b. "Dosis de orden y libertad." *El Espectador*, November 16.
———. 2010. "Marihuaneros cívicos." *El Espectador*, May 23.
Plata, E. 2009. "Hay dosis más urgentes." *El Tiempo*, March 29.
Revista Cambio. 2008. "País de metelones." August 27.
Revista Semana. 2001. "Iglesia contra las drogas." September 17.
———. 2002a. "A un *cacho* de la penalización." October 6.
———. 2002b. "En contravía." November 3.
———. 2002c. "*Cachos* libres." November 3.
Rodríguez, C., and D. Rodríguez. 2010. *Cortes y cambio social: Cómo la Corte Constitucional transformó el desplazamiento forzado en Colombia*. Bogotá: Centro de Estudios Derecho, Justicia y Sociedad-Dejusticia.
Rodrigues Torres, J. H. 2009. *La política de drogas y su confrontación en el ámbito judicial: Una experiencia brasileña*. Washington, DC: Washington Office on Latin America and Transnational Institute, Series on Drug Reform Legislation, no. 2.
Samper, D. 2002. "Ojo a la droga." *El Tiempo*, October 2.
Samper, E. 1980. *La legalización de la marihuana*. Bogotá: Tercer Mundo.
Santos, E. 2009. "Contratiempo dosis mínima." *El Tiempo*, March 15.
Secretaría de Cultura de Bogotá. 2008. *Encuesta de Cultura Ciudadana*. Bogotá: Secretaría de Cultura.
Svampa, M. 2006. *El dilema argentino: Civilización o barbarie*. Buenos Aires: Taurus.
Thoumi, F. 2002. "Adictos a las drogas." *Revista Semana*, July 15.
United Nations. 2009a. Report of the UN Working Group on Arbitrary Detention—Mission to Colombia, October 1–10, 2008. A/HRC/10/21/Add.3. February 16, 2009.
———. 2009b. UN Committee against Torture, Final Observations (Colombia), November 19, 2009. CAT/C/COL/CO/4.
———. 2010. Annual Report of the UN High Commissioner on Human Rights on the Human Rights Situation in Colombia, March 4, 2010. A/HRC/13/72.
Uprimny, R. 2009. "Una dosis mínima de cordura." *El Espectador*, March 30.
Valencia, L. 2002. "Sobredosis de justicia." *El Tiempo*, October 14.
Waquant, L. 2001. *Los parias urbanos*. Buenos Aires: Ediciones Manantial.
———. 2007. *Los condenados de la ciudad. Gueto, periferias*. Madrid: Siglo XXI.
Zaffaroni, E. R. 2003. *Criminología. Aproximación desde un margen*. Bogotá: Temis.

10 The Penal Treatment of Narcotics Trafficking and Associated Crimes

Manuel Iturralde and Libardo José Ariza

During the past three decades, the Colombian state has regarded drug trafficking as a national security problem that must be confronted with force. The penal system has played a leading role in this as the spearhead of the fight against drugs. The criminalization of activities related to trafficking has been the main feature of this criminal policy. The definition of new crimes, harsher punishments, the granting of extraordinary judicial powers to administrative entities, the limiting of procedural guarantees, the reduction of penal benefits, and the attack on the assets of narcotics traffickers have been some of the measures repeatedly introduced to strengthen the punitive system of the state and check the violence and impunity associated with narcotics trafficking.

Nevertheless, the criminal justice system (and the continual reforms to which it has been subjected) has not been effective in significantly reducing the criminal activities associated with narcotics trafficking, nor the high levels of violence and impunity accompanying it (Ariza et al. 1997; García 2001; García and Uprimny 2006a; Iturralde 2010; UNIJUS 1996). This explains, in part, the political strategy of continually reforming the penal system with the aim of strengthening it and making it more effective (Uprimny 2001, 392).

But there are at least two other factors that have had a strong influence on shaping the penal policy that attacks narcotics trafficking. For one thing, there are the agreements the international community has established to confront it. The United Nations Convention Against Illicit Traffic in Narcotics Drugs and Psychotropic Substances of 1988 (the Vienna Convention) got the signatory states (Colombia among them) to agree on strategies to confront the illegal trafficking of narcotics. The member states committed themselves to coordinating their juridical frameworks in order to harden the punishments of narcotics trafficking and related crimes, establish collaborative mechanisms for exchanging information and evidence, and attack new kinds of crimes associated with that activity, such as the laundering of assets.

For another, the leading role played by the United States in defining and implementing Colombia's anti-drug policy in the past three decades, through its logistical, economic, and military support, has been a central aspect of the war on drugs in Colombia. But in exchange for that support, the United States has wound up imposing its own vision of the problem and the way to deal with it (Rojas 2006, 2009; Iturralde 2010; Rodríguez 2009; Rodríguez and Uprimny 2006; Sousa Santos 2001).

Manuel Iturralde: Associate professor, Faculty of Law, Universidad de los Andes.

Libardo José Ariza: Assistant professor, Faculty of Law, Universidad de los Andes.

In both cases, narcotics trafficking is regarded as a form of transnational organized crime that assaults the security of the state, threatens the health and well-being of people, and undermines the economic, cultural, and political foundations of society. As a consequence, from that viewpoint, drug trafficking must be attacked in a joint manner by all the affected states, mainly through their mechanisms of control and security.

The above implies that the Colombian state's policy on drugs has been framed within the terms established by the United States and the international community, which narrows the range of responses it may attempt. Thus an eventual policy of decriminalizing or legalizing the trafficking of narcotics is not a feasible option in the middle term and does not exclusively depend on Colombia, even though the results of the fight against the narcotics trafficking industry have not been encouraging; the criminal organizations that control the trade have become powerful and violent (Comisión Latinoamericana sobre Drogas y Democracia 2009, 7).

In view of the above-mentioned considerations, the aim of this chapter is to present a brief description and assessment of the criminal policy employed by the Colombian state against drugs during the past three decades. On the basis of that analysis, we will then present a series of recommendations on public policy.

MAIN KINDS OF PENAL MEASURES USED AGAINST NARCOTICS TRAFFICKING (1984–2010)

Before explaining what the main penal measures implemented by the Colombian state to fight against narcotics trafficking in the past three decades have been, it is important to mention two main features of them that have influenced both the design and application of criminal policy and the results obtained up to now.

On the one hand, during most of this time, these measures have been adopted by the executive branch through powers granted to it under states of emergency (*estados de excepción*). This has led to negative effects: such policies have not been discussed by the legislative branch and public opinion, which noticeably limits the political control and evaluation of their suitability. The measures adopted have strongly restricted the constitutional rights of the accused, due to the exceptional powers given to penal justice, and by becoming permanent, they have undermined the democratic character and guarantees of the penal system (Iturralde 2010).

On the other hand, due to the large number of legislative decrees issued by different governments and the numerous legislative reforms of the penal framework,[1] there has been an inflation of norms, which threatens the effectiveness, stability, and coherence of the penal system. The respective norms are so numerous and change so frequently that those who implement the system find it difficult to understand and apply them, and the continuous changes of procedure affect the progress of investigations and trials, as well as legal certainty. All of this is taken advantage of by the members of criminal organizations, who are able to hire skillful lawyers who take advantage of the flaws and gaps in the system, while the rights to defense and due process of those who do not have the resources to hire experienced lawyers are harmed.

Within this scenario, which affects the legitimacy and effectiveness of the penal system, the following are the main features of the penal measures used against narcotics trafficking during the past thirty years.

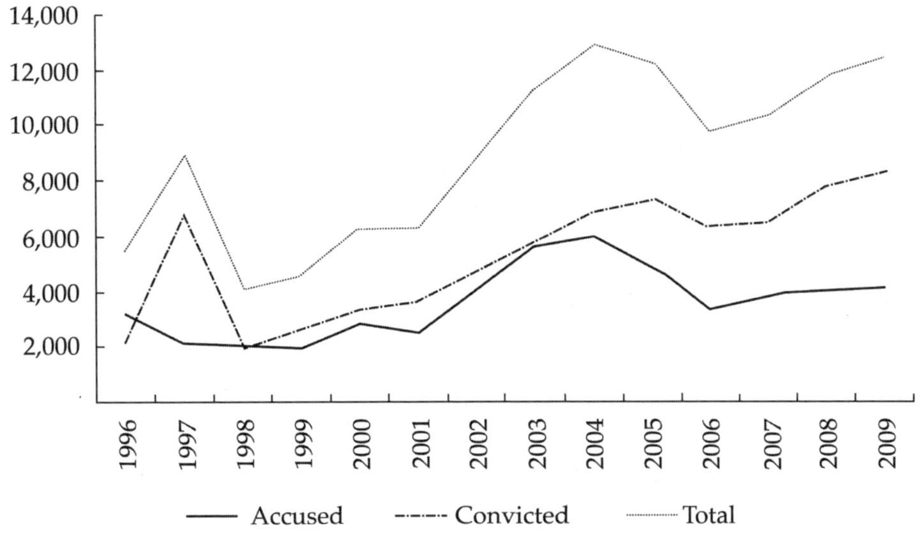

FIGURE 10.1. Population of those imprisoned (accused and convicted) for narcotics trafficking and associated crimes (1996–2009). Source: Inpec (2009)

Stiffer Sentences and More Arrests

Stiffening sentences has been the usual response when trying to correct the penal system's ineffectiveness in reducing the production and trafficking of narcotics and combating the criminal organizations that profit from it. Thus it seems that both the executive and legislative branches base themselves on the same erroneous premise that the high indexes of impunity are due to a lack of severity, rather than of effectiveness, in the penal system. From the beginning of the war on drugs in 1984,[2] narcotics trafficking and associated crimes have tended to show some of the longest sentences in the penal regulations.

The Penal Code currently in force (law 599/2000) originally set the maximum sentence for crimes meriting imprisonment at forty years. The sentences for narcotics trafficking and related crimes were the highest laid down in the code[3] and were harsher than those established by the National Narcotics Statute (Estatuto Nacional de Estupefacientes, law 30/1986).[4] With the introduction of the accusatory criminal justice system in Colombia (through legislative act 03/2002, which came into force on January 1, 2005), law 890/2004 increased all sentences by a third with respect to the minimum and by half with respect to the maximum.

This reform has had a significant impact on the people jailed for narcotics trafficking (Figure 10.1). Thus the maximum sentence in Colombia was fixed at fifty years (sixty years in the case of concurrent crimes). For narcotics trafficking and associated crimes, the prison sentences were set at between five and thirty-three years (which may be notably lengthened if there are concurrent crimes and aggravating punitive circumstances).

During the past thirteen years, the harsher punishments, creation of new kinds of crimes, and the punitive action of the state have given rise to a notable increase in the number of persons accused and convicted for this and related crimes (see Figure 10.1). This has turned narcotics trafficking into the third most common crime, on average, for

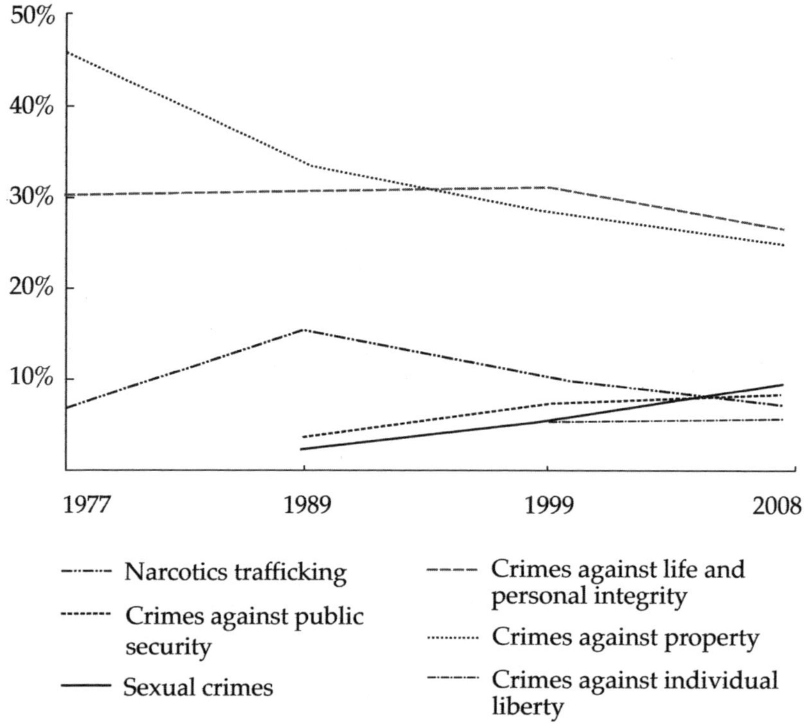

FIGURE 10.2. Percentage of those arrested for narcotics trafficking compared to other crimes (1977–2008). Source: Inpec (2009)

which people have been sent to prison during this period (after crimes against life and personal integrity and against property) (Figure 10.2).

There is no evidence that this criminal justice policy based on a stronger repression of narcotics trafficking has led to an easing of the problem, nor has it checked the criminal organizations devoted to that trade. According to the records of the Colombian Police (Policía Nacional), narcotics trafficking offenses and the number of those arrested for them have risen in the past two decades (particularly between 2000 and 2005, though the figures notably fell between 2006 and 2007) (Figure 10.3). As the socioeconomic profile of the prisoners usually shows (youngsters and/or those with low levels of education), on many occasions those who are convicted of such crimes are not members of criminal organizations or only have a marginal position in them (UNIJUS 1996, 153–54).

Creation and Broadening of Types of Criminal Offenses

One of the main features of the criminal justice policy used against narcotics trafficking is the constant creation of new types of criminal offenses or the broadening of the definition of those already in existence, so that they cover a greater number of acts, circumstances, and active agents. This penal strategy has been repeatedly employed by different governments under states of emergency[5] and also by the Colombian Congress.[6]

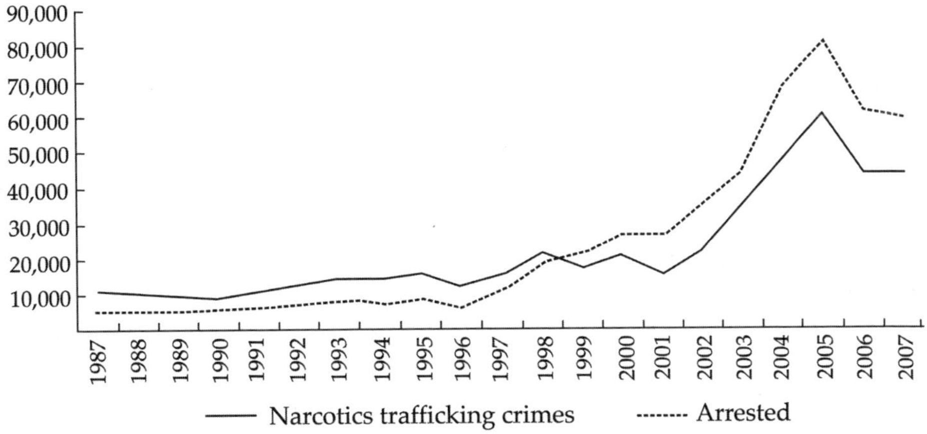

FIGURE 10.3. Narcotics trafficking crimes and total of arrests reported by the Colombian police (1987–2007). Source: Colombian police (2008)

The continual change in the definition of crimes has also caused problems: the terms in which they are drafted are vague and ambiguous, which causes problems of interpretation and application and violates the principle of legal certainty. This in turn weakens the right to defense of the accused. In addition, the improvised way these kinds of measures are adopted does not take into account the possible consequences of their implementation, like the clogging of the courts and the increase in the prison population, which exceeds the capacities of the authorities and leads the penal and penitentiary system to become even more congested.

Toughening of Procedures and Restriction of the Guarantees and Benefits of the Accused

On the assumption that those who are tried for narcotics trafficking and associated crimes represent a grave threat to society, numerous penal reforms have established measures that restrict their rights, with the aim of ensuring investigations and convictions as well as the protection of judicial officials, witnesses, and victims. The best known are those that were in force under the system, employed in the 1990s, known as Regional Justice or "faceless justice" (*justicia sin rostro*). These measures included the use of secret judges, prosecutors, and witnesses; the elimination of a public hearing during the trial stage; preventive imprisonment as the only means of securing the appearance of the accused; the lengthening of the period allowed for the stage of investigation and trial during which the accused were detained; and the limitation or elimination of punitive alternatives (probation and suspended sentences) (Ariza et al. 1997; García 2001; Iturralde 2010; UNIJUS 1996).

Although the most restrictive aspects violated constitutional rights and gradually disappeared, several have remained, like the use of preventive imprisonment as the main means of handling the risk of flight, the restriction of probation (given the presumed gravity of the punishable offense), and the elimination of the suspended sentence for these kinds of crimes. This confirms that the criminal justice policy of the state resorts to a harshening of penal measures as a way to confront narcotics trafficking instead of improving the effectiveness of the system and using the available resources more efficiently.

Exceptional Powers Granted to Administrative Authorities

Different Colombian governments, particularly under states of emergency, have granted extraordinary powers to the state security bodies (especially the armed forces) so they can capture suspects, gather evidence, confiscate goods, search premises and use wiretapping without a court order, and even judge people accused of narcotics trafficking and associated crimes.[7] By virtue of the 1991 Constitution, and thanks to several decisions by the Constitutional Court (Ariza and Barreto 2001; García 2001; García and Uprimny 2006b; Iturralde 2010), these kinds of powers have been strongly limited, with the aim of guaranteeing fundamental rights and the supremacy of the Constitution.

Despite these constitutional restrictions and their reinforcement by the Constitutional Court, different governments have tended to resort to these kinds of strategies in the fight against narcotics trafficking.[8] This can be explained by the complex political situation of Colombia in recent decades, under the combined influence of narcotics trafficking, armed conflict, and terrorism. Thus, as these governments and officials who deal with these problems firsthand usually claim,[9] implementing judicial procedures in conflict zones is risky given the power of the armed subversive groups.

With the introduction of the accusatory penal system, regulated by the current Code of Penal Procedure (law 906/2004),[10] this controversy has eased, at least for the time being, since the new system emphasizes constitutional guarantees and establishes that the public prosecutor (*fiscalía general de la nación*) has the sole authority to direct penal investigations. Therefore, only the *fiscalía* can ask for arrest warrants from the supervisory judges (*jueces de garantías*)[11] and carry them out, in collaboration with the judicial police.[12] It is only in exceptional cases, which must be established by law, that the *fiscalía* may capture people without a judicial order.[13] The *fiscalía*, in collaboration with the judicial police, is also responsible for carrying out searches, raids, confiscations, and wiretaps, subject to a subsequent judicial review of constitutional guarantees.[14]

Under the new accusatory system, it is clear that except in cases where criminals are caught in the act, the judicial police is a specialized body that must operate under the directions and instructions of the *fiscalía*, whose decisions and actions in turn are subject to judicial control. This control is exercised prior to acts related to arrests and subsequently in the case of searches, raids, seizures, and wiretaps.

On the basis of the above-mentioned information, one might think that the situation of violence and territorial control of regions where narcotics are grown and produced by illegal armed groups, along with the introduction of a new accusatory system, would hinder the effectiveness of searches and seizures by security agencies fighting against drugs.

Nevertheless, and despite ups and downs, the figures published by the national police and the armed forces show increasing seizures of narcotics and the inputs needed to produce them. This trend has been notable during the past decade in relation to cocaine, coca base, coca leaf, and heroin (see Chapter 3).

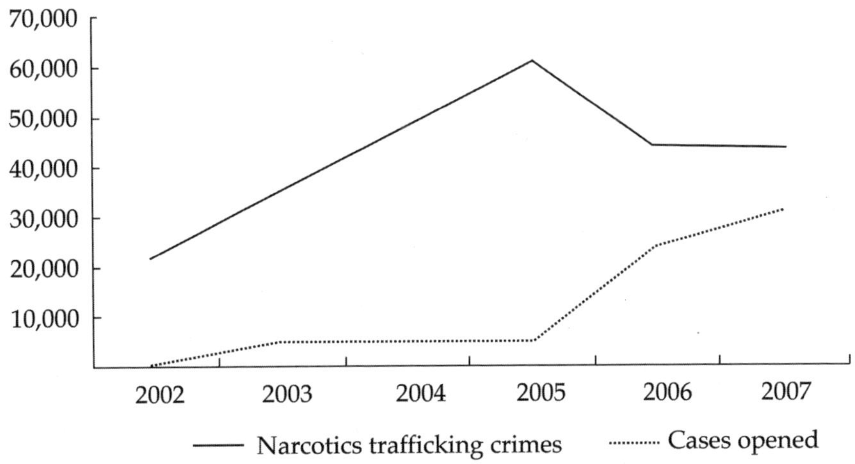

FIGURE 10.4. Criminal proceedings opened against narcotics trafficking crimes and reported narcotics trafficking (and associated) crimes (2002–2007). Source: Consejo Superior de la Judicatura (2009), Colombian police (2008)

The Creation of a Special Jurisdiction

With the aim of attacking the crimes and criminal organizations that cause the strongest social impact (particularly in relation to narcotics trafficking, terrorism, kidnapping, and other crimes associated with the armed conflict), different Colombian governments, under emergency powers, consolidated a system of exceptional penal justice (*justicia penal de excepción*) (Ariza et al. 1997; García 2001; García and Uprimny 2006a; Iturralde 2010). This system has been responsible for prosecuting such crimes and has been governed by its own procedures, which as we have seen restrict the rights of the accused, with the intent of protecting witnesses and judicial officials and strengthening its effectiveness. What was originally conceived of as an exceptional system of justice became permanent (Iturralde 2010).

While official figures on the rates and results of the cases in this system (the jurisdiction of which has always included narcotics trafficking) are incomplete,[15] certain significant trends over the past fifteen years can be seen.

With the establishment of the accusatory system, the number of registrations and clearances of penal trials for narcotics trafficking and related crimes has risen at a rate higher than the number of crimes reported (Figures 10.4 and 10.5). The number of convictions and persons convicted has also risen considerably since the introduction of the accusatory system in 2005 (Figures 10.6 and 10.7).

Extradition

Particularly in the past eight years, extradition has become a fundamental tool in the fight against narcotics trafficking. Established as a mechanism of international cooperation in the fight against crime, it has in practice been a substitutive form of Colombian penal justice, particularly when used against narcotics trafficking and requested by the United States. The number of Colombians and foreigners extradited to that country for

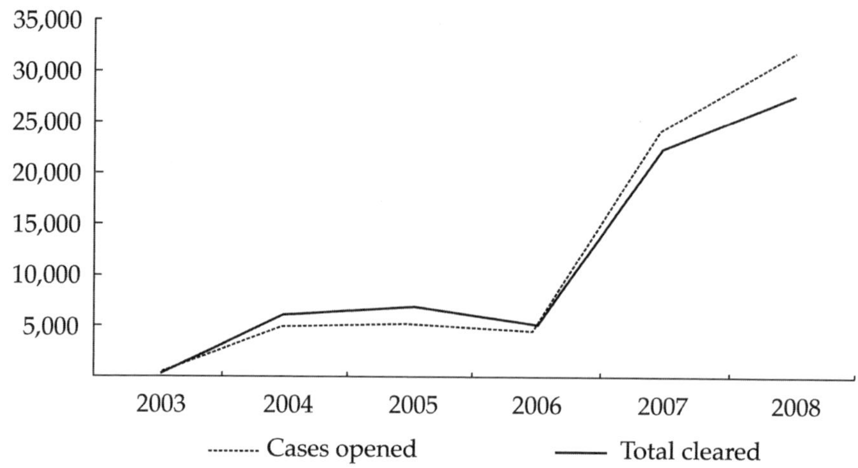

FIGURE 10.5. Criminal proceedings against narcotics trafficking (and associated) crimes opened and cleared (2003–2008). Source: Consejo Superior de la Judicatura (2009), Colombian police (2008)

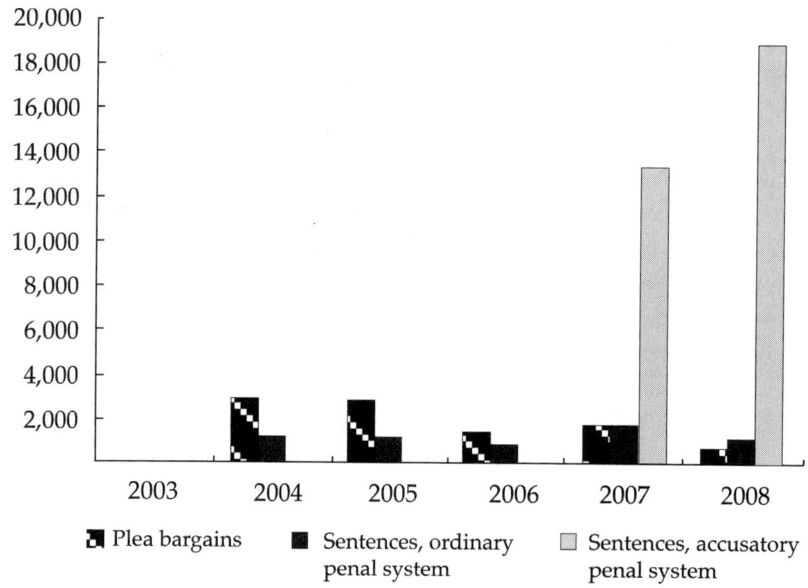

FIGURE 10.6. Main types of guilty sentences in penal proceedings against narcotics trafficking and related crimes (2003–2008). Source: Consejo Superior de la Judicatura (2009)

narcotics trafficking and related crimes has considerably risen since 2002 and is much higher than the total of all extraditions to other countries (Figures 10.8 and 10.9).

Article 35 of the 1991 Constitution prohibited the extradition of Colombian citizens, a mechanism that had become a fundamental tool in the fight against narcotics trafficking in the 1980s (particularly extradition to the United States). This prohibition was revoked by a legislative act in 1997 under the diplomatic and economic pressure of the United States. At the time, relations between the Colombian and US governments

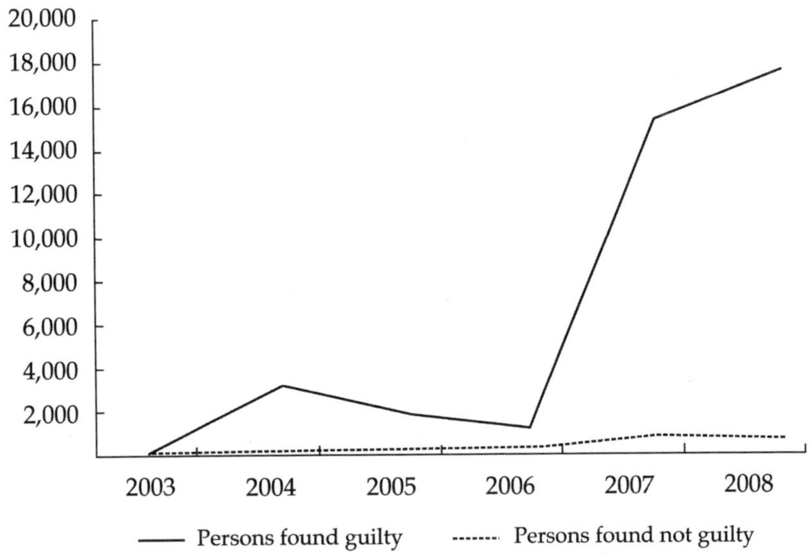

FIGURE 10.7. Persons convicted and absolved in penal proceedings for narcotics trafficking and related crimes (2003–2008). Source: Consejo Superior de la Judicatura (2009)

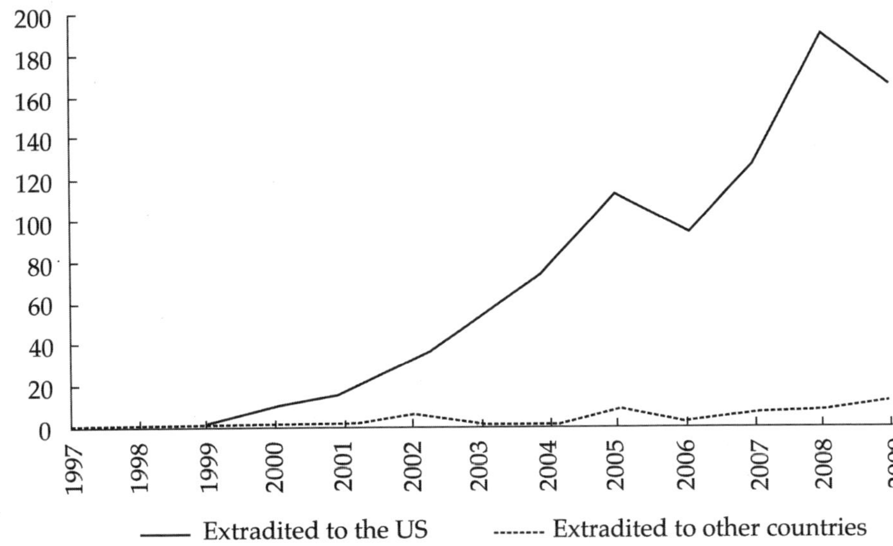

FIGURE 10.8. Colombians extradited for narcotics trafficking (by year) (1997–2009). Source: Colombian Ministry of the Interior and Justice (2009)

were troubled because of the political scandal arising from the financing by narcotics traffickers of Ernesto Samper's presidential campaign (Iturralde 2010, 171–72).

Although the 1997 constitutional reform re-established the extradition of Colombians, neither the Colombian nor the US governments showed interest in signing an extradition treaty. Extradition procedures have been regulated by the Codes of Penal Procedure laid down in the years 2000 and 2004. The Supreme Court of Justice must

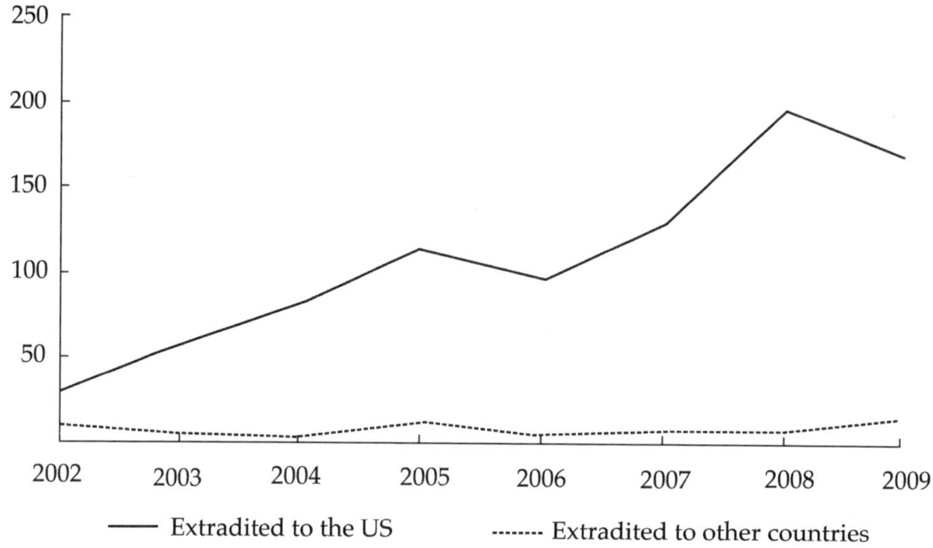

FIGURE 10.9. Colombians and foreigners extradited for narcotics trafficking, by year (2002–2009). Source: Colombian Ministry of the Interior and Justice (2009)

authorize the legality of every request for extradition (in accordance with the parameters established by the Code of Penal Procedure),[16] and the Colombian government is free to grant or deny the request, based on the national interest.

THE LAW AND PROPERTY DERIVED FROM NARCOTICS TRAFFICKING: AN ANALYSIS OF PROCEDURES FOR THE EXTINCTION (CONFISCATION) OF PROPERTY

As the previous sections showed, from the juridical point of view the Colombian state has tried to deal with the phenomenon of narcotics trafficking by mainly focusing on two legal rights: the liberty of and the property rights of the persons engaged in that activity. The procedure for the extinction of property, as known at the present time, is an autonomous and independent juridical mechanism that lies in a gray area between civil and penal law and between the ordinary and exceptional system of justice.

The Extinction of Property: Precedents and the Formation of the Mechanism

In general terms, the juridical debate has revolved around the question of whether a person may be convicted for illicit gain or subjected to a trial for extinction of property (where the state may seize all of the person's assets without any kind of compensation), regardless of whether that person has been convicted of a crime that enabled him or her to acquire the assets. In the most orthodox versions of penal doctrine, illicit gain on the part of individuals had been regarded as a predicate crime, that is, in order for it to apply it was necessary to prove that the goods and assets that made up the illicit gain came from an illegal activity.

This required a prior penal procedure in which the following had to be proved: (a) that the gain resulted from narcotics trafficking; (b) that the person being accused of illicit gain had been convicted of the crime. The fundamental proof, therefore, was a judicial conviction of the crime of narcotics trafficking, as well as proof of a causal relationship between that activity and an increase of wealth (Supreme Court of Justice 1989). The practical difficulties that arose from this definition forced judicial officials to find alternative solutions that would allow them to more effectively confiscate property related to narcotics trafficking.

Years later, the juridical thesis (defended by the Supreme Court of Justice) that regarded illicit gain as a subsidiary crime suffered a significant, polemical defeat when the Constitutional Court decided that illicit gain on the part of individuals must be regarded as an autonomous crime. This pronouncement states that illicit gain is a special crime that arises "without the need to recur to another penal category" (Constitutional Court 1996).

This implies that the burden of proof is reversed; it is up to the accused person to show that the increase in wealth is legitimate. The court emphatically upheld the idea that an increase in wealth deriving from illegal activities "in no manner must be interpreted in the sense that it has to originate from an individual previously convicted for the crime of narcotics trafficking or any other crime" (Constitutional Court 1996).

The proceedings for extinction of property have basically followed this same line of reasoning, as is plain from the wording of article 34 of the Colombian Constitution (Constitutional Court 2006). Constitutional jurisprudence, as in the case of illicit gain, regards the extinction of property proceeding as an autonomous institution, of constitutional rank and proprietary nature, which seeks through sentencing to refute that

> he who appears as the owner of properties acquired in any of the circumstances laid down by the norm is so in reality, since the illegal and spurious origin of their acquisition, insofar as it is contrary to juridical order or collective morality, excludes [the right] to property. (Constitutional Court 1997)

Although this procedure basically copies those pertaining to penal jurisdiction, an important jurisprudential and doctrinal effort has been made to show that it does not have that character, even though it is under the jurisdiction of penal justice (the *fiscalía* and the specialized penal judges).

The proceeding for the extinction of property is not what it seems to be, and it is difficult to determine its exact nature; it is an exceptional provision that has been turned into permanent legislation. It has its place in penal jurisdiction, but its nature is more similar to a private law procedure insofar as it not regarded as punitive in the strict sense. Thus it is not surprising that this confusion is reflected in the actions of juridical officials and the people who are subjected to extinction of property proceedings.

Narcotics Trafficking, Personal Assets, and the Extinction of Property

Insofar as the object of extinction are the personal assets of the affected persons, it is crucial to determine which properties owned by an individual or an entity are actually related to narcotics trafficking and the different changes they may go through. For that reason, the legislation has established three categories: legal properties, illegal properties, and equivalent assets.

The main problems with this classification are the equivalent assets. These assets are those that replace assets (obtained illegally with financial resources originating in criminal actions or that were used as means to commit such actions) that no longer belong to the patrimony of the titleholder by virtue of a contractual transaction.

Law 793/2002 establishes that the act of the extinction of property not only applies to illegally acquired properties, but also those used to undertake the illegal activities that resulted in acquiring the illegal properties. Under these premises, the act is not defined by the illegitimacy of the property right but by devoting the affected properties to activities different from the social and ecological function of the respective property. Narcotics trafficking includes both properties acquired at the cost of a grave deterioration of social morality (covered by narcotics trafficking and related crimes), that is, illegally acquired properties, but also those used for activities alien to the function of the property.

In statistical terms, it is pertinent to take into account the work of two categories of specialized penal circuit courts. The first, created in 2004, are meant to ease the overload of cases (*juzgados de circuito especializados de descongestión*) and have led to a significant increase in the number of proceedings finished. Since that time, both the number of proceedings assigned to those courts and the number of cases ending in sentences have remained relatively constant (on average, 214.2 assigned proceedings and 163.6 finished proceedings per year, or a 76.38 percent rate of clearance).[17] In the case of the second category of specialized penal courts (ordinary courts already in existence before 2004), the number of cases assigned between 2004 and 2009 has been relatively constant (between 201 and 222 per year), and there has not been a great variation in the number of cases cleared, an average of 169.5 per year. The total number of cases assigned to these courts up to June 18, 2009, has been 1,202, with 901 cases ending in sentencing, or a fairly efficient clearance rate of 74.96 percent.[18]

The Properties

The change of legislation caused a considerable increase in the properties[19] that, once extinguished, were transferred to the National Narcotics Administration (Dirección Nacional de Estupefacientes, DNE).[20] This increase may be explained by the definition of the properties subject to extinction; law 333/1996 established a more restricted definition of the categories and kinds of these properties, whereas the one laid down by law 793/2002 is much broader. Since 2004 there has been a significant increase in the total number of properties transferred to the DNE in comparison with 2003.[21] While in 2003 there were 918 new properties, the figure rose to 2,163 in the following year and to 4,948 in 2005. Between then and 2009, the number of properties transferred to the DNE has been more or less constant, with an average of 4,932 new ones per year.[22] As of February 28, 2010, the total number of properties administered by the DNE was 75,440 (DNE n.d., 25). Nevertheless, the increase in the seizure and transfer of properties to the DNE has not necessarily meant that there has been an increase in judicial proceedings or extinction of property orders; the judicial institutions are not flexible in the face of the increased activity of police agencies. Instead, it reflects the broadening of the kinds of properties that may be liable to extinction under new legislation.

TABLE 10.1. Legislation under which extinction of property proceedings are initiated

Legislation	Number of sentences	%
Old	60	32.61
New	124	67.39
Total	184	100.00

Source: The authors.

The indicators of the Observatorio de Drogas de Colombia (a government institution that monitors drugs in Colombia) show a reduction in the number of extinction of property proceedings in relation to the seized properties. For example, "whereas in 2003 the number of extinction or confiscation of property [*comiso definitivo*] sentences in favor of the state represented 5.6 percent of the total of the goods seized and placed at the disposition of the DNE, in 2006 that percentage fell by half, to 2.3 percent" (Observatorio de Drogas de Colombia 2008). This, says the monitoring entity, is because the number of properties seized from narcotics traffickers rises at a rate higher than the growth of the judicial system's capacity to clear cases and issue sentences.

Case Study: The Functioning of the Extinction of Property Proceedings

Between the issuance of law 333/1996 and of law 793/2002, the National Unit for the Extinction of Property and the Prosecution of Asset Laundering (Unidad Nacional para la Extinción del Derecho de Dominio y contra el Lavado de Activos) of the Public Prosecutor's Office (Fiscalía General de la Nación) undertook a total of 674 extinction of property proceedings. On average, a third of the cases (202) were dismissed. In 298 cases, the proceedings were judged valid and passed to the trial stage. It is worth emphasizing the increase in the number of cases that have been assigned to the unit since the passing of law 793/2002, a total of 5,892, although most are in the preliminary phase (3,423) and a good number of others are in the investigation stage (1,084). Only 120 cases have gone on to judgment (2.04 percent of the total).[23] We present a preliminary analysis of the data related to the sentences in the proceedings under study as follows (Table 10.1).[24]

As can be seen, the large majority of the sentences (86.7 percent) have been issued by judicial bodies located in Bogotá (Table 10.2). The significant difference between the assigned cases and the capacity to clear them, depending on the city, also indicates a heavy work load and a weak capacity, on a local and regional level, to resolve these kinds of cases, seen for example in practical limitations on jobs like the gathering of proofs, citations, and inspections of properties, which have to be carried out by a judicial entity different from the one familiar with the case.

This difference is equally evident when the local judges, in order to enforce the extinction of property sentence, have to take possession of the properties and similar measures, circumstances that favor the use of intimidation by narcotics traffickers in conditions that hinder the administration of justice.

That most of the sentences under analysis affect private individuals (93.05 percent) would, in theory, point out that it is easier to determine illicit gain in such cases than in

TABLE 10.2. Cities where extinction of property sentences have been pronounced.

City	Number of sentences	%
Bogotá	163	86.71
Medellín	9	4.79
Pereira	5	2.66
Cali	4	2.13
Barranquilla	2	1.06
Ibagué	2	1.06
Cúcuta	1	0.53
Villavicencio	1	0.53
Tunja	1	0.53
Total	188	100.00

Source: The authors.

TABLE 10.3. Types of properties subject to extinction of property sentences

Type of property	Number of mentions in sentences*	%
Furnishings	129	60.0
Real estate	70	32.5
Derived from narcotics trafficking	7	3.3
Intangible	9	4.2
Total	215	100.0

*In the 186 sentences analyzed, which furnished this information.

Source: The authors.

the ones that involve corporate entities. As for the kind of property that is the object of the sentence, one observes a preponderance of personal properties over real estate. Of the 190 sentences that were studied, there was information about the kind of property in the case of 186. Approximately 60 percent of these sentences involved personal properties and a little more than 32 percent involved real estate. Only 7.5 percent of the sentences included equivalent assets, shares and the like, or intangible properties (Table 10.3). We should take into account that there are important differences between these goods, such as their commercial value, the legal regime that applies to them, and the subsequent implications of the execution of the sentence and the liquidation of the economic value of each property.

On the basis of these figures, it can be said that the judicial resolution of personal properties is less cumbersome. As a general rule, the ownership of personal properties is proved by possession, except for those whose ownership must be registered with a government agency. In fact, the formalities pertaining to the juridical regime for real estate may not only affect the outcome of the case itself but also the subsequent execution of the sentences. When, for example, there are third parties who occupy the real estate, it is necessary to carry out further proceedings, such as eviction, to enforce the expropriation sentence.

An analysis of the uses of the properties subject to extinction may help to make the above clearer. As Table 10.4 shows, most of the properties listed in the sentences

TABLE 10.4. Properties subject to extinction of property, in terms of use

Type of property	Number of mentions in sentences*	%
Result of crime	66	32.0
Means or instrument of crime	101	49.0
Destined for illegal activity	37	18.0
Subject to proceedings	2	1.0
Total	206	100.0

*In the 169 sentences analyzed, which furnished this information.

Source: The authors.

TABLE 10.5. Equivalent assets

Equivalent assets	Number of sentences	%
No	175	97.22
Yes	5	2.78
Total	180	100.00

Source: The authors.

(49 percent) have been used as tools to undertake activities pertaining to narcotics trafficking. This may also explain the preponderance of personal goods over real estate in these kinds of proceedings, which would indicate that, judicially speaking, the judicial prosecution of activities directly related to the production and trafficking of drugs has been more successful than the attack on their economic results.

The latter interpretation gains momentum when one examines the processing of the so-called equivalent goods. As Table 10.5 shows, a quite reduced number of sentences (2.78 percent) concerns these kind of goods. In this sense, the initial conclusion is that the cases of expropriation that actually end in convictions mainly affect personal goods that have been used as a tool for narcotics trafficking by a private individual who does not respond to the summons of the court and therefore must be represented by an *ad litem* curator.[25]

Procedure and Length of Extinction of Property Cases

The large majority of the cases that end in sentencing are ex officio proceedings and they decree the suspension of the right to dispose of the properties in question. In a significant number of sentences (71.9 percent), third-party individuals were summoned (people with some relation to the property), while in 39.1 percent of the cases the titleholders or presumed titleholders of the properties had to be found and notified. This is related to the kind of defense presented, since in 68.33 percent of the sentences there is a curator *ad litem*, which has important consequences for the results of the case. In fact, because on the reversal of the burden of proof and the absence of the accused, the judge assumes that the property subject to extinction is of an illegal origin, since there is no showing of a legal increase in wealth. Thus, in the absence of the accused, the judges tend to conclude that due to the difficulty of gathering proofs, they must turn to circumstantial evidence, from which they usually conclude that the property originated from an illegal activity or had been destined for one.

TABLE 10.6. Average length (in days) of the extinction of property proceedings, in accordance with legislation (law 333/1996 and law 793/2002)

Type of legislation	Length	From the beginning of the case to decision to proceed (remit to public prosecutor)	From remittance to public prosecutor to sentencing
Law 333/1996 (124 sentences)	967 (100%)	729 (75.38%)	238 (24.62%)
Law 793/2002 (60 sentences)	1,570 (100%)	1,066 (67.89%)	504 (32.11%)
Average of total (184 sentences)	1,163 (100%)	839 (72.14%)	324 (27.86%)

Source: The authors.

Finally, regarding the length of the cases, it is important to point out that law 793/2002 implied a notable reduction in the terms of the proceedings, most of which were halved, although they continued to be long if one compares them with the terms prescribed by the law. The entity that seems to be most congested is the *fiscalía*, since the proceedings there are much longer than in the stage of judgment (a situation seen under both the old and the new legislation) (Table 10.6).

FINAL RECOMMENDATIONS

On the basis of the above analysis, these are the main recommendations for public policy on the penal treatment of narcotics trafficking and related crimes:

1. A serious analysis of the results of the criminal justice policy used to fight the trafficking of narcotics will provide fundamental grounds for making reasonable adjustments, many of which do not require legal reforms, which have been excessive. For example, the stiffening of jail terms is a strategy that has shown poor results in the fight against narcotics trafficking and usually creates more problems than it solves and should be abandoned. The current punishments for narcotics trafficking are sufficiently severe. The priority is to strengthen the effectiveness of the system (which would actually lead to a higher number of captures and convictions), not its severity (stiff sentences serve little if the state is not able to capture, judge, and condemn criminals). To achieve that, the penal system needs to be made more stable, which means that we should avoid the temptation of undertaking continual reforms in the search for better results. The key to this is to identify the weak points of penal justice and criminal policy, following an evaluation of its performance, in order to take the necessary corrective measures, most of which are of an administrative nature.
2. The new accusatory system introduced fundamental changes in penal procedure. The meager data we have up to now seems to indicate the new system has been more effective than the previous regime in the fight against narcotics trafficking (at least as measured by the increase in the number of cases processed by the penal system and of convictions and convicted persons). The same can be said of captures and seizures of goods. Thus, for the moment, making great normative

reforms of the accusatory system does not seem essential. The emphasis should be on strengthening the budget, human resources, and technical aspects of the system. To do that, there is a need for skilled personnel who receive suitable training and the means to fulfill their functions.

3. Interviews of prosecutors and officials of the national police have revealed difficulties in carrying out seizures and searches, and legalizing captures, that are more of a logistical than a normative kind. This is mainly because the accusatory system represents a radical and recent transformation of the Colombian penal system. For that reason, both judges and prosecutors and members of the judicial police need more experience and, above all, preparation to apply it. According to those interviewed, the judges responsible for overseeing constitutional guarantees interpret the new procedural norms in very diverse ways, which in many cases means their actions are ruled illegal. More than regulating or reforming such norms, the criteria for interpreting them should be unified (the jurisprudence of the Supreme Court of Justice plays a crucial role in this) and made known to the respective officials.
4. There is a widespread belief that the security agencies must have stronger powers and fewer legal controls in order to effectively confront organized delinquency and the armed groups dedicated to narcotics trafficking. The experience of the exceptional penal justice system has shown that such powers have not resulted in a more effective penal system, but on the contrary have given rise to the continual violation of the fundamental rights of the accused (Ariza et al. 1997; García 2001; García and Uprimny 2006a; Iturralde 2010; UNIJUS 1996).

   The deficiency of resources and personnel (prosecutors, judicial police, and judges who monitor constitutional guarantees),[26] and the difficult physical terrain of Colombia are important obstacles for the legalization of captures, seizures, wiretaps, and searches, since the respective formalities cannot be undertaken within the thirty-six hours laid down by the Constitution. The way to solve this problem is to make efficient use of the existing resources as well as improve them. The use of new communications technologies may facilitate communication among officials and may expedite the holding of hearings.
5. Given the characteristics of narcotics trafficking in Colombia (which is closely linked with criminal organizations and powerful armed groups that control remote parts of Colombian territory), the judicial police and prosecutors require special instruction and equipping to carry out their tasks in difficult situations. One possibility is the formation of special corps, dependent on the *fiscalía* and the national police, that could act in a joint manner and have a strong capacity to mobilize and react. This may turn out to be more expensive and cumbersome than reforming norms in the name of harsher procedures, but it is a more effective way to fight narcotics trafficking. The deficiencies of the state cannot be remedied by the continual restriction of the constitutional rights of citizens.

   The constitutional requisite that arrest warrants have to be previously authorized by a judge overseeing constitutional guarantees (or, in exceptional situations, by the *fiscalía* and subject to a subsequent authorization of their legality), and their legality established within thirty-six hours following the seizures, searches, and wiretaps, are reasonable conditions for effectively realizing penal investigations and guaranteeing the protection of the constitutional rights of all the affected persons.

Therefore, there is a need for more judges to carry out this task and for them to be better trained and more widely available throughout the country (or to be able to travel more easily to the places where they are required), so that they may exercise their functions in an effective manner.

6. Considering that the penal system specializing in the prosecution of narcotics trafficking and other crimes with a strong social impact has become permanent, it should not be distinguished by its restrictive approach to the guarantees and rights of the accused, but its specialized skills for prosecuting complex crimes and powerful criminal organizations. The specialized penal circuit judges, as well as the prosecutors and members of the judicial police who deal with these types of cases, must have a high degree of training and experience, and there must also be a sufficient number of them so they can efficiently assume the heavy burden of work placed on them.[27]
7. It would be worth the trouble to revive the debate on the signing of a new extradition treaty with the United States (Fundación Ideas para la Paz n.d., 28).[28] This is a frame of reference that is indispensable for defining the conditions in which the authorities of both countries may collaborate in attacking delinquency, especially narcotics trafficking, in a way that heeds the needs and interests of both countries. The high degree of discretion given to the Colombian government and the pressure of the US authorities have made extradition more of a tool to replace Colombian penal justice than a means of collaboration.

   An overwhelming majority of high- and middle-ranking leaders of the criminal organizations devoted to narcotics trafficking are extradited to the United States. Meanwhile, the Colombian authorities do not make a serious effort to clear up and judge the criminal acts these persons commit in Colombia. This weakens Colombian justice and affects the rights of the victims to truth, justice, and reparations. For that reason we must establish clear rules that give priority to the investigation and judging in Colombia of crimes that have a stronger social impact than narcotics trafficking itself and for that reason must be given priority.
8. The extinction of property proceeding is especially complex. On the one hand, it is not a penal proceeding although it is undertaken under the penal jurisdiction. On the other, neither is it a strictly civil matter, although certain aspects, like recovering properties in the hands of third parties, follow the norms pertaining to the possession of goods. For that reason, it is indispensable to unify the norms and procedures that govern the whole process, both in an organic and normative sense.
9. Due to the special characteristics of extinction of property proceedings, the absence of an effective technical defense during the trial affects its outcome, which is generally a sentence in favor of expropriation. Insofar as the burden of proof falls on the person whose title to the property is questioned, whenever that person is absent and the defense is left to a court-appointed attorney, a sentence that annuls the property right is the usual result. Therefore, it would be convenient to strengthen the work of the public defenders.

NOTES

For the gathering of information and drafting of earlier versions that served as the basis for this chapter, the work done by the research assistants Marcela Abadía, Felipe Jaramillo, and Camilo

Barrera was decisive, as well as that done by the researchers of the Cijus, Juan Pablo Mosquera and Hernán Ramírez, in organizing and systematizing the database that gave rise to the case study. We would like to thank all of them for their commitment and diligence in undertaking the different tasks assigned to them.

1. For example, the Penal Code currently in force (law 559/2000) has been subjected to twenty-nine legislative reforms in less than a decade.
2. The beginning of the so-called "war on drugs" in Colombia was marked by the assassination of the minister of justice, Rodrigo Lara Bonilla, ordered by the cartel of Medellín (Ariza et al. 1997; García 2001; Iturralde 2010).
3. They ran from four to twenty years.
4. Under that statute, the sentences ran from one to twelve years. Numerous legislative decrees, issued under states of emergency, increased these sentences. Law 365/1997 increased the sentences for offenses related to organized crime, among them narcotics trafficking (Iturralde 2010).
5. For example, under legislative decree 1895/1989, the Barco government created the crime of illegal enrichment.
6. By means of law 365/1997, which laid down "norms for fighting against organized crime," the crime of asset laundering was established.
7. Between 1984 and 1987 the military courts were allowed to investigate and sentence civilians for the crime of narcotics trafficking. That kind of measure was declared unconstitutional in 1987 by the Supreme Court of Justice (which ruled that it violated the constitutional right to due process) (Iturralde 2010, 86–87), and it was later prohibited by article 213 of the 1991 Constitution, which states that "In no case may civilians be questioned or tried by martial law."
8. At moments of their respective administrations, this was attempted by César Gaviria, Ernesto Samper, Andrés Pastrana, and Álvaro Uribe (Iturralde 2010). In the latter case, it was by means of a legislative act 02/2003, better known as the Antiterrorist Statute, which sought to give a constitutional status to the possibility that the security forces, including the military ones, would count on permanent emergency powers to fight against terrorism and related crimes (which usually include narcotics trafficking): they were authorized to arrest people, undertake wiretaps, and carry out raids and seizures without a judicial order. The Constitutional Court, in a ruling issued on August 30, 2004, declared that legislative act unconstitutional due to procedural flaws (Constitutional Court, sentence C-816/2004).
9. Interviews of prosecutors from the antinarcotics and extinction of property units, and with officers of the antinarcotics police, undertaken on December 10 and 15, 2009, and February 10, 2010.
10. It came into force on January 1, 2005, and has been subjected to seven legal reforms in less than six years.
11. According to article 39 of the Code of Penal Procedure, the municipal penal judges are responsible for overseeing constitutional guarantees.
12. Nevertheless, article 32 of the Constitution lays down an exception to this rule: if an individual is caught in flagrante delicto, he may be apprehended and brought before a judge by any person.
13. There is a subsequent judicial oversight of constitutional guarantees, undertaken within thirty-six hours following the capture (Colombian Constitution, article 250, number 1).
14. This must be done within thirty-six hours following the action.

15. Although the Superior Council of the Judiciary (Consejo Superior de la Judicatura, responsible for compiling statistics on the judicial branch) has databases on penal justice, organized under the "Statistical Information System of the Judicial Branch" (SIERJ), the available information for the period between 1997 and 2002 is incomplete. This is partly because that system does not include data related to the regime of Regional Justice that was in force between 1991 and 1999. Furthermore, that information has many gaps and there is little clarity in the definition of the variables and categories of its measurements. While the database we consulted covers the period of 1997–2008, there is only complete information from 2003 onwards. The establishment of the accusatory system (January 2005) also creates problems of measurement, since the introduction of new legal concepts and the elimination of others implies fundamental changes in the categories and variables used in the calculations. In addition, the elimination of the previous regime has been a gradual process; the proceedings that began before January 2005 are still governed by it. The databases we consulted are not sufficiently clear about this, which makes it difficult to compare and interpret data to determine whether significant changes have occurred.
16. The crime for which extradition is requested must be covered by Colombian penal legislation and have a minimum prison sentence of four years, so that it is not open to probation or a suspended sentence. Furthermore, the sentence laid down in a foreign country may not exceed the maximum sentence laid down by Colombian law. Thus, death sentences and life imprisonment must be commuted.
17. In the analysis of the information supplied by the Superior Council of the Judiciary, the year 2009 was not taken into account since it does not provide definitive data (the information only runs up to June 18 of that year).
18. Information provided by the Superior Council of the Judiciary (Administrative Chamber—Unit of Statistical Development and Analysis), in a response to a right-to-information request by the members of the research team. Once again, these figures refer to all the trials for extinction of property, that is, those arising from any of the motives established by law.
19. The statistical analyses of the assets liable to extinction of property generally include the following: aircraft, boats, works of art, money, rural properties, companies, precursor chemicals, urban properties, and vehicles.
20. The DNE is the state agency responsible for administering confiscated properties and properties over which the extinction of property action falls.
21. See figure 15, "Properties placed at the disposition of the DNE (2003–2008)" (DNE 2009).
22. The Colombian national police's System for Statistics on Delinquency and Crime (Sistema Estadístico Delincuencial y Contravencional de la Policía Nacional, SIEDCO) breaks this down into two categories: the assets transferred to the DNE under extinction of property sentences and the assets held by the authorities of the judicial police. This means that an asset may be held without necessarily being subject to a judicial order.
23. These figures include all of the proceedings for extinction of property, that is, those arising from any of the motives laid down by the law, not only for the crime of narcotics trafficking.
24. The sample was made up of 190 sentences for extinction of property (most, but not all, for assets related to narcotics trafficking crimes), taken from the archive of the Fund for Rehabilitation, Social Investment, and the Fight against Organized Crime (Fondo para la Rehabilitación, Inversión Social y Lucha contra el Crimen Organizado, FRISCO), which is part of the National Narcotics Administration. Although the number of sentences chosen

was 190, in several instances not all of them are included in the statistical analysis, since the information was not sufficient or clear.

25. The *ad litem* curator, named by the judge in charge of the case, is a licensed lawyer who in the extinction of property trial represents the owner of the asset, who may or may not be present or does not want to be.
26. For example, considering that there are 1,101 municipalities in Colombia, there do not seem to be enough municipal judges to oversee the guaranteeing of constitutional rights. According to the Superior Council of the Judiciary (in response to a right-of-information request), at the present time there are in the whole of Colombia 259 municipal penal judges and 1,048 municipal general judges (*jueces promiscuos municipales*) who, because they deal with penal, civil, and labor cases, usually lack the requisite specialized knowledge of penal law.
27. According to the Superior Council of the Judiciary (in response to a right-of-information request), at the current time there are in the whole of Colombia sixty-six specialized penal circuit court judges, who are responsible for most of the proceedings involving narcotics trafficking and related crimes. When one takes into account that in 2008 alone 31,480 proceedings involving narcotics trafficking were begun in the penal system (according to the data of the Superior Council of the Judiciary), it is easy to see that these judges are over-burdened with work, especially since they are also responsible for dealing with other serious crimes, like terrorism and human rights violations.
28. The Fundación Ideas para la Paz (Ideas for Peace Foundation) has been responsible for an important advance in this sense thanks to its study of extradition and its impact on the armed conflict and the fight against drugs, about which it also presents recommendations to the governments of Colombia and the United States.

REFERENCES

Ariza, L., et al. 1997. *Estados de excepción y razón de Estado en Colombia*. Bogotá: Estudios Ocasionales Cijus, Universidad de los Andes.

Ariza, L., and A. Barreto. 2001. "La Corte Constitucional frente a la excepcionalidad: Diez años de control material laxo y discursivo." In *Derecho constitucional. Perspectivas críticas*, edited by A. Barreto. Bogotá: Observatorio de Justicia Constitucional, Universidad de los Andes-Legis.

Comisión Latinoamericana sobre Drogas y Democracia. 2009. *Drogas y democracia: Hacia un cambio de paradigma*. Retrieved from *www.drogasedemocracia.org/Espanol/Destaques.asp?IdRegistro=1*, accessed February 27, 2010.

Corte Constitucional. 1996. Sentencia C-319.

———. 1997. Sentencia C-374, M.P. Hernández, J. G.

———. 2004. Sentencia C-816.

———. 2006. Sentencia C-821, M.P. Sierra, H. A.

Corte Suprema de Justicia, Sala Constitucional. 1989. Sentencia del 3 de octubre de 1989.

DNE (Dirección Nacional de Estupefacientes). N.d. "Bienes administrados por la DNE a febrero 28 del 2010." Quadrennial report 2007–2010, 25. Retrieved from *www.dne.gov.co/?idcategoria=10891&download=Y*.

———. 2009. *Resultados lucha contra el problema de las drogas Colombia (2008–2009). Informe ejecutivo*. Bogotá: Observatorio de Drogas de Colombia, Dirección Nacional de Estupefaciones, 30. Retrieved from *www.dne.gov.co/tools/marco.php?idcategoria=633*, accessed February 27, 2010.

Fundación Ideas para la Paz. N.d. "Investigación usos y abusos de la extradición en la lucha contra las drogas." Área Construcción de Paz y Posconflicto. Retrieved from *www.ideaspaz.org/portal/index.php?option=com_docman&task=cat_view&gid=49&Itemid=55*.

García, M. 2001. "Constitucionalismo perverso. Normalidad y anormalidad constitucional en Colombia: 1957–1997." In *El caleidoscopio de las justicias en Colombia*, edited by B. Sousa Santos and M. García, 317–70. Bogotá: Colciencias / Instituto Colombiano de Antropología e Historia / Universidad de Coimbra / CES / Universidad de los Andes / Universidad Nacional de Colombia / Siglo del Hombre.

García, M., and R. Uprimny. 2006a. "Sistema judicial y conflicto armado en Colombia." In *¿Justicia para todos? Sistema judicial, derechos sociales y democracia en Colombia*, edited by R. Uprimny, M. García Villegas, and C. Rodríguez Garavito. Bogotá: Norma.

———. 2006b. "El control judicial de los estados de excepción." In *¿Justicia para todos? Sistema judicial, derechos sociales y democracia en Colombia*, edited by R. Uprimny, M. García Villegas, and C. Rodríguez Garavito. Bogotá: Norma.

INPEC. 2009. *Estadísticas penitenciarias 2009*. Bogotá: INPEC.

Iturralde, M. 2010. *Castigo, liberalismo autoritario y justicia penal de excepción*. Bogotá: Siglo del Hombre, Universidad de los Andes, Pontificia Universidad Javeriana/Instituto Pensar.

Ministerio del Interior y de Justicia. 2009. *Respuesta a derecho de petición. Cifras y estadísticas de extradición por narcotráfico y conexos*. OFI09–44841-DVJ-0300, Bogotá: December 29.

Observatorio de Drogas de Colombia. 2008. *Gasto del Estado colombiano en la lucha contra el problema de las drogas 2005–2006*. Departamento Nacional de Planeación. Dirección de Justicia y Seguridad, Grupo de Estudios de Gobierno y Asuntos Internos, Dirección Nacional de Estupefacientes. Subdirección Estratégica y de Investigaciones, Bogotá, 35.

Policía Nacional. 2008. *Revista Criminalidad* 50, no. 1.

Rodríguez, C. 2009. *La globalización del Estado de derecho*. Bogotá: Universidad de los Andes, Colección Estudios Cijus.

Rodríguez, C., and R. Uprimny. 2006. "¿Justicia para todos o seguridad para el mercado? El neoliberalismo y la reforma judicial en Colombia." In *¿Justicia para todos? Sistema judicial, derechos sociales y democracia en Colombia*, edited by R. Uprimny, M. García Villegas, and C. Rodríguez Garavito, 109–46. Bogotá: Norma.

Rojas, D. M. 2006. "Estados Unidos y la guerra en Colombia." In *Nuestra guerra sin nombre. Transformaciones del conflicto en Colombia*, edited by IEPRI. Bogotá: Norma.

———. 2009. "El taller del imperio global: Análisis de la intervención de Estados Unidos en Colombia." *Análisis Político* 65: 111–26.

Sousa Santos, B. 2001. "Derecho y democracia: La reforma global de la justicia." In *El caleidoscopio de las justicias en Colombia*, vol. I, edited by B. Sousa Santos and M. García, 151–207. Bogotá: Colciencias-Instituto Colombiano de Antropología e Historia-Universidad de Coimbra-CES-Universidad de los Andes-Universidad Nacional de Colombia-Siglo del Hombre.

UNIJUS (Unidad de Investigaciones Jurídico-Sociales Gerardo Molina). 1996. *Justicia sin rostro. Estudio sobre la justicia regional*. Bogotá: Universidad Nacional de Colombia.

Uprimny, R. 2001. "El laboratorio colombiano: Narcotráfico, poder y administración de justicia." In *El caleidoscopio de las justicias en Colombia*, edited by S. Boaventura and M. García, 371–414. Bogotá: Colciencias, Universidad de los Andes, Universidad Nacional, Siglo del Hombre, ICAHN, Universidad de Coimbra.

11 The Fight against Money Laundering

Institutions, Results, and Disincentives

Carlos Caballero and Alfonso Amaya

The process of hiding the origins of illegally obtained revenues and turning them into legitimate ones is known as money laundering. In this chapter we provide an analysis of the problem and the control exerted by the state in Colombia in recent years. First, we make an estimate of the size of the cocaine business in the country, which is one of the most profitable illegal activities. Second, we identify the channels through which such resources may be entering the country. Third, we calculate the seizure of criminal proceeds. Finally, we review the legal framework and the main types of court rulings on seizures that have been implemented in the past decade. Institutional control has become stronger in recent years, but the forfeitures are not significant. Even though the value of the assets seized has been increasing since 2004, they are not representative in comparison with the estimated revenues of the drug trade.

INTRODUCTION

In all economies there are illegal activities that infringe on the procedures and regulations established by countries to organize trade, apply ethical codes, protect their citizens, and finance government expenditure (Naím 2006, 16). The violators must legalize their revenues from cocaine trading, arms trafficking, and sexual slavery in a way that does not allow for their origins to be traced (Reuter and Truman 2004). This process of hiding the origin of illegally obtained funds is known as money laundering.

Due to the importance of the drug trade in Colombia, the conversion of the revenues into Colombian pesos has a significant role as an associated crime. Drug traffickers are obliged to launder money to cover the production costs: the inputs, purchase of coca leaves from growers, and transportation to the embarkment points, among others (see Chapter 1).

It is extremely difficult to identify and seize money from illegal activities. According to the National Money Laundering Strategy report of 2002 by the Treasury Department, the seizure of assets related to money laundering in fiscal year 2001 were around US$381 million. Meanwhile the illegal economy as a whole might have been worth around US$800 billion (Reuter and Truman 2004, 9–14). As Reuter and Truman note, these figures are only useful as a way to call attention to the magnitude of the phenomenon and do not serve to guide public policies (Reuter and Truman 2004, 10). Nevertheless, it is important to make estimates so that government decisions may be as suitable as

Carlos Caballero: Dean, School of Government, Universidad de los Andes.

Alfonso Amaya: MBA/MPP student, University of Chicago.

possible. In this chapter we seek to evaluate the significance of the results of state control in terms of forfeitures compared to the revenues of the cocaine trade.[1]

For Colombia, there have been several estimates of the repatriated revenues of the drug trade (Mejía and Posada 2010; Rocha and Ramírez 2004; Rocha 2000; Steiner 1997; Caballero and Junguito 1978). In this chapter, after we calculate the revenues from the trafficking of cocaine and the channels through which these resources may return to the country, we analyze the control exercised by the Colombian state. We estimate the forfeitures and review the legal framework and types of cases related to money laundering that have been tried by the courts in the past decade.

The chapter is divided into four sections. In the first, we present an account of the evolution of the country's legal and institutional framework in the fight against money laundering. In the second, we quantify the potential size of revenues from the trafficking of cocaine, using a methodology similar to the one used by Rocha and Ramírez (2004) and Mejía and Rico (Chapter 1). In the third, we calculate the revenues that might enter the country through two of the three main channels of money laundering. In the fourth, we present an analysis of the current institutional results and estimate the forfeitures. In the final section we present the conclusions.

INSTITUTIONS TO DETECT AND FIGHT MONEY LAUNDERING

In the 1980s money laundering stopped being a marginal concern of the international community and turned into a central part of the fight against drugs, terrorism, and organized crime (Alldridge 2003). Ever since, the efforts to achieve national and international institutional designs that create disincentives for money laundering and the illegal activities it conceals have been numerous. International organizations like the United Nations and countries like the United States have led the initiatives of the main institutional changes that the Colombian government has implemented to fight money laundering.

In the 1980s, with the leadership of the United States, the policy of "follow the money trail" gained recognition in law enforcement (Blickman 2009, 4). President Ronald Reagan intensified the war against drugs and in 1986 made money laundering a criminal offense (Blickman 2009, 4). Anti-laundering legislation then started in Colombia with the issuance of the National Narcotics Statute, which declared that the profits derived from the drug trade, as well as the assets used for the trade, would be expropriated and transferred to the National Narcotics Council (law 30/1986).

The United Nations Convention against Illicit Traffic in Narcotic Drugs and Psychotropic Substances was adopted in Vienna in 1988, and the signatory parties agreed to trace the goods acquired with the revenues of the drug trade. In 1989, the G-7 urged all countries to ratify the convention and created the Financial Action Task Force (FATF) on money laundering. In 1990 this new institution presented forty recommendations for combating money laundering. Even though they weren't binding, the objective was to harmonize and strengthen national legislations to secure a greater control of money laundering by the world's financial entities (Blickman 2009, 6).

The United Nations convention came into force in Colombia through law 67/1993 passed by the Colombian Congress (Hernández 2002, 39). Four years later, through law

365/1997, the Congress issued the Anti-Corruption Statute, which formally defined the conduct known as money laundering (Penal Code, article 247).

In 1999, the Colombian government, urged by the International Monetary Fund (IMF), created the Financial Information and Analysis Unit (Unidad de Información y Análisis Financiero, UIAF). The unit's main objective was to analyze, prevent, and gather information on money laundering.[2] In 2002, through law 793, the legislation for seizing assets related to the drug trade was reinforced and simplified. The law followed another recommendation of the FATF and established that any asset could be seized if the owner couldn't legally justify its origin. The authorities no longer needed a conviction for money laundering to proceed with expropriations.[3] These forfeitures were allowed on seven grounds, some of which were an unjustified increase in patrimony, the ownership of assets directly or indirectly derived from an illegal activity, the ownership of assets used for the commission of a crime or obtained because of a crime, and the possession of properties used to hide goods of illegal origin (law 793/2002).

These international concerns and demands about the problem of money laundering were essential to shaping the country's legal framework to combat it. Law 793/2002 may be regarded as the final stage of the process to establish the legal tools needed to fight the phenomenon. Despite this dynamic attitude on the legal and administrative fronts, it is doubtful whether the results of these public initiatives have been sufficiently effective. The revenues from the drug trade and other crimes continue to be large and they must be analyzed with the greatest possible rigor in order to gauge the effectiveness of the current institutional framework to combat money laundering.

THE INCOME FROM THE COCAINE TRADE

The main revenues from the drug trade that enter Colombia are from cocaine (Rocha 2000, 61). Therefore, this section focuses on estimating the income from cocaine exports.

The amount of cocaine produced and the prices at which Colombian traffickers sell it is difficult to quantify (Mejía and Posada 2010; Rocha 2000). The two main sources of information about cocaine production are the United Nations Office on Drugs and Crime (UNODC) and the White House Office of National Drug Control Policy (ONDCP). UNODC takes satellite images of almost all Colombian territory and corrects the biases and errors of interpretation of the pictures of illegal crops (Mejía and Posada 2010, 6–7). The ONDCP, on the other hand, only takes satellite images of a sample of the country. Therefore, we use the estimates made by the UNODC.

To estimate the export prices of cocaine and the amounts sent to the United States and other markets, we used the data of Mejía and Rico (Chapter 1). We assumed that the price remained within the range they established for the whole decade and used the average exchange rate for each year. The price for the US market fluctuated between eighteen and twenty-four million pesos per kilo, and the price for Europe between fifty and sixty million pesos per kilo. Then we assumed that the amounts exported to each market were stable; 55 percent of the total production was exported to North America and 45 percent to the European market. Finally, we assumed that the seizures of cocaine and coca leaves did not affect the incomes of the traffickers. The official figures on these seizures usually have accounting problems and the amounts are inflated,[4] so it is best to ignore them. With these assumptions about the price, the production, and the

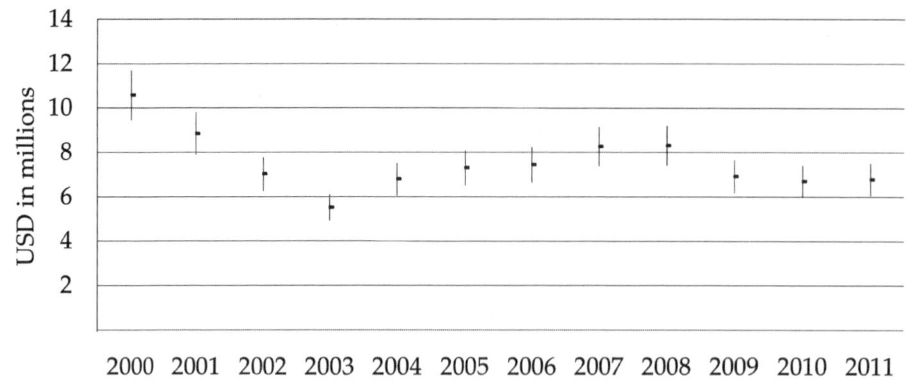

FIGURE 11.1. Estimation of money generated by cocaine trafficking (in millions of US dollars). Source: Our own estimates, based on the UNODC and Mejía and Rico (2011)

composition of the international Colombian cocaine market, we estimated the revenues, in US dollars, from the exports between 2000 and 2011 (Figure 11.1). After the increase and decrease cycle between 2000 and 2008, cocaine income seems to have stabilized around US$7 billion per year.

The traffickers need to turn an important portion of these earnings into local currency to cover the costs incurred at the different stages of the production chain.[5] In the next section we estimate the amount of earnings that might be brought into the country and turned into local currency.

THE AMOUNTS OF MONEY LAUNDERED

The revenues from the cocaine trade, like those from other illegal international transactions, may be brought into the country through three different mechanisms: the financial system, smuggling of goods, and shipments of foreign currency in cash.[6]

The financial system has been the most controlled. The initiatives against money laundering taken by the United States government and the international community since the 1980s triggered several reforms to strengthen the controls of the Colombian financial system. The banks were obliged to report suspicious activities to the UIAF and to play a more active role in the detection of money laundering.

Fictitious exports and overinvoicing exports are ways to channel illegal revenues through the financial system. According to the former director of the DIAN (the Colombian tax and customs agency), Juan Ricardo Ortega, the authorities should follow gold, cattle, and palm tree oil exports more closely.

There is an increasing and alarming gap between the gold production estimates and the exports. In 2011 gold exports were US$2.77 billion, which corresponded to the sale of 66.5 tons. The local production, however, only reached 56 tons. This might be due to the sale of old inventory, but the pattern has continued for several years, which makes this highly unlikely. Since 2009 the difference between production and exports has widened, and in 2011 it reached a difference above US$350 million (Figure 11.2).

Currently, there is no data on local production and consumption for certain products. Accordingly, cattle, palm tree oil, and other export gaps should be estimated to account for part of the money laundered through the financial system.

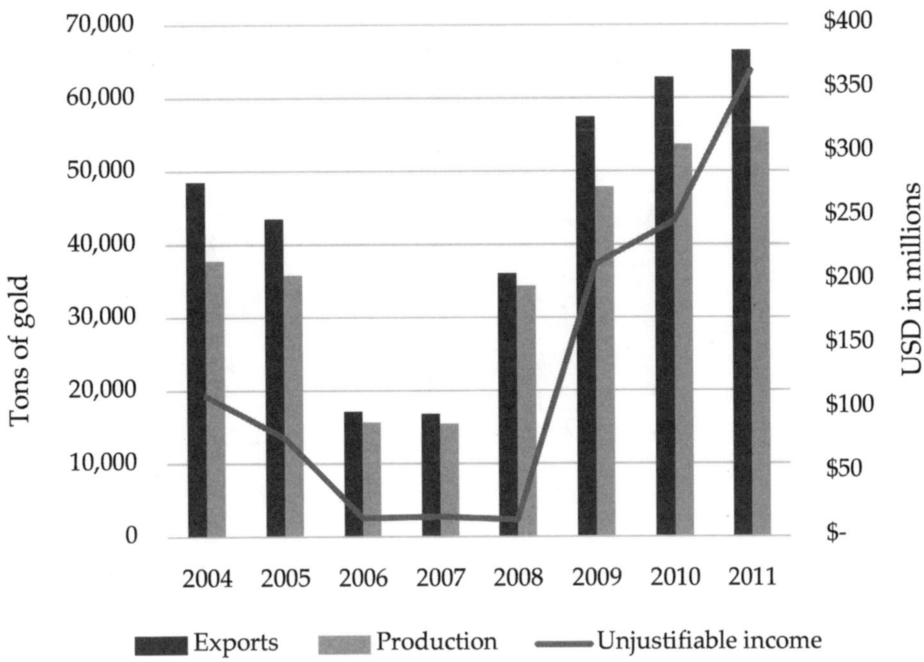

FIGURE 11.2. The difference between gold production and its exports. Source: Ministerio de Minas y Energía, Ingeominas, DIAN

The second channel, smuggled goods, includes outright smuggling, technical smuggling, and underinvoiced imports (Rocha and Ramírez 2004; Rocha 2000; Steiner 1997). We define technical smuggling as a tariff misclassification. This scheme is used to pay lower tariffs on import products with higher values. In this scheme, traffickers can introduce merchandise, which they sell cheaply and thus turn revenues from their cocaine sales into Colombian pesos. On May 16, 2002, the director of the DIAN said that "the smugglers are changing their strategy for laundering dollars. They are no longer importing big household appliances like refrigerators or televisions to the country, but they are bringing small articles, through the scheme of technical smuggling" (Hernández 2002, 37).

Outright smuggling—importing goods without any registration in the customs or any other government agency—is another method frequently used to launder money. Some government officials believe that containers full of dollars from the drug trade in the United States arrive at countries like Aruba and Panama. In these countries they are received by a number of illegal currency dealers, known as "pesos brokers," who legally buy cigarettes, liquor, and other goods with the money and smuggle them into Colombia (Hernández 2002, 37). Outright smuggling from Panama is the most significant. In the past years, its value has grown from around US$400 million annually to US$1.2 billion, and from representing 82 percent of all the outright smuggling to 99 percent (Rodríguez 2013, 10).

The underinvoicing of imports is another common mechanism for money laundering. The importer invoices the merchandise at a lower value, pays an inferior tax without raising much attention from the authorities, and sells the merchandise locally to obtain Colombian pesos. He thus manages to get more money in pesos than the value registered with the customs office.

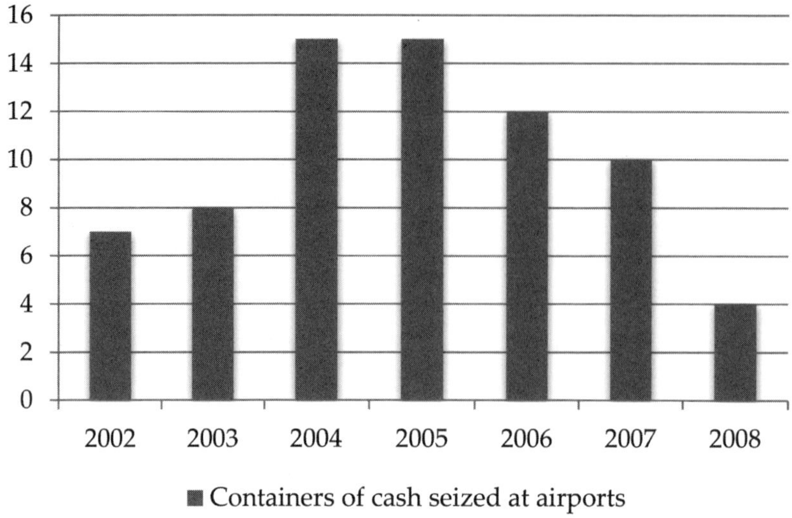

FIGURE 11.3. Extinction of property sentences for money in cash confiscated at airports. Source: Our own estimates based on sentences of the DNE

Outright smuggling, technical smuggling, and underinvoiced imports are often used for tax evasion, but there are several reported cases of these mechanisms being used for money laundering. The stronger controls applied to the financial system are probably the reason why imports have been the main mechanisms for money laundering since 2003. The DMG holding group is the most recent well-known case. The Colombian financial system refused to allow DMG to open bank accounts due to its dubious reputation. In 2009, the authorities established the illegal origin of the company's resources. The company used US dollars from the drug trade to buy and import goods from countries like Panama and sell them cheaply in the country.[7]

Cash shipments of foreign currency that are changed into Colombian pesos are the other common mechanism. On September 12, 2009, the Cali (Colombia) newspaper *El País* reported the discovery of a container with US$27.8 million in the port of Buenaventura (Colombia) and another with US$5.4 million in Manzanillo, Mexico, destined for Colombia. The police also report several cases of people who arrive at Colombian airports with suitcases full of foreign currency (Figure 11.3). When the authorities do not seize the shipments, the money is converted into pesos by local moneychangers and currency exchange offices. These moneychangers send a large part of the cash back to other countries through companies that offer cash transport services. This is how they keep their operation going.

With data from the Colombian central bank and the DIAN, we estimated the amount of two of the above-mentioned channels of foreign money laundering between 2000 and 2010 (Table 11.1). The estimates for technical smuggling, the subinvoicing of imports, and outright smuggling are taken from Rodríguez (2009) and cover the commercial partners that represent 86.9 percent of Colombian trade. To calculate the flow of drug trade revenues, which enter the country through cash shipments, we took into account the data on foreign currency in cash that was transported to other countries

TABLE 11.1. Estimates of money laundering on the basis of its main channels (in thousands of US dollars)

	2000	2001	2002	2003	2004	2005	2006	2007	2008	2009	2010
Laundering through goods imports											
Open smugglings	791,601	531,493	519,342	494,204	709,252	829,555	955,342	942,218	1,007,316	856,704	1,138,348
Sub-invoicing of imports	1,151,372	1,120,723	1,065,036	982,719	1,410,950	1,865,446	1,757,214	2,664,766	2,653,059	2,126,553	3,381,005
Technical smuggling	2,057,213	1,827,275	1,764,513	2,140,554	2,290,535	2,890,764	3,083,223	4,140,260	3,772,389	3,362,211	3,612,951
Total laundering with goods	4,000,186	3,479,491	3,348,891	3,617,477	4,410,737	5,585,765	5,795,779	7,747,244	7,432,764	6,345,468	8,132,304
Laundering with cash imports											
Seized cash	NA	NA	2,838	8,519	9,686	5,440	20,584	12,676	6,819	8,172	3,435
Seized securities	NA	NA	—	34	218	2,002	336	48	20	637	—
Cash sent abroad by transportation companies	702,968	1,228,943	1,455,719	2,544,200	2,554,400	2,622,619	2,257,351	991,801	237,021	186,032	132,247
Tourists cash imports	83,669	115,993	87,360	113,484	105,918	114,240	109,513	108,010	103,039	98,519	110,365
Total laundering with cash	619,299	1,112,951	1,371,197	2,439,269	2,458,386	2,515,820	2,168,758	896,515	140,821	96,322	25,317
Total	4,619,485	4,592,442	4,720,088	6,056,746	6,869,123	8,101,585	7,964,537	8,643,759	7,573,585	6,441,790	8,157,621

Source: Estimates based on Rodríguez (2013), DIAN y Banrep.

and the cash seized at Colombian airports.[8] Then we discounted the foreign currency tourists report when they enter the country. Usually tourists change their currencies into Colombian pesos at hotels, moneychangers, and foreign exchange offices. We assume these estimates are accurate, but it is possible that certain tourists who figure in these reports bring revenues from the drug trade. The corresponding figures are shown in Table 11.1, and we can see that they have been shrinking over time.

According to the figures shown in Table 11.1, technical smuggling may have fluctuated yearly in a range between US$1.8 and 4.1 billion in the period between 1998 and 2010. It is important to underline that not all the merchandise smuggled should be associated with the laundering of cocaine revenues. Nevertheless, the data is useful in providing an estimate of the magnitude of money laundered through the smuggled goods and currency exchange businesses. Calculating the difference between the customs statistics of the countries that export merchandise to Colombia and Colombian statistics on imports enables the estimates of money laundered through smuggled goods. The estimates also show that between 40 and 50 percent of the imports tagged as technical smuggling come from the United States, which is the main market for Colombian cocaine (Rodríguez 2009, 9).

To our money laundering estimates should be added the money laundered through the financial system, which we cannot estimate completely with the available data. We should also add the value of cocaine bartered by illegal groups, such as FARC, for weapons and other goods such as Venezuelan gasoline. According to the researcher Daniel Mejía, weapons transactions amount to approximately 15 percent of the incomes from the drug trade (Chapter 1).

Our estimates are rough figures of an activity for which there is no reliable information. The smuggling of goods and the cash shipments are also channels frequently used for tax evasion. Nevertheless it is important to state that since 2003, the estimated trend of the money laundered through the smuggling of goods and cash shipments is similar to the estimated income from cocaine trafficking (Figure 11.4). Since 2009, as the mismatch between imports and the production of certain products such as gold increases, our estimated trend starts to differ. We could infer that a great part of the revenues from cocaine trafficking were introduced into the country through smuggled goods and cash shipments until about 2009, and the financial system is now once again getting more pressure to get money laundered.

The UIAF and the financial system controls have required the drug lords and cartels to bring in most of their earnings in merchandise. Drug lords, however, are always looking for different mechanisms. The controls on the financial system and foreign cash currencies in the market should be kept strong and revised frequently.

THE INSTITUTIONAL NETWORK: RESULTS AND DISINCENTIVES

The current institutional framework is made up of several entities focused on prevention, control, and repression, and its objective is to discourage and penalize money laundering as well as the crimes it conceals.

The main state body working against these felonies is the Commission for the Interinstitutional Coordination of the Control of Money Laundering (CICLA), created in 1995. The commission is in charge of coordinating the actions and strategies of the

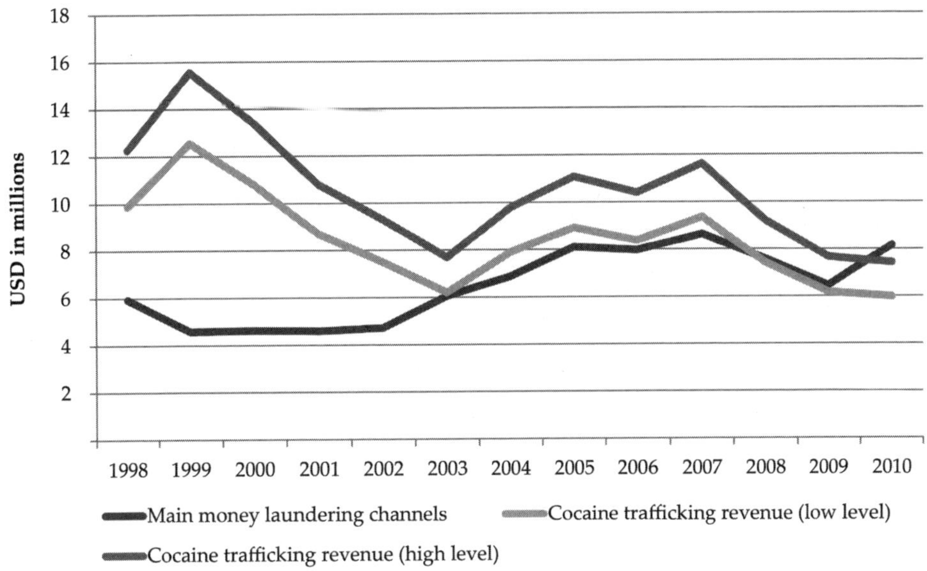

FIGURE 11.4. Cocaine trafficking revenue and money laundering estimates. Source: Our own estimates based on Mejía and Rico (2011), Rodríguez (2013), UNODC, DIAN, and Reportes del Emisor (Central Bank Reports, 2006)

different public organizations involved in this struggle. None of these organizations is exclusively devoted to prevention, control, or repression, as was acknowledged in 2003 by María Cristina Chirolla, then the chief prosecutor for the National Unit for Expropriation and the Fight against Money Laundering (Chirolla 2003), but there is a degree of specialization in the functions carried out by each one.

The main institutions responsible for prevention are the Financial Superintendency (Superintendencia Financiera), the Corporations Superintendency (Superintendencia de Sociedades), and the DIAN. These organizations have to deal with the three channels cocaine traffickers use to bring in their earnings. They are in charge of controlling the financial system, commercial trade, and cash shipments that may be entering the country or managed by corporations.[9] The Financial Superintendency implemented the Integral System for the Prevention and Control of Money Laundering (SIPLA), which was later transformed into the System for Managing the Risk of Asset Laundering and Financing of Terrorism (SARLAFT). The system's main objectives are to prevent money laundering in the financial sector and to control and detect suspicious financial operations. The Corporations Superintendency is in charge of supervising the external indebtedness of Colombian companies and their foreign investments. Finally, the DIAN prevents laundering by fighting against technical and outright smuggling. Furthermore, the superintendencies and the DIAN must submit monthly SARs (Suspicious Activity Reports) to the UIAF (Balen 2001, 3–4).

The police, the armed forces, the national intelligence agency, the UIAF, and even the Public Prosecutor's Office (Fiscalía General de la Nación) are in charge of detection. Certain foreign organizations like the DEA also support local efforts of detection. The police, armed forces, and the intelligence agency investigate and identify the crimes (Chapter 10). In turn, the UIAF receives SARs from the financial sector, the industrial sector, and notaries public, among others, and analyzes them and sends confidential

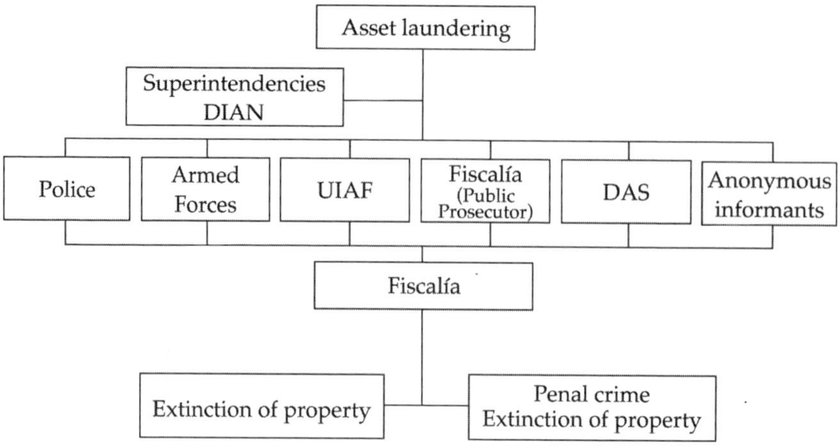

FIGURE 11.5. The institutional framework for combating money laundering

reports to the judicial police and the prosecutor's office. The latter studies these reports, as well as the internal ones of its Technical Investigation Body (Cuerpo Técnico de Investigación), and, if it finds merit, pursues a conviction. All criminal proceedings against money laundering and forfeitures are handled by the prosecutor's office, in accordance with their investigations and the reports filed by other prevention and detection institutions (Balen 2001, 6–8).

At first sight, the flows of information through the different institutions might seem adequate and efficient. The prosecutor's office is meant to play a crucial role in the whole process of discouraging money laundering. The office has to gather all the information about suspicious activities from the agencies of detection: the Financial Information and Analysis Unit, the intelligence agency, the police, the armed forces, and anonymous informants, among others. Then the office must sift through the information and when the case merits it and there is sufficient evidence, seek a conviction (Figure 11.5).

The prosecutor's office receives a flood of reports of suspicious activity that may lead to forfeitures or criminal indictments. The office has a huge responsibility, and its investigative and operational capacity is not up to the task. In February 2010, the Division for Seizures and the Control of Money Laundering had only thirty-three prosecutors available to prosecute members of a criminal enterprise whose worth, according to our estimates, is equivalent to between 2 and 3 percent of the GDP.

Since 2002, judges of the criminal courts have been given the power to order extinction when there is an unjustified increase in patrimony without having to prove links with the crimes. Before then, only in a few cases was it possible to prove the relationship between the resources and the crimes of narcotics trafficking. Thus, since the passing of law 793/2002, the number of extinction cases has risen. Attacking the earnings of the traffickers and criminals would be an important disincentive for illegal activities and would help to reduce them, but some authors have expressed their concern for this law's possible violation of the constitutional rights of the accused, among other risks (Chapter 10). The leaders of some of the main detection agencies such as the UIAF have

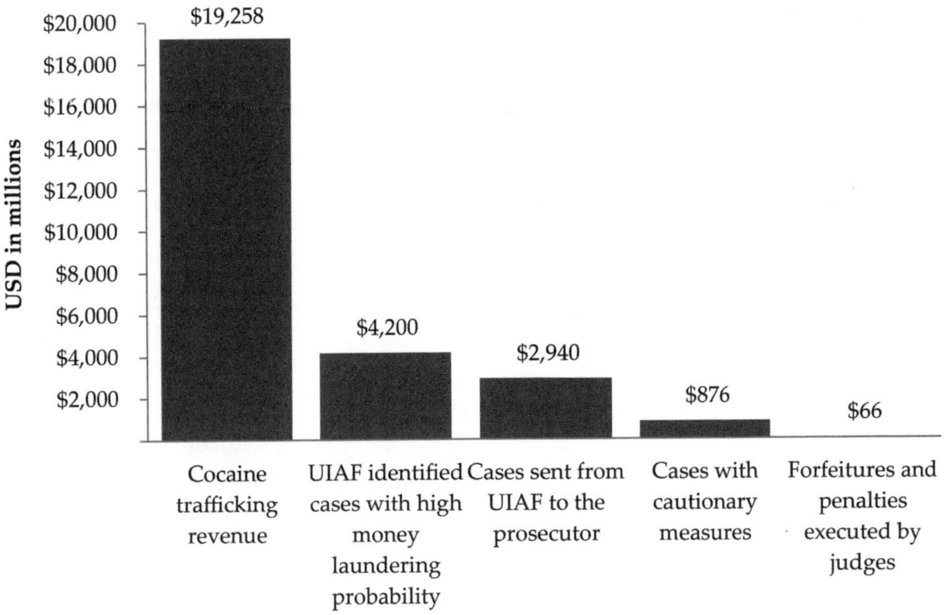

FIGURE 11.6. Cocaine production estimation and the confiscatory role of the state from 2011 to 2013 (in millions of US dollars). Source: UIAF. The cocaine revenues are based on UNODC and Mejía and Rico (2011). We assumed that the cocaine production in 2013 was the same as in 2012

been prosecuted and convicted. A former director was prosecuted for wrongly handling personal information.

Since 2011, the UIAF has been reshaped, but the results, in terms of actual expropriations, do not yet seem to be significant (Figure 11.6). The UIAF has built from SARs 268 cases with a high probability of money laundering. These cases represent properties with a cadastral value of US$1.4 billion and an estimated commercial value three times that. From this group of cases the UIAF has found compelling evidence in 131 cases and has sent them to the prosecutor's office. The cadastral value of the assets considered in these cases is US$980 million with an estimated commercial value three times that. From these 131 cases, the prosecutor's office ordered interim measures in 15 cases. The estimated value of the assets involved in these cases is US$292 million, with an estimated commercial value of US$876 million. Most of the cases with cautionary measures are associated with the cases against the Alvarez Meyendorff brothers, which have been considered by the media as the biggest antimafia operation in the history of the country. Finally, from the fifteen cases with cautionary measures only two cases have had convictions. The assets forfeited have an estimated commercial value of US$21 million, and the fines charged to the people involved have been US$45 million. From a business that we calculate generated around US$19.3 billion between 2011 and the beginning of 2014, only US$66 million have been captured by the state, or about 0.3 percent (UIAF interviews).

The seizures of smuggled merchandise reported by the DIAN have not been significant either (Table 11.2). The value of the goods that might have been smuggled into the

TABLE 11.2. Seizure of merchandise in US dollars (subdirectorate of customs supervision)

Year	Value of Merchandise
2002	$51,675,866
2003	$47,777,261
2004	$65,208,558
2005	$103,887,806
2006	$126,770,318
2007	$134,641,001
2008	$171,504,191
2009	$181,355,787
2010	$204,048,207
2011	$269,065,432
2012	$131,255,906

Source: DIAN

country is estimated at around US$8 billion in 2010, while the value of the goods seized was US$204 million. The DIAN might only have captured between 1.4 and 2.5 percent of the value of the goods that illegally entered the country between 2004 and 2010. Moreover, we should take into account that in several cases the merchandise is returned to the smugglers by judges and the statistics are not adjusted.

Finally, the forfeitures authorized by court rulings since 1999 also do not show encouraging results. The type of rulings can be divided into six categories, according to the grounds for the seizure: assets acquired with drug trade revenues, assets used in the drug trade, restricted inputs for drug production, assets robbed or used in a theft, foreign currency in cash retrieved in airports, and others. The categories and their trends since 1999 are presented in Figure 11.7.

Just after law 793 was passed in 2002, there was a significant increase in forfeited assets allegedly acquired with drug trade revenues. As shown in Figure 11.8, however, since 2004 the number of rulings in this category decreased. Only in 2002 and 2003 were there more rulings of this kind than rulings related to the assets used in the drug trade. Since 2004, most rulings on seizures have been aimed at assets used in the production, transportation, possession, or sale of illegal drugs. Usually such seized assets are fast boats, houses used for small local drug sales, and others of little value. They are usually not the kind of assets the seizure of which would discourage the drug lords or cartel members. The assets used in the drug trade are easier to detect and do not represent great sums of money. Law 793/2002 only had a temporary effect; court rulings on the forfeiture of assets allegedly acquired from the drug trade only rose for a couple of years. Nevertheless, we do not know how much money these seizures represent and we should note that the authorities report that the number of assets has been rising. Therefore, there are two possibilities: either the fewer rulings on assets acquired from the drug trade represent more money, or the assets seized on other grounds are more valuable and the financial disincentives against the drug trade are not really working.

The number of people brought to trial for money laundering follows the same pattern as the rulings on assets acquired with drug trade revenues, a rising trend between 2002 and 2004 and a fall until 2008 (Figure 11.8).

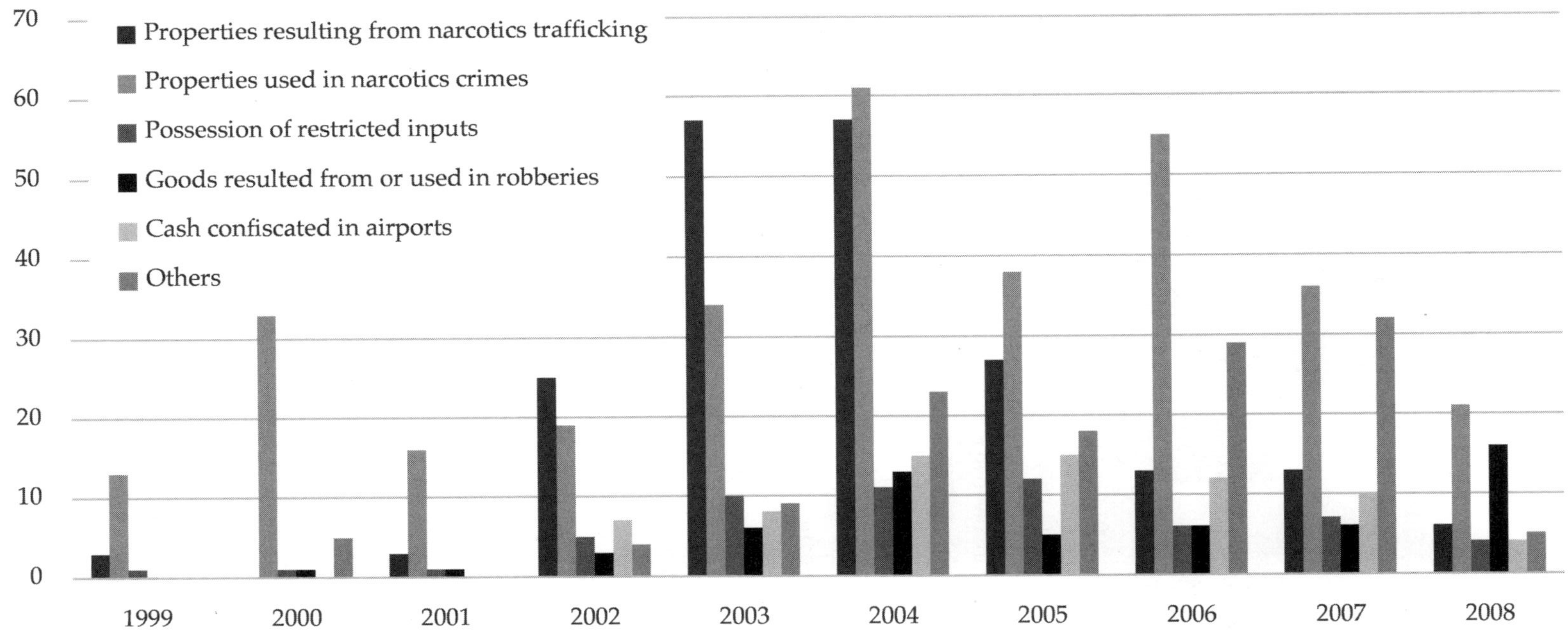

FIGURE 11.7. Breakdown of sentences for extinction of property. Source: Estimates of the authors based on DNE sentences

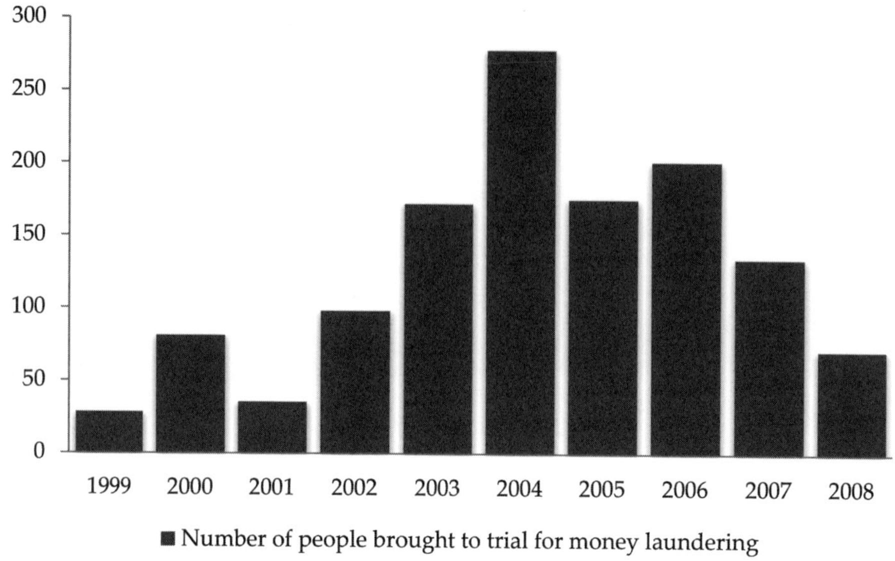

FIGURE 11.8. Persons involved in extinction of property sentences. Source: Estimates of the authors based on DNE sentences

The institutional framework for controlling money laundering is complex and focused on the main areas of concern: prevention, detection, and repression. Nevertheless, the results, measured by the seizure of a significant percentage of the revenues of illegal businesses, are still not significant. The issuance of law 793/2002, in terms of people brought to trial for money laundering and the number of sentences of seized properties, seems to show only a transitory change that has probably worn out.

CONCLUSIONS

In 1986, the fight against money laundering started in Colombia. The country formulated certain policies to follow the international community's concern and its harmful effects on society. The results are not significant yet.

Despite advances in the eradication of illegal drug crops, the cocaine trade continues to represent a large amount of money, around US$8 billion annually, most of which the traffickers must bring into the country in order to sustain the trade cycle.

These revenues mainly enter the country through three channels: the financial system, smuggled goods, and shipments of foreign currency in cash. The UIAF and the Financial Superintendency have strengthened their controls of the financial sector since 1999. The differences between the exports and the local production of certain goods, such as gold, should be carefully reviewed by the state. Gold seems to be one of the products used to launder money through the financial system. According to our estimates, in 2011 around US$350 million were laundered using gold in the financial system. Nevertheless, the number of SARs in this sector has been declining, and it is possible that a great part of the revenues are entering the country through smuggled goods and a declining portion through cash shipments. The estimate of how much money that may be entering the country through these two channels from 2003 to 2009 is close to that of the revenues from the cocaine trade. Although this is a broad ceiling estimate, the state should toughen its control.

Very few of the rulings on forfeitures issued between 1999 and 2008 dealt with smuggled goods. Instead, they usually involved real estate, foreign currency in cash, bank accounts, local commercial companies, and fast boats. The revenues entering the country through smuggled goods may be high, and the results of state efforts in this field are not significant. Between 2004 and 2010, the value of the smuggled goods that were seized did not surpass 2.5 percent of the estimated total of drug revenues. In 2010 the authorities ordered the forfeiture of merchandise valued at around US$104 million, whereas US$8 billion might have entered the country in smuggled goods. The DIAN, the customs police, and the prosecutor's office must pay more attention to this money-laundering channel. Judges frequently return the forfeited merchandise for simple legal procedural mistakes. Such control would also have a positive effect on the Colombian manufacturing sector, which is harmed by the smuggling of cheap products.

The legal and institutional frameworks have been toughened in the past decades. Nevertheless, the value of the forfeited assets is not significant compared with the estimates of the revenues of the cocaine trade. According to the UIAF estimate of the value of the forfeited assets, and our calculations of the revenue of the drug trade, since 2011 only 0.3 percent of the revenues have been captured by the state. The role of the prosecutor's office is important because it receives the suspicious activity reports of all the other state entities and seeks convictions. The effectiveness of its work depends on the availability of resources. There are not enough prosecutors in the National Expropriation Division.

Thus, while institutional controls have improved, the results in terms of forfeitures are not overwhelming. The "follow the money trail" policy is not working properly as a disincentive for the traffickers.

The adoption of the United Nations Convention against Illicit Traffic in Narcotics Drugs and Psychotropic Substances in Vienna in 1988 marked a commitment by the international community to enforce measures to trace the assets acquired with illegal revenues. Colombia followed its recommendations and modified its legislation, first when it ratified the Vienna Convention in 1993 and later in 2002 when it implemented procedures to seize assets without a criminal conviction.

Colombia currently has adequate legislation against money laundering, but its institutional network for obtaining convictions is still very weak. The main problem is the weak coordination between the agencies and their need for greater technical and human resources. Recently, the UIAF is coordinating better with the prosecutor's office and has moved from considering the number of SARs as a performance indicator to the difference between the value of the assets under investigation and the value of the assets seized in court rulings. This is an important step to keep improving the effectiveness of the state.

The Colombian state can still organize the institutional framework more efficiently. The government should centralize more responsibilities in an anti-drug czar office, responsible to the Colombian presidency with the status of an administrative department. This office would coordinate all government actions related to fighting the drug trade and money laundering. It would evaluate the efficiency of the whole institutional scaffolding and be in permanent contact with the heads of the armed forces, national police, intelligence agency, the DIAN, and the UIAF. To efficiently coordinate the different state agencies and their money-laundering controls, the anti-drug czar would be responsible for supervising the work of the National Narcotics Council and the National Narcotics Administration.

The office would also establish solid indicators to evaluate the results of the different institutions. It would also have to compile and annually publish information about illegal drug activities and money laundering. The office could establish rigorous indicators on smuggled goods, cash shipments, exports versus local production of goods, the efficiency of the prosecutor's office, and the value of the assets seized in court rulings. The office could also make annual estimates of the size of the drug trade and money laundering business.

These are merely suggestions that may turn out to be effective in the fight against this scourge. This chapter is only an approach to the subject. It seeks to call attention to a problem of great magnitude and complexity, with the aim of stimulating further studies and helping to improve the efforts of the state.

NOTES

To undertake this study it was necessary to interview officials of several state agencies: The National Tax and Customs Administration (DIAN); the National Narcotics Administration (DNE); the Banco de la República (central bank); the Fiscalía General de la Nación (Public Prosecutor's Office); the Unidad Administrativa Especial de Información y Análisis Financiero (Special Administrative Unit for Information and Financial Analysis) (UIAF); the United Nations Office on Drugs and Crime (UNODC); and the National Administrative Statistical Department (DANE); Daniel Mejía and Daniel Rico of the Faculty of Economics; and Libardo Ariza and Manuel Iturralde of the Faculty of Law. We would like to thank them all and especially the Banco de la República, which in addition to technical support provided the funding for this chapter. We would also like to express our thanks to Santiago Lizarralde for his help in processing the forfeitures information.

1. Forfeiture refers to the judicial proceeding (*extinción de dominio*) aimed at assets obtained through illegal activities. A rigorous analysis of this proceeding is found in Chapter 10.
2. For a more in-depth understanding of the UIAF's mission, see law 526/1999 and law 1121/2006.
3. The legislative process that established the current legal and institutional framework for detecting and combating narcotics trafficking and asset laundering is discussed in Chapter 10.
4. In the drug seizures, problems of double counting have been detected. In certain cases coca paste has been classified as cocaine and impure cocaine as pure cocaine. The degree of purity of seized cocaine varies between 60 and 95 percent.
5. According to Chapter 1, "The workshops (*cristalizaderos*) where cocaine sulphate (base) is transformed into cocaine chlorhydrate require an important investment in physical infrastructure, lodging and food for the operatives, distribution networks and storerooms for chemical equipment, early warning systems to avoid attacks by the authorities or even other criminal gangs, and a supply of electricity and safe (and dry) places to store the final product."

6. Within these three channels for bringing revenues into the country in foreign currency, the criminals may use different strategies to make their incomes seem legal. The UIAF has identified some of them, which are published on its web site: *www.uiaf.gov.co*. In this chapter we focus on the channels not on the strategies.
7. Between 2008 and 2009 it was discovered that the DMG Corporation illegally obtained deposits of money in Colombia, paid high interest rates to its depositors, and gave them different goods.
8. Resolution 6/2004 of the Board of Governors of the Banco de la República (central bank) established that "the inflows or outflows of foreign currencies or Colombian legal tender in cash for an amount higher than ten thousand United States dollars (US$10,000) or its equivalent in other currencies, may only be undertaken through securities transport companies authorized in accordance with the regulations which govern this activity." Likewise, it was decided that those who send money through securities transport companies are obliged to declare those operations to the DIAN. Before the Board of Governors issued this resolution, the bank acquired foreign currencies from the commercial banks, some of whom bought them in turn from money exchange offices that shipped them to foreign countries. They figured in the accounts as "deposits of American dollars in cash." The money exchange offices couldn't use the bank's service to ship foreign currency overseas undertaken by the Banco de la República until September 2004. They didn't have deposit accounts in the bank. Cf. *Reportes del Emisor* (2006).
9. The other superintendencies are also important in the prevention of money laundering, but they do not work directly against the three channels under discussion.

REFERENCES

Alldridge, P. 2003. *Money Laundering Law.* Portland, OR: Hart Publishing.

Balen, M. T. 2001. *Lavado de activos-el caso colombiano*. Washington, DC: XXIII Congreso Nacional LASA 2001. Retrieved from *lasa.international.pitt.edu/Lasa2001/BalendePerezToroMaria.pdf.*

Blickman, T. 2009. "Lucha contra los flujos de capitales no regulados." TNI Debate Paper. Amsterdam: Transnational Institute.

Caballero, C., and R. Junguito. 1978. "La otra economía." *Coyuntura económica* 8, no. 4.

Chirolla, M. C. 2003 "Presentación sobre el papel de la Fiscalía dentro del Sistema contra el Lavado de Activos en el Banco de Bogotá." Public Prosecutor's Office, March 4. Retrieved from *www.fiscalia.gov.co/pag/divulga/Decla02/lavact.htm*.

Colombia. 1998. Código Penal, artículo 247a, 102 (3rd ed.). Bogotá: Legis.

El País. 2009. "Los dólares decomisados ya suman 27,8 millones." September 12. Retrieved from *www.elpais.com.co/elpais/ediciones.php?p=sep122009*, accessed March 7, 2011.

El Tiempo. 2009 "Extradición de David Murcia Guzmán and William Suárez a E.U. fue firmada por el presidente Uribe." November 20. Retrieved from *www.eltiempo.com/archivo/documento/CMS-6637548*, accessed March 7, 2011.

Hernández, H. 2002. *El lavado de activos*. Medellín: Ediciones Jurídicas Gustavo Ibáñez Ltda.

Ley 793/2002, *Diario Oficial* 45.046 27 Dic. 2002. Retrieved from *www.secretariasenado.gov.co/senado/basedoc/ley/2002/ley_0793_2002.html.*

Ley 365/1997, *Diario Oficial* 42.987 21 Feb. 1997. Retrieved from *www.secretariasenado.gov.co/senado/basedoc/ley/1997/ley_0365_1997.htm.*

Ley 30/1986. Retrieved from *www.cnrr.org.co/interior_otros /pdf/ley_30_1986.pdf.*

Mejía, D., ed. 2006. "Movimientos de divisas en efectivo en Colombia: 2003–2005." Reportes del Emisor, Número extraordinario. Bogotá: Banco de la República.

Mejía, D., and C. Posada. 2010. "Cocaine Production and Trafficking: What Do We Know?" In *Innocent Bystander: Developing Countries and the War in Drugs*, edited by P. Keefer and N. Loayza. World Bank.

Naím, M. 2006. *Ilícito: Cómo traficantes, contrabandistas y piratas están cambiando el mundo.* Barcelona: Debate.

Reportes del Emisor. 2006. *Movimientos de divisas en efectivo en Colombia 2003–2005.* Bogotá: Banco de la República.

Reuter, P., and E. Truman. 2004. *Chasing Dirty Money: Progress on Anti-money Laundering.* Washington, DC: Institute for International Economics.

Rocha, R. 2000. *La economía colombiana tras 25 años de narcotráfico.* Bogotá: Siglo del Hombre Editores.

Rocha, R., and M. C. Ramírez. 2004. *Drogas ilegales en Colombia: Experiencia reciente e implicaciones de política.* Bogotá: Informe Final para comentarios Usaid.

Rodríguez, M. Y. 2013. "Medición de la distorsión en el valor de las importaciones." Documento Web 035. Bogotá: Subdirección de Análisis Operacional, DIAN. Retrieved from *www.dian.gov.co/descargas/Servicios/OEE-Documentos/Cuadernos/Cuaderno_de_Trabajo_035.pdf.*

Steiner, R. 1997. *Los dólares del narcotráfico.* Bogotá: Tercer Mundo Editores.

UN Office on Drugs and Crime (UNODC) and Government of Colombia. 2010. *Colombia: Monitoreo de cultivos de coca.* Retrieved from *www.unodc.org/documents/crop-monitoring/Colombia/Colombia-Censo-2009-web.pdf*, accessed May 12, 2015.

PART V: INSTITUTIONS AND NARCOTICS TRAFFICKING

12 Colombian Institutions and Narcotics Trafficking

Mutations and Politics

Álvaro Camacho

Given the critical juncture it has brought the country to, narcotics trafficking is suitable for study as an element of Colombian history. Along with the existence of guerrilla groups, narcotics trafficking is in fact one of the aspects that have most strongly shaped current Colombian society, and to see it as a juncture helps us to understand its role in the social, political, cultural, and economic arrangements that mark this stage of its history. Narcotics trafficking has invaded vast fields of the collective activities of Colombian society; construction, commerce, industry, architecture, sports, and politics have not been alien to its penetration. Along with the activities of the guerrilla, its effect has been seen most notably in the rise in murders, the disturbances in the judicial system, and the instability of the country's institutions. In fact, until a few years ago it was said that Colombia could be called a "failed state," and a director of the DEA labeled the country a "narco-democracy."

In this chapter we use the notion of a juncture (*coyuntura*) to indicate a period time when there arise phenomena that significantly alter the course of a society's history (Braudel 1974). In fact, in recent years there have been interactions of economic, social, and political processes, driven by narcotics trafficking and a guerrilla war, that have changed the face of the country. While the history of Colombia shows previous instances of the growing and clandestine export of illegal crops (Sáenz 1997), both their domestic consumption and contraband were no more than relatively isolated phenomena, limited to some towns and regions of the country. Nowadays, on the other hand, Colombia has turned into the world's biggest producer and exporter of cocaine, coca leaf is grown in several regions of the country, and the product is consumed in many countries of the world. For this reason, the business of illegal drugs is one of the major expressions of the way in which the country has inserted itself into the global picture.

Álvaro Camacho: Former director of the Center of Socio-Cultural and International Studies (CESO), Universidad de los Andes. Dr. Camacho passed away in December 2011. He was one of the first scholars in Colombia to study narcotics trafficking and its relation to crime and violence in Colombia. Daniel Mejía revised the English translation of this chapter and is responsible for any omissions or mistakes.

Narcotics trafficking has also had a history of its own and has gone through several transformations. They indicate that the phenomenon modifies its structures and organizational forms, yet meanwhile conserves its nature as an illegal and highly profitable business. It shows a great capacity for mutation, which enables it to develop shifting strategies that tend to neutralize state efforts to do away with it (Kenney 2000).

NARCOTICS TRAFFICKING: A MUTATING ACTIVITY

Narcotics trafficking arose in the 1960s with the production and export of marijuana from the Sierra Nevada de Santa Marta (ANIF 1980). This period was marked by the sudden development of an economy with a wide circulation of money. It embodied a new kind of agro-exporting economy and gave rise to a new social actor, the trafficker of marijuana, known as the *marimbero*. The presence of the *marimbero* led to different reactions. To begin with, there was the idea of a rising or "emerging class" that supposedly threatened the declining or "submerging" class, made up of the traditional elites. The phenomenon provoked heated debates about the best way to handle it, including proposals for the legalization of marijuana (ANIF 1980). Although these debates were of interest to some sectors of society, the proposal was strongly opposed and failed as a result.

Narcotics trafficking underwent a substantial change with the development of the cocaine trafficking networks in the 1970s. If the marijuana trade was limited to one region of the country and a particular social group, the cocaine trade turned into the maximum expression of the export of illegal drugs. Some contrabandists in the region of Antioquia, joined by other groups located in the Valley of Cauca, formed what later became known as the Medellín and Cali cartels. The key to the business now consisted of importing coca paste or raw cocaine from Peru and Bolivia, transforming it into cocaine in Colombian laboratories, and exporting it to consumer markets, mainly located in North America.

For this market to function, it was indispensable to create a number of organizations that would be able to the control the whole process, including controlling the import and export routes, organizing groups of wholesalers to supply the international market of consumers, and forming armed gangs willing to protect their bosses and take on both rival gangs and the policing organizations that constantly pursued them.

The so-called cartels resorted to different strategies to expand the business and insert themselves into legitimate spheres of society. Some, like the Medellín cartel, built up different networks of social relations, despite the criminal records of some of its main heads. To gain influence with the poorer sectors of society and attain some kind of social legitimacy, they engaged in philanthropic activities like sponsoring low-cost housing and building sports fields in poor neighborhoods. They inserted themselves into political networks and used these activities as mechanisms to infiltrate the spheres of the state. This strategy was largely undisguised, so they quickly made enemies of many politicians and members of the police and judiciary, insofar as they resorted to the use of violence and corruption, both to promote their business and protect themselves from state persecution.

In this undertaking, they resorted to different kinds of violence, from the type used to resolve internal disputes to the open deployment of violence against the enemies they had made in the world of politics and the judicial system. This was seen in the murders of police officers, judges, government officials, and politicians that had turned hostile to their activities. They did not hesitate to employ terrorism, which went as far as killing judges and presidential candidates and, along the way, hundreds of innocent civilians.

One characteristic of some of the leaders of these cartels was their hunger for political power. At times they linked themselves with already existing organizations, and at times they started their own. Within a short time, this had an impact on public opinion, which provoked the strong opposition of some journalists and politicians who denounced their criminal backgrounds and regarded their presence as a real threat to democracy and the country's institutions. For example, in the Colombian Congress and the media, Rodrigo Lara Bonilla, minister of justice under president Betancur, repeatedly denounced Pablo Escobar and his partners and exposed them as the heads of the Medellín cartel.

Two cases had a strong political resonance. Carlos Lehder, who became known for his role in transporting drugs from Cayo Norman, an island in the Bahamas he controlled, decided to start his own political movement, the National Latino Movement (Movimiento Latino Nacional), a strange mixture of socialist ideology and sympathy for Adolf Hitler. Following a campaign, some of his candidates were elected to the city councils of Armenia and other municipalities, and to the Departmental Assembly of el Quindío. After a failed kidnapping attempt by the M-19 guerrilla group, he went into hiding and left for the Llanos Orientales, where he tried to start a guerrilla force. He soon returned to Medellín, where he was captured by the police and quickly extradited.

Pablo Escobar was another notable case. He managed to get named as a candidate for the House of Representatives by the Nuevo Liberalismo Party. Soon, its head, Luis Carlos Galán, expelled him from the party, and Escobar was nominated by another party. Once he was elected a congressman, his criminal activities became public knowledge, and the Congress removed him from his seat. It did not take him long to retaliate, and the chain of terrorist attacks he unleashed shook the country. Escobar was responsible for the death of two ministers of justice, the director of the newspaper *El Espectador*, four presidential candidates, top officials of the police, judges, and magistrates, a general prosecutor, and numerous police officers in Medellín. He also ordered the kidnapping of important public figures (Castro 1996).

The Colombian government, headed at the time by César Gaviria, thus faced a double threat: on the one hand, the exporting of cocaine, which compromised it before the government of the United States; and on the other, the terrorist assaults of Escobar and his henchmen. Although he did not neglect the first challenge, it was clear that Gaviria gave priority to confronting terrorism. Some of his measures—like the creation of what was known as "faceless" judges (in order to protect them from being identified), the formation of an elite antinarcotics force, and a series of decrees that sought to facilitate the surrender of the main narcotics traffickers—showed limited results. In fact, some members of the Medellín cartel, the Ochoa Vásquez brothers, did give themselves up, and after the National Constituent Assembly responsible for the new Constitution prohibited extradition, Pablo Escobar did the same. A short while later, however, when the government found evidence that he continued to engage in his criminal activities from the jail he was in, they tried to move him to another prison, which led him to escape. It was only some time later, after he was killed, that the Medellín cartel was finally dismantled (Cañon 1994). Several organizations of narcotics traffickers, most notably the Cali cartel, played a crucial role in the war against Escobar.

Another striking characteristic of some members of that cartel was their hunger for lands. To acquire them, they resorted to paying inflated prices or forcibly evicting their owners or occupiers, setting off a process of mass forced displacement of the rural population. To achieve this objective, they formed alliances with local landowners, business owners, and politicians to deal with the threat of guerrilla organizations, which in turn abused the local population and helped to worsen the exodus. They thus managed to create armed groups devoted to eliminating such organizations, an enterprise in which they did not hesitate to kidnap or murder innocent civilians.

This alliance with antisubversive political groups on a local level took on a rapid momentum of its own, which turned them into the organizations later known as the paramilitaries. Counting in some cases on the tolerance or outright collaboration of local politicians and sectors of the armed forces, these organizations eventually became the most highly developed expression of organized crime that the country has experienced in recent years.

The heads of the Cali cartel chose another way of exerting political influence. Instead of playing a personal role, they collected funds from their companions in the Norte del Valle cartel to finance political campaigns. In the hope of obtaining legislation favorable to their interests but without showing themselves in public, they finally managed, it is assumed, to finance the campaign that ended in the election of Ernesto Samper as president of Colombia. That, in turn, was the start of one of the most notable judicial processes in recent political history: what was known as the Proceso 8,000 (Indictment no. 8000), which led to the jailing of some well-known politicians and the ruining of the careers of others.

The strong response of the US government didn't take much time. It countered the presumed financing of the campaign by narcotics money by "decertifying" Colombia for two years in a row, that is, removing it from the list of partners in its anti-drug fight. As a result, the United States withheld its support for Colombia's efforts to win funding from international credit organizations, cancelled president Samper's visa, and maneuvered to make him the object of widespread international criticism. Samper's response was to intensify the persecution of the leaders of the cartels, which resulted in the surrender or capture of the most important ones (some of whom were later murdered), or, in other cases, to extradite them, the most notable being the Rodríguez Orejuela brothers, alleged chiefs of the Cali cartel.

The most important leaders of the Cali cartel had chosen to link themselves with the world of legitimate business and cast their nets into those waters (Rodríguez and Rodríguez 2005). Without renouncing the use of violence, they ran their affairs in a more virtuous way, which helped them to rise socially into the richest sectors of society and protected them from prosecution. They devoted themselves to organizing legal commercial and financial companies and bought soccer teams, among other channels for laundering money. They hired business executives and other experts, which further widened their social networks and facilitated their economic rise; meanwhile they won acceptance and popularity from broad segments of the population.

It was during the 1980s and early 1990s that narcotics trafficking went through its greatest growth. Joe Toft, a top DEA agent, came to call Colombia a "narco-democracy" around that time, and the growing magnitude of its drug trade provoked a strong reaction from the United States, which intensified its pressures on Colombians in order to check the movement of drugs across its borders.

It might be said that a strong international reaction, especially on the part of the United States, was needed for the Colombian authorities to increase their efforts to eliminate or capture the heads of the drug trade, which finally occurred in the mid-1990s.

By that date, it had been evident for some time that Colombian narcotics trafficking was taking on a new face. The importing of coca paste from Peru and Bolivia was substituted by local growing and production after the closure of the air bridge connecting cultivation regions in Peru with cocaine processing facilities in the southern part of Colombia, and the Colombian traffickers entered into alliances with Mexican traffickers to export the drugs to the United States. Meanwhile they strengthened their exports to the European market, where the price of cocaine was substantially higher. Several regions that were especially apt for growing coca leaf were supplied with improved varieties of the plant, which meant a proliferation of the laboratories or "kitchens" (*cocinas*) for processing the leaves into cocaine. All this indicated that the dismantling of the cartels did not mean that production had been reduced. The most important effect of this shift was the formation of new, fragmented trafficking organizations, which the then director general of the Colombian police called "baby cartels" (*cartelitos*) (Serrano 1999), and their rapid expansion in different regions of the country. One of the most important examples of this occurrence was the strengthening of the so-called Cartel del Norte del Valle, some of whose members specialized in heroin exports, which were combined with those of cocaine. While they had close links with the heads of the Cali cartel to start with, they tried to break away from their guardianship, although some still maintained their contacts with the Cali organization. The rivalries worsened, however, and the former alliance turned into a turf war, marked especially by the bloody fight the northern valley group waged against its former allies. Investigations have shown how those narcotics traffickers came to control broad areas of Valle and Risaralda (Anonymous 1994) and unleash widespread violence (Comisión de Memoria Histórica 2008) that scourged the local populations and included occasional battles with different guerrilla organizations. Meanwhile, they employed existing companies as a legal façade for exporting drugs.

Not all of their rivals, however, were from the Cali cartel. They were beset by internal feuds and experienced a series of betrayals and murders of their heads, which accelerated the process of fragmentation as second-rank leaders rose to the top and formed new gangs.

FROM BUSINESSMEN TO LEADERS OF SELF-DEFENSE AND PARAMILITARY GROUPS

As we have just said, large organizations gave way to more dispersed ones, run by subalterns who displaced the leaders of the former groups and were experts at both handling the exporting routes and the use of violent tactics. These new traffickers quickly formed alliances with self-defense groups that had arisen to defend lands and territories from the guerrilla forces. Although some of the former drug chiefs had had a role in this process, which was not always peaceful and had led to some fights with the self-defense groups, the new ones gave it a strong push by financing such organizations, and they grew at a dizzying rate. Well-armed and well-trained, they were capable of violent actions.

The linking of narcotics trafficking with the self-defense groups thus played a double role; on the one hand, it multiplied the latter's offensive capacity, and on the other, it furnished the traffickers with a political kind of discourse, at least in more public realms. The mixture of antisubversion and drug exporting gave a new meaning to these organizations. In the first place, their role as eradicators of the guerrilla threat gave them a certain legitimacy in the eyes of some sectors of the armed forces, landowners, and regional politicians; in the second place, narcotics trafficking was able to openly confront the law and the judicial system.

In fact, the amalgamation of the self-defense forces and the narcotics traffickers provided the former with the financial resources they needed to increase their capacity for territorial control and expansion to other regions. The self-defense groups, for their part, supplied the narcotics traffickers with an argument that supposedly gave them a certain legitimacy vis-à-vis the state, insofar as the two sides shared the same interest in ending the guerrilla threat. The result of this combination was the emergence of two kinds of social agents: first, what became known as the *paranarcos*, that is, the members of the *autodefensas* who regarded narcotics trafficking as a mechanism for financing groups of combatants, and second, the *narcoparas*, the narcotics traffickers who sought the shelter of the self-defense groups in order to give themselves political justification (Camacho 2009).

The regions in which these organizations established themselves became arenas for attaining political power, both for the guerrilla groups, who exerted hegemonic control over some through the use of armed violence, and for the traditional politicians, whose control was based on clientelism and the appropriation of the financial resources of the state. This meant that both the local guerrilla fronts and political chieftains had, in some manner or another, to count on new armed wings. In the regions where the self-defense groups already had a presence, they had established links with local political leaders. In others, the new organizations were open intruders, and it was their military capacity that led some politicians to make use of them and force the guerrilla groups to shift to other regions. It was necessary to combine traditional skills at leading and mobilizing the local population with an ability to check the guerrilla groups and eliminate their supposed sympathizers.

The nature of these links has been the subject of arduous debates. It has been argued that the politicians were forced to use the paramilitaries to protect themselves from the subversives' threats to their proselytizing activities. But it has also been said that the paramilitaries used the politicians to gain social legitimacy and the local resources of the state. It would seem that the first argument is more plausible, given that the armed might of the paramilitaries was a weighty and powerful argument. But it is also necessary to take into account that it would have been difficult for these organizations to attain the hegemony they sought without the support of the local politicians and that the latter in turn won them a voice on a national level.

Some heads of the new organizations stood out for becoming real warlords, that is, politico-military leaders who consolidated their power on the basis of their rule over armed groups, appropriation of the functions and financial resources of the state, and exploitation of the illegal drug economy (Duncan 2007). With their military and financial might, they ended up dominating the regional politicians, though the latter benefited from this alliance.

This phenomenon was becoming consolidated when Andrés Pastrana became president of Colombia. Elected for his willingness to achieve a peaceful settlement of the war with the guerrilla organizations, Pastrana focused his policy on negotiations with the FARC guerrilla group, backed by parallel strategies. On the one hand, he strengthened the financial and technical capacities of the armed forces, which were enormously advanced in both quantitative and qualitative terms. On the other, he played a leading role in the adoption of Plan Colombia (PC), which called for a costly social investment to attack the underlying causes of the country's violence. During the stage of negotiations with the United States, the plan underwent a radical change and was basically transformed into an antinarcotics program. Once again, the government of the United States made it clear that its main concerns were the trading and consumption of illegal drugs.

The biggest obstacle in the peace negotiations was the guerrilla group's charge that the government was doing little to check the alliance between narcotics traffickers and self-defense groups that was strengthening the paramilitary phenomenon, but in reality the guerrilla group took advantage of the demilitarization of a vast territory (one of their preconditions for negotiating) to strengthen themselves both in military and political terms. That, in turn, provoked strong criticisms of Pastrana, who finally broke off the negotiations in face of increasing evidence (from kidnappings, for example) of the guerrillas' true intentions. Plan Colombia thus partly recovered its aim of openly fighting against the guerrillas and at the same satisfying the demands of the United States. It was no longer necessary for the Pastrana administration to link the FARC with narcotics trafficking, an emphasis that different Colombian governments had given to the problem for a number of years. So the idea that this was a war against drugs was strengthened, even though some US congressmen were opposed to combining the two aims and favored a strategy that gave priority to the aerial fumigation of illegal drugs and intensified the war against the guerrilla armies.

The latent risk that the peasant-farmers whose coca plots were eradicated would feel resentful and regard it as an enemy was not an obstacle to the expansion of the spraying. Pastrana's policy was plagued by the following dilemma: strengthening its legitimacy in the eyes of the United States would weaken it in the eyes of many peasant-farmers, and vice versa. This paved the way for the election of Álvaro Uribe, whose campaign focused on attacking Pastrana's ambiguities.

IMPACTS ON A LOCAL AND NATIONAL LEVEL

The alliances described above led to the building of bastions of local power based on corruption, violence, the protection of illegal crops, and the domination of electoral choices. They thus erected barriers against the central state's efforts to reclaim its legitimacy and act as the guarantor of the citizenry's right to democracy and political participation.[1]

They were further hindered by the support given to the paramilitaries by some government officials and members of the armed forces, so that on a national level the state was split between those who defended democracy and the rule of law and those who supported corruption and violence (Camacho et al. 2009).

One of the local effects of these social arrangements was the massive use of violence, which led to the widespread displacement of local peasant farmers and the seizure of their lands, with the resulting worsening of poverty and inequality. The violent actions of these new organizations, along with those of the FARC, brought about a situation where, in a number of regions of the country, no one who was not an open sympathizer of one band or the other was allowed to live. The author of one of the most rigorous studies of forced displacement estimates that 3.5 million people may have become victims of this phenomenon (Ibáñez 2008). Some studies indicate that approximately 6.8 million hectares of land have been forcibly seized from the peasantry (Salinas 2009). The monopolization of lands and displacements was accompanied by massacres and the selective murders of civilians suspected of having any kind of link with guerrilla groups. The latter, for their part, also played a part in this displacement and brutally attacked supposed sympathizers of the paramilitaries. According to the Commission on Historical Memory, of the National Commission for Reparation and Reconciliation (Comisión de Memoria Histórica de la Comisión Nacional de Reparación y Reconciliación), there were 2,505 massacres between 1973 and 2008, perpetrated by the paramilitaries, guerrilla groups, and members of the armed forces. The national government estimates that 932,626 Colombians died in massacres between 1998 and 2005.[2]

A second impact has been on corruption, which has been seen in the appropriation of public resources through the control of local government revenues and transfers of funds from the central government to local governments, as well as the weaknesses of the judicial system, whose delays and not guilty verdicts have helped to bring about an enormous level of impunity. Thus, in several departments of the country, the paramilitaries managed to control the resources for public health and education. They were likewise able to place relatives, sympathizers, yes men, and members of their coalitions in key positions of local government. The guerrilla groups employed these same tactics in the areas they controlled as a way of strengthening their hegemonies and financing their military wings.

A third expression of local domination was the organization of mafias, which, in exchange for forced taxes, guaranteed rural landowners, businessmen, and merchants the security of carrying on with their enterprises. In several regions and cities they won control of sectors of the informal economy, where they regulated prices and eliminated unwanted competitors. In some cases it was a matter of alliances with businessmen, in which extortion and kidnapping were used to eliminate competitors, persecute trade unionists, and seize lands from the peasants.[3]

A fourth aspect of the problem was the deep-rooted influence that some warlords and their political associates partly established in some regions. Despite being a business that concentrated wealth in a few hands, narcotics trafficking led to a wide circulation of money in several ways, among them the increased income of peasant farmers who grew illegal crops, and so different sectors of the population stimulated local markets and acquired consumer goods previously beyond their reach. The absence of legal investments both in the private and public sectors of the economy allowed the warlords to win the loyalties of those who benefited from this increase in buying power.

PARA-POLITICS: THE VULNERABILITY OF THE STATE

The paramilitary organizations that rapidly expanded and dominated several regions of the country founded what was known as the "United Self-Defense [Groups] of

Colombia" (Autodefensas Unidas de Colombia, AUC). President Uribe and the Colombian Congress later authorized negotiations with the AUC, aimed at their demobilization and surrender of weapons. The result was law 975 (on "Justice and Peace"), which laid down the parameters for the talks, headed by the high commissioner of peace. The main paramilitary chiefs accepted the offer and the meetings for an agreement on demobilization were held in a rural district of the department of Córdoba, with the support of a mission from the Organization of American States (OAS).

As a result, the information that became available to the public in the form of official statements from the two parties and press coverage revealed several dimensions of the problem. For one thing, it became clear that the paramilitary leaders were emphatically opposed to the possibility of being extradited. They also demanded that any sentences imposed on them would be no longer than eight years and served in special agricultural colonies, in exchange for which they would hand over the properties they had illegally obtained, surrender their arms, give up their subordinates, and confess their crimes.

Their main aim, which was to be regarded as political prisoners, was opposed by the Colombian government, with the support of the media, which did not accept that that status be given to persons accused of exporting cocaine, carrying out massacres, forcibly displacing peasant-farmers, and seizing their lands.

During the course of the negotiations it was evident that the warlords had formed alliances with politicians of national importance who exploited the warlords' military might and networks of sympathizers to win elections in exchange for subsidies and favors for the paramilitaries. What has been called "armed clientelism" turned into an effective political tool to uphold the warlords' domination of certain regions and their national influence.

The exposure of these harsh truths turned into one of the biggest scandals in recent years. These alliances were behind what was known as "para-politics," which had a sinister influence on national politics. The scandals grew when a number of warlords stated that they controlled nearly 30 percent of the members of the Colombian Congress, which meant that they had a fair chance of getting laws passed that favored their own interests.

As was to be expected, all this led to heated debates, especially because many of the politicians accused of entering into these alliances were members of parties that supported the government,[4] which tended to color everything that had been discussed before the controversies reached hitherto unsuspected dimensions. A partial result of these occurrences has been the arrest of many members of congress, several of whom have been jailed.

With the aim of clarifying these events, we present a number of statistics about the 2002–2006 legislative term. They are taken from the most reliable resources and are based on a comparison of the figures published by two human rights NGOs on the one hand (the Corporación Nuevo Arco Iris[5] and Indepaz[6]), and the Public Prosecutor's Office on the other (Fiscalía General de la Nación). They are the three most important sources and provide comparable statistics. In order to give the comparison the required specificity, five points have been taken into account: (1) the total number of "para-politicians" (*parapolíticos*), (2) atypical voting patterns, (3) the judicial situation of the para-politicians, (4) the departments in which they won elections, and (5) the political parties to which they belonged.

TABLE 12.1. Judicial situation of the para-politicians

	CNAI	Indepaz	Fiscalía
Members of Congress involved	82	78	83
Senators	45	43	46
Representatives	37	35	37
Convicted	9: 5 senators 4 representatives	No information	10: 5 senators 5 representatives
Prior investigations	28: 15 senators 13 representatives	40: 24 senators 16 representatives	27: 14 senators 13 representatives
Preliminary investigation	16: 7 senators 9 representatives	No information	1: 1 senator
Called to trial	16: 11 senators 5 representatives	No information	15: 11 senators 4 representatives
Writ of prohibition	No information	No information	7: 4 senators 3 representatives
Under investigation	No information	No information	16: 7 senators 9 representatives
Issue preclusion	No information	No information	2: 1 senator 1 representative
Case dismissed	No information	No information	2: 2 senators
Arrested	No information	38: 19 senators 19 representatives	No information

Source: The author.

- Total number of senators and representatives. One of the problems with the figures has to do with the total number of representatives who are listed as having links with the paramilitaries. Thus, for example, when one looks at the data of the Corporación Nuevo Arco Iris (CNAI), one finds that 45 percent of the accused (37) are representatives and 55 percent (45) are senators. According to the data compiled by Indepaz, however, there are 78 in all: 43 senators and 35 representatives. And in the opinion of the public prosecutor, 83 legislators are linked to the paramilitaries: 46 senators and 37 representatives.

  In the end, nevertheless, these discrepancies are minor and in general terms leave little room for misunderstandings or problematical results. The difference between the CNAI figures and the *fiscalía* ones only amounts to one representative, and the difference between those two entities and the data of Indepaz is only four and five representatives, respectively (Table 12.1).
- Atypical voting patterns. There are two sources for the figures on what are known as atypical voting patterns: those of the CNAI on the one hand, and those of Indepaz and the *fiscalía* on the other. The former are shown as the number of votes for candidates with atypical voting patterns (it is worth mentioning that the idea of using this criterion originated within the CNAI). The latter, the figures of Indepaz and the *fiscalía*, are not broken down into atypical voting patterns but include the votes for all of the representatives accused of having links with paramilitary groups.

When we compare the figures on atypical voting patterns (those of the CNAI) with the general figures on votes for para-politicians, we find that the figures of the three entities clearly coincide in this respect.

- Judicial situation of the para-politicians. When we compare the figures on this situation, we find certain differences between the data of the CNAI and of Indepaz, compared to those of the *fiscalía*. It may be that the latter are more up to date than those of the former two. We present the differences we have found between the three.

  Except for the category "acquitted," where there is a marked difference in the figures, the difference is one or two representatives, more or less, in the other categories. For that reason, the discrepancy could be attributed to the fact that the figures of the *fiscalía* are more up to date. In a similar manner, the figures of the *fiscalía* add a number of other legal categories that neither the CNAI nor Indepaz take into account. These are: writ of prohibition (*auto inhibitorio*), under investigation (*instrucción*), preclusion (*preclusión*), case dismissed (*archivo*), and arrested (*detenidos*). There are also other categories that Indepaz does not take into account: guilty (*condenados*), preliminary investigation and summoned to trial (*llamados a juicio*). That is why the figures of the *fiscalía* seem to be more detailed and complete than those of the CNAI, which stands to reason since the source of the information for the CNAI is the *fiscalía* itself. Hence, it is preferable to directly refer to the figures provided by the latter.
- Departments in which para-politicians were elected. The difference between the figures of the CNAI, *fiscalía*, and Indepaz is minimal. For example, in the case of para-politicians elected in Antioquia, the CNAI and *fiscalía* cite seven, while Indepaz claims five. The difference perhaps is explained by the total number of representatives that each takes into consideration: 82 for the CNAI, 83 for the *Fiscalía*, and 78 for Indepaz.
- Political parties to which the para-politicians belonged. On this point, as in the previous one, the difference in the information is minimal. Once again, the data of the CNAI agree with those of the *fiscalía*. Likewise, those of Indepaz show small differences from those in the other two sources. In the case of the Cambio Radical party, for example, Indepaz states that ten senators from that party got to the Congress, whereas the CNAI and the *fiscalía* say there were only eight.

By way of a conclusion, we might say that the differences between the data of the three sources we have used are a matter of form rather than content. They owe more to the way they are presented or errors that lead to discrepancies between the results of some sources and others. Thus, in general terms, the information found in the three sources is consistent and they do not contradict each other (see Table 12.2)

It is necessary to mention that in the face of this debacle of the Congress, some commentators and political figures called on the judiciary to undertake a parallel investigation of the representatives who might have committed crimes due to their links with the FARC. The investigation of what became known as "Farc-politics" (*Farcpolítica*) did not yield significant facts, but that does not exclude the possibility that there have been elected officials and politicians involved in some kinds of talks or agreements with the insurgents. It would be more a question of local figures, whose

TABLE 12.2. Para-politicians, by department

	CNAI	Indepaz	Fiscalía
Amazonas	1 representative	1 representative	1 representative
Antioquia	7 senators 3 representatives	5 senators 2 representatives	7 senators 3 representatives
Atlántico	5 senators	4 senators	5 senators
Bogotá		1 senator	
Bolívar	1 senator 3 representatives	2 senators 3 representatives	1 senator
Boyacá	1 senator	1 senator	1 senator
Caldas	2 senators	2 senators 5 representatives	2 senators 4 representatives
Caquetá	1 representative	1 representative	1 representative
Casanare	1 representative	1 representative	1 representative
Cauca	1 senator	1 senator	1 senator
Cesar	2 senators 2 representatives	2 senators 2 representatives	2 senators 2 representatives
Córdoba	5 senators 2 representatives	6 senators 1 representative	5 senators 2 representatives
Cundinamarca	1 senator	1 senator	1 senator
Chocó	1 representative	2 representatives	1 representative
Guainía	1 representative	1 representative	1 representative
Huila	1 representative	1 representative	1 representative
La Guajira	1 senator		1 senator
Magdalena	1 senator 6 representatives	2 senators 6 representatives	1 senator 6 representatives
Meta	1 senator	1 senator	1 senator
Nariño	1 senator 1 representative		1 senator 1 representative
Norte de Santander	4 senators	3 senators	4 senators
Putumayo	1 representative		1 representative
Risaralda	1 senator	1 senator	1 senator
Santander	3 senators 2 representatives	4 senators 2 representatives	3 senators 1 representative
Sucre	4 senators 3 representatives	3 senators 3 representatives	4 senators 3 representatives
Tolima	3 senators 3 representatives	2 senators 3 representatives	3 senators 3 representatives
Valle	2 senators 1 representative	2 senators 1 representative	2 senators 1 representative

Source: The author.

actions have not had repercussions on a national level, although they worsened the situation on a regional level. In fact, some regions are so dominated by the FARC that they prevent the holding of free elections, appropriate public resources, and profit from cocaine trafficking. To achieve this, the FARC would need to have local accomplices, be they voluntary or forced.

THE DILEMMAS FACED BY THE JUDICIAL SYSTEM

Extradition was one of the mechanisms the national government used to show its determination in liquidating the paramilitary criminal organizations. When it was proven that several of their leaders continued with their criminal activities from prison, and given that the government reserved its right to use that sanction during the original negotiations, President Uribe extradited fourteen of the main paramilitary chiefs. Since the judicial authorities of the United States had asked for their extradition based on narcotics trafficking charges, the government's decision implied that being a trafficker was a more serious crime than being a paramilitary leader. This caused strong criticisms in some sectors of public opinion; many people believed that the massacres, collective murders, forced displacements, and violent seizures of land they were accused of were more serious crimes than exporting illegal drugs.

These extraditions also showed that while it strengthened both bands and increased their power on a regional level, the alliance between the traffickers and the self-defense groups was the key to their defeat. The excessive visibility they attained and their cruel treatment of the civilian population went beyond a fight against the insurgent forces, and their actions made it clear that it was also meant to protect the lands they had forcibly seized and used to grow illegal crops, broaden their control over export routes, and appropriate public resources. That is, the profit motive and political ambition were revealed to be the driving force of their outrage and the effort to do away with the insurgents was shown to be a lesser motive.

This aspect also provoked a heated debate on a national level, as some sectors of public opinion believed that the extraditions closed the door to the confessions that were expected to ensue. Thus, a new consideration arose: in order for the Colombian justice system to gain access to the prisoners and obtain their confessions, they now had to win the cooperation of the judicial authorities of the United States.

At the present time, some of those who were extradited have been questioned by Colombian judicial officials and their statements have shown their involvement with several regional and national politicians.

THE NEW MUTATION: THE *BACRIM*

Just as the dismantling of the so-called cartels caused narcotics trafficking to be transformed into a paramilitary enterprise, the events that led the main paramilitary leaders to be imprisoned or extradited implied not a reduction of the activities related to illegal drugs, but a new mutation. To understand this new situation, is it necessary to acknowledge that the negotiations between the alliance of "*narcoparas*" and "*paranarcos*" on the one side and the national government on the other did not mean the complete dismantling of their organizations. On the contrary, several of the second-rank leaders stepped into the shoes of the extradited ones, and at the same time new chiefs arose in different regions. Some of these organizations have a considerable number of footsoldiers and some also have a coverage of several regions of the country. A number of their leaders were subalterns or relatives of the heads of the large organizations that entered into negotiations with the government, and in that sense there has been a certain continuity.

Nevertheless, the national government has insisted that these organizations, known as "criminal bands" (*bandas criminals*, hence the acronym "*bacrim*," used by the national police) do not represent new forms of paramilitarism. Rather, it believes, they are gangs of new narcotics traffickers who lack political ideas or aims and whose criminal activities derive from their need to control areas where narcotics are grown or export routes. This interpretation is logical up to a point, once it is acknowledged that many of the subalterns who are now chiefs belonged to the "*narcopara*" wing of the movement and therefore never had political motivations either. In addition, several of these new organizations are offshoots of the cartel of Norte del Valle, whose members did not join the ranks of the AUC and thus did not have political motives to start with. Recent statements by some members of that organization, however, have shown they did engage in political activities, like financing the presidential campaign of Ernesto Samper and playing a role in the assassination of the Conservative Party leader Álvaro Gómez Hurtado.

Furthermore, there are a number of indications that show how complex alliances are being formed between the new narcotics traffickers and some guerrilla fronts, something that would have been unthinkable when the AUC was flourishing. In fact, the national government is constantly releasing information that backs the hypothesis, shared by the government of the United States, that the FARC are the biggest exporters of cocaine nowadays and to attain that position they have needed the help and expertise of the narcotics traffickers who belong to the new *bacrims*.

The other side of the coin, though, shows that the persecution of trade union leaders and supposed sympathizers of the subversives continues, and in the current political situation it is likely that relatives or front men for the politicians involved in the parapolitics scandals will be candidates for the Colombian Congress. We are thus at a critical stage of the whole process.

A consequence of dismantling the narco-paramilitary groups has been the emergence of a new type of confrontation, which involves urban gangs that fight to protect their profits from the retail sale of illegal drugs and consolidate their territorial control over different urban neighborhoods. At the present time, several gangs of young men from poor neighborhoods of several cities are using extreme forms of violence, and some official reports indicate that despite being scattered over different districts, these bands have a hierarchical structure and are led by new or old bosses linked in some way with the organizations of the original bosses. Everything thus seems to indicate that despite the organizational changes and new fields of action, there is a line of historical continuity.

FINAL COMMENTS

The main aim of this chapter has been to show how the biggest threat to Colombian stability, justice, and democracy—narcotics trafficking—has displayed an extraordinary capacity to transform itself, which indicates that the ruthless hunger for profits that upholds it is never satisfied and that the policies of the Colombian state and the international community have not produced the results they sought, despite the enormous investments of money and effort.

What is more, a survey of the different phases of the phenomenon shows how narcotics trafficking may assume many organizational forms and that in this case the form does not determine its content. Some of these changes have arisen precisely as a response to state and international policies, in what seems to be a contest between the narcotics traffickers and the state, with the latter pursuing and the former escaping. The transition from organizations led by one person or small groups to others with a more dispersed leadership—from gangs basically devoted to the business to others that combine trafficking with violent political activities and from there to smaller bands that seek to control the domestic market—demonstrates this constant metamorphosis. Furthermore, the rapidity of these changes means that state actions are dilatory and ineffective in the medium term. While the authorities have managed to eliminate some organizational forms of narcotics trafficking, the fact that stands out is that trafficking has an enormous capacity to mutate. In this sense, Michael Kenney's thesis about the enormous capacity of criminals to keep a step ahead of the authorities is still fully relevant.

From all that, it must be clear that narcotics trafficking is more than a form of organized crime. For the peasant-farmers at the base of the trade, it is a cash crop that brings an income they cannot obtain from ordinary agricultural products. For other inhabitants of the areas where there is a strong presence of traffickers, the trade provides them with an income that would be difficult to obtain through legal commercial activities. Some inhabitants of the cities also benefit from trafficking, be it through money laundering, selling luxury goods to the traffickers, or acting as their lawyers. In short, it is a way of life that goes beyond the business of exporting cocaine.

But while these transformations are a testimony to the dynamism of narcotics trafficking, we need to emphasize that it has always been accompanied by violence. That has turned into its dominant trait and, at the same time, the gravest threat that Colombian society has faced in recent years. It is the nature of the country's current situation.

With regard to our main theme—the impact of narcotics trafficking on politics—the former's use of massive violence and corruption to defend itself from the state, win impunity for its crimes, and promote policies that serve the interests of those who run the business and their associates, that will all necessarily assume new forms, and it is highly unlikely that they will be drastically reduced. The experiences of recent years must serve as a warning about the risks run by Colombian society and its institutional framework.

The fields of action the Colombian state must work in are many. The Colombian government has to confront all the features and stages of the phenomenon, from the growing of coca leaves to the exporting of cocaine, not forgetting the fight against the monopolization of lands, the forced expulsion of the peasantry, and their displacement to cities.

Furthermore, it has to operate in the field this study specifically focuses on; acting against narcotics trafficking and its influence on politics requires taking drastic measures. It is necessary to strengthen the judicial system so it can deal with the linkage of politicians and traffickers in a timely and effective way. It must also implement a more drastic and radical political reform, with severe punishments for the politicians who enter into alliances with those involved in illegal drug trafficking and other forms of corruption. There are many tasks in the field of domestic policies and also in the international sphere where the Colombian government should seriously consider the many proposals and suggestions for policy changes advanced by different experts in the field of drug policy.

I am fully aware that these ideas are just that and that the options that would enable the country to free itself from narcotics trafficking are subject to substantial changes in international policies, as seen in the United Nations and its specialized conferences. In this field Colombia must act firmly and denounce the ineffectiveness of the prohibitionist regime that is periodically advanced and that prevents us from attaining a clear vision of these problems and implementing more effective measures.

NOTES

1. The literature on paramilitarism is abundant. In addition to Duncan's text, one may consult the following: Castro (1996); Corporación Observatorio para la Paz (2002); Cubides (1998); Duncan (2005b); Garzón (2005); Gutiérrez and Barón (2006); Kenney (2007); Medina (1990); Melo (1990); Téllez (2009); Romero (2003); and Reyes (1991).
2. Cf. *www.sigob.gov.co/est/indicador.aspx?id=*, accessed February 10, 2010.
3. Indepaz, a nongovernmental research institute, mentions 35 companies or businessmen who, in one way or another, were linked to paramilitary organizations. It also presents a list of 116 companies that are on the U.S. Office of Foreign Assets Control. Cf. *Punto de Encuentro* 2008.
4. The most heated debate had to do with attacks on the report of the Corporación Nuevo Arco Iris.
5. Consolidated figures of the Supreme Court and Fiscalía General (Public Prosecutor) on "para-politics," compiled by the Corporación Nuevo Arco Iris, Observatorio del Conflicto Armado (Monitor of the Armed Conflict), 2007–10.
6. *www.indepaz.org.co/?p=1139*, accessed September 2009.

REFERENCES

ANIF. 1980. *Marihuana: Legalización o represión*. Bogotá: Fondo Editorial ANIF.

Anonymous. 1994. "Estructura de una narcocracia regional. Villa Pujante, un estudio de caso." in *Drogas, poder y región en Colombia*, edited by R. Vargas, 283–313. Bogotá: Cinep.

Aranguren, M. 2001. *Mi Confesión. Carlos Castaño revela sus secretos*. Bogotá: Editorial Oveja Negra.

Bourdieu, P. 2002. *La distinción. Criterios y bases sociales del gusto*. Madrid: Taurus.

———. 2007. *El sentido práctico*, México, DF: Siglo XX.

Braudel, F. 1974. *La historia y las ciencias sociales*. Madrid: Alianza Editorial.

Camacho, Á. 2006. "De narcos, paracracias y mafias." In *En la encrucijada. Colombia en el siglo xxi*, edited by F. Buitrago. Bogotá: Coediciones Editorial Norma and CESO, Universidad de los Andes-Norma.

———. 2009. "Paranarcos y narcoparas: Trayectorias delincuenciales y políticas." In A. Camacho et al., *A la sombra de la guerra. Ilegalidad y nuevos órdenes regionales en Colombia*. Bogotá: Uniandes, CESO.

Camacho, Á. et al. 2009. *A la sombra de la guerra. Ilegalidad y nuevos órdenes regionales en Colombia*. Bogotá: Uniandes, CESO.

Cañón, M. L. 1994. *El Patrón. Vida y muerte de Pablo Escobar*. Bogotá: Planeta.

Castillo, F. 1987. *Los jinetes de la cocaína*. Bogotá: Ediciones Documentos Periodísticos.

Castro, G. 1996. "Los paramilitares." In *En Secreto*. Bogotá: Editorial Planeta.

Comisión de Memoria Histórica de la CNRR. 2008. *Trujillo, una tragedia que no cesa*. Bogotá: Editorial Planeta.

Corporación Nuevo Arco Iris. 2007. *Parapolítica. La ruta de la expansión paramilitar y los acuerdos políticos*, 2nd ed. Bogotá: Intermedio Editores.

Corporación Observatorio para la Paz. 2002. *Las verdaderas intenciones de los paramilitares*. Bogotá: Intermedio Editores.

Cubides, F. 1998. "De lo privado a lo público en la violencia colombiana: Los paramilitares." In *Las violencias: Inclusión creciente*, edited by J. Arocha et al. Bogotá: Universidad Nacional de Colombia.

Duncan, G. 2005a. "Del Campo a la ciudad en Colombia. La infiltración urbana de los señores de la guerra." Bogotá: Universidad de los Andes, Documento CEDE 2.

———. 2005b "Paramilitares puros e impuros." Bogotá: CESO, Universidad de los Andes, Documento CESO, no. 153.

———. 2005c. "Narcotraficantes, mafiosos y guerreros. Historia de una subordinación." In *Narcotráfico en Colombia. Economía y violencia*, edited by A. Rangel, 19–86. Bogotá: Fundación Seguridad y Democracia.

———. 2007. *Los señores de la Guerra*. Bogotá: Editorial Planeta.

Garay, L. J., et al. 2008. *La captura y reconfiguración cooptada del Estado en Colombia*. Bogotá: Fundación Método, Fundación Avina, and Transparencia por Colombia.

Garzón, J. C. 2005. "La complejidad paramilitar: Una aproximación estratégica." In *El poder paramilitar*, edited by A. Rangel. Bogotá: Planeta and Fundación Seguridad y Democracia.

Gaviria, C., F. Cardoso, and E. Zedillo. 2009. *Drogas y Democracia: Hacia un nuevo paradigma. Declaración de la Comisión Latinoamericana sobre Drogas y Democracia*. Retrieved from *www.drogasedemocracia.org/Arquivos/livro_espanhol_04.pdf*, accessed May 12, 2015.

Gibson, E. 2004. "Subnational Authoritarianism: Territorial Strategies of Political Control in Democratic Regimes." Paper prepared for presentation at the 2004 Annual Meeting of the American Political Science Association, September 2–5, 2004.

Gutiérrez, F., and M. Barón. 2006. "Estado, control territorial paramilitar y orden político." In *Nuestra guerra sin nombre. Transformaciones del conflicto en Colombia*, edited by F. Gutiérrez, M. E. Wills, and G. Sánchez. Bogotá: IEPRI-Norma.

Ibáñez, A. M. 2008. *El desplazamiento forzoso en Colombia: Un camino sin retorno hacia la pobreza*. Bogotá: Universidad de los Andes.

Jaraba, J. G. 2007. *Confesiones de un paraco*. Bogotá: Intermedio.

Kalyvas, S. 2004. "La ontología de las violencias políticas, acción e identidad en las guerras civiles." *Análisis Político* 5, no. 52 (September–December).

Kenney, M. 2000. "La capacidad de aprendizaje de las organizaciones colombianas del narcotráfico." *Análisis Político* (September–December).

———. 2007. *From Pablo to Osama; Trafficking and Terrorism Networks, Government Bureaucracies, and Competitive Adaptation*. University Park: Pennsylvania State University Press.

Legarda, A. 2005. *El verdadero Pablo. Sangre, traición y muerte . . .* . Bogotá: Ediciones Dipón and Ediciones Gato Azul.

Martínez, G. 2004. *Salvatore Mancuso. Su vida*. Bogotá: Editorial Norma.

Medina, C. 1990. *Autodefensas, paramilitares y narcotráfico en Colombia*. Bogotá: Ediciones Documentos Periodísticos.

Melo, J. O. 1990. "Los paramilitares y su impacto sobre la política." In *Al filo del caos*, edited by F. L. Buitrago and L. Zamosc. Bogotá: IEPRI-Tercer Mundo.

Pécaut, D. 2009. "Colombia en la tormenta." In D. Pécaut, *Crónica de cuatro décadas de política colombiana*. Bogotá: Grupo Editorial Norma.

Punto de Encuentro. 2008. No. 52 (December).

Reyes, A. 1991. "Paramilitares en Colombia: Contexto aliados y consecuencias." *Análisis Político*, no. 12 (January–April).

———. 2009. *Guerreros y campesinos*. Bogotá: Editorial Norma.

Richani, N. 2007. "Caudillos and the Crisis of the Colombian State: Fragmented Sovereignty, the War System and the Privatisation of Counterinsurgency in Colombia." *Third World Quarterly* 28, no. 2 (2007): 403–17.

Rodríguez, G., and M. Rodríguez. 2005. *Las confesiones secretas de Gilberto y Miguel Rodríguez Orejuela*. Bogotá: Quintero Editores and Editorial Oveja Negra.

Romero, M. 2003. *Paramilitares y autodefensas, 1982–2003*. Bogotá: IEPRI.

Sáenz, E. 1997. "La prehistoria del narcotráfico en Colombia. Temores norteamericanos y realidades colombianas durante la primera mitad del siglo xx." In *La crisis socio-política colombiana: Un análisis no coyuntural de la coyuntura*, edited by L. G. Arango. Universidad Nacional and Fundación Social.

Salinas, Y. 2009. "Elementos mínimos de un modelo rural incluyente y de una política de restitución de los bienes usurpados a las víctimas." *Cien días vistos por Cinep*, no. 67 (August).

Serrano, R. J., with S. Gamboa. 1999. *Jaque mate*. Bogotá: Editorial Norma.

Téllez, F. 2009. "¿Paras o narcos?: Intereses compartidos, trayectorias divergentes." Master's thesis, Universidad de los Andes.

13 Illegal Crops, Political Participation, and Institutional Trust

Miguel García

The existence of a relationship between the phenomenon of narcotics trafficking and Colombian politics has been the subject of many academic studies that have shown that the criminal organizations devoted to growing, producing, and commercializing illegal drugs have had a strong impact on the increase of political violence (Thoumi 2002b, 165), levels of corruption (Tullis 1995), and the quality of democracy (Hartlyn 1993). Likewise, these organizations have "captured" some state structures and modified the country's political culture. Nevertheless, this body of academic studies on the link between narcotics trafficking and politics has ignored the impact of this phenomenon on the behavior and political attitudes of individuals. This chapter tries to fill that gap by providing empirical information on a relationship that is highly relevant to an understanding of the magnitude of the political impact of the drug business. If narcotics trafficking, as a sociological phenomenon, conditions the way citizens behave politically and form their opinions on public institutions, it may be possible using microlevel data to validate the argument that the development and consolidation of narcotics trafficking in Colombia have helped to strengthen important changes in the country's political culture.

The general question this chapter tries to answer is: Are the behavior and political opinions of citizens who live in regions affected by narcotics trafficking radically different from those of people who live in regions not affected by this phenomenon? More specifically, what influence do the presence of illegal crops and the different strategies for eradicating them have on individuals' political participation and the degree of trust citizens have in state and nonstate agents?

This chapter is based on the assumption that political behavior cannot be exclusively understood in terms of individual factors but must also take into account the relationship between citizens and their social and political environments (Huckfeldt 1986). If the phenomenon of narcotics trafficking has created what some have called a "mafioso culture," the political behavior and attitudes of citizens who live in contexts affected by different manifestations of the drug business must be different from those who do not live in those contexts. The qualitative literature on the social effects of illegal organizations has shown that narcotics trafficking has been able to modify the mores and values of certain sectors of the Colombian population (Duncan 2009). If that is so, it would be feasible to argue that the structural transformations brought about by narcotics trafficking would have to express themselves in changes in the political behavior and attitudes of citizens.

Miguel García: Assistant professor, Department of Political Science, Universidad de los Andes.

This chapter is made up of six sections. Following this introduction, the second one offers a brief review of the literature on the political impacts of narcotics trafficking, with an emphasis on the studies that point to a link between the drug trade and political culture. The third presents a theoretical discussion about the relationship between the phenomenon of narcotics trafficking and the political attitudes of citizens. The fourth describes the data and introduces the analytical strategy. The fifth section discusses the empirical results. The final one offers the conclusions of this study and discusses their main implications in terms of public policies.

NARCOTICS TRAFFICKING, POLITICS, AND SOCIETY

Research on the social and political repercussions of narcotics trafficking in Colombia has shown that the effects of this phenomenon have been big as well as diverse. In general terms, the authors who have studied the link between narcotics trafficking, society, and politics can be classified into at least three groups. First, there are those who have studied the relationship between narcotics trafficking and the many political crises Colombia has gone through since the 1980s. Second, there are those who have focused on the relationship between narcotics trafficking, illegal armed groups, and the increase of political violence. Finally, there are the studies that show the role of narcotics trafficking in altering social and political practices. This chapter, in a certain manner, falls into the final group.

The studies on the relationship between narcotics trafficking and social and political practices have tried to understand, on the one hand, the link between narcotics trafficking mafias and certain characteristics of Colombian society, like clientelism, the illegal economies linked to contraband, the institutional weakness of the state, the lack of modernity, and even what some authors have called the "imaginaries" of illegality (Betancourt and García 1994; Hernández 1997; Salazar 2001). A second line within this analytical trend is made up of studies that have analyzed the social and political changes resulting from the so-called culture of illegality. These studies focus on the formation of agreements between illegal agents and representatives of the legal order, as well as mafioso practices on the part of some state agents.

Here, a good part of the academic literature has shown how, in an effort to protect its investments, narcotics trafficking has developed networks of influence over political and state power, giving rise to generalized corruption, the mafioso infiltration of some state agencies, and the financing of politicians with illegal monies, and has wound up promoting models of social order based on a "brutal armed domination" (Camacho 1988; Camacho, López, and Thoumi 1999; Thoumi 2002a). Recent studies that have concentrated on analyzing the political impact of local illegality have gone further by arguing that narcotics trafficking, in conjunction with the armed actors (particularly the paramilitaries) and some local politicians, have wound up consolidating what some have called new "social orders" (Camacho 2009). This idea assumes that narcotics trafficking has had the capacity to locally redefine modes of production, the exercise of political power, social groups and relations, the apparatus of the state, and even the values and mores of the population (Duncan 2009, 165).[1]

While the framework of this chapter are studies that show the capacity of narcotics trafficking to modify social and political contexts, in contrast to those studies it emphasizes the relationship between narcotics trafficking and individual political behaviors and attitudes. If the influence of the drug phenomenon in some regions of the country has given rise to transformations of the social order, it may be argued that the conduct and attitudes of individuals will also have undergone significant modifications.

POLITICAL PARTICIPATION AND INSTITUTIONAL TRUST UNDER THE SHADOW OF NARCOTICS TRAFFICKING

In Colombia, the drug mafias, political violence, and the armed actors, as phenomena capable of altering the functioning of the state and society, have brought out processes of crisis and have been able to change the social and political context in which individuals shape their decisions and political attitudes. Individual-level factors cannot entirely explain the actions and opinions of citizens. Along with them, political behavior should be understood in terms of the relationship between people and their surroundings, and the environmental factors that affect individual decisions (Huckfeldt 1986).

According to the studies on the impact of social contexts on political behavior, there are at least two mechanisms by which political and social environments may affect citizens' political preferences and actions. In the first place, there are structurally imposed contexts (Huckfeldt 1986; Huckfeldt and Sprague 1987). These are social and political conditions that are external to the individual and may have a direct effect on political conduct insofar as they limit the experiences and decisions of citizens. In addition, there are the social and political contexts that are defined in terms of social networks. These are interpersonal interactions that, while they result from individual decisions, are affected by the opportunities and limitations of the social context (Huckfeldt and Sprague 1987).

Narcotics trafficking would modify what has been called the structural context, to the extent that this phenomenon is capable of changing aspects such as the functioning of the economy, social relations, or the use of violence, and may even redefine the "social orders." As a consequence, citizens may adapt or modify their political behaviors and attitudes in response to the structural changes stimulated by narcotics trafficking. To evaluate the possible relationship between narcotics trafficking and individual conduct and attitudes, this chapter analyzes the influence of illegal crops—a key component of the narcotics trafficking chain—and strategies for eradicating them on citizens' decisions to get involved in electoral (voting) and nonelectoral (protests) forms of political participation.[2] It also analyzes the degrees of trust people have in the local executive, the police, the FARC, and the paramilitaries.[3]

Participation and institutional trust as the main dependent variables of this chapter are two central expressions of the functioning of modern politics at the individual level. Political participation, especially in its electoral form, represents the citizen's acceptance, belief in, and link with elections as one of the central mechanisms of the functioning of democracy. For its part, trust in public institutions measures citizens' feelings about the state, which is central for the functioning of governments, since where the citizenry trusts its institutions, these institutions can act without resorting to the use of force and do not need to consult the population about each decision they make (Mishler and Rose 1997; Espinal, Hartlyn, and Morgan 2006).

If narcotics trafficking had helped to weaken the state and encourage the emergence of structures and policies opposed to the idea of a modern society in those regions where the drug business has a strong influence, the levels of electoral participation and citizens' trust in state institutions would be significantly lower than in those where the drug mafias do not have a strong influence. The nature of this relationship may be understood when we take into account that the modifications of the political and social context caused by narcotics trafficking would make it clear to the citizen that the functioning of politics is not being mediated by state procedures and institutions. If the electoral processes are manipulated or have been exploited by the drug mafias, or by an alliance between the mafias and armed actors, political participation would lose importance for the citizen, insofar as his or her vote would not have much influence on the definition of political power. Furthermore, if the mafias' influence on the local social orders has been linked to the dynamics of territorial control by the armed actors (Duncan 2009), one would expect the regions influenced by the narcotics trafficking phenomena to be politically homogeneous, given that the territorial control of the armed actors would produce what Gibson (2005) has called subnational authoritarianisms. As recent studies have shown, when the political environment tends toward homogeneity, the flows of political information and the political parties' efforts to mobilize the electorate decrease, causing a reduction in electoral participation (Gimpel and Lay 2005, 210). In fact, empirical evidence on the impact of illegal agents on political participation has shown that in areas where the paramilitaries have consolidated territorial control, citizens tend to participate less in electoral processes than in areas where that armed actor does not enjoy such an influence (García Sánchez 2009).

In the case of nonelectoral forms of participation, it is possible to argue that the local influence of narcotics trafficking would strengthen the probability that citizens will get involved in marches and protests. Assuming that state structures are precarious in areas affected by illegal crops, it would be safe to say that the citizenry in such regions daily face the coercive side of the Colombian state. If that coercive aspect is on many occasions associated with state efforts to eradicate illegal crops, it would be feasible to argue that the citizenry would enter into a contentious relationship with the state due to its role in attacking economies based on the production of illegal drugs. To sum up, citizens who live in areas influenced by narcotics trafficking would be more inclined to participate in the public sphere through protests than through voting.

With regard to the subject of institutional trust, it is clear that those who represent the Colombian state at the local level would not count on the trust of the citizenry if the former are at the service or under the influence of illegal actors. It would be the illegal actors who would count on the trust of the population, which would be even more evident when the local economy and supply of goods and services are mediated by illegal agents such as mafioso networks. This expectation is supported by the results of comparative studies on trust in governmental institutions, which have shown that such trust is a function of the performance of governments in fields like the economy and the provision of security (Espinal, Hartlyn, and Morgan 2006; Mishler and Rose 2001).

As mentioned above, this chapter also seeks to evaluate the impact on participation and trust of some of the strategies for eradicating illegal drugs. These strategies, which basically amount to manual eradication or aerial spraying, would have different effects on the participation of citizens in the public sphere and their degree of trust in state and nonstate agents. In areas where illegal crops are the basis of the local economy and local orders have been built up around them, eradication in any form would bring decreased participation and trust in state institutions. The negative effect would be stronger, however, in the case of aerial spraying.

The theoretical speculations formulated thus far assume that narcotics trafficking, understood as a structural context, would have a homogeneous effect on the political behavior and attitudes of citizens. Nevertheless, the specialized literature has shown that the effect of structural contexts is mediated by certain individual characteristics (Huckfeldt and Sprague 1993; Weatherford 1982; Gimpel and Lay 2005). From that point of view it is valid to ask: what kind of people would be more resistant to the influence of narcotics trafficking? A recent study showed that the followers of minority parties in Colombia were more susceptible to the effect of violent contexts than those who said they belonged to the traditional parties (García Sánchez 2009). Despite that finding, it is difficult to give a specific answer to the question we have just mentioned, considering that the political identities and aims of the mafioso networks would not be as clearly defined as those of the armed actors. For that reason, we do not formulate any hypothesis about the kind of citizens whose political behaviors and attitudes would be more affected by narcotics trafficking. It might simply be said, in this respect, that some characteristics of the citizens would be sensitive to the effect of narcotics trafficking. The empirical analyses are meant to identify some of these characteristics.

DATA AND METHOD

This chapter makes use of a hierarchical structure of data. These kinds of databases compile information to at least two units of analysis. In this case, we work, on the one hand, with individual-level factors (level 1), and on the other, with municipal-level variables (level 2). Through a hierarchical structuring of data, it is possible to evaluate the impact of contextual factors, like illegal crops, on the political conduct of people, while also controlling for the effect of individual variables.

The information on the individual level comes from a representative national survey carried out in 2005 by the Latin American Public Opinion Project (LAPOP) of Vanderbilt University. The study interviewed 3,083 adults from seventy-five Colombian municipalities.[4] At the contextual level, this study includes data on the area of coca plots, type of eradication strategy, levels of territorial control by the armed actors, and the socioeconomic characteristics of the seventy-five municipalities included in the survey.

Description of the Variables

This chapter analyses three kinds of dependent variables: voting, participation in protests, and trust. "Voting" is a dichotomous variable that measures whether an individual participated in the local elections of 2003. The variable "Protests" is also a dichotomous one that determines whether the surveyed person has participated in public marches or protests. Finally, "Trust" measures the degree to which citizens trust the local executive, the police, the FARC, and the paramilitaries.[5]

The focus of this chapter is the relationship between narcotics trafficking and political behavior at the phase of growing. Therefore, the main independent variables, each of which was measured at the municipal level, are hectares of coca and eradication strategy. The first is a continuous variable that measures the number of hectares where coca was grown in 2005 in each of the seventy-five municipalities studied.[6] The second variable uses a three-point scale to measure the kind of strategy for eradicating illegal crops used between January 2004 and May 2005, the month in which the LAPOP study was conducted, in each of the municipalities included in this chapter. The three-point scale seeks to determine the "toughness" of the eradication strategy used. Zero (0) indicates that no eradication strategy was applied in the municipality in question. One (1) indicates that manual eradication of illegal crops was used in the municipality. Finally, two (2) means that in a given municipality, only aerial spraying was used to eradicate or the two eradication strategies were combined. This last case represents the most "radical" scenario.[7]

This analysis will control for other contextual and individual-level factors. At the contextual level two variables are included (control by the guerrillas and control by the paramilitaries) that measure the intensity of the territorial control enjoyed by guerrillas and paramilitaries on a municipal level.[8] In the second place, this article also takes into account contextual economic conditions,[9] by means of the unsatisfied basic needs (UBN) index. At the individual level, a series of factors are included that would have a significant impact on political participation and institutional trust. These are education, age, gender, socioeconomic status, urbanization, support for the political system, external political efficacy,[10] political sophistication,[11] involvement in party politics, identification with the traditional parties, sociotropic evaluations of the economy, and an index of the provision of public goods.[12]

Empirical Strategy

The relationship between illegal crops and strategies of eradication, political participation, and citizens' perceptions of trust was evaluated through several two-level hierarchical models (Raudenbush and Bryk 2002). These models allow for a simultaneous evaluation of the effect of contextual and individual factors on people's political opinions and behaviors, which would be problematic in the case of a standard regression analysis.[13] In this chapter, two kinds of hierarchical models are employed. In the first, the units of analysis at level 1 are individuals, and the value of the dependent variable for each person is a function of his or her individual characteristics. At level 2, the units of analysis are municipalities. Here, the intercept (average outcome) of the level-1 equation is the dependent variable that is modeled as a function of contextual factors (Raudenbush and Bryk 2002). These models are suitable for testing the extent to which a variation in the municipal incidence of illegal crops and the type of eradication strategy may predict significant changes in the municipal average of political participation and trust, while controlling for individual-level factors.

In the second kind of hierarchical model used in this chapter, both the intercept and some slopes of the level-1 equation are modeled as functions of contextual factors. Level-1 slopes correspond to individual-level variables; therefore when level-1 slopes are treated as dependent variables and they are explained using contextual variables, interactions between level 1 and level 2, or cross-level interactions, are formed. Through these interactions one can determine the extent to which the effect of individual-level variables on the outcome variable is conditioned by contextual factors. In other words, the interactions among levels prove to be useful for identifying which kinds of persons are more or less susceptible to the influences of the social context. For all the dependent variables, the first kind of hierarchical model was estimated, while the second was only applied in certain cases.[14]

RESULTS

This section presents the results of a series of hierarchical models used to study the impact of municipal-level variables associated with narcotics trafficking on individual political participation and citizens' degrees of trust in different organizations. The first part studies the relationship between contextual factors associated with narcotics trafficking and the individual probability of participation in local elections and public protests. The second part focuses on the impact of illegal crops and eradication strategies on citizens' degrees of trust in the municipal executive, the police, the FARC, and the paramilitary groups.[15]

Illegal Crops, Eradication Strategies, and Political Participation

The hierarchical models for voting in the local elections of 2003 and participation in protests include a series of individual variables at level 1[16] and model the intercept of the equation of level 1, using five contextual variables: UBN, level of guerrilla control, level of paramilitary control, hectares of coca, and eradication strategy.

The empirical analysis presented in the first column of Table 13.1 revealed that the individual probability of voting is negatively related to an increase in the area devoted to coca growing. This indicates that there are significant differences in the pattern of electoral participation between municipalities affected by illegal crops and those that are not. In accordance with the expected probabilities of voting, we find that this probability is more or less 0.57 in areas where there are no illegal crops. When the number of hectares of coca reaches the average, which is 110 for the municipalities included in the sample used in this chapter, the reduction in the probability of voting is practically nonexistent.

Nevertheless, in those municipalities with the maximum level of hectares of coca, the probability of participating in local elections falls to nearly 0.30.[17] It is important to take into account that in most municipalities included in this analysis the negative effect of illegal crops on electoral participation is small, not surpassing a reduction of 0.05 points in the probability of voting. Only in extreme cases, where coca plots reach very high proportions, do we find that the probability of voting suffers an important reduction. In these cases it may be assumed that the influence of the illegal drug business has come to affect the functioning of the social and political spheres and that in those scenarios citizens marginalize themselves from electoral participation. In these cases the drug mafias may have manipulated the political sphere in such a way that the votes of citizens do not have much influence on the definition of political power. Among the municipalities included in the sample used in this chapter, the town that shows the highest number of hectares where coca is grown is Tumaco, a municipality that has had difficulties integrating itself into the nation, in institutional and economic terms, and

TABLE 13.1. Hierarchical models for electoral participation and participation in protests

	Vote				Protests	
	Model 1		Model 2 With cross-level interactions		Model 1	
Fixed effects	**Coefficient**	**EE**	**Coefficient**	**EE**	**Coefficient**	**EE**
Level 2 Predictors						
Intercept	0.313*	0.133	0.312*	0.133	−1.688***	0.172
UBN	0.008**	0.003	0.008**	0.003	0.002	0.005
Guerrilla control	0.028	0.111	0.026	0.110	−0.053	0.123
Paramilitary control	−0.142*	0.069	−0.143*	0.068	0.181	0.139
Hectares of coca	−0.000***	0.000	−0.000**	0.000	0.000	0.000
Eradication strategy	0.157	0.116	0.158	0.115	−0.007	0.142
Level 1 Predictors						
Education	0.063***	0.014	0.063***	0.014	0.076***	0.014
Hectares of coca			0.000*	0.000		
Age	0.024***	0.003	0.024***	0.004	−0.001	0.004
Support to the system	−0.001	0.002	−0.001	0.002	−0.006*	0.003
Hectares of coca			0.000**	0.000		
Gender	0.032	0.105	0.028	0.105	0.103	0.113
Socioeconomic status	0.000	0.003	−0.000	0.003	0.005	0.003
Urban vs. rural	0.083	0.139	0.081	0.141	0.273	0.146
External efficacy	0.232**	0.078	0.237**	0.078	0.012	0.131
Hectares of coca			−0.000***	0.002		
Sophistication	0.001	0.002	0.001	0.002	0.006**	0.002
Identify with traditional party	0.445***	0.096	0.445	0.096	−0.145	0.108
Hectares of coca			0.000	0.000		
Political involvement	0.020***	0.096	0.020	0.003	0.015***	0.002
Random Effects	**Coefficient**	**EE**	**Coefficient**	**EE**	**Coefficient**	**EE**
Variance Components						
Municipal level effects	0.138		0.136		0.314	
Individual level effects	0.372		0.369		0.561	
Reliability of intercept	0.436		0.432		0.553	
Percentage explained†	0.284		0.296		0.031	

** $p < 0.05$; ** $p < 0.01$; *** $p < 0.001$; † Percentage of the variance among municipalities explained by the Level 2 Predictors.

has historically been under the influence of diverse illegal agents, like contrabandists, armed actors, and mafiosos.

One result that was highly surprising was the absence of a relationship between the hardening of strategies for eradicating illegal crops and participation in elections. Those individuals who live in municipalities where manual eradication and aerial spraying are combined did not show probabilities of participating in elections that were significantly lower than those who live in municipalities where only manual eradication was employed.

Additionally, the results coincide with previous studies, as they show that the individual probability of voting is negatively related to the level of paramilitary control and positively associated with poverty (UBN). From another angle, the results of the individual level variables indicate a positive and significant effect on the probability of voting in local elections of the following factors: education, age, external political efficacy, party identification, and political involvement.

But what kinds of citizen participation are seen to be more or less affected by the influence of narcotics trafficking as a contextual phenomenon? The results of model 2 for voting (Table 13.1) suggest that people who are better educated show a higher level of support for the system and that members of the traditional parties would be less susceptible to the negative effect of an increase in illegal crops on the probability of participating in local elections. In the case of education, results indicate that while persons who are less educated have a lower probability of voting in local elections, among individuals with a college degree (sixteen years of education), the negative impact of the increase in illegal crops on the probability of voting is practically nonexistent (0.03 points when you go from the minimum to the maximum number of hectares of coca). By contrast, among people without any education, when you go from municipalities without coca to those with the highest number of hectares of coca, the probability of voting falls by approximately 0.27 points.

Even more interesting is the case of the variable of support for the system. Among people who consider the Colombian political system as illegitimate, the increase in coca crops produces a collapse in the probability of participating in elections. In this case, the expected probability of voting falls from 0.56 to 0.35. This result suggests that the changes in the political behavior of the citizenry that would be influenced by narcotics trafficking grow stronger when there are negative perceptions of the Colombian state. Thus a phenomenon like the emergence of new political orders would be upheld by the growth and consolidation of phenomena like narcotics trafficking and the minimal belief of citizens in the legitimacy of state institutions.

Party affiliation is a third factor of the individual type that moderates the effect of the contextual variables associated with narcotics trafficking. As the area devoted to coca growing passes from the minimum to the maximum, the fall in the probability of voting is about 0.12 units among members of the Liberal and Conservative parties.[18] Among members of other parties, this fall is more or less 0.26 units.[19] How may we interpret this result? One possible answer has to do with the role the traditional parties have played in the reconstruction or redefinition of the local political order. In many areas of the country, the influence on local politics of narcotics trafficking and other illegal enterprises has taken place through pacts with local political leaders, most of whom belong to the Liberal or Conservative political networks (Zúñiga 2007; López 2007). The political pacts between mafias and traditional politicians would encourage the emergence of local political monopolies that coexist with routine political practices in which the nontraditional parties would have little weight. Hence the supporters of those parties would be discouraged from participating in electoral processes.

The results of the analysis of the relationship between illegal drugs, eradication strategies, and participation in protests indicates, as Table 13.1 (column 5) shows, that none of the contextual factors seems to have a significant impact on the probability of involvement in nonelectoral forms of participation. Neither the municipal incidence of illegal crops nor the hardening of strategies for eradicating them is correlated with citizens' involvement in protests. This result is baffling, given that there is qualitative evidence that suggests there have been important demonstrations against the state in areas with a presence of illegal crops (Ramírez 2001). This result may make sense, however, from two points of view. First, the qualitative evidence may be identifying exceptional events and in fact the link between narcotics trafficking and nonelectoral participation would be nonexistent. Second, what this result might indicate is that participation in protests takes place in multiple contexts. That is, it is not a resource exclusive to the inhabitants of marginal areas or those under the influence of illegal agents.

The results suggest that the individual factors are the ones that show a significant effect on participation in protests. The citizens who are more educated, more politically sophisticated, or more involved in party-political activities, and the individuals who have a negative opinion of the legitimacy of the state, would be more likely to get involved in demonstrations and protests. In contrast with the model on electoral participation, political sophistication and a critical opinion of the state are variables that only have an explanatory role for participation in protests. This has intuitive support insofar as the people with a more highly developed political knowledge may be dissatisfied with the functioning of the state and the public sphere, and those with lower levels of support for the political system would be more prone to confront it.

Illegal Crops, Eradication Strategies, and Trust

The hierarchical models for trust in the local executive, police and illegal armed actors include a series of individual variables at level 1,[20] and use the same five contextual variables (UBN, level of control by the guerrilla, level of control by the paramilitaries, hectares devoted to coca and eradication strategies) to model the intercept of the level-1 equation.

The results on trust in state institutions presented in Table 13.2 suggest that only the contextual variables associated with narcotics trafficking have an impact on the citizens' degree of trust. In the case of the municipal executive, the only statistically significant contextual variable is the presence of illegal crops. An increase in the area devoted to growing coca lessens the degree of trust in the local executive. In areas where there are no illegal crops, the average degree of trust is around 57 (on a scale of 0 to 100). When the variable of hectares of coca reaches 110, the average level for the municipalities in the sample, the reduction in the degree of trust is minimal. It is only in those municipalities where the number of hectares devoted to coca approaches the maximum level (more than 4,500 hectares) that the degree of trust falls, by a little more than ten points. That the negative effect of illegal crops becomes more evident in areas where they reach maximum levels may mean that the larger the area devoted to coca, the more social and political influence narcotics trafficking acquires. This would work against trust in the local executive, since that institution would lose its capacity for action and management. Furthermore, trust in the mayor's office may fall if citizens perceive that with the strengthening of the power of narcotics trafficking, the local executive branch winds up at the service of the drug mafias instead of the citizenry.

In the case of the police, both illegal crops and the eradication strategy appear to have a significant impact on citizens' trust in that institution. Contrary to what one may expect, the rise in the area of illegal crops increases trust in the police; this rises by almost ten points when one goes from municipalities without coca plots to those with the maximum level. Nevertheless, this relationship stops being significant when you introduce a number of interactions between individual-level variables and illegal crops. In another aspect, the statistical analysis showed that trust in the police does become affected by the strategy for eradicating illegal crops undertaken in the municipality. In areas where no eradication strategy is employed, the average degree of trust in the police is 62. When one turns to areas where only manual eradication is used, trust in the police falls to 57. Finally, in areas where both manual eradication and eradication by aerial spraying are combined, trust in the institution falls to 53. This result suggests that citizens clearly understand that the responsibility for eradicating such crops lies with the police, since the degree of trust in that institution was the only thing affected by the hardening of the strategies for fighting against illegal crops. It seems that the citizenry blames the institution that implements the eradication strategy, rather than the political agent that formulated it.

With regard to the role of the individual variables, the results indicate that trust in the mayor's office appears as a function of perceptions about the performance of the government, some political factors, and certain sociodemographic factors. The citizens who have a positive opinion of the provision of public goods and think that the national economy is on the right path tend to trust in the municipal mayor's office. The same is true of those who identify with the traditional parties. For their part, the citizens who are politically sophisticated tend to have less trust in the municipal executive than their counterparts who know less about politics. Trust in the police, in turn, is positively associated with opinions of political and economic performance, likewise with age, and negatively with socioeconomic status. Although the police are not responsible for managing the economy or providing certain public goods (apart from security), they would benefit from the good opinion citizens have of the performance of the government.

As in the models of electoral participation, an examination was made of some interactions between individual-level variables and contextual factors. Only the interactions between hectares of coca and individual-level variables were statistically significant. In the case of trust in the local executive, we found that opinions about the future of the national economy had a mediating effect on the relationship between illegal crops and trust. Thus the negative effect of illegal crops on trust in the mayor's office is only sustained in the case of people who think that the national economy is on the wrong path. For those individuals, the degree of trust falls from 57 to 46 when you turn from the minimum to the maximum number of hectares devoted to coca. In an opposite manner, for those who think that the economy will improve in the future, the increase in the area of illegal crops coincides with an increase of 17 points in the degree of trust in the

TABLE 13.2. Hierarchical models for trust in state institutions

	Trust in Mayor's Office				Trust in Police			
	Model 1		Model 2 With cross-level interactions		Model 1		Model 2 With cross-level interactions	
Fixed effects	Coefficient	EE	Coefficient	EE	Coefficient	EE	Coefficient	EE
Level 2 Predictors								
Intercept	57.429***	2.595	57.400***	2.587	60.998***	2.253	60.861***	2.251
UBN	0.035	0.035	0.358	0.035	–0.033	0.045	–0.034	0.046
Guerrilla control	2.011	1.440	1.963	1.440	1.258	1.659	1.178	1.674
Paramilitary control	0.946	1.234	0.945	1.224	1.729	1.161	1.721	1.163
Hectares of coca	–0.002**	0.001	–0.002**	0.001	0.002*	0.001	0.000	0.001
Eradication strategy	–0.667	1.400	–0.613	1.406	–4.502*	1.998	–4.376*	2.032
Level 1 Predictors								
Education	0.096	0.260	0.113	0.262	–0.135	0.212	–0.112	0.212
Age	0.194***	0.056	0.201***	0.055	0.158**	0.050	0.157**	0.050
Hectares of coca			0.000***	0.000			–0.000*	0.000
Gender	–4.011***	1.061	–4.165***	1.051	–1.462	1.232	–1.559	1.230
Socioeconomic status	–0.153***	0.042	–0.156***	0.042	–0.058	0.033	–0.059	0.033
Urban vs. rural	–2.065	2.917	–2.010	2.902	–1.331	2.002	–1.256	2.002
Sophistication	–0.067***	0.026	–0.067**	0.025	–0.036	0.031	–0.035	0.031

Identify with traditional party	2.923*	1.365	3.061*	1.360	2.867	1.467	2.860	1.503
Sociotropic evaluation, present	0.068	0.036	0.072*	0.036	0.023	0.030	0.025	0.030
Sociotropic evaluation, future	0.049**	0.020	0.050*	0.020	0.065***	0.019	0.065***	0.018
Hectares of coca			0.000***	0.000			0.000***	0.000
Provision of public goods, index	0.475***	0.056	0.482***	0.055	0.348***	0.062	0.346***	0.062
Hectares of coca							−0.000***	0.000
Random effects	**Coefficient**	**EE**	**Coefficient**	**EE**	**Coefficient**	**EE**	**Coefficient**	**EE**
Variance Components								
Municipal level effects	32.660		32.826		53.644		54.782	
Individual level effects	5.715		5.729		7.324		7.402	
Reliability of intercept	0.459		0.461		0.559		0.564	
Percentage explained†	0.420		0.414		0.245		0.234	

* $p < 0.05$; ** $p < 0.01$; *** $p < 0.001$; † Percentage of the variance among municipalities explained by the Level 2 Predictors

local executive.[21] Along the same lines, the effect of the same interaction on the degrees of trust in the police showed that for those who think the economy will improve and for those who think it will stay the same, there is an important increase in the degree of trust in the police, as you turn from the minimum to the maximum area devoted to coca in a given municipality. For the first group of citizens, the degree of trust rises from 67 to 95, and for the second group it rises from 64 to 68. For those who think the economy will worsen, the degree of trust in the police practically does not change with the increase in the area of illegal crops. These two results suggest that in contexts where narcotics trafficking has a strong influence, the changes in citizens' opinions of the national economy will produce an important variation in people's perceptions of trust. In areas where illegal crops predominate, citizens criticize the local executive more harshly when they see economic problems and praise them more generously when the economy goes well. The degree of trust in the police, on the other hand, is not affected by negative views of the economy. These results are probably due to the fact that economic ups and downs have a more radical and notorious impact on areas dominated by the drug economy than other areas.

Turning to the models on trust in the FARC and the paramilitaries (Table 13.3), we note that the results suggest that only the degree of trust in the paramilitaries is positively affected by an increase in illegal crops. When you go from areas without illegal crops to municipalities with large areas devoted to growing coca, trust in the paramilitaries rises by 10 points more or less, from 7.6 to 17.5. Although the degree of trust in the paramilitaries, for any level of illegal crops, lies on the lower part of the scale of trust, this result indicates that the paramilitaries have a higher social acceptance when there is a stronger influence of the drug business.

With regard to the impact of individual variables on trust in the armed actors, the results show that opinions about governmental performance do not influence opinions about trust in these illegal groups. That is, it cannot be said that problems of governmental performance favor the illegal agents. That citizens feel that the economy is in bad shape, or that the government does not provide adequate public services, does not imply a strengthening of the degree of trust in the illegal armed actors. This result suggests that the citizenry knows very well that the criteria for judging state and nonstate organizations cannot be the same, even in contexts where the state is weak. The variables on an individual level that show a significant effect on degrees of trust in the FARC and the paramilitaries were mostly of a sociodemographic kind. In the case of the guerrilla, education and urbanization have a positive effect on citizens' trust in that organization, while political sophistication has a negative impact. Education and urbanization likewise have a positive effect on trust in the paramilitaries. Similarly, men and active members of the traditional parties show a significantly higher trust in that illegal organization than women and supporters of independent or left-wing parties.

The link between political affiliation and trust turns out to be interesting, since in some manner it shows that the support the paramilitaries have received from many liberal and conservative elites is matched by an equally important support from the citizenry. Furthermore, if one assumes that the emergence of new social orders in Colombia went hand in hand with the formation of the coalition between the paramilitaries and drug lords, then the greater trust in the paramilitaries on the part of active members of the traditional parties would indicate that the new social orders count on the same

TABLE 13.3. Hierarchical models for trust in illegal armed organization

	Trust in FARC		Trust in paramilitaries			
	Model 1		Model 1		Model 2 With cross-level interactions	
Fixed effects	**Coefficient**	**EE**	**Coefficient**	**EE**	**Coefficient**	**EE**
Level 2 Predictors						
Intercept	6.247***	1.152	7.764***	1.291	7.647***	1.457
UBN	0.012	0.031	0.042	0.042	0.043	0.039
Guerrilla control	1.067	1.352	0.116	1.061	0.067	1.383
Paramilitary control	−0.623	0.844	0.881	1.311	0.859	1.086
Hectares of coca	0.001	0.000	0.002**	0.001	−0.002*	0.002
Eradication strategy	1.036	1.019	−0.741	1.305	−0.683	1.313
Level 1 Predictors						
Education	0.588***	0.123	0.407**	0.142	0.418**	0.158
Age	0.045	0.025	−0.034	0.042	−0.029	0.040
Gender	0.278	0.957	1.950*	0.915	1.960*	1.027
Socioeconomic status	−0.034	0.027	−0.032	0.031	−0.033	0.031
Urban vs. rural	3.479**	1.077	3.531**	1.000	3.466**	1.369
Sophistication	−0.055**	0.016	−0.015	0.023	−0.016	0.022
Identify with traditional party	1.220	0.907	2.639**	1.023	2.749**	1.059
Hectares of coca					0.005***	0.002
Sociotropic evaluation, present	0.011	0.022	0.038	0.023	0.039	0.025
Sociotropic evaluation, future	−0.008	0.011	0.015	0.018	0.015	0.014
Index provision of public goods	0.030	0.034	0.049	0.046	0.049	0.038
Random effects	**Coefficient**	**EE**	**Coefficient**	**EE**	**Coefficient**	**EE**
Variance components						
Municipal level effects	16.090		20.929		20.998	
Individual level effects	4.011		4.575		4.582	
Reliability of intercept	0.493		0.462		0.464	
Percentage explained†	0.274		0.290		0.284	

* $p < 0.05$; ** $p < 0.01$; *** $p < 0.001$; † Percentage of the variance among municipalities explained by the Level 2 Predictors

bases of citizens' support as the preceding social orders. That is, the citizenry adapts to changing social contexts.

Finally, for the case of trust in the paramilitaries, we found that the effect of illegal crops on the degree of trust in that organization is mediated by party affiliation.[22] Among the people who say they are liberals or conservatives, trust in the paramilitaries grew from 10 to 26 when one moved from the minimum to the maximum area devoted to coca. By contrast, among active members of the other parties, the increase in illegal crops produced a fall from 7 to 0 on the scale of trust in the paramilitaries. This result is highly relevant, since it reveals that in areas where there is a strong influence of illegal crops, paramilitaries are mostly supported by members of the traditional parties. Nevertheless, this finding is not that surprising when one takes into account the evidence for a link between the traditional parties and paramilitary organizations. What is interesting is that it confirms how narcotics trafficking encourages the growth of the bases of support for the criminal organizations and indicates the kind of people who support them.

CONCLUSIONS AND RECOMMENDATIONS FOR PUBLIC POLICY

In general terms, the empirical evidence presented in this chapter indicates that there are significant differences between the political opinions and behaviors of citizens who live in areas under the influence of illegal crops and those who live in areas that are free of it. Compared to the people who live in areas free of coca crops, the citizens who live in areas where they exist tend to participate less in electoral processes, show significantly lower degrees of trust in state institutions, and tend to have more confidence in the paramilitaries. It is important to underline that the differences in political behavior and political attitudes we mention are more evident in those municipalities where the influence of illegal crops is very high. In other words, for its relationship to political conduct and opinions to be noticeable, there needs to be a consolidation of the narcotics trafficking phenomenon.

The results of this chapter also indicate that when the Colombian state hardens its strategy for eradicating illegal crops, the levels of citizens' trust in the police show a significant decline. In addition to the negative effects on ecosystems and human health of such strategies as aerial spraying (IDEA 2005), one has to take into account the price the state would be paying in political terms through the weakening of trust in the police. This price may be irrelevant (a four-point fall in trust) when compared to the effectiveness of the eradication method, but in a context of a weak state and the emergence of new local orders promoted by illegal agents, this result becomes more relevant and should lead to a more profound and detailed study of the political impact of eradicating illegal crops through aerial fumigation.

This chapter also revealed how some individual factors moderate the effect of narcotics trafficking on people's political behavior and opinions. For example, among those who don't believe in the state's legitimacy, the electoral demobilization associated with the increase of illegal crops becomes stronger. That is, the negative consequences of the drug trade nourish themselves on the doubts some citizens have about the legitimacy of the Colombian state. Here it was also shown that the people who have a high opinion of the work of local governments in providing public services have more trust in state institutions.

These results provide us with clues about how the national, local, and regional governments may be able to minimize the negative effects of narcotics trafficking through public policies. Public investments in improving the provision of public goods and services, like the justice system or health services to give only two examples, could lead to a stronger trust in the state among citizens, which would in turn minimize the effect of narcotics trafficking on electoral abstention. In other words, improvements of government performance in the field of public services would optimize citizens' opinions about the legitimacy of the state and meanwhile minimize the influence of the drug mafias on the political conduct and opinion of those citizens.

In this respect as well, it was shown that the effect of the electoral abstention produced by the increase in coca plots was mainly seen among the supporters of the political minorities. Furthermore, evidence arose about the way the increased trust in the paramilitaries that follows the increase in the area of coca is exclusively found among the supporters of the traditional parties. These results are not surprising, since they are a manifestation of the relationship between narcotics trafficking, the armed actors, and the political elites. What is interesting is that they suggest, in the first place, that in the "partnership" between legal and illegal actors, the politicians linked to the traditional parties are the leading figures on the "legal" side. This, in turn, means that the independent and left-wing sectors lose ground in the political game, which results in a massive electoral abstention among the supporters of these parties. In second place, the links between politicians and illegal agents have specific effects on the bases of support for the illegal agents. While certain political sectors benefit in elections from their relationship with narcotics trafficking and the illegal organizations, the latter politically benefit from their relationship with the politicians, insofar as they enlarge their bases of support among the followers of those parties with which they are politically associated.

In the face of these results, it is fundamental for the Colombian state to maintain and increase its efforts to prevent the penetration of the drug mafias into local and national politics, since this affects the political scope and opportunities for electoral success of the small parties and helps the illegal agents to widen their bases of support among the citizenry. The Colombian judicial system must be given strong political, technical, and economic support to unmask and disjoint the relations between illegal agents and politicians. Toward this end, it might stiffen political, economic, and juridical sanctions on the parties that welcome people linked with the drug mafias or the armed actors into their ranks.

To restate, the results of this chapter suggest that there are three fields of action for public policies that would lessen the impact of narcotics trafficking on political behavior and citizens' degrees of trust in state institutions. In the first place, there should be an evaluation of the strategies for eradicating illegal drugs that balances their political convenience against their effectiveness. In the second place, in the governmental ambit there should be a stronger effort to achieve a more effective and efficient provision of public services in the areas affected by illegal crops, with the aim of preventing the illegal organizations from enlarging their bases of support. Finally, the Colombian state and the country's political parties should work to undo the political influence of the drug mafias.

NOTES

Help in the research for this chapter was provided by Diego Felipe Gómez and Janneth Angélica Vargas. I would like to thank Adriana Camacho, Daniel Mejía, Elvira María Restrepo, and an anonymous commentator for their comments on the preliminary versions of this chapter.

1. To be more precise, the construction of these "new social orders" assumes the dismounting of the central state and the appearance of social and political structures and relations that are opposed to the idea of a modern society.
2. These "forms" of participation are not mutually exclusive. That is, the fact that a citizen votes in election does not mean that he or she may not be involved in marches or protests.
3. The phenomenon of narcotics trafficking assumes a chain that ranges from the growing of illegal crops to the commercialization of drugs. This study's emphasis on the phase of growing implies that it evaluates only one among many dimensions of the phenomenon of narcotics trafficking and individual political opinions and behaviors. This choice is upheld by the availability of empirical information about the influence of illegal crops at the municipal level. Similar quantifications do not exist for other phases of the drug business.
4. This survey worked with two samples. The first is a representative national study that included 1,487 adults in forty-seven municipalities. The second is a sample of 1,596 adults from twenty-eight municipalities.
5. Each measure of trust was placed on a scale running from 1 to 7, where 1 represents a total distrust in the institution or organization that was evaluated and 7 represents a complete trust. The original scale was transformed into a scale of 0 to 100.
6. Although this variable does not take into account the size of the municipality, the correlation coefficient between this variable and a measure of the influence of coca crops that controls for the size of each municipality (hectares of coca / area of the municipality in hectares) was 0.9445 ($p < 0.001$). Despite this correlation, the effects of the two versions of the variable for illegal crops were estimated. Given that the results of the two versions of the variable in question were very similar, and the interpretation of the results is more intuitive if one works with the unweighted version of the measure of illegal crops, this article only reports on the results of the ratio between unweighted hectares of coca and the dependent variables. Results of the models with the measure of illegal crops weighted for the size of the municipality can be obtained upon request from the author.
7. Since aerial fumigation was exclusively used in only one municipality in the sample, it was decided to put this kind of municipality and those where the two strategies were combined in the last category.
8. These variables are measured on a scale from 0 to 3, where the lower value (0) indicates the absence of control of the armed agent in question, whereas a value of three (3) indicates that the armed agent exerts a complete territorial control over the municipality. With the use of a geographically weighted count of the armed incidents and violent acts undertaken by each armed agent, we came up with a classification of municipalities in terms of their levels of violence, by means of a methodology known as a "a semi-parametric, group-based approach to longitudinal analysis" (Nagin 2005). On the basis of this classification we came up with the variables that capture different levels of guerrilla and paramilitary control. For a detailed description of the process of operationalizing these variables, cf. García Sánchez (2010).
9. This is one of the contextual variables that, in different investigations, are shown to have a significant effect on individual behavior, particularly on political participation. In this

regard, cf. Giles and Dantico (1982); Huckfeldt (1979); Kenny (1992); and Mondak, Mutz, and Huckfeldt (1996).

10. This refers to the belief that voting can change things.
11. This refers to the quality and coherence of a person's political knowledge.
12. The variables of socioeconomic status, urbanization, system support, sophistication, involvement in party-political activities, and the provision of public goods are continuous and were measured on a scale of 0 to 100. If the reader so wishes, the author can provide a detailed description of the operationalization of level-1 variables.
13. For example, for an estimation made with the ordinary least-squares method to be efficient and precise, it is necessary that the errors are independent, normally distributed, and have a constant variance. These assumptions are violated, however, when the characteristics of the context are attributed to the individuals. For example, if a municipality's level of development is treated as though it were a characteristic of each person surveyed in a certain municipality, the errors of these observations will not be independent.
14. Since this study does not set forth any specific theoretical expectations about how the contextual factors associated with narcotics trafficking condition the impact of the individual-level variables on the dependent variables, the definition of which slopes of the level-1 equation were going to be modeled on the basis of contextual factors followed an inductive path. In theory, it would have been possible to model all the slopes by using contextual factors, but hierarchical models with several cross-level interactions tend to lose efficiency in the estimation of the parameters (Raudenbush and Bryk 2002). Therefore, we chose a strategy that consisted of only including interactions among levels in those cases where the contextual variables had t scores higher than 1.5. Authors like Lee and Bryk (1989) and Weldon (2006) followed similar strategies when they worked with cross-level interactions.
15. The variables for participation in local elections and participation in protests were estimated by using a two-level model for binary outcomes, while the models for institutional trust used a two-level estimation for continuous variables. Before undertaking the empirical analysis shown in this section, several *nonconditional models* were estimated. These predict the dependent variable in each unit of level 1, with only one level-2 parameter (the intercept), which represents the average of the variable dependent among municipalities. The variance components of these models provide information about whether the factors of the contextual level must be taken into account when modeling the dependent variable. For all the dependent variables analyzed in this chapter, the results of the *nonconditional models* indicated the need to take contextual factors into account in order to understand their variation.
16. The conditional models for participation control for the following individual-level factors: education, age, system support, gender, socioeconomic status, urbanization, external efficacy, political identification with a traditional party, and political involvement.
17. For the calculation of the predicted probabilities, the variables included in the model were left equal to zero. For all of the calculations shown in this section, the minimum of hectares devoted to coca is zero, the average is 110, and the maximum is 4,800. These data correspond to the average and maximum area of coca crops for the seventy-five municipalities included in the LAPOP sample.
18. Goes from 0.67 to 0.55.
19. Goes from 0.57 to 0.31.
20. The individual level variables which are included in the models of trust are: education, age, gender, socioeconomic status, urbanization, sophistication, identification with a traditional

party, current sociotropic evaluation of the economy, prospective sociotropic evaluation of the economy, and an index of public goods provision.

21. For these persons, the rating of trust rises from 62 to 79 when you go from the minimum to the maximum of hectares of coca.
22. For the model of trust in the FARC, cross-level interactions were not explored, since the contextual variables were not significant.

REFERENCES

Betancourt, D., and M. García. 1994. *Contrabandistas, marimberos y mafiosos. Historia social de la mafia colombiana (1965–1992)*. Bogotá: Tercer Mundo Editores.

Camacho, Á. 1988. *Droga y sociedad en Colombia. El poder y el estigma*. Bogotá: Cisde, Universidad del Valle, Cerec.

———. 2009. "Paranarcos y narcoparas: trayectorias delincuenciales y políticas." In *A la sombra de la guerra. Ilegalidad y nuevos órdenes regionales en Colombia*, edited by Á. Camacho et al. Bogotá: Ediciones Uniandes, CESO.

Camacho, Á., A. López, and F. Thoumi. 1999. *Las drogas: Una guerra fallida. Visiones críticas*. Bogotá: IEPRI, Tercer Mundo Editores.

Duncan, G. 2009. "El dinero no lo es todo: Acerca del narcotráfico en la persistencia del conflicto colombiano." In *A la sombra de la guerra. Ilegalidad y nuevos órdenes regionales en Colombia*, edited by Á. Camacho et al. Bogotá: Ediciones Uniandes, CESO.

Espinal, R., J. Hartlyn, and J. Morgan. 2006. "Performance Still Matters. Explaining Trust in Government in the Dominican Republic." *Comparative Political Studies* 39, no. 2.

García Sánchez, M. 2009. "Political Violence and Electoral Democracy in Colombia. Participation and Voting Behavior in Violent Contexts." PhD dissertation, University of Pittsburgh.

———. 2010. "Bajo la mira de los actores armados. Contextos violentos, participación política e intención de voto en Colombia." In *Conflicto armado, seguridad y construcción de paz en Colombia: Cuatro décadas de Ciencia Política en la Universidad de los Andes*, edited by A. Rettberg. Bogotá: Departamento de Ciencia Política, Ediciones Uniandes.

Gibson, E. L. 2005. "Boundary Control: Subnational Authoritarianism in Democratic Countries." *World Politics* 58, no. 102.

Giles, M., and M. Dantico. 1982. "Political Participation and Neighborhood Social Context Revisited." *American Journal of Political Science* 26, no. 1: 144–50.

Gimpel, J. G., and C. Lay. 2005. "Party Identification, Local Partisan Contexts, and the Acquisition of Participatory Attitudes." In *The Social Logic of Politics. Personal Networks as Contexts for Political Behavior*, edited by A. S. Zuckerman. Philadelphia: Temple University Press.

Hartlyn, J. 1993. "Drug Trafficking and Democracy in Colombia in the 1980s." Working Paper no. 70. Barcelona: Institut de Ciènces Polítiques i Socials.

Hernández, M. 1997. "Comportamientos y búsquedas alrededor del narcotráfico." In *Drogas ilícitas en Colombia. Su impacto económico, político y social*, edited by F. Thoumi. Bogotá: United Nations Development Programme (UNDP), Ministerio de Justicia y del Derecho, Dirección Nacional de Estupefacientes, Editorial Ariel.

Huckfeldt, R. 1979. "Political Participation and the Neighborhood Social Context." *American Journal of Political Science* 23, no. 3: 579–92.

———. 1986. *Politics in Context: Assimilation and Conflict in Urban Neighborhoods.* New York: Agathon Press.

Huckfeldt, R., and J. Sprague. 1987. "Networks in Context: The Social Flow of Political Information." *American Political Science Review* 81, no. 4: 1197–1216.

———. 1993. "Citizens, Contexts, and Politics." In *Political Science: The State of the Discipline II*, edited by A. Finifter. Washington, DC: American Political Science Association.

IDEA (Instituto de Estudios Ambientales). 2005. *Observaciones al 'Estudio de los efectos del programa de erradicación de cultivos ilícitos mediante aspersión aérea con el herbicida (pecig), y de los cultivos ilícitos en la salud humana.'* Bogotá: Universidad Nacional de Colombia, IDEA.

Kenny, C. B. 1992. "Political Participation and Effects from the Social Environment." *American Journal of Political Science* 36, no. 1: 259–67.

Lee, V. E., and A. Bryk. 1989. "A Multilevel Model of the Social Distribution of High School Achivement." *Sociology of Education* 62, no. 3: 172–92.

López, C. 2007. "La ruta de la expansión paramilitar y la transformación política en Antioquia 1997 a 2007." In *Parapolítica. La ruta de la expansión paramilitar y los acuerdos políticos*, edited by M. Romero. Bogotá: Intermedio Editores.

Mishler, W., and R. Rose. 1997. "Trust, Distrust and Skepticism: Popular Evaluations of Civil and Political Institutions in Post-Communist Societies." *Journal of Politics* 59, no. 2: 418–51.

———. 2001. "What Are the Origins of Political Trust: Testing Institutional and Cultural Theories in Post-Communist Societies." *Comparative Political Studies* 34, no. 1: 30–60.

Mondak, J. J., D. Mutz, and R. Huckfeldt. 1996. "Persuasion in Context: The Multilevel Structure of Economic Evaluations." In *Political Persuasion and Attitude Change*, edited by D. C. Mutz et al. Ann Arbor: University of Michigan Press.

Nagin, D. S. 2005. *Group-Based Modeling of Development.* Cambridge, MA: Harvard University Press.

Ramírez, M. C. 2001. *Entre el Estado y la guerrilla: Identidad y ciudadanía en el movimiento de los campesinos cocaleros del Putumayo.* Bogotá: Icanh, Colciencias.

Raudenbush, S. W., and A. Bryk. 2002. *Hierarchical Linear Models. Applications and Data Analysis Methods.* Thousand Oaks, CA: Sage Publications.

Salazar, A. 2001. *Drogas y narcotráfico en Colombia.* Bogotá: Planeta.

Thoumi, F. 2002a. *El imperio de la droga. Narcotráfico, economía y sociedad en los Andes.* Bogotá: Planeta, IEPRI.

———. 2002b. "Illegal Drugs in Colombia: From Illegal Economic Boom to Social Crisis." *Annals of the American Academy of Political and Social Science* 528: 102–16.

Tullis, L. 1995. *Unintended Consequences: Illegal Drugs and Drug Policies in Nine Countries.* Boulder, CO: Lynne Rienner Publishers.

Weatherford, M. S. 1982. "Interpersonal Networks and Political Behavior." *American Journal of Political Science* 26, no. 1: 117–43.

Weldon, S. A. 2006. "The Institutional Context of Tolerance for Ethnic Minorities: A Comparative, Multilevel Analysis of Western Europe." *American Journal of Political Science* 50, no. 2: 331–49.

Zúñiga, P. 2007. "Ilegalidad, control local y paramilitares en el Magdalena." In *Parapolítica. La ruta de la expansión paramilitar y los acuerdos políticos*, edited by M. Romero. Bogotá: Intermedio Editores.

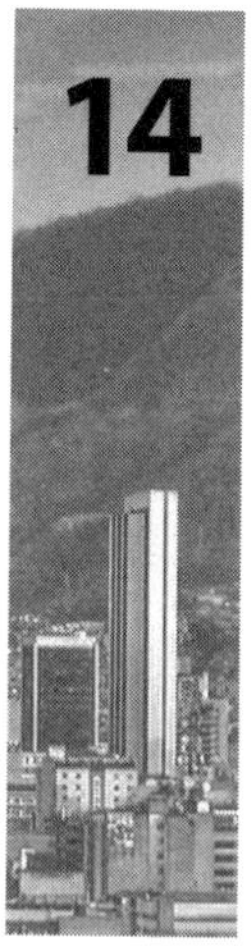

14 The Failure of Decentralization in the War on Drugs

Juan Carlos Echeverry and María Paula Gómez

INTRODUCTION

The events occurring with organized crime in Colombia, Mexico, and the United States have led us to evaluate the effectiveness of the so-called "war on drugs." Our main contention is that strategies based on decentralization abound and are prone to be costly failures with long-lasting consequences. We stress that phenomena with an "aggregate" or national character should not be handled with decentralized strategies.

The types of questions we try to answer are the following: What costs does a society incur when some phenomena broaden their size to reach a national scale? Are there "breaking points" in the process of "aggregation" from the local to the national level which mean that, once past a certain point, linear additions of inputs lead to a geometrical growth of production and profits? Can the concept of economies of scale be applied to like crime?

We draw on reflections derived from the Keynesian revolution in economics. Part of Keynes' contribution (1936) to economic analysis was an emphasis on phenomena that occur at an aggregate level and create new conditions that surpass the simple addition of micro-units, in which the whole is greater than the sum of the parts.

The conclusion we arrive at is that aggregation is in fact crucially important. The reason is that according to the Keynesian model, there are economic instruments with the capacity to induce systematic errors in the perception of individual agents, who cannot thereby determine whether what is observed originates in local and "real" causes or, by contrast, in aggregate or "nominal" ones. This is the case of changes in prices caused by inflation, as opposed to those reflecting variations in their own local markets. The former are due to monetary policy, when the monopoly over the issuance of money creates nationwide or aggregate shocks.

We apply this idea differently, but with sufficient similarities to make the parallel interesting. Namely, we contrast the "national" or aggregate character of narcotics

Juan Carlos Echeverry: This chapter was written while he served as an associate professor at the Economics Faculty of the University of the Andes. As of the time of original publication, he is the Colombian minister of finance (ministro de hacienda).

María Paula Gómez: This chapter was written while she was studying for a master's in economics at the Economics Faculty of the Universidad de los Andes. As of the time of original publication, she is studying for a master's at the University of Chicago.

trafficking, vis-à-vis the local or state strategies developed to combat such crimes, at least at the early stages of incidence, stages that typically last more than a decade. The earnings of a narcotics trafficker may grow at a geometrical rate, with a small addition of inputs, by virtue of surpassing the institutions at the local level. Why? Because the local police and judicial system soon reveal their uselessness once their tools for enforcing the law are surpassed by a new type of crime.

Thus, economies of scale lead to enormous profits for criminal enterprises (see Chapter 3). But when the crime has precisely to do with a product that must be exported—which requires national and international transport and commercialization networks and surpasses municipal, provincial, and national frontiers—the criminals discover the huge hidden potential of leaping to national and international scales.

In the first phase of narcotics trafficking, which lasted a decade or more in Mexico, Colombia, and Central America, law enforcement relied on the traditional techniques of police and the judiciary. They mostly had a provincial scope, often merely a municipal one.

This disparity between the scope of crime and the scope of the forces responsible for enforcing the law is the focus of our research. We used the analytical tools that economics has developed to clarify the difference between shocks of a micro or local nature and those of an aggregate or national one. A particularly relevant tool is known as the Lucas Islands Model, presented in a series of articles published in the 1970s by Robert Lucas, winner of the Nobel Prize in economics (Lucas 1973, 1976).

In our opinion, Lucas' ideas throw light on crucial aspects of the ineffectiveness of the fight against organized crime, in particular that related to cocaine trafficking in Colombia, Mexico, and the United States. We present a summary of the analytical and empirical study we wrote in 2009 based on a paper written with Zeinab Partow in 1998. It is followed by a discussion of strategies for fighting organized crime. Our conclusions are relevant for countries around the world with different incidence of the drug trafficking or mafia-type phenomena.

THE ANALYTICAL MODEL

Since the mid-1970s, mafioso crime, nourished by the profitability of the narcotics trafficking business, has had reckless effects in some regions of Colombia, Mexico, and the United States. For example, there were approximately 5,800 murders in Colombia in 1975, which amounted to a homicide rate of 26 per 100,000 inhabitants. Crime took off during the 1980s, and in 1991 and 2002, the years in which violence reached its historic peak, the number of homicides surpassed 28,000 and the homicide rate had risen to more than 80 per 100,000 inhabitants (Figure 14.1). According to the DEA, by 1980, 80 percent of the cocaine reaching the United States came from Colombia. This led to the assumption that that rise in crime could be attributed to the narcotics trafficking boom and the escalation of the armed conflict.[1] What is more, the fact that poverty declined during this period suggests that the rise in crime was not related to it (Echeverry and Partow 1998).

As Figure 14.1 shows, while murders shot up in Colombia between 1975 and 1991, the provision of justice, measured as the number of arrests per murder, stagnated.

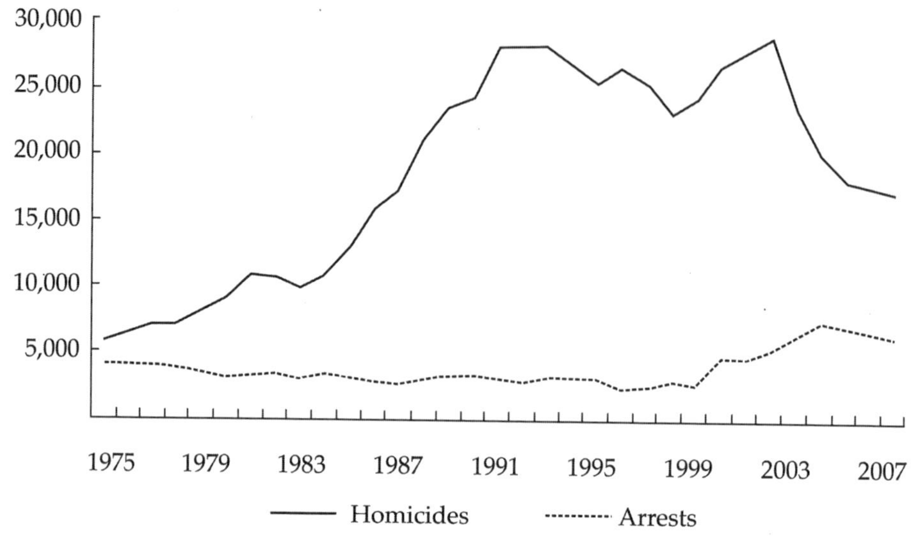

FIGURE 14.1. Homicides and arrests per homicide in Colombia (1975–2007). Source: *Revista Criminalidad*

According to Gaviria (1999), this can be explained by a multiple equilibria model, where the judicial system becomes clogged by an initial rise in crime, caused by the narcotics trafficking boom, which means that the authorities are unable to do their jobs. Another possible explanation is that local authorities recognize that the crime wave is related to narcotics trafficking and understand that their best strategy—and the best "judicial technology" needed for confronting this kind of crime—would be to focus on the leaders of the criminal organizations, and thus conclude that they cannot deal with that kind of crime. In the end, as the models of Gaviria (1999) and Echeverry and Partow (1998) show, this will lead to a weaker provision of justice and the endogenous emergence of impunity.

Note, however, that murders began to fall in Colombia in 2002 and the number of arrests began to rise. While in 1990 the homicide rate was 7.5 times the rate of arrests, in 2007 it was 2.7 times. This is the result of the strategy adopted by the Colombian authorities in collaboration with the United States.

By 2002, the violence related to drug trafficking was out of control despite the authorities' efforts. In that year, presidents Andrés Pastrana and Bill Clinton signed an agreement known as Plan Colombia, by which the US government would provide economic and military support to Colombia for the fight against the guerrillas and narcotics traffickers. The relative success of this strategy caused a change in the balance of power in the cocaine business (Mejía and Restrepo 2010).

The Colombian cartels were weakened and their traditional routes through the Caribbean were strongly patrolled. This led to the creation of new drug trafficking corridors through Central America and the Colombian Pacific coast, controlled by the Mexican cartels (Garzón 2008). Since then, Mexico has faced a situation similar to that of Colombia in the 1980s and 1990s. Additionally, the violence related to drug trafficking has permeated the frontiers of the United States and spread through several states.

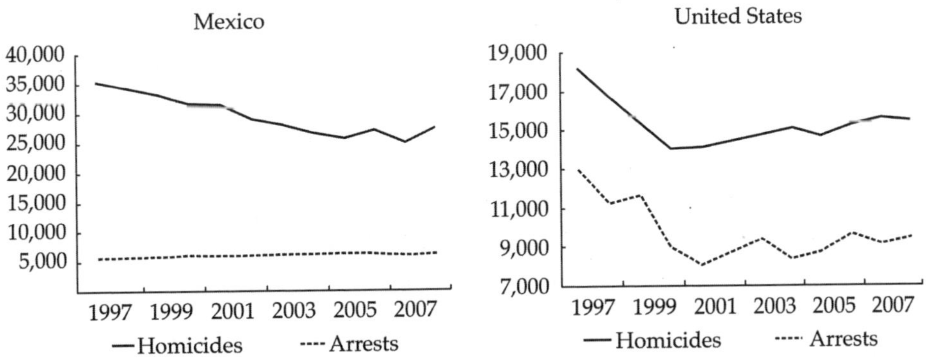

FIGURE 14.2. Homicides and arrests per homicide in Mexico (1997–2007) and the United States (1997–2007). Source: INEGI and Bureau of Justice Statistics

Despite the efforts of Mexican president Calderón, which have led to the arrest of thousands of traffickers and the seizure of many of their properties, crime is rising in Mexico. According to INEGI (the Mexican statistical agency), the homicide rate reached 26 per 100,000 inhabitants in 2008. In the United States, and especially in border states, crime rose during the first decade of the century. That doesn't show, however, in aggregate figures. In 2000 there were 5.5 homicides per 100,000 inhabitants nationwide, a rate that rose to 5.6 in 2009 (Figure 14.2).[2]

Nevertheless, these national figures conceal the fact that there are substantial differences in crime levels between different states or provinces of Colombia, Mexico, and the United States (Figure 14.3).

The United States, Mexico, and Colombia (Figure 14.4) faced a similar situation in different periods: an increase in crime impelled by the presence of narcotics trafficking, with substantial regional differences within each country and a weak response from the police and judicial authorities. To analyze this, we estimated a decision-making model where agents are geographically distant from each other and face a generalized crime wave on a national level, about which they lack sufficient information at the start.

The Lucas model (1973, 1976) considers the possibility of different responses by agents who are geographically separated (on different islands or in different regions, provinces, states, or departments) in the face of the observed shocks. The main hypothesis is that faced with a crime upsurge, local authorities will respond in an active or passive manner to the shock of violence, depending on their different perceptions of its origin. If they believe that the upsurge of violence is due to causes pertaining *only* to their particular locality (the so-called "idiosyncratic" causes), the judicial system will show an active response. The reason is that the "technology"[3] of the police and the judiciary system will have the tools needed to confront this kind of crime, given that the person how actually committed the crime (its "material author") and the person who designed or planned it (its "intellectual author") will most likely be the very same individual.

With the passage of time, if authorities discover that the origin of the shock is of a supra-regional mafioso kind, the local police and justice system will change their response to a "passive" one. If the local authorities conclude that the rise in crime has to do with criminal organizations linked to drug trafficking, they will conclude that the

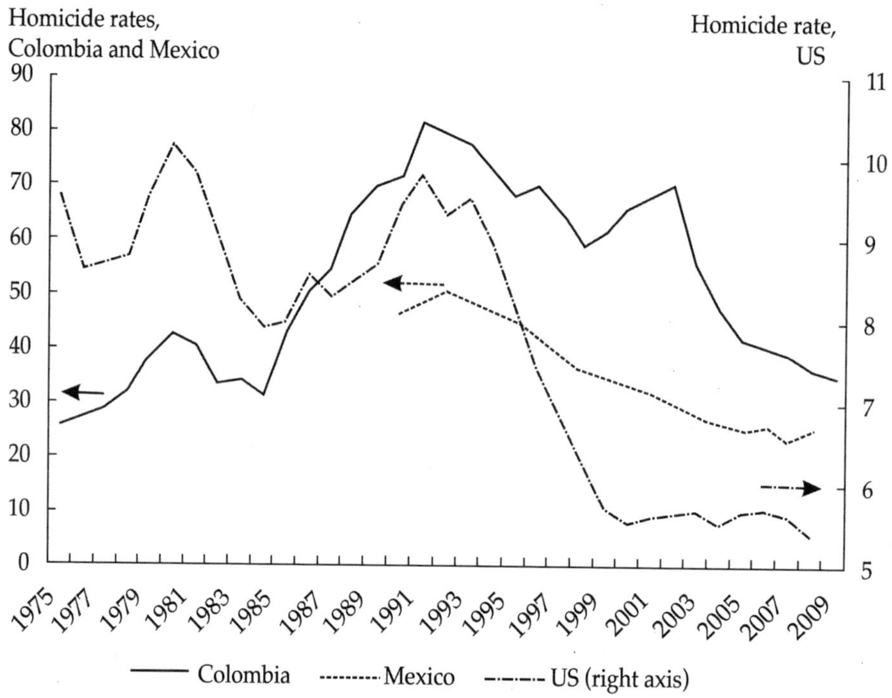

FIGURE 14.3. Homicide rate per 100,000 inhabitants in Colombia, Mexico, and the United States (1975–2009). Source: *Revista Criminalidad*, INEGI, and Bureau of Justice Statistics

appropriate strategy for fighting it should focus on attacking the leaders of those organizations and their illegal activities. Typically, this would need new laws or constitutional reforms, as in Colombia in the 1980s and 1990s or in the United States in the 1970s; or the involvement of the military, as in Mexico and Colombia; or international agreements like the Plan Colombia.

Indeed, the activities of mafias typically surpass the capacity of local police and judicial authorities and belong to the domain of those who formulate national policies. Therefore, the futility of combating the crime linked to drug trafficking with the traditional tools of the local authorities becomes evident. Thus, when the local authorities notice that the rise in crime has roots of a national character, they will substantially reduce their efforts to combat it.

Figures 14.5, 14.6, and 14.7 show the results of the key coefficients estimated for Colombia, Mexico, and the United States, which show the responsiveness of the law enforcement authorities to the crime shock. Note that in all cases the prediction of the model is fulfilled. In the first years of the crime shock, the coefficient is positive and statistically significant. That is, local authorities actively responded to the rise in crime with more arrests. As time passed, however, they stopped. In all cases, this happens with a time lag in the regions where the impact of narcotics trafficking is weak.

Now it is important to note that the coefficient of the judiciary's response to the relative increase of crime in the United States is nearly five times as high as in Colombia

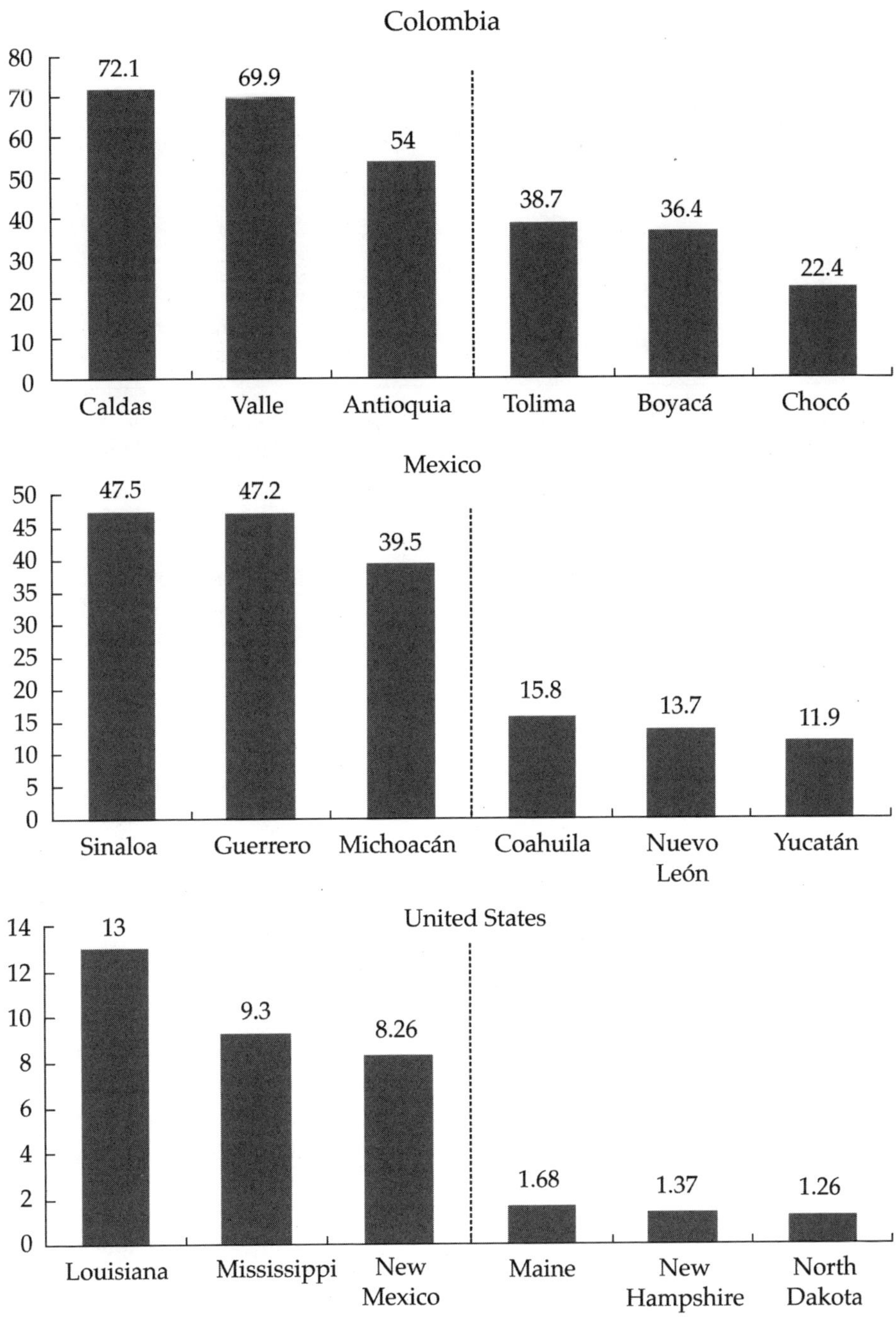

FIGURE 14.4. Homicide rate per 100,000 inhabitants in Colombia, Mexico, and the United States. Selected regions. Average (1996–2007). Source: *Revista Criminalidad*, INEGI, and Bureau of Justice Statistics

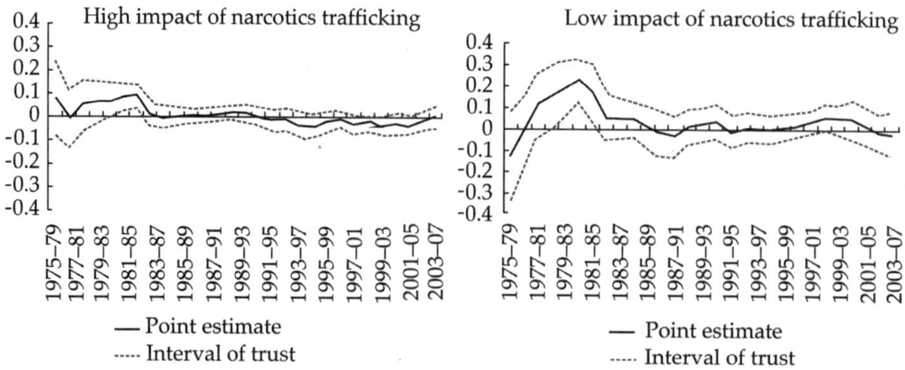

FIGURE 14.5. Response of justice to relative crime in Colombia. Source: Our own estimates. Note: The intervals of trust are calculated as the point estimate of the coefficient plus (minus) two standard deviations

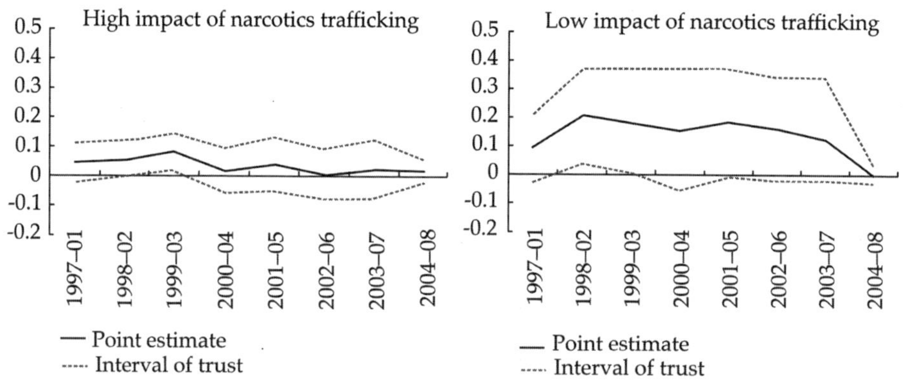

FIGURE 14.6. Response of justice to relative crime in Mexico. Source: Our own estimates. Note: The intervals of trust are calculated as the point estimate of the coefficient plus (minus) two standard deviations

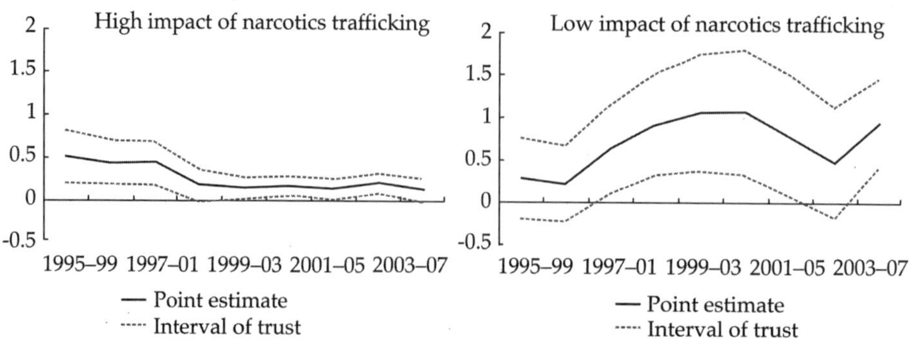

FIGURE 14.7. Response of justice to relative crime in the United States. Source: Our own estimates. Note: The intervals of trust are calculated as the point estimate of the coefficient plus (minus) two standard deviations

and Mexico. We conjecture that while the boom in mafioso-type crime in the United States in the 1950s and 1960s led to the 1973 RICO Act, which provided that country with an arsenal of law enforcement institutions at the federal level that did not exist in Mexico and Colombia at that time. Colombia developed its own new institutions between 1984 and 1999. Mexico started only recently.

THE KEY VARIABLES: TIME, SPACE, AND INFORMATION

This approach makes explicit the temporal and spatial dimension in combating narcotics trafficking, in particular the fact that authorities respond to a crime shock in different ways over time, depending on their geographical location and the available information. The key to the change in their response is the process of learning about the nature of the crime they are fighting. This learning process takes time. This is not only valid in the first stages of the appearance of narcotics trafficking in Colombia, Mexico, or the United States. It continues to happen daily, thirty years after the emergence of that phenomenon.

Mafioso crime is a lucrative activity, which, like any business, constantly modifies some of its technologies and learns to become more efficient and gain a better idea of its competitors and the environmental conditions in which it operates. The strategies and effectiveness of the authorities are part of these environmental conditions, an essential part, since they are perhaps the biggest determinant of the costs and risks of an illegal business and thus of its profitability. Therefore, the authorities are also always learning about the phenomenon they confront and its continuous mutations.

An anti-drug strategy must be aware of this evolutionary nature of the crime phenomenon and the speed with which it must adapt its own capacities to fight it. If in the sphere of tactics, strategies, and policies, the anti-drug fight is not understood as a constant learning process, which is both costly and complex and which requires continuous innovation by the authorities, it runs the risk of being overtaken by the dynamism of crime. In other words, an effective anti-drug strategy must anticipate the strategic responses of the criminal organizations, with the aim of preventing those responses from rendering their tactics ineffective.

Our argument centers on the learning process at the initial stages of the mafioso phenomenon; the authorities, even in the absence of corruption, were increasingly overtaken by the new type of crime, both in technological and juridical terms, which undermined their morale in the fight or their incentives for undertaking it. Specifically, a policeman risks his life to capture a hired assassin who committed a crime in his municipality, but within days or months learns that the criminal is only the direct or material perpetrator and the intellectual authors are far away, both in geographical and juridical terms. The reward for his bravery is not really the solution of the crime but the breaking of a small link in the criminal chain that in no way will change the phenomenon responsible for the wave of deaths he faces. In this case, when another murder occurs in his town, neighborhood or locality, this policeman will not act so decisively and his resolve will continue to weaken as the mafioso phenomenon intensifies.

Naturally, he will need the help of national or international authorities that have the required technological intelligence tools, and he will need new and more appropriate juridical tools to deal with the new phenomenon, something we will speak of later. For the moment, we would like to emphasize the crucial nature of the passing of time, the learning process, and changes in the morale of or incentives for waging the fight, factors often overlooked in the strategies adopted in the war on drugs.

As for the matter of space or geography, the initial shock of crime had different regional effects in the three counties we studied. While in some provinces it took off, in others it stayed at relatively low levels. For that reason, we proposed an explanation for this stylized fact that puts an emphasis on the lack of incentives, on the part of decision makers who are geographically separated, to confront what they regard as a problem that either transcends the limits of their jurisdiction or originates beyond their local or regional frontiers.

Although the strength of criminal shock is not evenly distributed in all regions, the worrying aspect of our empirical results is that both in the provinces where narcotics trafficking has a strong impact and in those where its impact is weak, the local police and judicial authorities no longer exert themselves once they understand the origin of the crime shock they are dealing with. To be sure, there is a difference in the duration of the learning process of the different local authorities. Whereas in the regions where there was a strong impact of narcotics trafficking, the authorities stopped actively responding to the crime after the first few years of the shock (say, a period of approximately six years in the case of some Colombian regions); by contrast, in those regions where there was a weak impact, this took more time (eight years in other regions of Colombia). This is what we call the *information effect*, as compared to the *learning effect*, which predominates in the low-impact regions.

Since the crime shock impelled by the narcotics trafficking boom does not directly reach distant or unrelated regions, the local authorities stop exerting themselves when information from the rest of the country reaches them. This usually indicates that the new mafioso phenomenon of a national or international scope has overtaken the authorities in other regions. It would be plausible to say that the frequency and profitability of all kinds of crime would increase where there is a widespread loss of morale and weak response from the authorities. In short, it is not surprising that, in addition to mafioso crime, other kinds of crime would also thrive, like street crime. Naturally, there are several communicating vessels between major and petty crime.

These results show that for the local judiciary system and police authorities—both in the 1980s in Colombia and in Mexico in the 2000s—recognizing the size and importance of the emerging cocaine industry was accompanied by the understanding that local crime-fighting efforts were insufficient in the absence of a national strategy.

Finally, the empirical results imply that in this situation the available information is crucial. If the origin of the crime is known in its earliest stage of growth, it may be checked before it has reached the point of thriving on economies of scale. This job is the responsibility of state intelligence agencies, which in most cases do not exist on a local level. Applying tools on a national level and forcefully and opportunely reacting in the first stages of the crime shock would do away with the need for the learning process for the local authorities and hinder the possibility of a national and international escalation of the activities of the criminal organizations. For that reason, it is important to know what lies behind the observed increase in crime before it is too late and to attack the crime with suitable tools from the beginning.

SPECIFIC ELEMENTS OF ORGANIZED CRIME AND STRATEGIES FOR COMBATING IT

Technologies

The approach we are advancing here puts an emphasis on the persistent asymmetries between the technologies available to the criminals, and to the police and judicial authorities who confront them.

The first asymmetry lies in the fact that it is best for the narcotics traffickers to go beyond the limited geographical reach of the authorities, since this enables them to exploit the growing yields of economies of scale, as we argued at the beginning of this chapter. Nothing like that is available to the local authorities.

The second asymmetry lies in the fact that it is best for each group of narcotics traffickers that there is a given level of policing/judicial activity, even a war on drugs, so long as it is aimed at its competitors in the narcotics trade. This point was eloquently stated by Becker, Grossman, and Murphy (1991), who showed how the authorities are doing the biggest possible favor to one drug cartel when they devote all their energies to attacking another.

This was the case in the war against Pablo Escobar and the Medellín cartel, undertaken by the Colombian authorities and the secret services of Colombia and the United States. Later we learned that the Cali cartel encouraged this strategy through networks of influence extending to the political class and the police and fueled by corruption.

In colloquial terms, if the war on drugs is not waged on all fronts with all the forces of the state, it is better not to wage it all. It is not clear whether or not a war of half-measures may be really serving the ultimate ends of some of the criminals. With the best intentions and the political objective of showing that "something is being done," a country may be worsening the problem it strives to solve. Combating mafioso crime with strategies that are national but of middling intensity may be the best thing that could happen for the criminals themselves, as it favors certain actors by eliminating their competition and raises the international price of drugs.

A Redesign of the Juridical Structures

A large body of literature has shown that for fighting drug trafficking crime, one must create a special normative juridical regime of a supra-regional nature. This is due to the "industrial organization" of these kinds of crimes; while it is easy to deal with ordinary crime with traditional police and judicial tools, these tools have little effect on the networks of organized crime (Bouchard 2007; Chabat 2002; Felbab-Brown 2009; Gaviria 1999; Matthiesen 2000; Mejía and Restrepo 2010; Thoumi 2001).

A crime shock on a national level must be dealt with through the issuance of new laws, or even constitutional reforms, suited to the operations of the criminal organizations. This was the case when the Colombian Constitution was modified to authorize extradition and the state established laws that define and punish illegal enrichment; mechanisms for the expropriation of properties acquired through illegal activities, including corruption; and even special measures and units to attack money laundering and force the operators of the financial and capital markets to be especially careful about suspicious transactions and persons (the Clinton List, control of money laundering, etc.).

If these actions are not taken in time, at a national level, the result will be to undermine the whole country's ability to deal with the problem. Given the geometric growth of organized crime due to its economies of scale, any delay in recognizing the national scope of the problem and acting with the right strategies will increase the institutional costs for the country.

The results of the empirical model show that the narcotics trafficking boom had a harmful effect on the response of the judiciary in Colombia and Mexico, and to a lesser extent in the United States. In our opinion, the main difference is that while the United States has faced many shocks from mafias, especially in the 1920s because of Prohibition, and the 1940s and 1960s when the Italian mafias were strong, Colombia only began to face a shock of this magnitude in the 1980s and Mexico in the 2000s.

Because they had previously confronted a similar shock, the US authorities, both federal and local, had the tools they needed to combat the violence caused by organized crime. To cite the examples given by Abadinsky (1985), the 1970 RICO Act and the creation of the DEA in 1973 broadened the field of action of federal justice and allowed it to directly attack the criminal organizations.

The most successful strategy for combating this type of crime in the United States and Colombia was the joint work of the local and national authorities. In the case of the United States, the passing of federal laws, with harsher punishments and judges, acted to dissuade and/or better attack organized crime. In the case of Colombia, the creation of the public prosecutor (*fiscalía*), the authorization of extradition, and the signing of the Plan Colombia agreement, accompanied by the institutional strengthening of the armed forces, fulfilled this purpose. As the three cases show, the local authorities have often been the victims of corruption, intimidation, or demoralization by these organizations and therefore have frequently turned out to be ineffective against the drugs cartels.

This finding has important implications for the fight against drugs and crime, both in Colombia and Mexico. The importance of a national (aggregate) strategy is undeniable, not only to directly attack the main capos but also to imprison those who work for them. Institutional tools (laws, extradition treaties) and innovations in intelligence and military techniques in general (dominating the area through the use of helicopters, planes, and radar) restore the power lost by the local governments to the national one.

To strengthen the comparison with economics, in the case of a monetary shock the institutional innovations consisted of constitutionally independent central banks, with inflation targets, endowed with technical bodies of experts who continuously monitor the state of the economy and its inflationary pressures. Learning and innovation were the key instruments used to tame inflation worldwide.

Need for an Early Warning System

A timely reaction by the central authorities is the most important factor in this scenario. An alarming consequence of the conduct we have described is that once it takes off, it weakens the will to confront crime in general, whether it is related to drug trafficking or not. The institutions lose credibility. Figure 14.8 shows a simple diagram that illustrates how crime evolves over time and may follow an *S*-shaped path rather than a straight

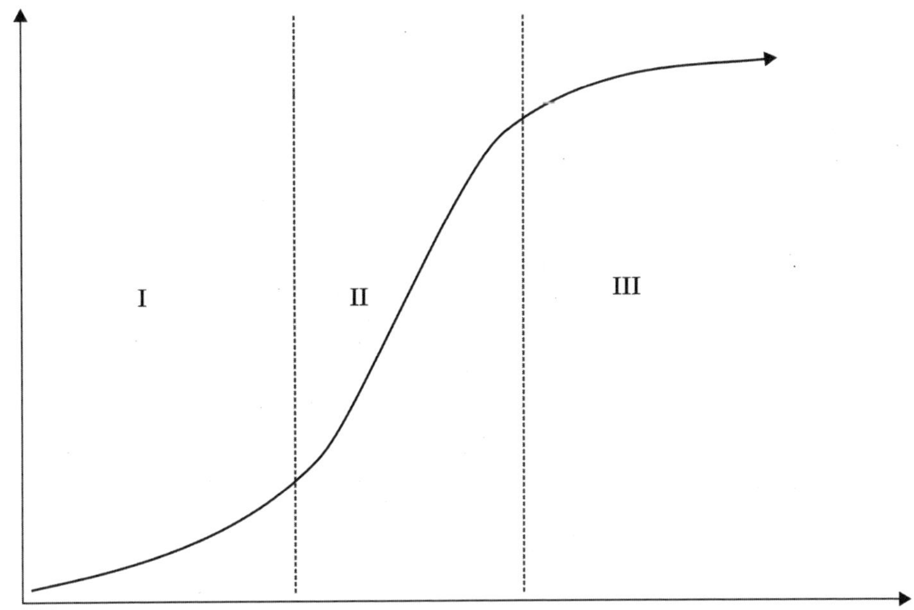

FIGURE 14.8. Evolution of earnings from crime over time

line (so that it is nonlinear). In the earliest stage, it grows at a slower rate than the one it may reach once it manages to break through the local barriers and rise to a national and international level. For that reason, the creation of an early warning system for crime is essential. This would seek to prevent it from reaching the third phase.

This does not only apply to countries that have not yet faced narcotics trafficking shocks—it may happen in Venezuela and Ecuador, or for that matter Brazil and Spain, we believe—but also those that have confronted this kind of crime for years, like Colombia and Mexico. According to Echeverry and Gómez (2009), the shock of narcotics trafficking that the United States currently faces as a consequence of the rise of the Mexican cartels has not had such dramatic effects on the crime rate and the implementation of justice, mainly because that country already counted on a national strategy that enabled it to act rapidly against that kind of crime.

Self-Defeating Strategies?

The case of Colombia shows how a direct attack on the drugs capos did not have significant long-term effects on the production and trafficking of cocaine, nor on the violence caused by the cartels, and that these organizations were quickly and easily replaced by others.

For example, in 1990 President Gaviria (1990–1994) understood that the tools available locally were not sufficient to deal with this kind of crime. He therefore began to pursue the leaders of the drugs cartels. In 1993, the police killed Pablo Escobar, and by 1995 the Cali cartel had been dismantled when, among other measures, its leaders, the Rodríguez Orejuela brothers, were arrested in Colombia. Ten years later, they were extradited to the United States (the only legal tool they feared). At this point, crime began to fall and the homicide rate reached a new level of 65 per 100,000 inhabitants (in the year 2000), still high by international standards.

Despite the falling crime rate, the dismantling of the Cali and Medellín cartels gave rise to the Norte del Valle cartel and the strengthening of the guerrilla and paramilitary groups' role as drugs traffickers. In addition, as Garzón (2008) documents, these events strengthened the Mexican mafiosos, who have had a more active participation in the drug business since then.

This shows that a halfhearted fight against this kind of crime, attacking only a single cartel and refusing to cooperate with neighboring countries, may be a self-defeating strategy. Fighting against a single cartel strengthens the ones not attacked, and this is valid both on a national and international level. It shows the danger of underestimating the capacity of the actors in question to adapt and rapidly change their strategy, export routes, and allies.

Crime is highly dynamic, and one expression of its adaptability and capacity for change has to do with the growing of coca. The local Colombia saying that "coca walks"—meaning that what is fumigated in one region reappears in another department or province—is evidence of this flexibility. In short, the police and judges have to be at least as mobile, agile, and resourceful as are their counterparts among the delinquents. Provinces of Colombia that were relatively free of illegal activities two decades ago have become the epicenter of the current war: Chocó and Nariño, for example. Likewise, nations that were free of such crimes two decades ago, such as El Salvador, Guatemala, Venezuela, and Ecuador, are emerging as bases for the narcotics traffickers, routes for the aerial shipment of drugs, and bridges for arms trafficking, among other criminal activities.

One of the key points of our study is precisely the geographical structure of organized crime and its effect on the response of the authorities, whether through the learning or information processes. The phenomena that characterized certain regions of Colombia two decades ago are now daily happenings in others. Circumstances pertaining to Colombia have been affecting Mexico for the past decade and will reach and grow in Venezuela, Ecuador, or Brazil in the near future. A popular saying captures the mobile nature of the drug trade: "When you see that someone is cutting your neighbor's beard, start wetting yours."

Cooperation and the Balloon Effect

The production of cocaine in Colombia, Peru, and Bolivia stayed at a relatively stable level between 1990 and 2007, rising from approximately 790 to 1,000 metric tons annually, according to the UNODC (Figure 14.9). Although cocaine production fell in Peru and Bolivia during this period, as a result of the efforts of their governments with the help of the United States, it rose by 500 metric tons annually in Colombia. This is known in the literature as the balloon effect. If the demand for cocaine does not fall, the success of a campaign to eradicate coca crops in a given geographical area will simply shift those crops to another one. This has happened with the geography of coca crops and cocaine trafficking since the 1980s.

It is natural to extend this argument when the country as a whole confronts cocaine trafficking on an international level. The incentives for acting diminish once it

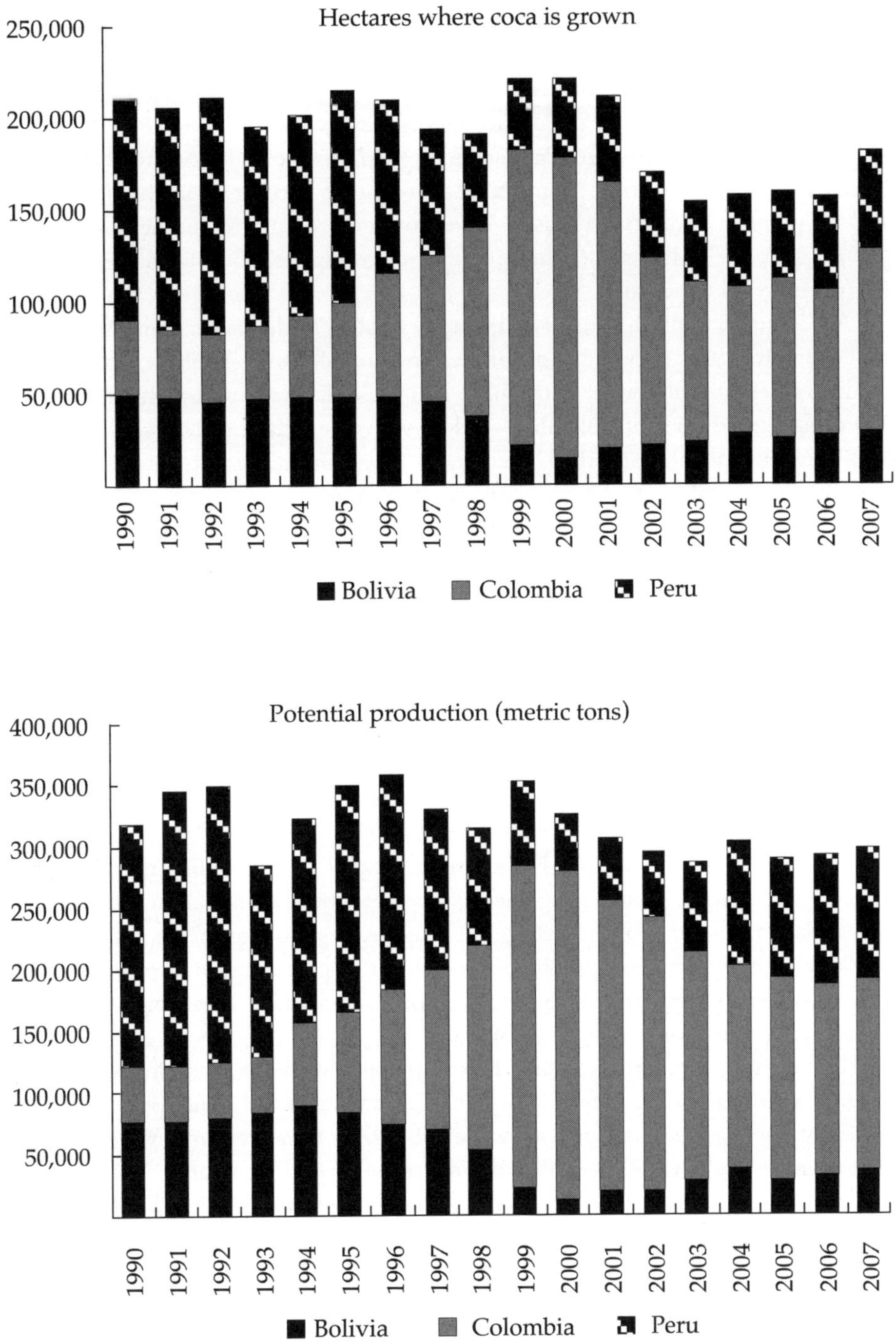

FIGURE 14.9. Cocaine grown (hectares) and potential production (metric tons) in Bolivia, Colombia, and Peru (1990–2007). Source: United Nations Office on Drugs and Crime (UNODC). Statistics and analysis

is understood that, given the criminal structure of the drug industry, national efforts lose much of their effectiveness if they are isolated. Those countries that are in the vanguard of the battle against drugs understand the futility of an approach to the problem that merely attacks the consequences and ignores the origins of the crime, which means weaker efforts to combat the problem in the end. For this reason, it is crucial that the neighboring countries also assume an active role in the fight, given that the problem of drugs may easily move from one country to another, as has been seen in the past. In this sense, the programs of coresponsibility in the fight against drugs are of vital importance.

Additionally, when the same argument is extended to the international sphere, the implication is that an important part of the provision of justice should be placed in the hands of international bodies, both police and judicial. The latter aspect—trying narcotics traffickers outside of Colombia—has been an especially sensitive issue in the relations between Colombia and the United States. There are reasons for arguing that these cases should be dealt with supra-nationally, for example, in the International Criminal Court. This might be able to ease the problems associated with a polemical feature of binational relations.

In Colombia the asymmetry of the war against drugs makes many people indignant. A bit of Colombian dark humor captures the country's feeling that the financial, political, and juridical efforts of Colombia are not matched by those of the United States: "the gringos will fight the war against drugs down to the last Colombian." Furthermore, Colombia has borne for a long time the enormous cost of being an international pariah, with a deteriorated national stereotype as a country plagued by corruption and insecurity. This hurt foreign investment and tourism and imposed physical and moral costs on its citizens when they traveled abroad.

Before Andrés Pastrana and Bill Clinton signed Plan Colombia, the attitude of the United States was denigrating and revolved around the annual "certification" of Colombia's collaboration in the war against drugs. A "regime change" came about when the Pastrana administration proposed the concept of coresponsibility to the Clinton administration and the latter accepted it as a justification for the launching of the broad binational agenda known as Plan Colombia.

This is not the place to explain the components or make an evaluation of Plan Colombia (Mejía and Restrepo 2010). In the context of our analysis, this kind of strategy should have been adopted since the mid-1970s. It took twenty-five years for the Colombian and United States authorities to see the light with regard to international cooperation; considering that Mexico has exported drugs to the United States since the 1920s, it took even longer for two bordering nations, the United States and Mexico, to establish the Mérida Initiative. The advantage gained by the narcotics traffickers from the absence of clarity and political vision among the authorities is incalculable.

Why Isn't There an Andean Plan?

The point just mentioned brings out the futility of recent events in the Andean countries, which have been dominated precisely by the consequences of their failure to cooperate and create an Andean plan for the past twenty years. On the contrary, influenced by ideological differences about fighting the guerrillas and corruption, their governments have established divergent views of the fight against narcotics and the mafias. As a result, instead of cooperating, in many circumstances the national authorities have been fighting diplomatic wars against each other.

This has been and still is advantageous to organized crime. The institutional cost borne by Venezuela, Ecuador, Peru, Bolivia, and Colombia for failing to cooperate with and trust each other and invest in the drug fight means that they will probably suffer decades of financial drain, loss of life, and institutional disorder before solving the problem.

These costs will be higher for the countries that are turning themselves into paradises for organized crime.

CONCLUSIONS

Our analysis is based on the empirical observation that the presence of narcotics trafficking caused an initial crime shock that quickly multiplied endogenously in Colombia, Mexico, and the United States. This fast reproduction of crime is largely due to the capacity for aggregation that the criminal organizations have and the economies of scale of their criminal activities. In Echeverry and Gómez (2009) we showed how the local authorities were not able to respond in a timely and effective way to the rise in crime. This is because if they are left to act on their own, they will have to go through a period of learning, which may take more than five years and will require information about the origin of the shock, an interval during which the criminal organizations will outstrip them. After that, attacking crime becomes more difficult and expensive.

A number of policy recommendations derive from this analysis. Taking into account that it is complicated to confront organized crime as the periods of shock grow longer, it is crucial to have an early warning system that enables a country to identify the criminal organizations before they have permeated society, the judicial system, and the police, as happened in Colombia in the 1980s. To achieve this, institutions exclusively devoted to organized crime are needed, organizations that count on suitable technologies for detecting the presence of drug trafficking in a given region and attack all the responsible actors.

In addition, it is important that the authorities react as strongly as possible—and even overreact—in the first stage of the crime, as Ecuador did in the 1970s when the first coca crops appeared. Given the nature of the shock, it is better to attack the earliest symptoms to saturation point to send the signal that the crime will not be tolerated locally. This kind of reaction should serve as a signal both for the local mafiosos who are emerging and for the authorities, so that the effects of learning and information act in favor of legality, and not the other way around. Also, organized crime should never be combated with half-measures. The greatest possible force and attack on all fronts should be used at the same time.

Given the constant mutation of the criminal organizations, it is important to keep up the dynamic of creating and designing police, judicial, and institutional tools for confronting organized crime on a national level. For example, the first strategy used to fight against narcotics trafficking in Colombia was the persecution of the leaders of the criminal gangs and the approving their extradition. While it was a relatively successful strategy at the time, it is no longer sufficient. With the establishment of Plan Colombia, the Colombian authorities began to focus on persecuting the armed groups and controlling the illegal crops (see Chapter 3).

Nowadays, according to the same author, the most efficient strategy for combating narcotics trafficking is to seize the precursor chemicals needed to produce cocaine. In short, there must be a continuous development of new tools to attack all the links of the value chain, from the precursor chemicals to money laundering and the acquisition of assets with illegal monies.

Finally, the ease with which the criminal organizations can transform themselves, along with their international character, means it is important to confront organized crime through internationally coordinated strategies, and it is important to sign international cooperation agreements with all the countries affected by drug trafficking.

NOTES

This essay summarizes the conclusions on public policies found in a study written by the authors, *Narcotrafficking and impunity in the Lucas Islands: The Evidence for Colombia, Mexico and the United States.*

1. Unfortunately, in the case of Colombia, there are no statistics for homicides specifically related to drug trafficking.
2. Ideally, we would have liked to work with statistics on homicides specifically related to drug trafficking, but the figures on homicides are not broken down in that way either for Colombia or for the United States. Therefore, with the aim of having comparable and homogenous figures, we used the figures on total homicides in the three countries. These figures reflect the behavior of the homicides related to drug trafficking.
3. "Technologies" is the name we have given to the set of practices, capacities, juridical tools, and forms of organization available both to the criminals who are members of narcotics trafficking groups and the police and judicial authorities who confront them.

REFERENCES

Abadinsky, H. 1985. *Organized Crime*, 2nd ed. Belmont, CA: Nelson Hall.

Becker, G., M. Grossman, and K. Murphy. 1991. "Rational Addiction and the Effect of Price on Consumption." Center for the Study of the Economy and the State. University of Chicago, February.

Bouchard, M. 2007. "On the Resilience of Illegal Drug Markets." *Global Crime* 8, no. 4 (November).

Chabat, J. 2002. "Mexico's War on Drugs: No Margin for Maneuver." *Annals of the American Academy of Political and Social Science*, vol. 582. Cross-National Drug Policy, 134ff.

Echeverry, J. C., and M. P. Gómez. 2009. "Narcotráfico e impunidad en las Islas de Lucas, Evidencia para Colombia, México y Estados Unidos." Universidad de los Andes.

Echeverry, J. C., and Z. Partow. 1998. "Why Is Justice Unresponsive to Crime: The Case of Cocaine in Colombia." In *Borradores de Economía, Banco de la República*. Bogotá. Spanish reprint in J. C. Echeverry and Z. Partow. 2002. *Las claves del futuro, economía y conflicto en Colombia.* Bogotá: Oveja Negra.

Felbab-Brown, V. 2009. "The Violent Drug Market in Mexico and Lessons from Colombia." Policy Paper no. 12 (March), Foreign Policy at Brookings.

Garzón, J. C. 2008. *Mafia y Co. La red criminal en México, Brasil y Colombia*. Bogotá: Editorial Planeta and Fundación Seguridad y Democracia.

Gaviria, A. 1999. "Increasing Returns and the Evolution of Violent Crime: The Case of Colombia." *Journal of Development Economics* 61 (2000): 1–25.

Keynes, J. M. 1936. *The General Theory of Employment, Interest and Money*. New York: Harcourt, Brace and Company.

Lucas, R. 1973. "Some International Evidence on Output Inflation Tradeoffs." *American Economic Review* 63, no. 3 (June): 326–34.

———. 1976. "Econometric Policy Evaluation: A Critique." *Carnegie-Rochester Conferences on Public Policy* 1, no. 3: 19–46.

Matthiesen, T. 2000. *El arte político de conciliar*. Bogotá: Fescol/Cerec/Fedesarrollo.

Mejía, D., and P. Restrepo. 2010. "The War on Illegal Drug Production and Trafficking: An Economic Evaluation of Plan Colombia." In *Documento CEDE*. Bogotá, Universidad de los Andes.

Thoumi, F. 2001. *Drogas ilegales, economía y sociedad en los Andes*. Unpublished. Bogotá. Retrieved from *www.notinet.com.co/pedidos/drogasilegales.pdf*, accessed May 12, 2015.

15 Violent Nonstate Actors and Narcotics Trafficking in Colombia

Arlene Beth Tickner, Diego García, and Catalina Arreaza

According to the United Nations Office on Drugs and Crime (UNODC 2010), the annual value of the global cocaine trade is some US$88 billion. The United States and Europe account for 84 percent of this market, with US$38 billion and US$34 billion respectively, and Colombia continues to be the main supplier, responsible for meeting about 50 percent of the demand.[1] Despite this, the boom in academic studies of illegal drugs that began in the late 1980s has waned in the present decade, so that current analyses of the subject are surprisingly meager. As a result, the state of our knowledge of the participation in narcotics trafficking of violent nonstate actors (VNSAs) is especially weak. This is due in part to the growing linkage of these actors and the armed conflict since the 1990s, the effect of which was to fuse the analysis of the two phenomena as well as the strategies adopted to combat them. Thus, narcotics trafficking has been mistakenly interpreted as an appendix of the conflict, so that little attention is paid not only to its complexity but also the roles the different VNSAs play in it.

Between the discovery of the coca-processing complex known as Tranquilandia in 1984 and the present, the relationship between narcotics traffickers, guerrilla and paramilitary forces, and the illegal drug business has gone through substantial mutations. The aim of this chapter is to evaluate the different roles played by the VNSA in narcotics trafficking. Toward that end, we briefly review the diverse stages of the problem in Colombia and speak of the main forces of continuity and change that have been seen during its historical development. We then present a more detailed analysis of the current situation. For that purpose, we focus on two different regions that exemplify some of its most important dynamics, one being Nariño, an area of production and trafficking, and the other Medellín, mainly one of trafficking. These case studies enable us to state that narcotics trafficking is structured as a network of transactions between national and international VNSAs, in which different types of intermediaries (whom we call "brokers") act as the main driving force of the phenomenon. To illustrate the different roles played by such actors in the narcotics trafficking chain and their different kinds of relatedness, the chapter also includes a series of three cartograms.[2]

Arlene Beth Tickner: Full professor, Department of Political Science, Universidad de los Andes.

Diego García: Alumnus of the Department of Political Science, Universidad de los Andes.

Catalina Arreaza: Coordinator, Center of International Studies (CEI), Department of Political Science, Alberto Lleras Camargo School of Government.

The market in illegal drugs takes the form of a chain, which, when its different links are broken down, reveals the division of labor among the different actors who participate in it, as well as the transformations that have taken place at different stages of the history of narcotics trafficking in Colombia. Up to twelve links can be seen in the chain that, taken together, represent the three stages of producing cocaine—the growing of coca leaves (links 1 to 4), and the processing (links 5 to 10) and commercializing of cocaine chlorhydrate (stages 11 and 12) (see Chapter 1): (1) supply and transport of inputs and precursor chemicals, (2) planting of coca, (3) growing of coca leaves, (4) fabrication of coca paste (cocaine base) in "kitchens" (*cocinas*), (5) purchase of coca paste, (6) administration of laboratories (*cristalizaderos*) and processing of base into cocaine chlorhydrate, (7) protection of or permission to operate the laboratories, (8) transport to collection centers, (9) security when moving the product (10) providing security for the collection centers and the routes toward the embarkation points, (11) sale of cocaine chlorhydrate to intermediaries, (12) overseas shipment of cocaine to intermediate points, which requires the development of smuggling techniques (for example, the use of semisubmersibles).

At each stage of the chain one sees a division of labor in which different actors participate. In the case of Colombia, the violent nonstate ones have historically played a role in most of the above-mentioned links, except for the planting and growing of coca leaves—which is generally assigned to peasant-farmers (*campesinos*) and specialist harvesters (*raspachines*)[3]—and, with a few exceptions, the international transporting of cocaine to intermediate points (though they frequently participate in the design of its methods). In addition to the roles associated with these links, there are a varied series of "brokers" or "link men" (*articuladores*) who act to intermediate or interconnect them and thus enable the chain to function as an integrated system. As we shall see below, the growing sectorization, specialization, and horizontality of narcotics trafficking in recent years has not only led to a multiplication of brokers on each level of the chain but has also given them more importance.

STAGES IN THE DEVELOPMENT OF NARCOTICS TRAFFICKING IN COLOMBIA AND THE ROLE OF THE VNSAS

Pioneers and Big Cartels

The assumption of a leading role in the illegal drug trade by diverse Colombian actors dates back to the early 1970s, when the implementation of crop eradication and interdiction programs in Jamaica and Mexico produced a "balloon effect" that caused a shifting of most of the crops to Colombia, along with the control of their sales to the US market. Marijuana was grown in the Sierra Nevada de Santa Marta and neighboring areas close to the Caribbean coast and exported along traditional smuggling routes from the part of the same coast known as la Guajira, with stages in some Caribbean countries, to southern Florida. After reaching a production peak in the 1980s, when Colombia supplied 75 percent of the marijuana consumed in the United States, the traffickers in Colombia began to focus their efforts on the production and trafficking of cocaine. This was due to a combination of factors: the application of antinarcotics strategies similar to the ones used in Mexico, the growing self-sufficiency of the United States in marijuana, and the marked difference in the profit margin of cocaine compared to other illegal drugs (Tokatlian and Bagley 1990; Tokatlian 1991; Thoumi 1994; Rocha 2000).

Toward that end, the Colombians developed routes for importing coca paste from Peru and, to a lesser extent, Bolivia—the main countries where coca leaves were grown up to the mid-1990s—and made use of agro-chemical inputs, transport systems, and distribution networks originating in the United States, an enterprise facilitated by the large number of Colombian immigrants in that country. They also established sophisticated systems for money laundering, largely based on networks of contraband trade developed before the advent of narcotics trafficking.[4] According to Thoumi (2002, 108), this production structure, which was fragmented on a transnational level but administered and controlled in a hierarchical way, was one of the factors that led to the forming of the big cartels, especially those of Medellín and Cali. In addition to these central organizations, an extensive network of actors formed part of the narcotics economy, among them the peasant growers and other unskilled workers, freelance professionals (like chemists, pilots, lawyers, financial advisors, and hit men), and organizations specializing in transport, money laundering, and processing, which undertook specific functions within a pyramidal structure (Clawson and Lee 1996, 20).

During this "founding period" the narcotics trafficking cartels adopted at least two different modus operandi, both based on a monopoly of the production chain (Gugliotta and Leen 1989; Clawson and Lee 1996; Bowden 2002; Chepesiuk 2003). On the one hand, the Medellín cartel and leaders like Carlos Lehder and Pablo Escobar acted with high visibility and openly employed violence in order to gain political influence (mainly aimed at preventing extradition) and attack the Colombian authorities (Cubides 2004, 18). On the other, the Cali cartel kept a low public profile in order to accommodate itself to the political establishment and conserve a façade of legality, meanwhile employing sophisticated managerial techniques that gave it more effective control of the cocaine trade, especially of the links related to its commercialization. As a consequence, by the beginning of the 1990s, the Cali cartel counted on a network of distribution cells in the United States and later in Europe, in collaboration with the Italian mafia. This enabled it to overtake the Medellín cartel even before the death of Pablo Escobar in 1993.

Parallel to this and alongside the private armies employed by the two cartels, this early stage of narcotics trafficking also witnessed the first attempts to establish paramilitary groups in Colombia. The mid-Magdalena River region (*el Magdalena medio*), where the narcotics traffickers invested in land and allied themselves with the traditional landowning class, became the birthplace of the model for later illegal antisubversive forces with the 1981 founding in the town of Puerto Boyacá of the Death to Kidnappers (Muerte a Secuestradores, MAS) group. Similar to what is currently happening as the paramilitary forces constantly realign themselves, the MAS spread to different parts of the country as a violent phenomenon without any internal coherence (González 2004, 14). Thus its structure was replicated in Córdoba and Urabá, first with the People's Liberation Army (Ejército de Liberación Popular, EPL) and later the FARC, with the aim of combating the guerrillas (Romero 2002).

Despite the antisubversive ideology of the narcotics trafficking organizations, especially the Medellín cartel, the first signs of business alliances between them and the guerrillas, mainly the FARC, became public knowledge almost simultaneously with the discovery in the jungles of the department of Caquetá in 1984 of Tranquilandia, a large complex for cocaine production that belonged to Pablo Escobar. The FARC's involvement in narcotics trafficking had emerged at the end of the previous decade when the Medellín cartel began to operate in Caquetá, then under the control of the guerrillas. While the guerrillas initially prohibited the cultivation of coca, the growing opposition of the local peasant-farmers led them to change their position. The growing of coca leaves and sale of coca paste was allowed and the guerrillas charged the farmers a tax of approximately 10 percent of the value of a kilo of cocaine base (ICG 2005, 9). This form of participation was consolidated at the FARC's Seventh Conference in 1982, when they made the strategic policy decision to use drugs to finance their armed fight, a tipping point in the history of that subversive organization's military and territorial expansion (Pizarro 2006; Pécaut 2008). Later, the FARC raised the tax on growers and harvesters, extended their role of providing security for the intermediaries to the small producers, and established measures like setting a single fixed price for the sale of cocaine base and encouraging the peasants to grow legal crops alongside the illegal ones. This policy culminated in taxes on the use of airstrips, agrochemical inputs, the building and maintenance of laboratories, and the protection of export routes (Pécaut 2008). At their Eighth Conference in 1993, their growing participation in narcotics trafficking was "operationalized" with the creation of fronts the specific function of which was to participate in different links of the chain, mainly the initial ones, and pay a monthly percentage of their revenues to the General Staff.

With regard to the international aspect of the trade, as mentioned above, during the marijuana boom the merchandise was mainly shipped through the Caribbean to southern Florida, with staging posts in a number of islands along the way. In 1984, with the aim of checking the flow of narcotics along that route, and as part of its recently announced "war on drugs," the US government established the South Florida Task Force. The breaking of the Caribbean connection shifted the movement of drugs to Central America and Mexico and led to the creation of strategic alliances with groups of Mexican traffickers such as the cartels of Juárez and Tijuana (Bagley 2009), who facilitated the use of the new routes and acted as intermediaries. Parallel to these events, following the assassination of the Colombian justice minister Rodrigo Lara Bonilla in 1984 and the government's intensification of the fight against narcotics traffickers, many capos sought refuge in foreign countries, especially Mexico and Panama (where they could enjoy the protection of its then president, general Manuel Noriega), which tightened their links with the different intermediaries they largely depended on to secure the continued success of their exports to the United States.

This restructuring of the transport routes and reorganization of the roles assigned to the different actors responsible for the commercialization of cocaine meant that the vertical integration that characterized the big Colombian cartels gradually gave way to the delegation of some tasks to third parties, especially the Mexican cartels. They, in turn, began to take over the shipping of cocaine through Mexico to the United States, where the cartels of Cali and Medellín were still in control. While the initial agreements involved paying the Mexicans a fixed fee for the services they provided, the situation changed when the latter began to be partly paid with cocaine. As their share in the US market grew, they demanded a larger slice of the business (Cook 2007; Bagley 2009).

The Independent Narcotics Traffickers and the Growing Participation of the VNSAs

The killing of Pablo Escobar in 1993, along with the surrender of some major figures of the Cali cartel two years later, ended the "classical" period of narcotics trafficking in Colombia and gave rise to a new stage in the business. In the case of the Medellín cartel, the elimination of Escobar was followed by a regrouping of the different branches of his organization, including both those who had become his enemies (the Pepes and the Doce del Patíbulo) and those who had kept their distance from the internal feuds. While the former continued to participate in the trade from the prisons where they had been sent, the latter, headed by Fabio Ochoa and Alejandro Juvenal, operated as a "reconstituted" cartel until 1999, when Operation Millennium culminated with the capture and extradition of the two capos. For their part, some members of the Cali cartel stepped into the shoes of their former bosses and reorganized themselves into the "*cartel del norte del Valle*" (northern Valle cartel). Meanwhile, a large number of independent organizations whose role in trafficking had been dimmed by the two big cartels began to re-emerge. This was the case, for example, of the cartels of Ibagué, Bogotá, La Guajira, the Atlantic coast, and the Llanos (allied to the trafficker whose alias was Martín Llanos), among others.

In contrast to their predecessors, the large majority of the new organizations—both those that arose from the dismantling of the Medellín and Cali cartels and those who had been overshadowed by the two—were characterized by their decentralization and assumption of specialized roles at specific points of the productive chain of narcotics trafficking (DEA 2004). The main result of the power vacuum left by the disappearance of the big capos and the simultaneous intensification of the "war on drugs" by the US and Colombian governments was the fracturing of the chain, especially seen in the initial penetration and later dominance of the final stages of the business by the Mexican cartels (that is, wholesale and retail sales of cocaine in the United States),[5] and the growing importance of the VNSAs as providers of security and transport on a national level who were also monopolizing the initial stages on a local level (the growing of coca and production of cocaine base). As a consequence, it was during this stage that there arose the conditions that allowed the armed groups to seize larger revenues from narcotics trafficking at a time when the internal armed conflict flared up again (Restrepo, Spagat, and Vargas 2006, 535).

One of the clearest examples of this trend was the creation of the United Self-Defense Forces of Colombia (Autodefensas Unidas de Colombia, AUC) by Carlos Castaño in 1997, the main objective of which was to consolidate the territorial control of the paramilitaries over the areas formerly dominated by the FARC and the National Liberation Army (ELN) guerrillas (Puentes 2009), especially those where coca was grown (the plots of which had been expanding exponentially since the mid-1990s). Toward this end, Castaño and his brother also formed an alliance with the northern Valle cartel to control the route for exports of cocaine from the Pacific coast (McDermott 2009).[6]

Between 2000 and 2003 many narcotics traffickers managed to establish or reinforce paramilitary blocks through a kind of franchise offered by the AUC, with a twin aim: to serve as private armies to control the regions where the trade was concentrated and to win a seat at the table where negotiations were taking place between the paramilitaries and the government of Álvaro Uribe Vélez (2002–2010). The prototypical case of this convergence between narcotics trafficking and paramilitarism is the Central Bolívar Block (Bloque Central Bolívar, BCB) (Arias and Prieto 2009), although many other traffickers also made use of the "AUC trademark" (FSYD 2006), among them those who used the aliases Gordo Lindo, Don Berna, Cuco Vanoy, los Mellizos, Juan Carlos Sierra, and Miguel Arroyave.

For their part, the participation of the FARC in the narcotics trafficking economy began to change in the mid-1990s, largely due to changes in its organizational model in its zones of influence (Vargas 2005, 29). In the period between 1996 and 1998, attacks against the armed forces were most intense and they required ample financial resources for arms and new footsoldiers (Vargas 2005). As a consequence, the guerrilla organization stepped up its activities in the region known as the "coca belt" ("*cinturón de la coca*"), which runs from southern Nariño through the northeastern part of the Amazon basin to the prairies of Vichada. By the beginning of 1999 that zone was responsible for 79.19 percent of the total number of hectares where coca was grown in the country (UNODC 2000), which is largely explained by the reduction of illicit crops in Peru and Bolivia. Thus, while in 1990 the hectares of coca in Colombia corresponded to 19 percent of the total number in the Andean region, a decade later it had risen to 72 percent. In addition to this exponential growth during this period, the number of departments (Colombian states) where coca was grown rose from twelve in 1999 to twenty-one in 2000 (Díaz and Sánchez 2004).

At the same time that the "narco-paramilitaries" shifted from taxing the "*traquetos*" (Colombian slang for "narcos") for the cocaine they shipped out of the areas they controlled to becoming partners in the production of the drugs and their export to the United States and Europe, the FARC also began to specialize in other links of the chain, mainly the growing stage. They began to gather, store, and sell large volumes of coca paste or cocaine base to select representatives of the many groups that had replaced the big cartels (ICG 2005, 10), including the paramilitaries. The diary of the trafficker whose alias is Don Mario, seized in March 2007 (to which we had access), shows the type of transactions that were going on between the guerrillas and the paramilitaries. According to that document, while the latter built their own laboratories for processing coca into cocaine, the former allowed trucks with inputs, arms, food, and medicine to travel through the zones controlled by the FARC (charging a tax for it) in exchange for purchases of specific amounts of cocaine base. The testimony of David Hernández López, given to the public prosecutor (*fiscalía*) when the Libertadores del Sur Block of the BCB paramilitary group demobilized itself under a peace agreement with the government, confirms a similar arrangement whereby the block bought cocaine base from the FARC, processed it in laboratories, and sent the cocaine to Tumaco for export to foreign markets.

In contrast with the above is the atypical case of the sixteenth front of the FARC (of the Eastern Block), when the commandant, whose alias was Negro Acacio, made an alliance with Luis Fernando da Costa, alias Fernandinho, one of the most powerful traffickers of Brazil, to produce and sell cocaine chlorhydrate.[7] Another case that departs from the general pattern of the FARC's role in narcotics trafficking has been that of John 40 of the 43rd front (Macarena), who established a relationship at the beginning of the 1990s with the narco whose alias is Loco Barrera, currently one of the most important "meta-brokers." In contrast with the Negro Acacio, however, his role has been limited to processing and selling cocaine to the Loco Barrera (*Eltiempo.com* 2005; *Semana* 2009).

One aspect of the readjustment of the international division of labor was that the Mexican cartels gained more control of the stage of commercialization, especially transport and distribution. In the same way that the dismantling of the big cartels shook up the structure of growing, production, and commercialization in Colombia, the anti-drug campaigns in Mexico, especially since the end of the 1990s, weakened the three most active cartels of narcotics traffickers (Tijuana, Juárez, and Golfo) and led to the emergence of several new ones to fill the gap, among them the Sinaloa, Beltrán Leyva, and Michoacana family cartels, as well as the reorganization of the existing ones (Bagley 2009).

Current Dynamics of the Role of the VNSAs in Narcotics Trafficking

With the agreements for "disarmament, demobilization, and reintegration" made between the government of Álvaro Uribe and the AUC between 2003 and 2006, the phenomenon of narcotics trafficking entered the stage of its greatest fragmentation in the past twenty-six years. In contrast with the "classical" period, the business currently operates through a multiple linkage of Colombian and foreign actors who participate in each link of the chain independently. In that sense, one of its most significant characteristics is the links' heterogeneity. A second important characteristic is the way it functions as a transnational network.[8] This type of linkage is different from the direct networks, which are created for specific purposes by a closed group of organizers, as was the case with the Medellín and Cali cartels (Williams 2008). Instead of centralized and hierarchical control, the "brokers" are now those who intervene in the multiple transactions that each stage of the narcotics trafficking chain requires for it to function as an integrated system. Among the roles now played in Colombia, there are the "*chichipatos*," the intermediaries in the transactions involving coca paste/cocaine base, the "*armadores*" ("assemblers") who handle domestic transactions of cocaine chlorhydrate, and the "meta-brokers" who manage the international ones.[9]

The change in the division of labor in narcotics trafficking has resulted from several different factors, among them the shifting nature of the armed conflict and changes in the presence and territorial control of the VNSAs (Ávila 2010a, 2010b; Camacho et al. 2009; Pécaut 2008; Duncan 2007; Pizarro 2006; Vargas 2005); diverse dynamics of globalization (Cusimano 2009); and the anti-drug policies of the governments of Colombia and the United States (Bagley 2009; Cubides 2004; Thoumi 2002). On a national level, the demobilization of the AUC had a decisive influence on this process. In addition to winning a seat at the negotiating table and thus changing their image from drugs barons to paramilitary commanders, another objective sought by the different leaders of the AUC was to transfer their illegal businesses to third parties and launder their profits (FIP 2010). The alternatives their members chose gave rise to several models for the realignment of narcotics trafficking during this third stage: (1) there were those who wanted to completely retire from the business (among them Cuco Vanoy, Jorge 40, and Salvatore Mancuso) by selling their holdings to independent groups of traffickers, (2) others who did not want to get out sold "franchises" in order to continue playing a role in the trade (the most prominent example being the BCB), and (3) those who did not demobilize or were not invited to the negotiations carried on with their activities (for example, alias Pablo of La Guajira cartel [FSYD 2006, 2007]).

The Bacrims

The power vacuum left in different areas of Colombia by the demobilization process—which ended in mid-2008 when the paramilitary chiefs were extradited to the United States—was filled by several kinds of regional actors, especially the emerging criminal gangs (*bacrims*).[10] By the end of the same year the *bacrims* were present in 246 municipalities of Colombia, organized into 100 armed nuclei with 21 different names (FIP 2008). Several kinds of groups can be distinguished in accordance with their origin and composition. There are the new or emerging ones, such as the Águilas Negras and the Organización Nueva Generación; reconfigured paramilitary ones, such as the one led by alias Cuchillo,[11] known as the Colombian Popular Revolutionary Anti-Terrorist Army (Ejército Revolucionario Popular Antiterrorista de Colombia, ERPAC); dissidents under the command of members of the AUC who did not participate in the peace negotiations, such as los Urabeños led by alias Don Mario (FIP 2008); and gangs working for traffickers like the Rastrojos, Paisas, and Machos, who act as the military wing of organizations like the Cartel del Norte del Valle and the Oficina de Envigado (McDermott 2009; FSYD 2007).

In contrast with the paramilitary groups, the *bacrims* are not confederated under a central body of administration or command. On the contrary, they follow a pattern similar to that of the purchase of franchises or blocks found in the case of the AUC and a number of traffickers. Thus while there are gangs with the same names in different regions of Colombia (Indepaz 2009), they are not organically related (under the mantle of an ideology, statute, set of regulations, or antisubversive mission), but rather maintain commercial relations or provide services to one another (ICG 2005; Matiz 2009; Indepaz 2009; FIP 2008; Ávila 2010a). The commercial nature of these groups also distinguishes them from the organic structure of the components of the AUC. Their criminal profile is much broader and more flexible, since they devote themselves to multiple activities such as the trafficking of cocaine, agricultural inputs, or fuel; kidnapping and extortion in rural areas; and microtrafficking and murder for hire in urban ones.[12] In addition, the *bacrims* participate in the intermediate phases of the narcotics trafficking chain, such as the purchase of coca paste, the production of chlorhydrate, the protection and transport of drugs; and the control of microtrafficking on the domestic market (FIP 2008; FSYD 2006).

The FARC

With regard to changes in the FARC's form and level of involvement in the current stage of narcotics trafficking, it is important to point out that in contrast with the paramilitaries and the *bacrims*, whose relationship with the business is of an organic nature, the guerrillas still have an opportunistic relationship with narcotics. That is, it nourishes itself on the resources from narcotics trafficking to finance its military activities (whether in the form of money, arms, or other kinds).[13]

The territorial presence of the FARC suggests that its relationship with narcotics trafficking is limited, in almost all cases, to the initial phases of the chain: the growing of leaves, production of coca paste, and, to a lesser extent, the protection of laboratories. It charges a tax on the activities in these links, in exchange for allowing them to continue and for providing security (see Chapter 1). In the above-mentioned cases, like that of the Negro Acacio, where links between the guerrilla and transnational criminal groups have been established, the relationship goes beyond taxing. The direct exchange of drugs for weapons shows that in contrast with what happens with other VNSAs like the AUC, whose commanders receive direct economic benefits from their involvement, the guerrillas place a priority on the functioning of its organization.

As an example of the transactional arrangements between different kinds of actors, which have multiplied in this stage of narcotics trafficking, a mention may be made of the relationship between the ERPAC and the FARC in the region of the Llanos Orientales, especially the department of el Meta, as well as the one in the municipality of Barbacoas, department of Nariño, between the ELN guerrillas and the Rastrojos. These are commercial-type transactions that have come about precisely because of the specialized roles the different VNSA have assumed in the different stages of the productive chain.

The International Level

As a result of the heightening of the Colombian armed forces' offensive against the VNSAs, especially the FARC, some of the laboratories in frontier zones (near Ecuador and Venezuela) have been shifted to the other side of the border as part of a balloon effect. As of July 2009, the Ecuadorian authorities had identified sixty narcotics trafficking facilities in their frontier zones, including laboratories for processing cocaine and a semisubmersible for transporting the merchandise (*Semana* 2010). There are also signs that Ecuador is turning into an important collection center for drugs originating in Colombia, which are then sent by ship to Mexico along routes that circle the Galapagos Islands, among others (see Cartogram 15.1) (*Semana* 2009).

As regards the role of the Colombian VNSAs in the production and trafficking of drugs in neighboring countries, it is worth underlining that on the frontier with Venezuela the ELN and the Águilas Negras are the ones who control the stages of shipments to that country (Ávila 2010b), which suggests that actors other than the FARC run the laboratories in Venezuela. In the same way, the increasing checks on the movements of fronts 48 and 32 of the FARC along the frontier with Ecuador indicate that there too the guerrilla group lacks the territorial control and military might needed to administer and/or protect laboratories.

It is estimated that the size of the cocaine market in Europe doubled between 2000 and 2009, while consumption in the United States stabilized, causing a shifting of some routes to Europe.[14] As Europe becomes an outlet as important as the United States, and even more lucrative due to Colombian control over more links of the trade (UNODC 2010), Venezuela and West Africa are becoming more important as transit

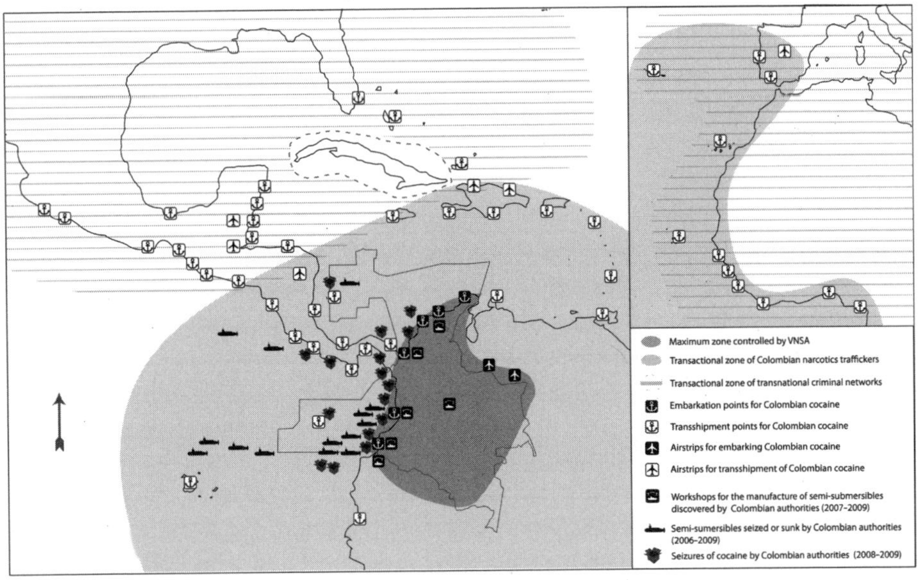

CARTOGRAM 15.1. Transactional zones of Colombian cocaine toward the United States, West Africa and Europe. Sources: Colombian police, Colombian navy, UNODC, Europol, European Monitoring Centre for Drugs and Drug Addiction. Drawn by Sebastián Díaz Ángel

points. According to the UNODC (2010), in 2008 more than 50 percent of the drugs seized on the Colombian Atlantic coast came from Venezuela. For its part, West Africa became a crucial link around 2004, when Nigerian mafia groups (who entered into the trafficking of narcotics from South America in the 1980s) began to provide logistical support to traffickers from Colombia and other countries. With the payments they receive in cocaine—as happened previously in Mexico and is now happening in Central America,[15] Jamaica, and the Dominican Republic, three central transit points—the West Africans have created their own structures for selling in the European market and are thus transforming the business once more.

Cartograms: A Visual Illustration of the Problem

Cartograms 15.1 and 15.2 illustrate the fragmentation that characterizes the current stage of narcotics trafficking on a Colombian and international level, as well as the roles played by each of the VNSAs in the different links of the chain. Cartogram 15.1 does a "zoom out," with an emphasis on exports from Colombia to the United States (through the Caribbean, Central America, and Mexico) and to Europe (with West Africa and the Iberian peninsula prominent), with the aim of showing that one of the most characteristic features of the phenomenon today is the breach between the initial and intermediate links in the narcotics trafficking chain on the one hand, and those of distribution and commercialization outside of Colombia on the other, at least with regard to the role of the VNSAs. One can identify three interfaces or radii of action of those actors: national, transactional, and international. In the first, as has been shown, the actors of a national nature participate; the transactional zone—which not only includes the moment when the drugs are transferred from the producers to the distributors, but also the negotiation of cargoes and prices—is in the hands of the brokers; and the international interface is controlled by the Mexican cartels and other transnational criminal organizations (including Colombian ones), which control the final links of the chain for distribution and sale in the United States and Europe.

Cartogram 15.2 illustrates the way the model is organized on a national level, especially with regard to the participation of the diverse VNSAs in each link of the chain. While the role of the guerrillas (essentially the FARC) is focused on the protection of crops and the production and transport of coca paste, the *bacrims* specialize in the processing of coca paste into cocaine in the laboratories, for which they provide protection and transport of the cocaine and its collection and embarkment. This is the point at which those actors lose control of the business and it falls into the hands of the meta-brokers, who, in turn, link up with transnational criminal organizations to complete the final link of the chain. The cartogram likewise identifies the main areas where the linkage among those actors takes place, thanks to the role played by the brokers. In this sense, it is important to note that each transaction in a link of the chain is mediated by middlemen who are less important than those mentioned and who link those actors' activities in the production and commercialization of both cocaine base and cocaine chlorhydrate. Finally, one can see how the key corridors for transporting the illegal drugs are secured by the different rings of security provided by different groups.

THE PRACTICES, ROLES, AND DYNAMICS OF THE VNSAS IN NARCOTICS TRAFFICKING

For the purpose of more clearly visualizing the subdivision of labor among the current different actors, it is useful to do a "zoom in" on two areas crucial for narcotics trafficking in Colombia: Nariño (Pasto/Tumaco) and Antioquia (Medellín). For that purpose we undertook a short period of fieldwork where we gathered descriptive and explanatory material through forty anonymous interviews between October and November 2009.

Nariño: The Epitome of Narcotics Trafficking in Colombia

The southern Pacific coast region of Colombia, and especially the department of Nariño, shows almost all the links of the narcotics trafficking chain—the growing of coca, the manufacture of coca paste, its processing into cocaine, the collection of the merchandise, its trafficking on a domestic level (microtrafficking), and its export—as well as a clear division of tasks and roles among the actors involved in the trade (Vicepresidencia de la República 2009; Observatorio Regional de Paz Cauca-Nariño 2008). The presence of multiple VNSAs there—the FARC and ELN, as well as several *bacrims* that are responsible for different kinds of violence in the department (Indepaz 2009), among them the Nueva Generación, Rastrojos, Urabeños-Autodefensas Gaitanistas de Colombia, Machos, Águilas Negras, Autodefensas Unidas de Nariño, and ERPAC—is no coincidence. Nariño is divided into two main areas of control. In the mountainous zone the FARC has a strong presence (*Semana* 2007), while the piedmont region and the river routes that run from the interior to the Pacific coast

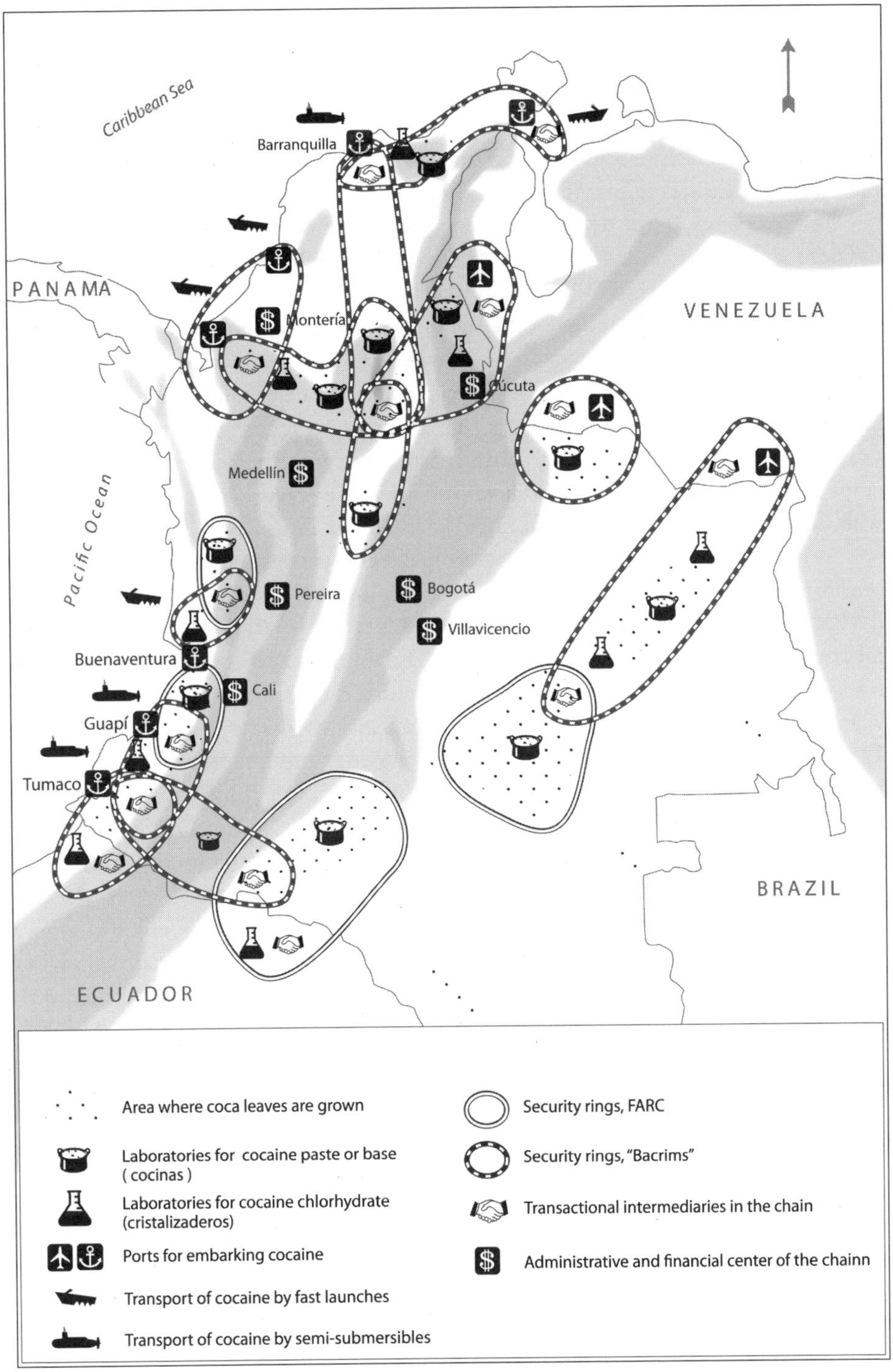

CARTOGRAM 15.2. Chain for the processing and trafficking of cocaine in Colombia. Sources: Colombian police, Colombian navy, UNODC. Drawn by Sebastián Díaz Ángel

are under the influence of the *bacrims*. In the gaps, especially in the municipality of Barbacoas, one finds the ELN, which, in alliance with the Rastrojos, has acted as a "hinge" for the military power that facilitates control of that territory. On the Pacific coast, where the collection and embarkment points are, both the *bacrims*, on the one hand, and the Águilas Negras and Rastrojos, on the other, are contracted by the brokers or linkers to provide protection.

The coca crops in the department are grown either on large plots controlled by the different VNSAs or, more frequently, on small plots by peasant-farmers who sell their harvests to the former (UNODC 2010). Workers who have emigrated from other parts of the country, the result (among other factors) of the government's forced eradication campaigns in the areas they come from, provide sufficient manpower for the harvesting and processing of the coca.[16] In 2007, 60 percent of the department's illegal crops were located in the coastal region, almost all far from paved roads, a situation that allows those actors to exercise territorial control. The areas with the highest density of coca crops include the north of the cordillera of Nariño, the Pacific coast up to the frontier with Ecuador, and the Putumayo frontier (Laverde and Tapia 2009, 31).

In addition to its large area of coca crops, the department is clearly important in processing,[17] and the processing, transport, collection, and embarkment links are also in the hands of the Águilas Negras, Rastrojos, and Nueva Generación, who fight each other for control of the territory. This is evident in the municipalities of Tumaco, Barbacoas, Roberto Payán, and Olaya Herrera, which are among the ten municipalities in Colombia with the largest areas devoted to growing coca and highest production of cocaine: 15.6 percent of the total area devoted to growing coca and a production of forty-nine tons per year (UNODC 2010, 12).

The zone near the frontier with Ecuador has an important function, since it serves as a strategic rearguard area for these actors, an entrance point for inputs and the site of laboratories, among other facilities. In 2009, the Ecuadorian National Anti-Narcotics Agency (Dirección Nacional Antinarcóticos de Ecuador) reported the destruction of seven laboratories in its territory, while some Ecuadorian press reports stated that fourteen more were destroyed in 2010 (*El Universo* 2010; *Expreso* 2009). In addition to the growing role of the Colombia-Ecuador border in processing,[18] several statements we gathered pointed to the city of Esmeraldas as an administrative center and operational base of the *armador*-type brokers, as Cali is.

The influx at the end of the 1990s of workers from other parts of the country who are skilled as harvesters (*raspachines*) and lab chiefs (*jefes de cocina*) coincided with the expansion of illicit crops in Nariño.[19] This encouraged the participation of the FARC in the production of coca paste, since they already had a presence in the mountainous zone and in the lower basin of the river Mira. The collection of taxes from growers, producers, and brokers of coca paste has enabled its front 29 to establish itself as one of the richest fronts of the FARC, comparable to number 45 in Norte de Santander and number 10 in Arauca (Ávila and Núñez 2008, 61). The small number of attacks on the armed forces, government institutions, and the region's infrastructure suggest that both the front 29 and the mobile columns in the region are more interested in using the coca business to finance their organization.[20]

Despite that, it is interesting to note that according to some of those interviewed, after encouraging the growing of coca for more than a decade, the FARC have begun to discourage it in some territories where Afro-Colombian communities enjoy collective rights to the land—as in the lower Mira river region—in order to avoid the incursion of the armed forces, while in other areas they continue to sell inputs to and buy coca paste from the peasant-farmers.[21]

For transactions involving the sale of paste, there are linkmen who facilitate the negotiations between the FARC and such *bacrim* as the Águilas Negras and the Nueva Generación.[22] Despite the interconnection of different groups, the region has also seen an effective alliance between the ELN, the Rastrojos, and also tacitly the armed forces to attack the FARC and wrest territory from them for the movement of illegal goods (Ávila 2010b).

Several interviewees stated that the ELN has gone through a reactivation in recent years, especially in municipalities like Barbacoas. After having been weakened in military terms, it took advantage of the arrival of the Rastrojos to establish an alliance for the purpose of territorial control, which has enabled it to participate in the first links of the narcotics trafficking chain. As Ávila and Núñez (2008, 25) point out, the ELN has recovered its military capacity in this region thanks to the acquisition of arms and increased recruitment. It is important to clarify, however, that the wings involved in narcotics trafficking are distanced from the Central Command (Comando Central, COCE), which does not approve of its participation in the business.

Although in historical terms the critical actors in the region have been the subversives, especially the FARC, the incursion of the Bloque Libertadores del Sur (BLS) paramilitary group—an organic structure of the Bloque Central Bolívar (BCB)—gave narcotics trafficking there new dynamics. As mentioned, as part of the strategy for consolidating and expanding the BCB, this block encouraged the establishment of all stages of the illegal drug business in Nariño. By 2011, it had gained control of the towns as well as the main transit corridors for the drugs and sites for laboratories (Garzón 2005; Arias and Prieto 2009).[23] The demobilization of the BLS did not reduce the presence of paramilitary-type structures in the department; in fact, control of specific links of the trafficking chain was taken over by some remnants that did not demobilize, like the Nueva Generación, and new groups that entered the zone to fill the places left by the BLS, such as the Rastrojos and Urabeños (Arias and Prieto 2009). While the yielding of control over different stages of the business took place through the sale of franchises by former leaders of the BLS, there is now a territorial dispute among the above-mentioned groups, especially in the estuaries on the coastal plain that serve as a route toward the embarkment points on the Pacific coast.[24]

The middlemen responsible for transactions involving illegal drugs in the region are other brokers from big cities like Cali and Medellín, who act as linkmen for narcotics trafficking in the southwestern part of the country and work in an area that runs from Tumaco through Guapí to Buenaventura. These cities are where the financial resources are administered, money is laundered, and the brokers blend in.[25] The roles played by the three cities exemplify the characteristics of the phenomenon in Nariño. The town of Llorente acts as a lesser administrative center, where the entrance of inputs and export of cargoes are negotiated. It is also a source of specialized manpower installed there by virtue of the municipality's location on the road network and complex topography of marshes and estuaries.[26] As well as being the main export point for cocaine, the city of Tumaco provides hired killers, while Cali operates as the center of gravity for the whole

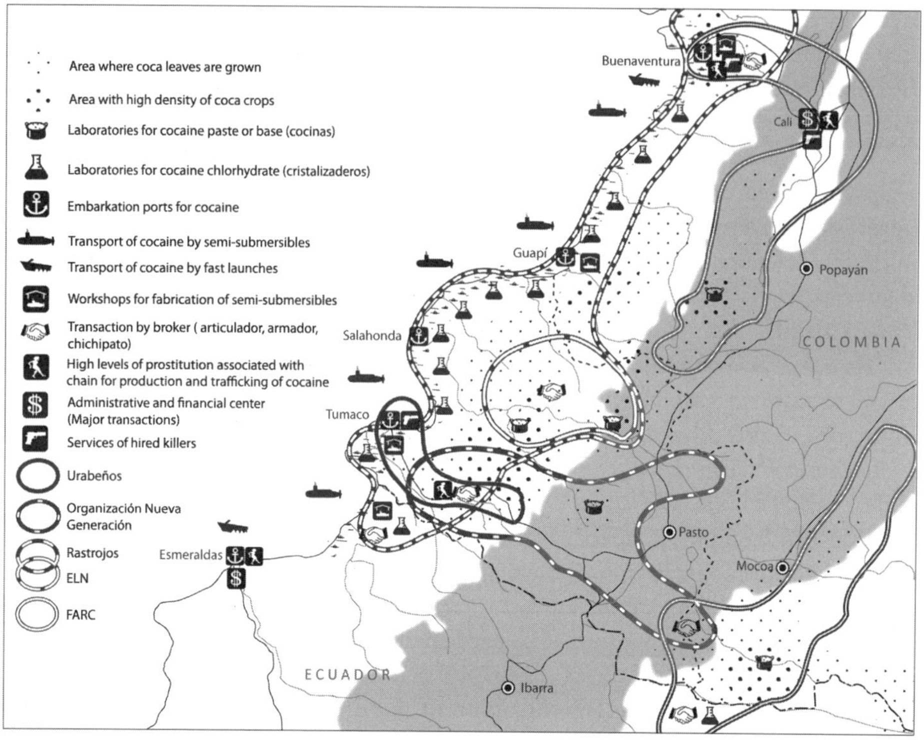

CARTOGRAM 15.3. Chain for processing and trafficking of cocaine in Nariño and southwestern Colombia. Sources: Colombian police, Colombian navy, UNODC. Drawn by Sebastián Díaz Ángel

phenomenon of narcotics trafficking in the department. Like Medellín, it is the administrative center where most of the negotiations about routes and embarkments take place (Cartogram 15.3).

Medellín: An Administrative and Regulatory Center

Like Nariño, the city of Medellín—which functions as an administrative and financial center for the different stages of narcotics trafficking—illustrates crucial aspects of the current relationship between the VNSAs and this illegal trade. The dynamics found there have been fundamentally influenced by the redeployment and breakdown of several fronts of the FARC that operated in the zone and the demobilization of the blocks of the AUC which began in Medellín in November 2003 (Restrepo 2010, 64).

The importance of Medellín for a number of illegal economies in the northwestern part of the country explains why different VNSAs have tried to control them from the city. In the metropolitan area of the valley of Aburrá, made up of nine municipalities apart from Medellín, one can identify three main aspects of their interest: (1) the area is a business center that controls illegal activities in the gulfs of Urabá and Morrosquillo and the north of Chocó, all important ports for the export of drugs, (2) it is the second most important center for money laundering, after Bogotá, and (3) the valley of Aburrá offers a geostrategic advantage for these actors, insofar as it provides access to and control over corridors for the shipment of illegal goods toward the Caribbean and the Pacific that run through regions such as the lower Cauca, the nudo de Paramillo, southern Bolívar, and the Magdalena medio (Grupo de Investigación Casa de Paz 2010, 78).

These features have led diverse VNSAs to compete for the control of the different links of the chain, as is shown by the growing presence of gangs like the Paisas and factions of the Oficina de Envigado.[27] Although the *bacrims* play an essential role in the current model of narcotics trafficking, they do not have the capacity to bring all the links in the chain together nor to negotiate with other such actors. Instead they are basically devoted to the production and transport of cocaine and to providing specialized services to diverse illegal economies.[28] The establishment of agreements and the holding of negotiations are in the hands of the brokers or bosses (*patrones*), as they are known in the region. We refer to individuals who in many cases are former members or heirs of expired organizations like the Medellín cartel and still act as links between narcotics trafficking in Colombia and commercial partners like the Mexican cartels.[29] The low profile the brokers maintain in their role as connectors is indispensable for the continuous functioning of the productive chain, even at times when the different VNSAs are at war with one another.[30] The brokers have acted with some autonomy in relation to the criminal organizations and violent actors involved in the drug trade, a situation that allows them to act as intermediaries and negotiators in the transactions that occur at each stage of the business.

The role played by the subversives in the city and surrounding department has been substantially reduced by the actions of the paramilitary groups prior to 2006, who benefited from the armed forces' attacks on the guerrillas to consolidate their control of the towns in the region and the production of cocaine (as happened with Operation Orion in the comuna 13 of the city of Medellín) (Grupo de Investigación Casa de Paz 2010, 80–82). At present, the areas controlled by the FARC in the department of Antioquia are distant from the Medellín urban complex. The group still has a presence in the corridor that connects the subregion of northwestern Antioquia with the department of the Chocó, where it maintains control over the growing of coca leaves and the production of cocaine base. Something similar occurs in the municipality of Ituango, where the political work of the FARC's militias continues to be strong and seems to be directly related to the shipment of drugs through that town toward collection and embarkment points (Ávila 2010a, 17). As in Nariño, however, the production of cocaine chlorhydrate, as well as its transport, collection, and embarkment, is generally under the control of other kinds of VNSAs, such as the Paisas.

Before their demobilization, the paramilitary organizations linked and controlled the activities of around four hundred gangs and groups located in the metropolitan area of the valley of Aburrá that undertook military actions and controlled the local illegal economies. These gangs had a two-headed structure: a boss who acted as broker in the transactions involving coca paste and the smuggling of cocaine chlorhydrate, and the head of the block, who was devoted to military and operational aspects (Giraldo 2008).[31] After the extradition of the former commanders of the AUC, those known as the *patrones* kept up their role in the negotiations between the VNSAs and the transnational criminal networks, whereas the military leaders of these gangs disappeared or were replaced.[32]

Once the different wings of the AUC were demobilized, there was a period when the illegal economies were tacitly controlled from Medellín by what are known as the "collection agencies" or "payment offices" (*oficinas de cobro*). When the main former commanders of the AUC in the region were jailed, extradited, or murdered, a vacuum arose in the work done by the paramilitary groups. This led to a war between factions of the Oficina de Envigado (heirs of the Medellín cartel), the Urabeños (a group founded by alias Don Mario after he demobilized along with the Bloque Élmer Cárdenas), and the ERPAC. This was the start of a period of a "violent realignment of forces" among the city's gangs, which continue to fight for control over specific territories and their share in different illegal economies (Restrepo 2010).[33] They also offer specialized services in the intermediate links of the narcotics trafficking chain: security, debt collection, murder for hire, and transport and collection. In exchange for these services, they are given the option of managing the local illegal economies: the extortion of public transport companies, safeguarding of allies, microtrafficking, and so forth. In the city, the control of and strong presence in different territories are fundamental to the survival of these actors (Giraldo 2008).[34]

Just as Nariño is the epitome of narcotics trafficking in Colombia, Medellín serves an illustration of its different historical stages. In the former, one can clearly see the current division of labor among diverse VNSAs, as Cartogram 15.3 shows. By contrast, Medellín illustrates the evolution of the phenomenon, from its start with the major cartels, through its transition toward organized and hierarchical armed groups like the AUC, and to present stage of fragmentation marked by competition and violent disputes between actors, along with its role as the operational center for the brokers.

CONCLUSIONS

As we have argued in the course of this chapter, the relationship between the VNSAs and narcotics trafficking is complex, changing, and difficult to classify. The increasing differentiation of the roles played by different local, regional, national, and foreign participants, as well as their atomization, have created a structure that is multidimensional and highly specialized. With the fragmentation of the productive chain and the existence of multiple poles of activity and power, the relevance of the brokers throughout all of this has considerably increased.

The above points to the need to design different policies for each of the stages of growing, production, and commercialization, as well as for the variations evidenced by the problem of narcotics trafficking in different areas of Colombia. It likewise suggests that one of the main strategies employed up to now to fight against narcotics traffickers—to foment their violent competition and mutual annihilation, a strategy currently in use in Mexico—may leave untouched the activities of the brokers, who are essential for the joint functioning of the different VNSAs.

Despite some atypical cases, like those of the Negro Acacio and John 40, the role played by the FARC during the three historical stages of narcotics trafficking has been relatively stable and corresponds to their participation in the phase of growing. What has changed is the guerrillas' capacity to charge taxes on different links, a reflection of their power to dominate certain territories and provide security, which, despite regional variations, has declined generally. A second aspect of continuity in the FARC that is worth underlining is the opportunistic attitude it still has toward narcotics trafficking, which is fundamentally used to finance its armed fight and has not yet led the guerrillas to abandon their ideology. To leap to calling them "the biggest drugs cartel," however, as different government figures in Colombia have, tends to hinder rather than help one to attain a clearer idea of the FARC's role in the business.

Finally, given the multiplicity of origins, radii of action, and functions performed by the different criminal gangs involved in narcotics trafficking, the homogenized interpretation of the new phenomenon of violence encapsulated in the term "*bacrim*" does not allow one to take into account the diversity of the different actors nor their varied regional expressions. In addition, it minimizes the new political identities that may be latent in some of them.

NOTES

1. It is worth noting that the country's share of the market has fallen over time. At the beginning of the 2000s it was more than 75 percent.
2. In contrast with maps with georeferenced data, cartograms allow one to give graphic expression to an idea, concept, or analytic model. The choice of this visual tool instead of maps was made because the information available about the relations between the VNSAs and narcotics trafficking is not only meager and contradictory but also corresponds to different sources and levels that are not comparable. The three cartograms included in this chapter were constructed on the basis of written information provided by the police and the navy, information offered during the interviews that were held, and data found in the annual reports of the UNODC.
3. Despite that, by exerting control over local populations, the VNSAs have also participated indirectly in this stage.
4. See Chapter 11 for a discussion and detailed quantification of money laundering in Colombia.
5. See Chapter 1 for a measurement of the earnings observed in the different stages of the production chain.
6. Around the same time, at the end of the 1990s, there was a war between alias Don Diego and Wilber Varela, both members of the norte del Valle cartel, one result of which was the creation of the private armies known as los Machos and los Rastrojos, respectively, which have gradually gained a power of their own within the business of narcotics trafficking, especially during the third stage.
7. For a broad analysis of the case of the Bloque Oriental and especially its Front 16, based on one hundred interviews with demobilized members of the FARC, cf. Rico (2009). It concludes that in addition to the capture of Fernandinho and the death of Negro Acacio, the disruption of the Eastern Block's territorial control by the armed forces caused it to lose its capacity to manage laboratories, so that its current function is limited to the purchase and sale of cocaine base.
8. This arises spontaneously with the aim of making the processes of commercial exchange efficient, especially through the linkage of intermediaries or brokers in each link of the chain, from production to retail sales (Williams 2008, 70).
9. Daniel el Loco Barrera is an example of this last type of linkman. Among his important commercial partners are the old norte del Valle cartel and paramilitary chiefs like alias Don

Mario and Cuchillo (current commandant of the ERPAC). Along with Luis Enrique and Javier Antonio Calle Serna (together known as "los Comba"), el Loco is acknowledged to be one of the big capos of the country today, the owner of most of the labs in the east and the microtrafficking trade in Bogotá.

10. Surprisingly, the ranks of the *bacrim* are not largely made up of demobilized members of the AUC. According to estimates by the police, only 12 percent are, a figure that corresponds to middle-rank militia members who have taken advantage of the military and narcotics trafficking know-how they acquired during their time in that paramilitary organization. FIP (2010) and personal interview, Policía Nacional, Dirección de Carabineros, Bogotá, October 22, 2009.
11. After demobilizing itself in 2005, it began to extend its influence through the southeastern region of the country, with control over crucial zones like Cauca and Nariño, which facilitated its access to the Pacific coast.
12. Personal interview, Policía Nacional, Dirección de Carabineros, Bogotá, October 22, 2009. Of the known *bacrims*, the Águilas Negras and the Organización Nueva Generación have a political profile similar to that of the AUC and which is expressed in the threats against and murders of social leaders of the left (FIP 2008).
13. Although it would be mistaken to conclude that the FARC is no longer motivated by political or ideological factors, its growing interaction with other actors who participate in narcotics trafficking indicates a potential transformation that may already be under way.
14. See the costs associated with each route, along with the expected profits, in Chapter 1.
15. Since 2003 and especially after the inauguration of Felipe Calderón, the seizures of cocaine in Central American began to surpass those of Mexico and the Caribbean (Bagley 2009), largely due to the Mexican president's anti-drug policy.
16. Official of Acción Social, personal interview, Pasto, Nariño, November 8, 2009.
17. Navy officer, personal interview, Tumaco, Nariño, November 7, 2009.
18. According to a contractor of the DEA, the Rastrojos have been contracted to ship a certain monthly tonnage of cocaine paste to the Ecuadorian side of the border to be turned into cocaine. Personal interview, Bogotá, December 10, 2009.
19. Officer of the Policía Nacional, personal interview, Nariño, November 7, 2009. Cf. Ávila and Núñez (2008, 31).
20. Ávila and Núñez (2008).
21. A similar process is seen in Arauca, where, according to the antinarcotics police, the FARC have discouraged the growing of coca leaves with the aim of making the processing of coca paste (cocaine base) more secure. Dirección de Antinarcóticos, Policía Nacional, personal interview, Bogotá, January 6, 2009.
22. These are individuals linked to narcotics trafficking networks who deal in coca paste or cocaine chlorhydrate. Intelligence agent of the Sijin, personal interview, Tumaco, Nariño, November 7, 2009.
23. Official of the office of the Governor of Nariño, personal interview, Pasto, Nariño, November 8, 2009.
24. In 2009, 37 percent of the laboratories that were found and destroyed in the country were located on the Pacific coast (UNODC 2010, 40).
25. Navy officer, personal interview, Tumaco, Nariño, November 7, 2009.
26. Llorente is located on the road between Pasto and Tumaco and is known in the region as the "Babylon of the Pacific."

27. Official of the office of the governor of Antioquia, personal interview, Medellín, Antioquia, October 14, 2009.
28. Official of the office of the governor of Antioquia, personal interview, Medellín, Antioquia, October 14, 2009.
29. Member of the armed forces assigned to the region, personal interview, Medellín, Antioquia, October 15, 2009.
30. Official of the office of the governor of Antioquia, personal interview, Medellín, Antioquia, October 14, 2009.
31. Social investigator, Mayoralty of Medellín, personal interview, Medellín, Antioquia, October 15, 2009.
32. Official of the office of the governor of Antioquia, personal interview, Medellín, Antioquia, October 14, 2009.
33. Former member of a group of VNSAs, personal interview, Medellín, Antioquia, October 14, 2009.
34. Former member of gangs in Medellín, personal interview, Medellín, Antioquia, October 14, 2009.

REFERENCES

Print Sources

Arias, G., and C. A. Prieto. 2009. "El Bloque Central Bolívar: Un caso de paramilitarismo y narcotráfico en Colombia." Bogotá: Fundación Ideas para la Paz. Unpublished.

Arrocha, R. 2000. *La economía colombiana tras 25 años de narcotráfico*. Bogotá: Siglo del Hombre / UNDCP.

Ávila, A. F. 2010a. "La guerra contra las FARC y la guerra de las FARC." *Arcanos*, no. 15 (April).

———. 2010b. "Las dinámicas territoriales del Ejército de Liberación Nacional: Arauca, Cauca y Nariño." *Arcanos*, no. 15 (April).

Bagley, B. 2009. "La conexión Colombia-México-Estados Unidos." In *Atlas de la seguridad y la defensa en México*, edited by R. Benítez, Ar. Rodríguez, and A. B. Rodríguez. Mexico, DF: Ford Foundation.

Bowden, M. 2002. *Killing Pablo*. New York: Penguin Books.

Camacho, Á. et al. 2009. *A la sombra de la guerra: Ilegalidad y nuevos órdenes regionales en Colombia*. Universidad de los Andes, Facultad de Ciencias Sociales, CESO. Bogotá: Ediciones Uniandes.

Chepesiuk, R. 2003. *The Bullet or the Bribe*. Westport, CT: Praeger Publishers.

Clawson, P. L., and R. Lee. 1996. *The Andean Cocaine Industry*. New York: St. Martin's Press.

Cook, C. W. 2007. "Mexico's Drug Cartels." CRS Report for Congress, October 16.

Cubides, F. 2004. "Narcotráfico y guerra en Colombia: Los paramilitares." In Instituto Francés de Estudios Andinos (IFEA), *Violencias y estrategias colectivas en la región andina: Bolivia, Colombia, Perú y Venezuela*. Bogotá: IEPRI-Norma.

Cusimano, M. 2000. *Beyond Sovereignty: Issues for a Global Agenda*. Boston: Bedford St. Martin's.

Díaz, A. M., and F. Sánchez. 2004. "A Geography of Illicit Crops and Armed Conflict in Colombia," Document CEDE 2004-19 (March), Universidad de los Andes.

Duncan, G. 2007. *Los señores de la guerra: De paramilitares, mafiosos y autodefensas en Colombia*. Bogotá: Planeta.

———. 2005. *Del campo a la ciudad en Colombia. La infiltración urbana de los señores de la guerra*. Bogotá: Universidad de los Andes–CEDE.

FIP (Fundación Ideas para la Paz). 2010. "¿Para dónde va el paramilitarismo en Colombia?" *Siguiendo el conflicto: hechos y análisis*, no. 58.

Garzón, J. C. 2005. *Desmovilización del Bloque Libertadores del Sur del Bloque Central Bolívar*. Bogotá: Fundación Seguridad y Democracia.

Giraldo, J. 2008. "Conflicto armado urbano y violencia homicida. El caso de Medellín." *Revista Latinoamericana de Seguridad Ciudadana*, no. 5 (March): 99–113.

Godson, R., and P. Williams. 2000. "Strengthening Cooperation Against Transsovereign Crime: A New Security Imperative." In *Beyond Sovereignty: Issues for a Global Agenda*, edited by M. Cusimano. Boston: Bedford St. Martin's.

González, F. E. 2004. "Conflicto violento en Colombia: Una perspectiva a largo plazo." *Controversia* 182 (Aug.): 10–17, Retrieved from *www.c-r.org/sites/default/files/2_Conflicto%20violente%20en%20Colombia.pdf*, accessed May 14, 2015.

Gugliotta, G., and J. Leen. 1989. *Kings of Cocaine: Inside the Medellín Cartel*. New York: Simon & Schuster.

Indepaz (Instituto de Estudios para el Desarrollo y la Paz). 2009. *Informe comparativo de nuevos grupos narcoparamilitares 2008–2009*. Medellín: Indepaz.

ICG (International Crisis Group). 2005. "Guerra y droga en Colombia." *Informe sobre América Latina*, no. 11 (January 27).

Laverde, Z., and E. Tapia. 2009. *Tensión en las fronteras. Un análisis sobre el conflicto armado, el desplazamiento forzado y el refugio en las fronteras de Ecuador, Venezuela y Panamá*. Bogotá: Consultoría para los Derechos Humanos y el Desplazamiento (CODHES).

López, A. 2006. "Narcotráfico, ilegalidad y conflicto en Colombia." In *Nuestra guerra sin nombre. Transformaciones del conflicto en Colombia*, edited by F. Gutiérrez. Bogotá: Norma-Universidad Nacional de Colombia–IEPRI.

MAPP-OAS. 2007. Eighth Quarterly Report to the Permanent Council of the Organization of American States. Washington, DC: Organization of American States.

Pécaut, D. 2008. "Las FARC: Fuentes de su longevidad y de la conservación de su cohesión." *Análisis Político*, no. 63 (May–August).

Pizarro, E. 2006. "Las FARC-EP: Repliegue estratégico o punto de inflexión?" In *Nuestra guerra sin nombre. Transformaciones del conflicto en Colombia*, edited by F. Gutiérrez. Bogotá: Norma-Universidad Nacional de Colombia–IEPRI.

Restrepo, J. A., M. Spagat, and J. F. Vargas. 2006. "El conflicto en Colombia: ¿Quién hizo a quién? Un enfoque cuantitativo (1988–2003)." In *Nuestra guerra sin nombre. Transformaciones del conflicto en Colombia*, edited by F. Gutiérrez, 534–35. Bogotá: Norma-Universidad Nacional de Colombia–IEPRI.

Rico, D. 2009. "Cambios en la estructura financiera de las FARC: El caso del Bloque Oriental." Bogotá. Unpublished.

Rocha, R. 2000. *La economía colombiana tras 25 años de narcotráfico*. Bogotá: Siglo del Hombre / United Nations Office on Drugs and Crime (UNDCP).

Romero, M. 2002. "Democratización política y contrarreforma paramilitar en Colombia." *Política y Sociedad* 39, no. 1: 273–92.

Thoumi, F. 1991. "La política exterior de Colombia hacia Estados Unidos, 1987–1990." In C. G. Arrieta et al., *Narcotráfico en Colombia*. Bogotá: Tercer Mundo Editores-Ediciones Uniandes, 277–367.

———. 1994. *Economía política y narcotráfico*. Bogotá: Tercer Mundo Editores.

———. 2002. "Illegal Drugs in Colombia: From Illegal Economic Boom to Social Crisis." *Annals of the American Academy of Political and Social Science* 582: 102–16.

Tokatlian, J. G. 1991. "La política exterior de Colombia hacia Estados Unidos, 1987–1990." In C. G. Arrieta et al., *Narcotráfico en Colombia.* Bogotá: Tercer Mundo Editores-Ediciones Uniandes, 277–367.

Tokatlian, J. G., and B. Bagley, eds. 1990. *Economía y política del narcotráfico.* Bogotá: Uniandes–CEI.

Vargas, R. 2005. *Narcotráfico, guerra y política antidrogas: Una perspectiva sobre las drogas en el conflicto armado colombiano.* Bogotá: Novib, Netherlands, and Transnational Institute; Acción Andina Colombia.

Vicepresidencia de la República, Observatorio del Programa Presidencial de Derechos Humanos and DIH. 2010. "Situación de Derechos Humanos de las Comunidades Afrocolombianas." Bogotá: Presidencia de la República.

Williams, P. 2008. *Violent Non-State Actors and National and International Security.* Zurich: International Relations and Security Network. Retrieved from *mercury.ethz.ch/serviceengine/Files/ISN/93880/ipublicationdocument_singledocument/940949e4-4f98-4eb6-8ca6-c1eb878a3721/en/VNSAs.pdf*, accessed May 14, 2015.

Online Sources

Ávila, A., and M. Núñez. 2008. "Expansión territorial y alianzas tácticas." Bogotá: Corporación Nuevo Arco Iris. Retrieved from *www.nuevoarcoiris.org.co/sac/files/arcanos/arcanos_14_Dic._2008_files/arcanos_14_informe_alianzas_farc.pdf.*

DEA (Drug Enforcement Administration). 2004. "History Book: 1999–2003." Retrieved from *www.justice.gov/dea/pubs/history/1999–2003.html.*

FIP. 2008. "En qué va la guerra." November 28. Retrieved from *www.verdadabierta.com/conflicto-hoy/50-rearmados /584-en-que-va-la-guerra.*

———. 2010. "12% de las Bacrim son desmovilizados." February 10. Retrieved from *www.verdadabierta.com/conflicto-hoy /50-rearmados/2122–12-por-ciento-de-las-bacrim-son-desmovilizados-policia-nacional.*

FSYD (Fundación Seguridad y Democracia). 2006. "Paras puros e impuros." Retrieved from *www.seguridadydemocracia.org/docConflicto.asp.*

———. 2007. "El rearme paramilitar." Retrieved from *www.verdadabierta.com/./8-documentos-sobre-rearme?.140%3Ael-rearme–paramilitar.*

Grupo de Investigaciones Casa de Paz. 2010. "Medellín, la inseguridad cíclica y la permanencia de la ilegalidad." Retrieved from *www.lacasadepaz.org/index.php?option=com_contentandview =categoryandlayout=blogandid=32andItemid=62.*

Matiz, S. 2009. "El poder de 'los rastrojos." Retrieved from *www.elespectador.com/noticias/judicial/articul0143154-el-poder-de-los-rastrojos.*

McDermott, J. 2009. "Generational Shift: Colombia's Evolving Drug Cartel." *Janes Intelligence Review* (December 29). Retrieved from *jir.janes.com/public/jir/organised_crime.shtml.*

Moreno, R. 2008. "Erpac, dolor de cabeza de Uribe." Retrieved from *www.elespectador.com/impreso/nacional/articuloimpres096022-erpac-dolor-de-cabeza-de-uribe.*

Observatorio Regional de Paz Cauca-Nariño. 2008. "Línea base municipio de Leyva, dimensión derechos humanos y paz." Retrieved from *observatoriodepaz.org/wp-content/uploads/2008/12/linea-de-base-leiva.pdf.*

Puentes, Á. M. 2009. "Narcotráfico y la creación de las AUC." Bogotá: FIP. Retrieved from *www.verdadabierta.com/narcotrafico-period03*.

Restrepo, J. D. 2010. "La selectividad de la seguridad democrática en Antioquia." July. Retrieved from *www.semana.com/noticias-opinion-on-line/selectividad-seguridad-democratica-antioquia/141507.aspx*.

UNODC (United Nations Office on Drugs and Crime). 2000. "World Drug Report 2000." Retrieved from *www.UNODC.org/pdf/report_2000–09–21_1.pdf*.

———. 2010. "World Drug Report 2010." Retrieved from *www.unodc.org/unodc/en/data-and-analysis/WDR-2010.html*.

Vicepresidencia de la República, Observatorio de DDHH. 2009. "Diagnóstico de la situación de los municipios habitados por las comunidades afrocolombianas priorizadas por la honorable Corte Constitucional en el departamento de Nariño." Bogotá: Presidencia de la República. Retrieved from *www.derechoshumanos.gov.co/observatorio_de_DDHH/documentos/DiagnosticoAfro/Narino.pdf*.

Press Reports

Armada Nacional de Colombia. 2008. "Destruidos precursores para la producción de cocaína en el sur del país." April 16. Retrieved from *www.armada.mil.co/?idcategoria=539955*.

Eltiempo.com. 2005. "Los cuatro capos de las FARC." March 7. Retrieved from *www.eltiempo.com/archivo/documento/MAM-1633923*.

El Universo. 2010. "En Ecuador logran ubicar 14 laboratorios que procesan cocaína." February 22. Retrieved from *www.eluniverso.com/2010/02/22/1/1355/ecuador-logran-ubicar-14-laboratorios-procesan-cocaina.html?p= 1355Aandm=256*.

Expreso. 2009. "Dos carteles controlan el narcotráfico." December 5. Retrieved from *www.expreso.ec/ediciones/2009/12/06/nacional/judicial/dos-carteles-controlan-el-narcotrafico*.

Semana. 2001. "La confesión de Fernandinho." May 28. Retrieved from *www.semana.com/noticias-nacion/confesion-fernandinho/17243.aspx*.

———. 2007. "El lento y persistente avance de la guerrilla y los 'paras' en Nariño." April 10. Retrieved from *www.semana.com/wf_InfoArticulo.aspx?idArt=102099*.

———. 2009 "Desbaratan red de narcotraficantes con militares en Ecuador." October 7. Retrieved from *www.semana.com/noticias-narcotrafico/desbaratan-red-narcotraficantes-militares-ecuador/129767.aspx*.

———. 2010. "Ecuador ubicó 60 instalaciones de FARC y narcos en su territorio este año." July 13. Retrieved from *www.semana.com/noticias-america-latina/ecuador-ubico-60-instalaciones-farc-narcos-su-territorio-este-ano/141669.aspx*.

INDEX